Collected Essays in Speculative Philosophy

New Perspectives in Ontology

Series Editors: Peter Gratton, Southeastern Louisiana University, and Sean J. McGrath, Memorial University of Newfoundland, Canada

Publishes the best new work on the question of being and the history of metaphysics

After the linguistic and structuralist turn of the twentieth century, a renaissance in metaphysics and ontology is occurring. Following in the wake of speculative realism and new materialism, this series aims to build on this renewed interest in perennial metaphysical questions, while opening up avenues of investigation long assumed to be closed. Working within the Continental tradition without being confined by it, the books in this series will move beyond the linguistic turn and rethink the oldest questions in a contemporary context. They will challenge old prejudices while drawing upon the speculative turn in post-Heideggerian ontology, the philosophy of nature and the philosophy of religion.

Editorial Advisory Board
Maurizio Farraris, Paul Franks, Iain Hamilton Grant, Garth Green, Adrian Johnston, Catherine Malabou, Jeff Malpas, Marie-Eve Morin, Jeffrey Reid, Susan Ruddick, Michael Schulz, Hasana Sharp, Alison Stone, Peter Trawny, Uwe Voigt, Jason Wirth, Günter Zöller

Books available
The Political Theology of Schelling, Saitya Brata Das
Continental Realism and its Discontents, edited by Marie-Eve Morin
The Contingency of Necessity: Reason and God as Matters of Fact, Tyler Tritten
The Problem of Nature in Hegel's Final System, Wes Furlotte
Schelling's Naturalism: Motion, Space and the Volition of Thought, Ben Woodard
Thinking Nature: An Essay in Negative Ecology, Sean J. McGrath
Heidegger's Ontology of Events, James Bahoh
The Political Theology of Kierkegaard, Saitya Brata Das
The Schelling–Eschenmayer Controversy, 1801: Nature and Identity,
   Benjamin Berger and Daniel Whistler
Hölderlin's Philosophy of Nature, edited by Rochelle Tobias
Affect and Attention After Deleuze and Whitehead: Ecological Attunement,
   Russell J. Duvernoy
The Philosophical Foundations of the Late Schelling: The Turn to the Positive,
   Sean J. McGrath
Schelling's Ontology of Powers, Charlotte Alderwick
Collected Essays in Speculative Philosophy, by James Bradley and edited
   by Sean J. McGrath

www.edinburghuniversitypress.com/series/epnpio

Collected Essays in Speculative Philosophy

JAMES BRADLEY

Edited by Sean J. McGrath

EDINBURGH
University Press

Edinburgh University Press is one of the leading university presses in the UK. We publish academic books and journals in our selected subject areas across the humanities and social sciences, combining cutting-edge scholarship with high editorial and production values to produce academic works of lasting importance. For more information visit our website: edinburghuniversitypress.com

© James Bradley, 2021, 2023
© editorial matter and organisation Sean J. McGrath, 2021, 2023

Edinburgh University Press Ltd
The Tun – Holyrood Road, 12(2f) Jackson's Entry, Edinburgh EH8 8PJ

First published in hardback by Edinburgh University Press 2021

Typeset in Garamond and Gill Sans
by R. J. Footring Ltd, Derby, UK

A CIP record for this book is available from the British Library

ISBN 978 1 4744 8586 9 (hardback)
ISBN 978 1 4744 8587 6 (paperback)
ISBN 978 1 4744 8589 0 (webready PDF)
ISBN 978 1 4744 8588 3 (epub)

The right of James Bradley to be identified as the author of this work has been asserted in accordance with the Copyright, Designs and Patents Act 1988, and the Copyright and Related Rights Regulations 2003 (SI No. 2498).

Contents

Acknowledgements   viii

Preface: Creative Order – James Bradley's Speculative Metaphysics   xi
Peter Harris

Introduction: James Bradley's Path to the Trinity   1
Sean J. McGrath

1. F. H. Bradley's Metaphysics of Feeling and its Place in the History of Philosophy   36
2. Whitehead, Heidegger and the Paradoxes of the New   50
3. From Presence to Process: Bradley and Whitehead   82
4. The Speculative Generalisation of the Function: A Key to Whitehead   100
5. Triads, Trinities and Rationality   115
6. The Triune Event: Event Ontology, Reason and Love   133
7. What is Existence?   149
8. Beyond Hermeneutics: Peirce's Semiology as a Trinitarian Metaphysics of Communication   173
9. A Key to Collingwood's Metaphysics of Absolute Presuppositions: The Trinitarian Creed   189
10. Philosophy and Trinity   245

Postscript: My Friend James Bradley   264
    Helmut Maaßen

Appendix A: James Bradley's Tables of Triads and Trinities   268

Appendix B: Complete List of James Bradley's Publications   272

Index   276

At the request of James Bradley, this book is dedicated to his children: Sonia, Julian, Isobel and Adrian

Acknowledgements

This book has been eight years in preparation and many people were involved at different stages of its production. The editor's thanks go Emily Jean Gallant, Michelle Mahoney and Jennifer Dyer. Helmut Maaßen, William Hamrick, Brian Henning, James Scott Johnston and Douglas Hedley each reviewed the manuscript, offered helpful comments to the editor, and unequivocally supported its publication. My heartfelt thanks to each of them for supporting Bradley's work and advancing speculative philosophy in their own ways. Special acknowledgement is due to the late Peter Harris, who eagerly awaited the publication of this book, and who was always available to discuss with me issues related to Bradley's work. Peter Harris was Bradley's oldest friend and colleague from his Cambridge days, and, like him, an inspired teacher of philosophy at Memorial. He read everything Bradley wrote, and on more than one occasion Bradley's writings emerged out of discussions with him. The two were planning on co-authoring a work in speculative philosophy, but life had other plans for both of them. Together Bradley and Harris made the MUN Department of Philosophy a true university in the medieval sense, 'a community of teachers and scholars' (*universitas magistrorum et scholarium*).

My final thanks go to my wife, Esther Squires. She has been key to getting this project off my desk and into press, both by assisting me with the final manuscript and putting up with my preoccupation with it in its final days of completion.

I would like to acknowledge the support of Memorial University in covering the costs of indexing this book.

The Introduction, Chapters 5, 7, 9, the Postscript and the Appendices are published here for the first time.
- Chapter 5 is an unpublished paper read at the Winter Colloquium of the Department of Philosophy of Memorial University, St John's, Newfoundland, in 2003.
- Chapter 7 is an unpublished paper prepared as chapter 1 of a book on ontology Bradley planned in 2011 but never completed. Bradley lectured on 'Strong and Weak Theories of Existence' in the 1996 Winter Colloquium at Memorial and again at the meeting of the Canadian Philosophical Association held in St John's, Newfoundland, in June 1997, and published some of this material in Bradley (1999). See Appendix B.
- Chapter 9 is a significantly extended version of material which Bradley published in 2011. See Appendix B, p. 275.

The other chapters were previously published as follows. Careful readers will notice the repetition of certain passages in these essays. I have retained these repetitions where they are essential to the flow of the argument.
- Chapter 1, 'F. H. Bradley's Metaphysics of Feeling and its Place in the History of Philosophy', first appeared in A. Manser and G. Stock (eds), *The Philosophy of F. H. Bradley* (Oxford: Clarendon Press, 1984), 227–42.
- Chapter 2, 'Whitehead, Heidegger and the Paradoxes of the New', first appeared in *Process Studies* 20.3 (1991), 127–50.
- Chapter 3, 'From Presence to Process: Bradley and Whitehead', first appeared in James Bradley (ed.), *Philosophy After F.H. Bradley* (Bristol: Thoemmes Press, 1996), 147–68.
- Chapter 4, 'The Speculative Generalisation of the Function: A Key to Whitehead', first appeared in *Tijdschrift voor Filosofie* 64 (2002), 253–71.
- Chapter 6, 'The Triune Event: Event Ontology, Reason and Love', first appeared in Roland Faber, Henry Krips and Daniel Pettus (eds), *Event and Decision: Ontology and Politics in Badiou, Deleuze and Whitehead* (Cambridge: Cambridge Scholars Publishing, 2010), 97–114.
- Chapter 8, 'Beyond Hermeneutics: Peirce's Semiology as a Trinitarian Metaphysics of Communication', first appeared in *Analecta Hermeneutica* 1 (2009), 45–57.
- Chapter 10, 'Philosophy and Trinity', first appeared in *Symposium: Canadian Journal of Philosophy* 16.1 (2012), 155–77. It originated in a paper Bradley read at the meeting of the Canadian Society for Continental Philosophy in St John's in the fall of 2011. Bradley's paper was part of a panel on the relevance of the late Schelling for Continental Philosophy.
- Peter Harris's preface first appeared in *Analecta Hermeneutica* 4 (2012) under the title, 'Creative Order: The Case for Speculative Metaphysics'.

Photograph by Stephen Crocker

Preface: Creative Order – James Bradley's Speculative Metaphysics

Peter Harris

It is an enormous honour to have been invited to give the first of a series of lectures in honour of James Bradley, my friend and colleague of some forty-four years.[1] This is not meant to be a very rigorous analysis of Jim's philosophical work but rather an informal attempt to put that work into some historical perspective. The closer analysis I leave to the distinguished lecturers who will continue the series. Consequently, this is more a kind of philosophical reminiscence than a lecture.

In the first place I would like to use the title *Creative Order* as a lead into what follows. About ten years ago Jim asked me whether I would be interested in collaborating on, as he argued, a study, much needed for insertion into current philosophical offerings – an area of philosophy much neglected in recent times, yet vital to the continuity of the grand tradition, stemming from the Greek philosophers, concerning the meaning of Being and Existence. It was his view that the idea of creation, rightly understood, was the key to the development of metaphysics in the post-medieval world. Although not always recognised, the re-conception of Being as *Esse* or Existence stemmed from the progression of Being as 'substance' to that of Being as activity, the activity of actualisation. Being was no longer to be thought of as the instantiation of unchanging essences or forms but rather as the origin of the new and unprecedented. It was with the nature of this most universal origination that speculative metaphysics must concern itself. The proposed book would begin with a theoretical introduction to the notion of speculative metaphysics, and would then be concerned with tracing something of the history of metaphysics understood in this way. From Aquinas and Scotus, through the speculative thought of Hegel and Schelling, onward to Bradley and Collingwood, Bergson, Whitehead,

---

1. Peter Harris gave this paper on 30 October 2012 as the first of the 'Bradley Memorial Lectures' begun at Memorial University in honour of James Bradley and continuing to this day – ed.

Peirce and Heidegger in a recognisable 'history', but also with a view to breaking some new ground in this field. This would be achieved by way of a harvesting of the implications of these thinkers. We did set to work on this project and parts of it have already seen the light of day in various articles. It remains incomplete.

This, however, is to reach the end before the beginning. What I propose to do just now (as the Scots would say) is to trace something of Jim's philosophical odyssey, from the time when we first got to know each other in Cambridge in 1968. Our rooms at St Edmund's House (now College), Cambridge, were next to each other. He was there as a boarding undergraduate of Christ's College and I as a refugee theologian who had been kindly welcomed and given a Fellowship by St Edmund's. It was a time perilous for Catholic theologians! Jim was reading English, and one of the papers he could choose for his 'tripos' was a philosophy paper – the set text, Kant's *Critique of Pure Reason*. As he set about reading the text, Jim was soon fascinated by Kant's close and cogent argument; and, while continuing to lead the life of a Cambridge undergraduate with great gusto, it was then that he acquired that passion for philosophy which never left him. He did not become a Kantian; but he recognised philosophical genius in what he read. Philosophy became his first and all-pervasive interest then and for the rest of his life.

After completing his MA and a postgraduate diploma in theology, Jim enrolled in the PhD programme in the Faculty of Divinity and was assigned as his supervisor the noted philosopher Professor Donald MacKinnon, who was at that time the Norris Hulse Professor of Philosophical Theology in the University of Cambridge. Philosophy in Cambridge at this level could be studied under the aegis of the Divinity Faculty, the Department of Philosophy or that of the History and Philosophy of Science. Movement between these faculties and departments was endlessly fluid. Jim chose as the subject of his thesis 'The Philosophy of Feeling of F. H. Bradley'. Apart from the attraction of synonymity, Jim was interested in the transposition of idealist thought from Germany to the more empiricist, down-to-earth soil of the British tradition. He was later to publish a pair of highly informative articles on British idealism under the title 'Hegel in Britain', which appeared in the *Heythrop Journal*.[2] To carry out this work he transferred to a new and, for him, very influential supervisor in the person of the Reader in History and Philosophy of Science, Dr Gerd Buchdahl, a refugee from Germany by way of Australia, I believe. He was the author of the important work,

---

2. James Bradley, 'Hegel in Britain: A Brief History of British Commentary and Attitudes, Part I', *The Heythrop Journal* 20 (January 1979), 1–24; Part II, *The Heythrop Journal* 20 (April 1979), 163–82.

Metaphysics and the Philosophy of Science – The Classical Origins Descartes to Kant.[3] From Buchdahl Jim learned concern for meticulous but enlightened scholarship. He eventually completed his thesis, and in 1983 was awarded the PhD degree. What I think he learned from his work on Bradley in particular was that metaphysics could just as well be grounded in the empirical as in the ideal and did not need to take flight into realms of pure idealism or *a priorism*.

In 1984–85 he was awarded a prestigious Humboldt Fellowship at the University of Munich. This began his 'continental' links and proved to be the beginning of a very large number of international connections from which Memorial and its philosophy department benefited enormously over the years.

In the intervening years I had found my way to the Department of Philosophy at Memorial University, where I first went at the invitation of J. G. (Peter) Dawson as a visiting lecturer, obtaining a regular tenure track appointment two years later. By 1986 I was finishing a six-year stint as head of department and we needed a replacement for the following academic year. The department was persuaded that Jim's background and interests made him an excellent candidate and invited him to accept this position. And to be thoroughly unoriginal and trite, 'the rest is history'. From here on Jim's philosophical career was linked inextricably with the life of Memorial's Department of Philosophy. Under the leadership first of Dawson and subsequently of F. L. (Lin) Jackson, the department had developed important strengths in historical philosophy for which Jim was ideally fitted. Apart from the occasional *faux pas*, as on one occasion saying, quite outrageously, 'of course in a real university…', by which he meant Oxbridge, Jim thrived and prospered in the department, not only through his powerful teaching capacity but also his attention to the availability of philosophical material in the university bookstore and the ongoing development of the philosophy collection in the university library. In the mean time he devoted his boundless philosophical energy to ongoing research and publication. He enriched the life of the department also by his overseas connections and arranged important liaisons, notably with the University of Hannover, with which there were a number of exchanges.

Although, as far as I know, the thesis on Bradley was never published as a whole, Bradley remained an influence in Jim's later work. Eventually in 1996 he edited and contributed to a symposium collection: *Philosophy After F.H. Bradley*, published by the Thoemes Press.[4] His own contribution

---

3. Gerd Buchdahl, *Metaphysics and the Philosophy of Science: The Classical Origins – Descartes to Kant* (Oxford: Blackwell, 1970).
4. James Bradley (ed.), *Philosophy After F.H. Bradley* (Bristol: Thoemmes Press, 1996).

to the symposium was entitled 'From Presence to Process: F. H. Bradley and A. N. Whitehead.'[5] This gives an interesting glimpse into the movement of his focus of interest in the years of his early work at Memorial. In his essay, Jim focuses on Bradley's method and highlights on the one hand the appeal to the principle of reason – about which more later – but also the experimental nature of his philosophical inquiries. In some circles it was assumed that metaphysics in the idealist tradition must inevitably be aprioristic and axiomatic. On the contrary, Bradley adopts an experimental approach which he describes in the following terms: 'I have assumed that the object of metaphysics is to find a general view which will satisfy the intellect, and I have assumed that whatever succeeds in doing this is real and true, and whatever fails is neither.'[6] In other words, the assumption of the inquiry is that it is the world that we are trying to understand, and that in some sense this world is intelligible. I quote this because as we shall see, Jim appeals to what he refers to as the 'principle of reason' and endorses the idea that metaphysics is of its nature experimental – characteristics that he will find spelled out by Peirce.

It is worth remembering that the philosophical world in which he had worked at Cambridge, in spite of notable exceptions such as his two supervisors, Dorothy Emmet, and a handful of others, was dominated by two schools of thought, both of which were essentially hostile to metaphysics: on the one hand, the logical positivists and their successors in the logical analysis school heavily influenced by the likes of A. J. Ayer and Gilbert Ryle; and on the other, the Wittgensteinians who had been gaining influence through thinkers such as Elizabeth Anscombe and Peter Geach. To both schools, metaphysics was essentially something that had died with idealism. To pursue metaphysical inquiry was therefore in those days very much to swim against the philosophical tide. The vogue of so-called 'continental' philosophy had not yet emerged in the schools of the 1960s and early 1970s in Britain. In such a context, the pursuit of metaphysical inquiry called for a singular degree of independence of mind. But Jim believed very strongly that the great Western tradition of metaphysics would survive these negative and perhaps passing reactions.

In his own work, he felt the need to move on from Bradley, from whom he had learned a great deal. Apart from the work of R. G. Collingwood – to which he would much more recently return – Jim's philosophical interest turned to the work of A. N. Whitehead and the notion of existence as 'process'. Whitehead's earlier career had been entirely in the field of

---

5. James Bradley, 'From Presence to Process: Bradley and Whitehead', in Bradley (ed.), *Philosophy After F.H. Bradley*, 147–68.
6. F. H. Bradley, *Appearance and Reality* (Oxford: Clarendon Press, 1930), 491.

mathematics and his first claim to fame was as the co-author with Bertrand Russell of the acclaimed *Principia Mathematica*. In fact his entire career until his appointment to Harvard in 1924 had been as a mathematician. But this appointment was as Professor of Philosophy – a post that reflected the divergence of his interests from those of Russell, and which he held until 1937. In this period he developed his theory of 'process'. As one writer suggests, his movement to the recognition of being as *process* rather than *substance* was as profound a development in metaphysics as his work with Russell had been in mathematics and logic.[7]

In Whitehead's work Jim believed that he had found an important key to the nature of existence as the activity of actualisation in which the dominance of the concept of essence had been finally overcome and existence as self-actualisation could be made comprehensible. In this respect, an article that epitomises this Whiteheadian phase in Jim's conception of speculative metaphysics is one he published in *Process Studies* in the autumn of 1994 with the title: 'Transcendentalism and Speculative Realism in Whitehead'. The article is notable in a number of ways. I think that at this stage Jim had recognised that the complexity of his arguments had become a barrier to a more general understanding, and he consequently presented his case in the form of a number of 'theses', which he proceeded to state, explicate and justify. This became a characteristic of his writing right up to his final article, to which I will later turn. In this article Jim outlines the importance as well as the limitations of Aquinas's notion of *esse* or active existence and the way in which these limitations were overcome by Whitehead:

> On the first question [on the rationality and intelligibility of things] Whitehead's position is perhaps best stated in this way: while with Aquinas he gives *esse* finitely understood as the act or occasion of being – primacy over essence, unlike Aquinas he does not hold the individual to be intelligible only in terms of essence; that is the subject or first substance is not defined in terms of eminent, exemplary structures. Rather, Whitehead develops a form of analysis in which, extraordinarily, *esse* itself becomes the principle of intelligibility; by defining *esse* transcendentally in terms of serially-related structures of self-actualization, *esse* is for the first time articulated as both what makes a thing to be and what makes it intelligible. In Whitehead, it is the structures of finite, serial self-actualization which themselves constitute the conditions of empirical intelligibility.[8]

Here we begin to see more clearly the outlines of what Jim came to term 'creative order'.

---

7. Peter Hare, 'Whitehead', in Ted Honderich (ed.), *The Oxford Companion to Philosophy* (Oxford: Oxford University Press, 1995), 909.
8. James Bradley, 'Transcendentalism and Speculative Realism in Whitehead', *Process Studies* 23.3 (1994), 155–90, at 182.

However, just as Whitehead had moved across the Atlantic to North America, so the next phase in Jim's philosophical progress took him to an American philosopher, the strange genius of Charles Sanders Peirce (1839–1914). There are many areas of Peirce's philosophy which to me present huge barriers, largely because of my weakness in mathematics and logic, in which Peirce excelled and to which he made important contributions. For the very same reasons he excited Jim, who found in him the more or less complete philosopher who, unlike many of his contemporaries and successors in the English-speaking traditions, was well acquainted with medieval thought as well as with German idealism, not least with that of Schelling. In one of his by no means rare 'cheeky' moments, Jim referred to Peirce, at least with regard to metaphysics, as 'cleaned-up Schelling'. What particularly excited Jim was the deployment of the principle of triunity, about which I will say more in the final section.

Peirce's name historically has been inseparable from what is known as pragmatism. This has often been understood as the theory that truth is nothing more than 'what works', and moreover that it stems from a profound scepticism about the nature of truth. When understood without refinement, this of course is entirely destructive of classical metaphysics, ethics and even logic. Precisely because of these misunderstandings, some of which are attributable to his colleague William James, Peirce adopted the rather strange label of pragmaticism by which he preferred his own philosophy to be identified. But the idea that, since 'reality' is unknowable in itself, whatever works goes was entirely alien to Peirce's thinking. It is true that Peirce dispensed with the cumbersome idealist appeals to an 'absolute'. But at the same time he endorsed what Jim refers to as the principle of reason. There is nothing in reality that defies possible explanation. We may not know the explanation, but it goes against reason to think that there are aspects of the real for which there really is no explanation.

This needs a word of qualification, since Peirce also embraced the idea which he referred to as 'tychasm' – that there are 'chance' events in nature, not least in cosmological evolution, which are indeterminate in the sense that they are unpredictable. This is not at all the same as claiming that they are 'unintelligible'. As I understand it, it is not the embracing of unintelligibility but the rejection of a purely deterministic cosmos that is the issue here. Chance events, however, can in their turn give rise to intelligible regularities, or probabilistic laws. It was this combination of flexibility and corrigibility in the formulation of explanations that provided a way out of the impasse of determinism versus unintelligible randomness. The notion or concept of 'creation', shorn of its mythological associations, allows for the coming to be of the new and unprecedented, without which any understanding of an evolutionary cosmology and biology would be incomprehensible. Hence the importance of the notion of 'creation' in its philosophical sense.⁹

Peirce is widely known for his deployment of the 'categories' of 'firstness', 'secondness' and 'thirdness'. I cannot begin to give an account of how these might be deployed, for example and most famously, in semiotics – for in this area, nothing 'stays still' and what is an example of 'firstness' in one context can metamorphose in the twinkling of a brain cell into 'secondness' or even 'thirdness' – it is all to do with the angle we are coming from – or something like that. In principle, however, it is a theory of the deployment of what Jim came to call the principle of 'triunity' – about which, more in a moment.

In Jim's philosophical career we have reached what was tragically to be its final stage. In the midst of enormously fruitful work, most particularly with regard to speculative metaphysics, Jim was taken ill with a deadly cancer that first invaded his lungs and then began to infect that incredibly fertile and productive brain. Work on the book on speculative metaphysics came to a halt. However, even in his latter days of increasing sickness, Jim oversaw the putting together of a great amount of this material, assisted in this as in so much of his life and work by his treasured wife and co-worker, Jennifer Dyer.

I think perhaps his last formal presentation was to the conference of the Canadian Society for Continental Philosophy, held at the well-known extension of Memorial University, the Guv'nor Pub.¹⁰ Eloquently and poignantly he ended his paper with the words: 'With this, I rest my case for speculative philosophy.' I think he knew that this would be his last word on speculative metaphysics. But the paper began with a piece of irrepressible cheek, an attack on the very concept of 'continental philosophy' – talk about bearding lions in dens! But the paper does put together in a concise but powerful manner the main lines of his final position – a position which, had he lived longer, would undergo endless revision. I feel sure that he would have responded with vigour to the subsequent explorations of his work by his colleagues, represented in this tribute to him.

How many of our conversations have ended with him saying something like: 'You can tear that one [probably of last week!] up – I have revised the whole thing!' or words to that effect. By which time I had probably worked through about half of a very densely argued article! He was himself his own most continual critic.

---

9. See Peter Harris, 'Can "Creation" be a Metaphysical Concept?', in William Sweet (ed.), *Approaches to Metaphysics* (Dordrecht: Kluwer, 2004), 155–64.
10. The conference was held on 6–8 October 2011. Bradley's paper, which was given on the afternoon of the 8th, was later published in the CSCP journal. See James Bradley, 'Philosophy and Trinity', *Symposium: Canadian Journal of Philosophy* 16.1 (2012), 155–77. It is reprinted here as Chapter 10 below.

I will end by trying to show how Peirce's triunity of firstness, secondness and thirdness was able to bring to an, at least provisional, conclusion the philosophical inquiry that was the substance of Jim's philosophical life. On occasion he would summarise the essence of these categories as 'origin', 'order', 'communication' – these were the fundamental categories of existence taken in the strong sense – as Jim would say, like tea! The whole notion of speculative philosophy depended on taking existence not simply as instantiation of a variable, nor, as Kant would have it, simply as a non-determining predicate, adding nothing to the determination of the object; but rather as the fundamental activity of actualisation, or as Aquinas would have it, of *esse* as opposed to *essentia*. The difference from Kant is subtle but at the same time absolutely crucial. In a particularly powerful paper delivered to the Claremont Conference on 'Metaphysics and Things' (2010), Jim wrote:

> It [existence] is not a real or determining predicate, for it does not add any determinate feature or content to the concept of an object [so far, complete agreement with Kant]. Rather '-exists' is a non-determining predicate; *It is taken to designate that activity which is the reason why things have any determining predicates at all. Existence is here understood as 'active' existence or 'actualization.*[11]

What Jim saw here as the brilliant thread running through Western metaphysical thought was the essentially relational nature of existence. What Aristotle had conceived as the highest and most perfect kind of 'divine' being' was the activity of νόησις νοήσεως or 'thought thinking itself'. The divine life in Christian theology and speculation was conceived indeed as essentially an activity rather than a 'substance' and as triune in its interrelations. In ordinary theology this triunity was known as the relationship of three 'hypostases' – Father, Son and Holy Spirit. The drawback of this personification – essential indeed to Christian worship – *lex orandi lex credendi* – was the obscuring of divine being as pure, relational activity. But, for Aquinas, for example, the divine nature or essence consists precisely in these interrelated, circumincessive, relational activities.

The significance of this I have already alluded to in the section on Whitehead. As Jim recognised, in the theological tradition this triunity could be conceived on a 'rationalistic' model, as in Aquinas, in whom divine knowledge precedes divine love; or, conversely, on a 'voluntaristic' model as in Bonaventure and Scotus, for whom divine love is the foundation of the trinitarian life. In modern, idealist philosophy, the former might be

---

11. James Bradley, 'The Semiotic Object: Speculative Philosophy, Nominalism and Triunity', paper given at 'Metaphysics and Things: New Forms of Thought', the Fourth International Conference of the Whitehead Research Project, Claremont University, 2–4 December 2010, unpublished.

exemplified in Hegel, with the primacy of the Absolute as idea, and the latter in Schelling with the primacy of the Absolute as potency. You might be surprised, and no doubt the clientele of Chapters and Starbucks would be astounded to know, that these differences formed the subject of numerous debates over lattes and cappuccinos at our fairly frequent, though latterly not quite so frequent, *causeries* – at which we discussed not only high philosophy but also the latest news from the university and the department. I am vain enough to believe that on both counts Jim valued my comment. We certainly enjoyed these, for me, post-retirement updates. I miss them dearly.

It would be boring at this point to rehearse the case for each of these positions. What is the point, however, is that in Jim's work the continuities between ancient philosophy, Christian theology and the subsequent cultural history of the Western world could enlighten our understanding of the nature of the world we live in and what is at stake in our civilisation, not merely what are the current trends in academic philosophy.

When I tried to sketch out what I might say about the culmination of over forty years of strenuous philosophical thought and research, I had thought that I might conclude by way of a fuller account of Jim's last and most recently published paper, 'Philosophy and Trinity'. When I took it up again to see what I might say about it, I realised that Jim had managed through a gargantuan effort to muster in one place just about everything that he had come to argue about the nature and importance of speculative metaphysics. Among other things I think it manifests an extraordinary command of the contemporary philosophical scene in so far as it has a bearing on the nature and vindication of speculative metaphysics. No single talk, least of all by myself, could do justice to the strength, rigour and wide-ranging nature of what is there put forward. It is not easy reading, but it is demanding, and not the easiest of introductions to his argument for the speculative metaphysics of triunity. I think that it will be up to the subsequent lectures in this series to get to grips with the detail of this argument.

As an alternative I have thought it might be worthwhile to raise and attempt to answer the question which, no doubt, some have asked and may continue to ask: Is this kind of speculative metaphysics simply crypto-theology? The repeated appeals to the notions of trinity and triunity surely betray a dependence on views that have passed with the passing of Christian faith in the Academy.

What I will try is something between the short answer and the long one.

When we philosophise, we philosophise inevitably and unavoidably in a *tradition*. Even as radical an anti-metaphysician as Martin Heidegger, who could herald the 'end of philosophy', recognised both the inescapability of that tradition and moreover that he had spent his philosophical life in dialogue with that tradition. One can indeed attempt to do philosophy ahistorically, and this would surely be true of many logical analytic philosophers and many post-Wittgensteinians, but that is a choice, not an unassailable rule – just as, for example, atheism and theism are choices, in spite of what, as Terry Eagleton has termed them, the Ditchkins shout from the contemporary rooftops – or the sides of London buses!

A great deal of Jim's work aimed to show the permeation of the *philosophical* tradition by the notion of triunity – the idea of the three-in-one is to be found in Plato as well as in Aquinas and Scotus.[12] It shapes the great critical system of Kant and passes over powerfully into Schelling and Hegel. It is fundamental in the thought of Collingwood and Peirce. There is no appeal in these philosophers to the authority of Christian doctrine or dogma. It will be interesting to see what subsequent contributors to this series will have to say on this question. It is here that I will end my sketch of Jim's 'Philosopher's Progress'.

Jim's contribution to the philosophy of our time is attested not only by his published work but also by the impressive list of his invitations to speak in universities across Europe, in Germany (Hannover, Munich, Bayreuth, Berlin, Wuppertal), Holland (Amsterdam, Nijmegen, Utrecht), Belgium (Brussels – the Belgian Academy, Leuven), Vienna and Bucharest, as well as universities in the UK, Canada and the United States. In addition to this, Jim arranged through these contacts for visits to Memorial by a number internationally known figures – it might be tedious to add another list. But the life of the philosophy department and its teachers and students, undergraduate and graduate, has been enviably enriched by the web of international philosophy that he wove. One hopes that the tradition will continue. But the influence on his students of his teaching and advice, not to mention his enrichment of their social life, is, I am sure, unrepeatable and will be sorely missed. For Jim the original meaning of 'university' at the time of their origin was its most profound meaning: 'the community of teachers and scholars', as exemplified in our department as well as in its Jockey Club,[13] and its marvellous blend of the academic and the social – at which Jim was indeed a genius.

---

12. Both of us were delighted when we read H.-G. Gadamer's essay, 'The Dialectic of the Good in Plato's Philebus', in H.-G. Gadamer, *The Idea of the Good in the Platonic–Aristotelian Philosophy*, trans. P. Christopher Smith (New Haven: Yale University Press, 1986), 104–25. Jim had quite strong reservations about Gadamer's hermeneutic philosophy, but certainly had a great admiration for his highly enlightening work on Plato and Aristotle.
13. The Jockey Club is an informal weekly philosophy discussion group that takes place in a pub in St John's. Bradley was one of its founding members and most faithful attendees – ed.

Introduction: James Bradley's Path to the Trinity

James Bradley's densely argued and sometimes cryptically compressed essays and lectures span the whole history of Western philosophy, from Plato to Deleuze. His main project was to understand this history as a coherent search for an explanation of why things are the way they are – and why they are at all – and he insisted to any who would hear him that 'the key' to understanding this history as an integrated whole, an uninterrupted conversation, is the Christian doctrine of the Trinity. Bradley's published essays, which were not numerous (depending on whether you include encyclopaedia entries and book reviews, just over thirty), chronicle his development, from his early, meticulous studies of a selection of problems in the history of modern philosophy, to his own systematic position, which constitutes an original and at once humanistic and realistic metaphysics, in both senses of the term 'realist': anchored in mind-independent beings and including the reality of universals or ideas among them.

This book has been edited in the hope that it will not be the last word on Bradley's philosophy; indeed it is my hope that the book shall begin the scholarly reception of his philosophy. Bradley's realism should be of interest to the many philosophers pursuing varieties of 'objective' metaphysics today, from the ontologies of objects to the many versions of realism and materialism that are introduced with regularity each year. I would hazard to say that Bradley's philosophy is more relevant now than it was when he was lecturing on it internationally in the 1980s and 1990s. For Bradley reminds us, in this 'post-human' era, that one can think an emergent, material order without denying human difference; that one can return to metaphysics without jettisoning the achievements of the linguistic turn in philosophy; and that one can think the divine without lapsing into so called 'onto-theology'. Whether anyone wants to hear this message is an empirical question that can only be answered by publishing and distributing Bradley's work as widely as possible. This book is only an introduction to this work. It should be soon followed by a collection of Bradley's seminal works on Whitehead (over a dozen substantial and strikingly original papers, some of them still unpublished). And then there are the dozens of presentations to the Memorial University community. Bradley approached the annual winter Philosophy Colloquium at Memorial University as a laboratory in which he would work out the ideas that he would later publish. But much of this material was never published, for Bradley was as selective in what he would publish as he was condensed and even laconic in his writing. I hope to see all of this material published as well, for in his occasional lectures to the university community in Newfoundland, Bradley endeavoured to explain his ideas to non-specialists. These lectures were carefully written up in his characteristically impeccable style and are eminently readable. But they will need readers. And it is my hope that with this volume, those readers shall be found.

While rooted in what he called the Anglo-American speculative tradition (British idealism, process philosophy, and certain key figures in American philosophy), Bradley's philosophy offers a fresh and extraordinarily comprehensive account of the basic principles of thought and being. These principles have not remained unknown until now, although they are always in danger of being forgotten. They are deeply embedded in the history of Western thought, which for Bradley includes both the history of philosophy and the history of theology. Bradley's philosophy governed his teaching, lecturing and writing until his early death in 2012. His work was cut short by illness just as it was crystallising into its clearest and most original formulation.

Bradley's philosophy was first hammered out in the context of a lonely but vigorous defence of British idealist positions among Cambridge analytical philosophers who wanted to hear nothing more about them, when he was a postgraduate student at Christ's College in the 1970s. When he got to Memorial in the late 1980s, Bradley found a welcoming community that was, at least among the students, enthusiastic to hear more about what he called 'speculative philosophy'. I first met Jim when I was 22 years old and an undergraduate in philosophy at Memorial. I remember his argument against scientism at that time (something that bothered me then and to some degree still does today): the scientific naturalists, Jim asserted, wish to settle philosophical issues by reference to facts, but they fail to see that this can never work, for in philosophy it is the facts themselves that are at issue. I have never forgotten that proposition, and I shall be thinking about it still in years ahead, for it says so much about why philosophy is at once so needed, and at the same time so unappreciated in the university of the twenty-first century.

I was on my way to a monastery – I had decided that the *vita contemplativa* was more authentically philosophical than graduate school. Jim did not disagree. His only concern was whether the monastery in question had a library. This exchange, which returns to me over thirty years later, sums up Jim's attitude to academic life in general (for he was a consummate academic), and to academic philosophy in particular, which he believed in without wavering. Academic success, fame, honours, well-placed publications and positions were not essential to a philosophical life for Jim. These things could no doubt become valuable additions to a life lived philosophically, but one ought never to confuse them with the thing itself. In short, philosophical achievement does not need public approval or widespread recognition. What it needs is books, the leisure to read them, and a community to discuss the ideas to which they give rise. Jim's words from that conversation all those years ago now shed light for me on his devotion to two central institutions in St John's: the Queen Elizabeth the Second Library of Memorial University, which Jim made sure had the best collection of philosophy books of any library in eastern North America, and the Jockey Club, the informal weekly philosophy discussion group which Jim co-founded in St John's in 1993. Jim seldom missed a session, and kept careful notes of the important things that were occasionally said. It was, he insisted, the heart of the department, and it remains so today.

Jim and I reconnected in 2003 when I was a newly minted PhD from Toronto teaching a couple of courses at Memorial in the summer to pay down my student debt and try to find a foothold in the academy. The monastic life had lost its appeal after a time – to make a long story short, there were not enough books there for me, nor the leisure to read and discuss them. I found Jim little changed, holding court in St John's, unquestionably the master of the vibrant discussion that sprang up around him wherever he went, but wielding his authority with an exquisitely light touch. When I joined the faculty at Memorial in 2007, largely because of his invitation to apply and his enthusiasm for my application, Jim became my regular interlocutor and one of my closest friends. I consulted him on all matters, academic, philosophical and personal. I looked forward to many more years of conversation. I had so much still to learn from him, not the least why he was so hard on the nominalists (among whom he included Aristotle and Aquinas), what he understood by God (which he often described as the explanation that explains itself), and why he insisted on explanations, when clearly they were always breaking down. He is no longer available for a chat. But he leaves behind him his papers, his questions, and above all the memory of his irrepressible zeal for philosophy.

In my first years at Memorial, I often wondered how Jim had adjusted so well to this environment, which was academically and intellectually miles distant from Cambridge. I realised only after he was gone that his response to Memorial, which had rescued him from the unemployment allotted to many British academics coming of age under Thatcher, was to bring as much of Cambridge to his Newfoundland institutional home as he could. If he could not influence the administration to create a space more conducive to free intellectual discussion (what else is a university for?), he could at least change the atmosphere around him. When I sat in his book-lined study, with the rich smell of years of tobacco smoke suffusing everything, I often felt as though we were in a medieval college at Cambridge or Oxford, rather than where we were, in a middle-ranking, remotely located, comprehensive Canadian university. As the discussion progressed Jim would produce volume after volume of things I had never read but which he insisted were intimately related to points I was clumsily and inadequately trying to make: T. H. Green, Bosanquet, Buchdahl and above all Peirce. For me, Jim embodied what George Grant describes as the necessary pre-condition of ethical and political life: love of one's own. Jim loved Memorial and his department, not because it was better than any other department, but because it was his. By loving it so unconditionally he changed it and made it better than it needed to be.

At Cambridge, Bradley studied English literature, theology and British idealism, in that order. He wrote his PhD thesis on F. H. Bradley (no relation), at a time, as I have said, when the British idealists were at their lowest ebb of popularity. Bradley's supervisor was the well-known philosophical theologian Donald MacKinnon, who in turn was a student of R. G. Collingwood. Bradley's work is thus historically situated in a line of twentieth-century Oxford and Cambridge philosophers who were in some way heirs to the nineteenth-century British idealists but who engaged the historical legacy of Nicene-Chalcedonian Christian theology (as the British idealists for the most part did not). They turned to theology, as Bradley himself did, not necessarily on confessional grounds, but because they perceived that the history of Christian theology was inextricably intertwined with modern Western rationality.

Bradley had deferred his plans to write a book until after he was free from chairing the Department of Philosophy at Memorial University, a duty to which he had given himself wholeheartedly for a decade. He was diagnosed with terminal lung cancer on his 63rd birthday, shortly after stepping down from the headship. On his deathbed, Jim passed me his outline of what he thought the book might be, and said, with his characteristic cheer: 'It's all yours, chief.' The idea for the book articulated then, it must be said, was not yet defined enough to be executed. For example, it included contributions from other authors that I believe would have distracted from the singular vision of which Bradley was possessed. Had he lived, Bradley would have written a monograph of profound originality and significance for contemporary metaphysics. In its absence, I have edited this selection of his most important essays, with the hope that something of his genius might be preserved for future thinkers. Many of these essays have been previously published in academic journals, but among them I am delighted to be able to include several unpublished pieces, including the first chapter of the book Bradley planned to write (Chapter 7, 'What is Existence?').

I have decided to publish the essays chronologically in order to show the logic of Bradley's development, the *ordo inveniendi* of his breakthrough to the Trinity as the key to the history of Western philosophy. The following essay is my attempt, no doubt inadequate (for Bradley's thought is not something to which I have ever felt equal), to reconstruct something of the origins of his philosophy in problems emerging out of British idealism, and its culmination in a speculative philosophy of the Trinity, conceived not only as the central dogma of historical Christianity but as a perennial theory of what Bradley referred to as 'self-actualising order'. For more information about the biographical roots of Bradley's unique approach to metaphysics, the reader is referred to the preface written by one of his oldest friends, the Cambridge graduate who preceded Jim to Memorial, and who was responsible for bringing him there in 1988, the late Peter Harris.

The Search for a Self-Explanatory Account

Speculative philosophy for Bradley is a modern, historically conscious and fallibilist metaphysics that follows the principle of reason as far as it can, without heeding any arbitrary limits imposed on it by empiricism or naturalism, phenomenology or existentialism, or, for that matter, without imposing premature closure on itself or foreclosing on the range of questioning in a rationalist fashion by presuming to have more certainty on ultimate matters than we can have in an evolving universe. 'Speculative metaphysics ... pushes philosophy's commitment to intellectual inquiry to its limits.'[1] It is first of all, a fallibilist metaphysics, that is, a philosophical search for first principles which proceeds neither inductively nor deductively, but, following Peirce, abductively.[2] The criteria of truth in speculative philosophy

---

1. 'What is Existence?', Chapter 7 below, 156.
2. See 'Beyond Hermeneutics: Peirce's Semiology as a Trinitarian Metaphysics of Communication', Chapter 8 below, especially 174–6.

includes not only or even primarily coherence and correspondence, but following Whitehead, 'adequacy'.[3] The sound speculative position is the one that is most adequate to experience, experience that is neither to be conceived atomistically, as in Scottish empiricism, nor individualistically, as in phenomenology, but to risk an overused word, holistically. Experience is simultaneously personal and collective and irreducibly historical. A speculatively philosophical explanation ought to leave nothing out that needs to be explained, and it ought to so explain things as to open itself to challenge, to the falsifying fact, setting up a condition for noticing the most surprising features of the real. The experience upon which speculative philosophical explanations are to be tested is the collective human experience of the evolving universe.

Speculative philosophy in Bradley's sense is first explicitly defined by the late Schelling, and developed in different ways and with great sophistication by Peirce and Whitehead. The Kantian demolition of deductive metaphysics freed philosophy from its classicist heritage so that it could begin its speculative career unhampered by either empirical reductionism or rationalist foundationalism. At issue in the late Schelling, Peirce and Whitehead is the very possibility of metaphysics after Kant, that is, the possibility of metaphysics in an era defined, on the one side, by the new quantifiable knowledge of an evolving nature granted us by advances in the hard sciences, and on the other side, by the greater linguistic precision afforded us in logic by what Bradley, following Cassirer, calls the 'generalisation of the function', the early twentieth-century move, spearheaded by Frege, Russell and Whitehead, from the immovable certainties of subject–predicate logic to a heuristic, algebraic logic that allows reason to map an *emerging* order.[4] The empiricist sceptic and the absolute idealist, the Humean empiricist and the Cartesian rationalist, each in their own way, but with equally damaging results for philosophy, presume to foreclose inquiry with a finality that according to Bradley is not in fact possible in a universe that originates in activity, a universe that is fundamentally characterised by 'creativity', as Whitehead puts it, that is, a universe that is endlessly productive of novelty, of unique and unrepeatable events that nevertheless manifest intelligible structure. This intelligibility, however, is not a property of the things that come to be, but rather of the process by which they come to be, and so speculative philosophy must follow modern logic in reorienting metaphysics away from settled terms and their abstract

---

3. A. N. Whitehead, *Process and Reality: An Essay in Cosmology*, ed. David Ray Griffin and Donald W. Sherburne (New York: Macmillan, 1978), 3–4.
4. See 'The Speculative Generalisation of the Function: A Key to Whitehead', Chapter 4 below.

generalisations, and, after the model of mathematics, towards the relations of variable terms to one another and their recurring triune patterns of self-actualisation.

Bradley's path to the Trinity is the theme of this book. As a criterion of selecting writings from Bradley's rich output of papers and lectures, while keeping the book at a manageable length, I have chosen texts that stand as milestones on that path, along with Bradley's important later essays in which he explicitly articulates his position as a philosophy of Trinity. The path, in rough outlines, is this. After his early work on F. H. Bradley (hereafter FHB), Bradley studied Whitehead's speculative method until he discovered the triune logic of Peirce, and through Peirce, came to accept Collingwood's thesis of the Trinity as the absolute presupposition of Western thought. This is hardly a straight line. But if one reads these materials the way Bradley does, never losing the forest for the trees but cutting to the very essence of the matter, one can see the coherence of the path. FHB makes relations, without which nothing can be thought or said, inexplicable in terms of the subject–predicate logic that had determined all previous metaphysics, and its presupposition, the ontology of substance and accident. But he does not offer an alternative explanation for relations, and leaves metaphysics in aporia with his odd gesturing towards reality as an eternal, non-relational unity disclosed only in feeling. Bradley calls this 'the monistic metaphysics of presence or identity' and he finds it singularly unsatisfying (to use FHB's own criterion for truth).[5] FHB's aporia of neither internal nor external relations is the springboard for both Russellian analytical philosophy and Whiteheadian speculative metaphysics. Both make relations constitutive of concepts but in opposed ways: Russell by reducing names to definite descriptions and existence to quantification, and Whitehead by pioneering a functionalist approach to a universe of self-actualising 'occasions' that can only be understood in terms of process not products. Collingwood points out in his late work, *An Essay on Metaphysics* (1940), that the primacy of relations over substances is not only the fundamental thought of contemporary formal logic, it is also the theme of the new natural sciences, from quantum physics to ecology. And most surprising, it is the basic thesis of the Niceno-Constantinopolitan Creed that remains binding on all major Christian denominations. God can be one in three persons, according to

---

5. The phrase is taken from Bradley's essay, 'Whitehead's Transcendental Cosmology', which remains unpublished in English but was published in French. See James Bradley, 'Le cosmologie transcendentale de Whitehead: transformation spéculative du concept de construction logique', *Archives de philosophie* 56.1 (1993), 3–28, at 22. Gilles Deleuze was so impressed by this essay that he wrote Bradley a note congratulating him on it, which Bradley would proudly exhibit at his frequent and always lively dinner parties.

the Church Fathers who gathered to define the Trinity at the Councils of Nicaea and Constantinople, because the criterion of distinction for the Church Fathers was no longer substance, *ousia*, or *essentia*, as it was for Aristotle; it was relation, which could no longer be regarded, as Aristotle had regarded it, as merely an accident of substance. The Church Fathers assumed that this concept of 'subsistent relation' only applied to God; modern mathematics, logic and natural science has come to see that it applies to everything. Collingwood concludes that the Trinity is therefore 'a basic presupposition' of Western philosophy and science, an assumption that cannot be truly doubted because it is the frame for the very questions in terms of which doubts about it could be expressed. Bradley seeks to demonstrate, abductively (following the method of speculative philosophy perfected by Peirce), the rationality of the trinitarian presupposition.

Like any original philosophical position, Bradley's cannot be reduced to its influences: the whole is more than the sum of its parts. Nevertheless, the influence of three thinkers on Bradley's development cannot be overstated: FHB, on whom he wrote his PhD at Cambridge, Whitehead and Peirce. I would hazard to say that much of what Bradley has to say in his programmatic papers ('The Triune Event', 'What is Existence?', 'Philosophy and Trinity') can scarcely be understood without some knowledge of these three. To sum up matters that require much greater elaboration than I can give them, FHB showed Bradley the inadequacy of substance metaphysics and the logic based on it, as well as introducing him to the ideal of a fallibilist metaphysics. He showed Bradley how 'satisfaction' could be elevated into a speculative criterion of truth, and revealed to him the ontological significance of feeling. Dissatisfied, however, with the ineffable eternity of non-relational 'reality' as FHB's best guess as to what might ultimately be true, Bradley turned with great vigour and perspicuity to process philosophy. Bradley found in Whitehead exactly what FHB did not have to offer, a metaphysics of an evolving and unfinished universe, and closely related to this, the speculative generalisation of the function as the method for such a metaphysics. Most importantly, Whitehead gave Bradley his first clue as to the nature of being as activity (in Whitehead's terms, 'creativity'). But it was in Peirce's philosophy, which he finally discovered at the turn of the new century, that Bradley was most at home. Here he found his speculative philosophical method, abductive logic; his explanatory hypothesis, the activity of being (love); and especially his triunity of explanatory principles: spontaneity, difference and order.

Bradley's path to the Trinity, then, belongs to a post-Kantian tradition of metaphysics. Bradley's thought is resolutely *metaphysical*, that is, a rigorously philosophical elaboration of first principles, but at the same time, *critical*, accepting as decisive certain key elements of the Kantian critique of classical metaphysics, above all, Kant's critique of deductive onto-theology and his reorientation of philosophy away from classical, *a priori*, deductive approaches to a reality assumed to be eternally accomplished, towards a more empirical approach that assumes as its primary task the explanation of the results of the natural and cultural sciences. The late Schelling pioneered this method, as Bradley pointed out to me on many occasions, and called it 'metaphysical empiricism'.[6] In his 1842 Berlin lectures, Schelling argues that while Kant had conclusively shut down rationalist, *a priori* metaphysics, he had left open the possibility of a fallibilist metaphysics which learns from new experiences, especially the new discoveries in the natural sciences and the historical-critical human sciences beginning in his day.[7] Schelling's metaphysical empiricism does not presume an eternally valid set of terms from which it deduces the structure of reality, such as matter and form, or substance and accident, for reality is not complete. It hypothetically constructs its terms, and revises them as it continues to learn from experience. But such a metaphysics is not *inductively* based on experience; rather it argues *towards* experience (as Schelling puts it, the method of metaphysical empiricism is neither *a priori* nor *a posteriori*, but *per posterius*).[8] Bradley describes this post-Kantian Schellingian project, which he made his own with his distinctive style and original formulations, as an explanatory metaphysics, a constructive and revisable metaphysics that recognises the provisionality of every successful explanation in a universe that has not yet finished unfolding, and yet still maintains the principle of reason, the assumption basic to all rational philosophy, that everything that occurs has its reason for occurring, even if this reason is not presumed to be 'sufficient' to what it causes, for the consequent in an emerging order always exceeds the causal power of the antecedent. An emerging order is one in which the effect, *pace* Descartes, contains 'more reality' than the cause. Such reasons, Bradley insists, over and over again in these essays, must be traceable back to a ground of being that explains itself, a self-explanatory first principle. In short, metaphysical empiricism, or in Bradley's terms, 'speculative philosophy', has made peace with historical consciousness, and yet has not, with Nietzsche, Weber and the 'postmoderns', given up on the pursuit of ultimate knowledge in the vortex of a Heraclitean flux of history in which nothing admits of a final explanation because no essential structures of intelligibility are stable enough to serve as the terms of a final explanation.

---

6. F. W. J. Schelling, *The Grounding of the Positive Philosophy: The Berlin Lectures*, trans. Bruce Matthews (Albany, NY: SUNY Press, 2007), 171ff.
7. Schelling, *The Grounding*, 147ff.
8. Schelling, *The Grounding*, 180.

Speculative philosophy finds its compass bearings in an evolving universe, not in any unchanging *terms* of reference, such as Aristotle's categories or Spinoza's axioms, but in the formal elaboration of the *relations* of terms to one another, and the recurring logical structure of such relations, which are proven (abductively) to be determinative of all that comes to be. Cassirer calls this the pivotal twentieth-century move from the logic of 'substance' to the logic of 'functions'.[9] Bradley agrees with Cassirer that the only real advance in logic since Aristotle is the generalisation of the function, the move from substance as the nexus of concepts, which are accordingly understood to be generalisations on the basis of an abstraction from difference, to relations as the nexus of concepts, which are now understood as concrete universals specifying the rules governing the serial iterations of differences. The *speculative* generalisation of the function, according to Bradley, is to be distinguished from the *analytical* generalisation of the function. With a few exceptions, analytical philosophers generalise the function so as to elide the question of being and reduce existence to quantifiable instantiation.[10] Speculative thinkers such as Whitehead take the point of the generalisation of the function to be to increase the capacity of philosophy to think novelty.

The late Schelling calls the functional relations determining anything that comes to be 'the three potencies of being'.[11] Peirce, who may well have drawn on Schelling in this regard (although the scholarly reconstruction of this debt has still not been done), calls them the three categories of thought.[12] Whitehead, using different expressions, makes the speculative

---

9. See Ernst Cassirer, *Substance and Function*, trans. W. C. Swabey and M. C. Swabey (Chicago: Open Court, 1923), 3–26. Cassirer shows how Aristotelian abstraction has the problem of achieving generality by prescinding from differences. A functionalist logic solves this problem. Instead of generalising what all instances of a class have in common, functionalist logic formalises the rule that any instance in an indefinite series must be expected to follow. This move, which Cassier finds so revolutionary (and Bradley follows him in this), is the philosophical application of the mathematical rule-based approach to variable numbers in a series to variable entities in an order of being conceived as emergent. 'To the extent that the concept is freed of all thing-like being, its peculiar functional character is revealed. Fixed properties are replaced by universal rules that permit us to survey a total series of possible determinations at a single glance' (Cassirer, *Substance and Function*, 22). One of Bradley's most original moves is to extend functionalism in logic to a non-substance-based realism of universals.
10. For an important reference to some of the analytical exceptions, see Chapter 10 below, note 8.
11. F. W. J. Schelling, *Philosophy of Revelation (1841–42) and Related Texts*, ed. and trans. Klaus Ottmann (Thompson, CT: Spring Publications, 2020), 41–52.
12. See C. S. Peirce, 'The Principles of Phenomenology', in *Philosophical Writings of Peirce*, ed. Justus Buchler (London: Routledge, 1940), 74–97, at 75. Peirce refers to Schelling in several places in his collected works, but never directly to the late lectures on revelation. Nevertheless, the methodological parallels are striking. See Paul Franks, 'Peirce's "Schelling-Fashioned Idealism" and "the Monstrous Mysticism of the East"',

philosophical method explicit through his generalisation of the function: what recurs invariantly in a universe whose most basic features are creativity and novelty cannot be the species and genera of the kinds of beings that exist, for these evolve and must be considered variables. But as in an algebraic equation, one might still discern the structure of a pattern of becoming, continuous with past 'occasions of experience', and so reliably true to that degree, even in the absence of the new terms that come to be, by disengaging the relations that any and all terms must have to one another.[13] The Canadian theologian Bernard Lonergan, who was equally committed to a move from classical metaphysics into a situation in which knowledge has fundamentally changed under the influence of relativity theory, quantum mechanics and statistical science, calls such a metaphysics 'heuristic' because it does not pre-decide what it is to be known but only stipulates the cognitive conditions that would need to be satisfied by anything that is to be known.[14] It is worth noting that Lonergan's cognitive conditions are also ordered as a triunity: experience, understanding and judging, and explicitly patterned on the psychological analogy of the Trinity in Augustine and Aquinas.[15] Bradley's work clearly belongs in this lineage, and scholars of the late Schelling, Peirce, Whitehead and Lonergan will find much in it that will interest them and further their own research.

Particularly in his later works (after the turn of the millennium), Bradley deploys the fallibilist method of metaphysical empiricism to the end of demonstrating the explanatory power of trinitarian thinking, and thereby proving the unity of Western philosophical and theological experience. The goal is not to vindicate Christianity above all other religious traditions, but to extract the logical core of the Nicene and Chalcedonian Christian theological traditions, and put it to work on the fundamental metaphysical

---

The British Journal of the History of Philosophy 23.4 (2015), 732–55. In 'Philosophy and Trinity', Bradley argues (without offering any textual evidence for the claim) that Peirce's three categories are based on Schelling's late doctrine of the Trinity (Chapter 10 below, 255). I believe Bradley is right – the parallels are too close, and Peirce never concealed his admiration for Schelling, which makes it unlikely that he would *not* have read the later work – but unfortunately Peirce's references to Schelling are all to the early Schelling, in which his theory of the three potencies is only nascent. Peirce's three categories manifestly do not map on to Schelling's *early* doctrine of potencies.

13. See 'The Speculative Generalisation of the Function', Chapter 4 below.
14. Bernard Lonergan, *Insight: A Study of Human Understanding*, vol. III of *The Collected Works of Bernard Lonergan* (Toronto: University of Toronto Press, 1992), 521ff.
15. Bernard Lonergan, *Verbum: Word and Idea in Aquinas*, vol. II of *The Collected Works of Bernard Lonergan* (Toronto: University of Toronto Press, 1997). The similarities between Lonergan and Peirce have been noted before. See Vincent G. Potter, 'Objective Chance: Lonergan and Peirce on Scientific Generalization', *Method: Journal of Lonergan Studies* 12.1 (1994), 91–108. It is not hard to read Lonergan's notion of experience as firstness, understanding as secondness, and judgement as thirdness.

question, articulated by Leibniz, and picked up in various ways by Schelling, Peirce, Whitehead and Lonergan: Why is there something rather than nothing? Why Christianity should have broken through to the functional, heuristic, explanatory categories, the triunity of ontological principles, which Christianity defines as the three divine persons in God, 'vestiges' of which are found in all that God has created, is a question that preoccupies Bradley to the end, one that neither Peirce nor Whitehead address to any important degree. The question leads Bradley back to his beginning, which was the study of theology at Cambridge. Bradley's last essays, it should be noted, are brilliant and original contributions to non-confessional philosophical theology. Bradley's position on the Trinity more or less aligns with the late Schelling's: the logic of the Trinity is universal even if its discovery as such was dependent upon Christian theology.[16] The Christian doctrine is not properly understood if it is too simplistically regarded as 'supernatural' and trans-rational. In fact, the doctrine is not only reasonable, but expressive of the essence of reason as such. But the Trinity is not for that reason reducible to logic.

Readers will note Bradley's important distinction between speculative descriptivists and speculative explanatorists (see Appendix A, Table 1). Both are opposed to the naturalism that reigns in analytical philosophy. Most naturalists espouse, explicitly or implicitly, a weak theory of existence as quantifiable instantiation, according to Bradley. All speculativists espouse, explicitly or implicitly, a strong theory of existence as activity. Some speculativists are determinists, assuming an already complete reality (Plato, Aquinas). Others are indeterminists, assuming an emerging or incomplete reality (Schelling, Peirce, Heidegger, Whitehead, Bergson, Deleuze). Some speculativist indeterminists are descriptivists, accepting implicitly or explicitly what Peirce calls 'the no hypothesis hypothesis'.[17] Bradley, like Peirce, is a speculative explanatorist, arguing abductively for the reasonableness of a self-explanatory origin of order. At the end of the day, the speculative descriptivist as much as the naturalist forswears an adequate explanation for why things are the way they are, arguing in effect that explanations at some point are no longer possible and the philosopher must accept things as given without explanation. Now it might turn out to be the case that

---

16. See F. W. J. Schelling, *Philosophie der Mythologie. Erstes Buch. Der Monotheismus*, in *F. W. J. Schelling, Sämtliche Werke*, ed. F. F. A. Schelling (Stuttgart/Augsburg, 1856–61), XII, 79: 'It was not Christianity which created this idea [of the Trinity], but on the contrary, this idea produced Christianity.'
17. See C. S. Peirce, MS 950, c. 1890, Harvard University Library, quoted in Helmut Pape, *The Irreducibility of Chance and the Openness of the Future: The Logical Function of Idealism in Peirce's Philosophy of Nature* (Roskilde: Roskilde Universitetscenter, 1996), 2.

no ultimate explanation of the universe is in fact possible, but this would have to be demonstrated. The search for such a demonstration would be nothing other than the search for a self-explanatory explanation: in other words, it would be speculative philosophy. To put it more succinctly: while an ultimate explanation remains possible, but not necessary, it cannot be decided upon in advance, either affirmatively or negatively.

Most importantly, speculative philosophy is postulatory rather than apodictic, and fallibilist without being merely pragmatic. As such, Bradley's speculative philosophy is prepared to think the new, to revise itself, continually, as it endeavours to offer more and more adequate explanations of a universe of emergent order. In Bradley's view, the tightrope walk between disruptive, novel event and adequate explanation is the proper task of metaphysics and the deepest challenge facing modern thought. Speculative philosophy must deploy a logic adequate to such a task, one that neither generalises, as does induction, nor concludes with certainty, as does deduction, but hypothetically explains in such a way as to leave nothing out that demands explanation while opening itself up in a very precise way to falsification. Peirce was the first to call this logic abductive, but he did not invent it.[18] The abductive tradition in logic begins in German idealism and gets an important impulse from British idealism, especially F. H. Bradley's criterion of 'satisfaction'.[19] It is outlined as the method of any metaphysics adequate to the discoveries of science in the first chapter of

---

18. C. S. Peirce, 'Pragmatism as the Logic of Abduction', in *The Essential Peirce: Selected Philosophical Writings, Volume 2 (1893–1913)*, the Peirce Edition Project (Bloomington: Indiana University Press, 1998), 226–41. Peirce also calls it 'retroduction'. See C. S. Peirce, 'A Neglected Argument for the Reality of God', in *The Essential Peirce*, II, 434–50, at 441. Peircean abduction is known as the logic of the hypothesis and the argument to the best explanation. It is also the logic of discovery and can be seen at work wherever human beings had to invent something radically new in order to achieve a desired result. Whereas deduction begins with sound premises and deduces valid or unshakable conclusions therefrom (arguing from antecedent to consequent), abduction begins with conclusions ('surprising facts' that need explanation), or desired outcomes (conclusions), and postulates the premises that could produce such results, arguing in effect from consequent to antecedent. When early humans needed to invent a way to safely kill a mammoth from a distance with a projectile weapon, they invented a thing that had never before existed, the hand-held wooden spear thrower. They began with the 'conclusion' or the consequent: spearing a mammoth from a distance, and on the basis of that proceeded to 'dream up' a technique (Peirce calls this move 'musement', 'A Neglected Argument', 436). I owe this example to Dietrich Dörner, Professor Emeritus at Bamber University.
19. See F. H. Bradley, *Essays on Truth and Reality* (Oxford: Oxford University Press, 1914), 317: 'The truth for any man is that which at the time satisfies his theoretical want, and "more or less true" means more or less of such satisfaction. The want is a special one. We do not of course know beforehand what it is and what can satisfy it. We only at first feel that there is something special that we miss or gain, and we go on to discover the nature of the want and its object by trial, failure and success.'

Whitehead's *Process and Reality*. Abduction has come to be associated with the logic of hypothesis formation in the philosophy of science, but it should not be restricted to that specialist line of inquiry. It is, as Bradley develops it over the course of these essays, the mode of reasoning proper to a situated rationality provisionally finding its way in a universe of emergent rather than predetermined order.

At the centre of the speculative tradition, Bradley discovers the recurring doctrine of the triunity of ultimate explanatory principles, which in his view is the logical root of the Christian doctrine of the Trinity and the key to understanding the nature of reality itself. The relationship of speculative philosophy to Christian trinitarian thinking will be for some readers Bradley's most dubious move, but it is not without precedent in the history of modern metaphysics. Here again Bradley follows the late Schelling, although Bradley never in fact wrote on Schelling.[20] To be brief on a matter that receives much greater elaboration in the essays to follow, every explanation works with three basic principles: possibility (formulated in the principle of identity), difference (the principle of non-contradiction) and order (the principle of reason, or what Schelling calls 'the law of the ground').[21] In the third-century doctrine of the Trinity, which is still maintained by all major Christian denominations, early theologians such as Clement and Origen of Alexandria, and Athanasius a century later, who won the day at the Council of Nicaea which defined the doctrine of the Trinity in 325, drew upon Jewish and pagan neo-Platonism to articulate the trinitarian structure of the divine, which they believed could alone adequately explain the Christ event.[22] The divine is not monolithic or homogeneously one, but comprises three hypostases or internal relations: a unitary principle of origin, the person of 'the Father'; a principle of duality based on that which originates from the first principle, the person of 'the Son' ('the only begotten' and the archetype and mediator of creation, that is, difference); and a principle that unites these two opposite divine principles of 'unbegotten' and 'begotten', the person of 'the Spirit', who constitutes the perichoretic relation between the Father and the Son, the circulation of self-effacing love, beginning with the self-abnegation of the Father in willing there to be another beside

---

20. At last we have a coherent presentations of the late Schelling on the potencies translated. See Schelling, *Philosophy of Revelation*, 41–52. I spent many hours discussing the late Schelling with Bradley, and vividly remember him studying Schelling's *Philosophie der Offenbarung* in the years 2007–12. Bradley used to say that Peirce was Schelling 'cleaned up', Schelling without the obscurity and 'darkness' of late Romanticism. I never quite agreed on this point, for I find Peirce even more obscure than the late Schelling.
21. F. W. J. Schelling, *Philosophical Investigations into the Essence of Human Freedom*, trans. Jeff Love and Johannes Schmidt (Albany, NY: SUNY Press, 2006), 17.
22. Charles Bigg, *The Christian Platonists of Alexandria* (Oxford: Clarendon Press, 1886).

himself, and continuing with the self-abnegation of the Son in willing that the Father should be 'all in all', as Paul puts it (*panta en passin*, 1 Cor. 15:28).

Schelling was not the first to argue that the trinitarian relations are in one way or another universally acknowledged by thinkers independently of one another in various traditions throughout history – that they are not only divine persons, they also represent principles of intelligibility. But, with Hegel and Franz von Baader, Schelling was among the first of modern philosophers to explicitly relate the structure of the divine Trinity to the principles of logic. Bradley always found Schelling's trinitarian thought superior to Hegel's, for the former held fast to the speculative project, and the latter, in Bradley's view, capitulated to rationalism.[23] This is a point that needs to be more carefully scrutinised in the rush of new works on German idealism (many appearing in the series in which the present book is published). Wherever the relationship of German idealism to trinitarian theology remains unknown, or even in some instances suppressed, this important research cannot happen.[24] Bradley's essays may prove crucial in this respect, for his work is an example of how philosophy can appropriate its Christian heritage while avoiding the Scylla of confessionalism and the Charybdis of essentialism. Modern philosophy, regardless of how atheist, immanentist or materialist it purports to be, remains indebted to theology, and in Bradley's last major work ('A Key to Collingwood's Metaphysics of Absolute Presuppositions: The Trinitarian Creed', Chapter 9, below), he unequivocally recognises the insuperability of this dependence.[25]

While Bradley's commitment to speculative or fallibilist metaphysics is as old as his doctoral thesis, the breakthrough to the speculative significance of the Trinity occurred relatively late in his career. It is manifestly absent in his early work on British idealism. In these early papers (only one of which we have been able to include in this collection, Chapter 1: 'F. H. Bradley's

---

23. 'Hegel's "new" is already contained in its beginning. "Immediate actuality" already has within itself, as the "inner", the possibility of the "new" reality as its "other" . . . In consequence, the "new" that emerges from this process is not a new in the sense of what has never been there before . . . He can thus ultimately conceive the movement of the absolute, all-containing totality as a "return" to itself and to regard it as the revolving circle after the fashion of Aristotle.' 'Whitehead, Heidegger and the Paradoxes of the New', Chapter 2 below, 58. For a similar critique of Hegel in Peirce, see C. S. Peirce, 'Evolutionary Love', in *Philosophical Writings of Peirce*, ed. Buchler, 361–74, at 365–6.
24. See Dale M. Schlitt, *German Idealism's Trinitarian Legacy* (Albany, NY: SUNY Press, 2016).
25. I recall how impacted Bradley was by his late realisation that Collingwood was right about 'absolute presuppositions'. We cannot get behind these historically contingent beginnings of speculation because they make possible whatever it is we think or know. This discovery occurred while Bradley was researching Collingwood in 2010–11. See Chapter 9 below.

Metaphysics of Feeling and its Place in the History of Philosophy'), one sees Bradley tracking a single thought, which first struck him as a question, the answer to which would give him the trinitarian key to the history of philosophy. This question made Bradley unsatisfied with the systems of Kant, Hegel and their British followers, which he read at Cambridge, even as he found it quite impossible to retreat to a pre-modern position, say that of Plato or Aristotle or one or other of their medieval followers. The pre-modern figures could not be ignored, and were in some respects more astute on the pitfalls of certain philosophical dead ends than their followers (nominalism, for example); but they wrote for a different age with different questions. Central problems that cannot be neglected in our time, above all the problem of the historicity of thinking or the eventfulness of time (what Bradley refers to below as 'the paradoxes of the new'), were non-existent for them. However, the question Bradley asked was not only a modern question, it was a question put to the whole history of Western philosophy, indeed, a question that put that whole history into question. The question allowed Bradley to conceive of the Western tradition as one unbroken trajectory, the significance of which had not yet been fully grasped by contemporary philosophers, isolated as they are in their analytical and continental silos. The question was this: What is the origin of the universe in all of its material and immaterial variety and dynamic productivity? Any answer worth considering would need to provide not only an explanation for why *things* exist; it would also need to provide an answer to the question of the *reason* for the existence of the origin itself. In Bradley's language, the only satisfactory answer to the question would be a self-explanatory account; anything less than this would be no account at all. There is no guarantee that such an absolute explanation exists: being might in fact be absurd. The principle of reason does not guarantee that it isn't; it only ventures, on postulatory grounds, that a self-explanatory explanation *might* exist, and that, in any case, reason is constitutively oriented to seeking one.

Self-explanatory explanations of existence have, of course, been offered in the past, notably by traditional philosophical theologians of the *actus purus*. However, if one concludes too quickly that the origin of the universe is God, or a first cause, one risks begging the question, for it can obviously still be asked, Why does *God* exist? Modern subjective idealist answers are no better than foundationalist metaphysical theories, according to Bradley, for they too suffer shipwreck on an unexplained ground; if not the creator God, then the synthesising subject, who produces a world out of the raw materials of sensation, but who himself is not produced and is thus inexplicably given. The naturalism that Bradley rails against and that dominates contemporary thought precludes the whole speculative enterprise by insisting that things are simply given as they are – there's no use asking why they are given thus and so and not otherwise. The question of existence according to naturalism leads nowhere and should be dropped in favour of more promising inquiries, invariably questions concerning language, science or politics.

Why has naturalism so taken hold of contemporary philosophy? Because, Bradley argues, contemporary philosophy has forgotten the question concerning the nature of existence. While readers of Heidegger will prick up their ears at this point, and Thomists might be inclined to cheer, it must be said that Bradley's turn to ontology has little sympathy for the early Heidegger nor for phenomenology in general, and he always remains suspicious of Thomists as closet nominalists. Theories of existence, according to Bradley, are either weak or strong. A weak theory of existence holds that 'being' refers to nothing other than *instantiation* and is to be dealt with via a functionalist *and* quantitative approach to ontology that is best pursued symbolically. A strong theory of existence, such as is typical of the speculative philosophical tradition from Plato to Hegel, holds being to be primarily *activity*. Instantiation is the product of this activity; it cannot therefore explain it. Being, for Plato and Aristotle (*einai*), as for Bonaventure and Aquinas (*esse*), has an originally verbal sense (as does the German *sein*, and the English 'being') and only secondarily, derivatively or analogously a nominal sense (*ousia/ens*). Before there are beings, there is the act of being which makes a being what it is. In Bradley's words, '"Being" does not denote a mysterious, impalpable abstraction. As a verbal noun, it is intended to capture the active existence of things. Thus a good general rule for the modern English speaker is to understand "being" as denoting activity of some sort.'[26] As Bradley's philosophy became better defined, the position taken on existence became the litmus test for whether a philosophy should or should not be regarded as 'speculative' (whether descriptivist or explanatorist): what is usually termed 'speculative metaphysics' characteristically defends a strong theory of existence. The differences between strong and weak theories of existence are so fundamental to any views we may have of the nature of reality that the debates between them are the driving force of Western philosophy. Indeed, these debates are at the centre of the conflicts and oppositions, the arguments and alternatives, which characterise not only Western philosophy but Western culture as a whole.[27]

Bradley gives several reasons for the contemporary forgetfulness of the activity of existence. Chief among these is the very generalisation of the function that makes modern speculative philosophy possible. For driven by Russell's nominalism, the generalised functional approach to logic has

---

26. 'What is Existence?', 162.
27. See 'What is Existence?', 149–56.

allowed for the emergence of a system of symbolic notation in logic that permits philosophy to elide the question of existence, to answer the question by making it nonsensical. Frege, Russell and Wittgenstein render the copula unnecessary by means of a system of symbols in which being means simply instantiation, effectively solving the problem of existence by rendering the question impossible. Many believe that Fregian-Russellian symbolic logic advances philosophy by closing off certain dead ends of traditional metaphysics that invariably lead to unanswerable questions. In Bradley's view, the move plunges Western philosophy into a deeper obscurity than had held sway in the 2,500 years of its history. Speculative philosophy is obstructed if not rendered impossible by first-order or predicate logic, for the meaning of existence is no longer a legitimate matter for questioning. But the error is not unique to the analytical traditions; the continentalist assumes as much when he or she refuses to inquire into the possibility of an infinite and self-explanatory ground of existence. The analyst formally precludes the question of being (or answers it without in fact asking it) when she mandates that existence is only a quantifier. To say that something exists is simply to posit some bearer of predicates or to introduce in front of the predicate F, the existential quantifier $\exists$, substituting $\exists x F x$ for the predicative judgement, which means, for the predicate F, there exists something, x, which answers to it. Elided by this notation, which has more or less determined analytical philosophy ever since, is the question of the nature of originary being.

From F. H. Bradley to A. N. Whitehead

Bradley's dissertation in philosophy is entitled 'F. H. Bradley's Metaphysics of Feeling'. It was defended in 1983 and has yet to be published as a whole. While Bradley became increasingly critical of the idealism of FHB and more or less broke with his philosophy in the 1990s, he never entirely escaped his influence. Bradley's style of writing in compressed and pithy sentences, direct and succinct to the point of being cryptic – a style so at odds with the verbose indirection of contemporary continental philosophy – owes much to FHB's masterly prose. One of the latter's great accomplishments is to have translated the terminologically obtuse theories of the German idealists into concise, jargon-free and compelling arguments. Whatever one might think of FHB's system, his *Ethical Studies* is a masterpiece of English philosophical writing. But more than a stylistic influence, Bradley's speculative philosophy of the Trinity is in many ways rooted in a critique of FHB. The latter's paradox-laden work demonstrated to Bradley both in method and result the insufficiency of dualistic metaphysics, that is, the need to transcend traditional metaphysical dualisms – mind/body, universal/particular, form/matter, identity/difference, noumena/phenomena, or in FHB's language, relations and terms – by means of a third, ordering principle, which would establish the dyad as constitutive of a triad. For FHB this transcendence of dualistic thought is ostensibly achieved through his doctrine of the absolute as the indescribable, indeed, unknowable unity of appearance and reality. The absolute for FHB is felt, and the feeling for totality is lost in reflection and only partially recovered in every true proposition.

According to Bradley the concept of feeling plays a far more significant role in FHB's thought than most commentators have noticed. Bradley is particularly impressed with how FHB's idealism strives to be adequate to the empirical, which is so much a theme of English philosophy, without capitulating to the abstractions, and ultimately the nominalism, of Scottish empiricism. Feeling in FHB does not reference sense data built up into complex ideas (the atomistic empiricism of Locke and Hume), but the pre-conceptual givenness of reality as a non-relational whole to sentience.[28] By making feeling central, Bradley believes that FHB made up for what was lacking in German idealism – notably due attention to the empirical. For Locke and Hume, conceptual reflection and predication is as secondary to immediate experience as it is for FHB, but the experience that empiricism would make foundational is the discrete experience of unrelated sense data, which are ostensibly assembled like building blocks into concepts. The atomistic empiricists would break the world up into discrete and unrelated bits, and thereby render predication, and indeed knowledge itself, impossible. What we originally 'feel' according to FHB is not patches of colour or sounds, nor is it the brute facticity of singular things, but the continuous and unbroken whole of the given, a unity of being in which everything is harmoniously united with everything else. If we were to speak truly and adequately of anything in the universe, FHB contends, we would have to exhaustively describe it in such a way as to show its internal relations to everything else that exists. This, of course, is not possible with discursive thought. It would be to see, with Blake, 'a world in a grain of sand', and to 'hold infinity in the palm of your hand'.[29] And yet while we cannot speak of the unity of reality, for every statement breaks up that which belongs together, we nonetheless *feel* it, and the feeling of it impels us to move beyond any single proposition in an endless search for the totality of true statements, which would alone be adequate to the whole.

After working on this concept of feeling throughout the 1970s, Bradley came to reject FHB's solution to the problem of predication because it

---

28. Bradley, *Essays on Truth and Reality*, 159–91.
29. William Blake, 'Auguries of Innocence'.

offers no account of how relations emerge from the absolute, and so can no more answer the question, why these discrete appearances and not rather unbroken reality, than a naturalist can answer the question (let alone ask it), why is there something rather than nothing?

> What the speculative philosopher asks is: 'Why are there instantiations of relations or connectivity?' 'Is it possible to establish any reason for the fact of connectivity?' The speculative philosopher's interest is in the fact that there are relations, and whether or not any account can be given of them over and above the fact that they are partial, incomplete, intrinsically connective objects. In asking 'Why are there relations?' or 'Why do relations relate?' speculative philosophers are not overlooking the intrinsic connectivity of relations. Rather, they are inquiring into the possibility of a self-explanatory account of connectivity in terms of actualising activity. Hence the strong question speculative philosophy puts to relations remains open and is perfectly intelligible.[30]

These and similar questions inspired Bradley to search for a more adequate approach to an *emerging* and unfinished order of being in Whitehead's process philosophy. For Whitehead, metaphysics must be adequate to *all* experience, particularly the experience of relations and so-called 'appearances'. Nothing, Whitehead says, can be left out. Above all metaphysics must be adequate to the modern experiences of evolution, of deep time, and on a cultural level, of historical consciousness. Whitehead tackles these 'paradoxes of the new' head on, and Bradley studied his work for over a decade. The decisive question facing Whitehead, and indeed, modern philosophy, in Bradley's view, is the puzzle of novelty. As Bradley puts it, 'How can metaphysical reason analyse that which in the nature of the case is unique and unrepeatable or genuinely new?'[31] One answer to this question, the one pursued by Heidegger and deconstruction, is that it cannot. Metaphysics, by which Heidegger means 'onto-theology', the deductive derivation of all beings from a first absolute being, is fundamentally incapable of thinking the event. Bradley took the Heideggerian answer very seriously, and accepted its

---

30. 'What is Existence?', 168. In the many philosophical debates that Bradley engaged in at Memorial University (for he was above all a philosopher of the spoken word), he would usually return to the question of nominalism. This often exasperated his interlocutors, who failed to see as he did the systematic consequences of nominalism for contemporary logic, metaphysics and ethics. For Bradley, nominalism was not only a dead end for *speculative* philosophy, it was a dead end for philosophy as such. If I were to venture a critique of Bradley on this point, I would point to the *ethical* significance of nominalism in the history of philosophy. Without nominalism of the late medieval variety, but before that, of an ancient Jewish stripe, the irreducible freedom of the rational individual would have remained unthematised. A historical relation exists between the conceptualisation of the freedom of the individual in Christendom and the nominalist tradition. Otherwise put, a strong doctrine of the realism of ideas is often at the expense of the intelligibility of the free act (as it was for Plato and Plotinus, for example).
31. 'From Presence to Process', Chapter 3 below, 94.

premise: that philosophy must become adequate to eventful time in a way in which onto-theology never was, even if he rejected the conclusion that metaphysics or the search for the ultimate *explanans* must be abandoned. Whitehead offered Bradley a way to approach an emergent order, a method for thinking eventful time that was rigorous, scientific and falsifiable.

While Peirce became even more important to Bradley in terms of thinking of meaning as objective event, it was Whitehead who showed him that the synthesis associated with meaning is not a cognitive act, as in Kant and atomistic empiricism, but a real and universal feature of a processively emerging reality. Bradley is not a Platonist in the usual sense: as numbers exist in virtue of an act of the mind that counts them (according to Brouwer's philosophy of mathematics), so to do universals exist in virtue of an act of the mind recognising meaning coming into existence through a series of events. The refutation of nominalism, therefore, need not be aligned with an ahistorical assumption of eternal essence. What Bradley calls Whitehead's constructivism is decisive for his moving beyond the impasse between nominalism and realism. On the basis of it, Bradley pursues what could be regarded as a speculative and evolutionary theory of universals.

> For Whitehead there is no such thing as a single occasion, for an occasion is nothing else than a medial movement of becoming from what precedes to what follows it. It is 'that which never really is' (*Process and Reality*, pp. 82, 84): when in becoming it does not exist, and its completion is its perishing. It is a site of transition, a relational connection or 'passage' (*Adventures of Ideas*, p. 303), a 'route of inheritance' (*Process and Reality*, p. 181) – a character which is most accurately described by saying that it combines the empiricist notion of the objective datum with the idealist notion of constructive activity by placing them on an horizontal plane as antecedent and consequent 'phases' or 'stages' of an occasion. An occasion, that is to say, has direct experience of past occasions, but the significance or 'status' (*Adventures of Ideas*, p. 226) of the antecedently given is 'decided' (*Process and Reality*, p. 43) by the occasion itself in its movement of becoming.[32]

Later Bradley sums this up as the move from the synthesising cognitive subject as the principle of the unity of judgements (the idealist view) to meaning as an objective synthesis. Wittgenstein takes this in a nominalist, weak-theorist direction (meaning as use); Bradley takes it in a realist, strong-theorist direction, and this is what most attracts him to Peirce's semiotics. When a sign is anything that stands for an object to anything else, and not only for a cognising subject, as in Peirce's triune theory of sign/object/interpretant, reality itself becomes constructivist. 'This is an extreme realism of objects and universals, in which the cosmos is an information exchange system . . . In short: Being is the event of communication.'[33]

---

32. Bradley, 'Le cosmologie transcendentale', 22.
33. Bradley, 'The Semiotic Object', unpublished paper given at Claremont Graduate University, 2010, 8.

Whitehead is not only a thinker of eventful time, according to Bradley: he is also a thinker who assumes a strong theory of existence, which he elaborates in terms of his master idea of 'creativity' to contest mechanistic and deterministic accounts of evolution. Bradley follows Whitehead in seeing FHB's non-processive notion of being as a consequence of the limitations of the subject–predicate model of logic and a failure to take seriously the advances made in the sciences, especially in mathematics and physics. The generalisation of the function, for which the empirical becomes a variable to the recurring patterns of categorial form, 'an analogical algebra of the new', allows Whitehead, in Bradley's reading of him, to articulate a strong theory of existence as processive or emerging order.[34] Difference for Whitehead is not mere *appearance*, a subjective defection from the rich positivity of the real, as it is for FHB; it is 'a matter of the pluralistic self-differentiating or self-actualising nature of things without reference to any principle of cause or production'.[35] Bradley sees a real advance in the thinking of the new in Whitehead. What is seen by Kant or Russell as synthesis, construction, a condition of cognition, is for Whitehead the serial or 'vectorial connections or transitions between occasions of self-actualisation'.[36] In a nod to FHB, Whitehead argues that we *feel* the connection between the occasions that make up an event. This feeling for the process of reality is no longer associated with a perfect or completely realised infinite, as it is in FHB, but with a progressively developing and emerging order. Whitehead's vectorial analysis of feeling maintains the internality of relations imperilled by Russell's atomistic empiricism, but without lapsing back into what Bradley reads as FHB's ahistorical monism. And with Russell, the asymmetry of serial relations is acknowledged but without rendering order a logical construction. 'Any subsequent occasion is internally related to its antecedent occasion, but its antecedent occasion (as completed or "perished") is not internally related to it. That is to say, the internal relations of occasions are serial or asymmetrical in character.'[37]

With the move from universally recurring forms (substance metaphysics) to functionally 'mappable', emergent variation (process metaphysics), Whitehead renders the occasion the base unit of ontology. Reason in the register of process metaphysics becomes abductive rather than deductive, a categorial mapping of events rather than a determination of the properties of things. Reason does not generalise or conclude with certainty; it rather explains what is occurring as best it can on the basis of what is given to be explained, and stands always ready to revise its explanation in the light

---

34. 'Whitehead, Heidegger and the Paradoxes of the New', Chapter 2 below, 59.
35. See 'From Presence to Process', 91.
36. See 'From Presence to Process', 92.
37. See 'From Presence to Process', 93.

of some new fact. In this way the postmodern slide into the irrationalism of pure difference (philosophy become mere description) is averted, but without retreating from eventful time to determination by concepts (that is, Hegel). The categorical is related to the empirical as 'an equation defining a function is related to the value of its variables'.[38]

C. S. Peirce and the Philosophy of Trinity

Bradley is keenly aware of the social-political context of the rise of what Gadamer calls 'historically effected consciousness' (*Wirkungsgeschichtliches Bewußtsein*), both the antecedent historical conditions of this paradigmatic shift, which according to Strauss defines the moderns over and against the ancients,[39] and the sociopolitical consequences of it, namely the emergence of liberalism and socialism as contesting but equally historically minded theories of social-political life.[40] While on the one hand, historical

---

38. See 'Whitehead, Heidegger and the Paradoxes of the New', 63.
39. Leo Strauss, *Natural Right and History* (Chicago: University of Chicago Press, 1953). Strauss calls the modern attitude, which understands reality to be as temporally variable as human opinion, as 'the historical sense' or 'historical consciousness'. He sums it up in the proposition, 'all human thought is historical and hence unable ever to grasp anything that is eternal' (p. 12).
40. H.-G. Gadamer, *Truth and Method*, 2nd rev. edn, trans. Joel Weinsheimer and Donald G. Marshall (New York: Continuum, 1995), 265ff. In 'Philosophy and Trinity', Bradley references R. J. Campbell, *Truth and Historicity* (Oxford: Clarendon Press, 1992), which he calls 'an indispensable work' (Chapter 10 below, 249, n. 7). Bradley published a review article on Gadamer's magnum opus in 1977, 'Gadamer's *Truth and Method*: Some Questions and English Applications', *The Heythrop Journal* 18 (October 1977), 420–35. In this seminal piece for the young Bradley, who was still a graduate student at the time, he praises Gadamer for recognising what Bradley calls 'the historical-linguistic finitude of man' (p. 434). But Bradley criticises Gadamer for leaving the nature of truth unclarified, and thereby surrendering the epistemic claims of the human sciences. 'It really is difficult to determine the relation of truth and method which is his [Gadamer's] concern . . . As a result the different "kinds" of truth that the human sciences achieve is left in obscurity' (p. 435). Of greatest interest in this review article is the immanent critique to which Bradley subjects Gadamer, and by implication, Gadamer's teacher, Heidegger. Gadamer does not take historical consciousness seriously enough, according to the young Bradley, for he explains language in terms of ontology with no reference to the social-political conditions that determine the various 'horizons' of meaning that make language at any given time intelligible. 'Going further, one can even ask (secondly) whether ontology as such is wholly adequate to the proper development of a theory of language. For although Gadamer in no way suggests that language determines natural or social reality, or reduces these latter to a linguistic phenomenon, he does appear to overlook the fact that language and understanding are fundamentally determined by political, economic and social structures. Again, our understanding of these structures is undoubtedly linguistic in nature but the ontological theory of language and understanding as such, avoids the actual historical conditions in which its transcendental

consciousness threatened philosophy and culture with truth-destroying relativism, as Nietzsche was among the first to point out, on the other hand, it allowed people to hope that the future could be better than the past. Values are no longer rooted in eternity but are as changeable as is everything in the universe. As such, the values of a previous era can no longer impede technical and social-political progress. To such a sense of history Bradley readily concedes many of the greatest advancements of modernity, for example the ascendancy of the ideal of human equality and liberty, dramatically manifest in the change in European attitudes to women and the rise of socialism in the nineteenth century. None of this emancipatory humanism seems to him to be possible in a classicist metaphysical frame that assumes an eternally stable, already realised normative order of nature and an unchanging essential human nature. Bradley also recognises with a small minority of historians of ideas the theological origins of historical consciousness, how the hope that the future can be better than the past, which is rooted in the concept of eventful time, finds its inception in Jewish-Christian eschatology.[41]

In 'Philosophy and Trinity', Bradley writes:

> A key feature of the Judaeo-Christian view of truth is that truth is not a timeless state of affairs. It must occur, and it must be unfolded and realised again and again in new situations that shed fresh light on it. It is as such intrinsically connected to actions in time. In consequence truth is not a reality that lies behind appearances, but is something that emerges in history and is nothing other than

---

conditions are constituted' (p. 434). When one sees how important Christianity as the social-historical context for explaining the rise of historical consciousness will become for Bradley at the end of his career, the significance of these remarks for his development becomes clear.

41. Two monographs in particular were important to Bradley in his tracing the rise of historical consciousness to the new attitudes to time and being that emerged from early Christianity: R. G. Collingwood's *The Idea of History* (Oxford: Oxford University Press, 1946), esp. 46–52, and Charles Norris Cochrane's *Christianity and Classical Culture* (Oxford: Oxford University Press, 1944), particularly Part III. Bradley is fully aware that the argument concerning the Christian discovery of historicity is a mainstay of German Romantic and idealist thought and can be found expressed by Schleiermacher, Friedrich Schlegel, Schelling and Hegel. The argument recurs in a less idealistic form in Wilhelm Dilthey's *Introduction to the Human Sciences*, trans. Ramon J. Betanzos (Detroit: Wayne State University Press, 1988), especially in Dilthey's analysis of the historical significance of Augustine's *Confessions* (pp. 228–39). The young Heidegger picks the thesis up from Dilthey, and with his characteristic flair sums it up in one short, pithy sentence, 'Christian religiosity lives temporality as such.' See Martin Heidegger, *The Phenomenology of Religious Life*, trans. Matthias Fritsche and Jenifer Anna Gosetti (Bloomington: Indiana University Press, 2004), 80. On the inception of Heidegger's phenomenology of temporality in his research into the nexus of historical consciousness and early Christianity, see S. J. McGrath, *The Early Heidegger and Medieval Philosophy: Phenomenology for the Godforsaken* (Washington, DC: Catholic University of America Press, 2006), 185–207.

its coming-to-be in the movement of history. On this account, because the real is to be found nowhere except in the movement of history, in the contingent materiality of socio-economic, institutional and cultural circumstances, the movement of history is itself the unfolding and construction of the real. As the movement of history itself, with all its potentialities, the real is more than any of its specific historical manifestations or formations. But the real is at least what the constructive movement of history has shown it to be, and is nothing less than that.[42]

In the short passage from which this excerpt is drawn (the third thesis in the article), Bradley articulates the basic presuppositions of his mature philosophical position on truth and historicity. They can be summed up as follows: Truth is primordially disclosure, unveiling, and not a relation between propositions and facts. Hence, correspondence is not its locus, rather, adequacy or 'coherence and comprehensiveness' is. While truth as disclosure is a primitive Greek concept (*aletheia*), truth is first conceived as a properly historical event of unveiling or revelation in Jewish-Christian theology. As such, truth is no longer expressed in terms of the appearance/reality dichotomy (which was basic to Greek thinking, and in which FHB remained caught); it is rather a personal event that cannot be abstracted from its situation of occurrence, and one that must be repeated and revisited in new situations. The truth must be personally appropriated over and over again. The event of truth is not a once and for all happening, but a processive unfolding that must be endlessly appropriated because reality is not eternal but processive, and the process includes the consciousness of the process. That is, it is not only truth that is an event, but the disclosure of truth as an event that is an event, and one that is still ongoing. Historicism has prematurely surrendered truth to the vicissitudes of history: what is needed is not the defeated perspectivism of Nietzsche, or the relativism of Weber, but rather a new theory of truth that can be adequate to both its eventful nature and to an evolving reality that is not yet finished and that includes the consciousness of that reality unfolding in human history.

But for Bradley it is not enough to say, as many others have, that the Jewish-Christian concept of history is the presupposition of social equality and natural scientific progress; one has to offer an account of the origin of the universe that is adequate to this experience, that is, an account that explains why the universe is emergent rather than cosmologically closed, and why in this emergent universe, beings such as ourselves exist, that is, beings who not only understand a processively emergent order, but who also hold themselves to be morally responsible, that is, free, and standing before a future of open possibility, rather than finding themselves embedded in an eternal hierarchy of being. The hermeneutical question cannot be avoided at

---

42. 'Philosophy and Trinity', Chapter 10 below, 232.

this point, the question Collingwood asks in his *Essay on Metaphysics*: Why is the breakthrough to historicity (eventful time) contingent upon a certain religious tradition, the Jewish-Christian tradition? Why is it not, rather, a common discovery of many cultures? The overwhelming evidence that our modern understanding of time is in its origin theological rather than philosophical or speculative, and that it continues to maintain itself on religious grounds, impacted Bradley deeply and drove him to take Collingwood's thesis of 'basic presuppositions', and indeed the whole 'hermeneutic turn' in twentieth-century philosophy, much more seriously than he previously had.

Towards the end of his career, the precise nature of the Christian break with the classicist cosmos became more evident to Bradley. It is not only our concept of God that changes under the pressure of the Greek and Roman reception of Christian revelation, it is also the concept of time that changes. And while the Christian conception of God remains a matter that is not widely understood outside theology, the Jewish-Christian conception of time as open, emergent and undetermined has permeated secular thought to its very core. Had Bradley lived longer, he would, I believe, have ventured to demonstrate the intrinsic and systematic connection between the two great ideas that Christianity bequeathed to Western philosophy, historical time and Trinity, for they are in truth essentially connected, as the late Schelling demonstrated. Only a God that is in himself differentiated and internally processive, Schelling argues, could be the source of an emergently ordered universe.[43]

But before he turned to Collingwood, Bradley discovered the only modern thinker whom he was inclined to regard as his master in speculative philosophy, C. S. Peirce.[44] Bradley has a very specific point of entry into the Peircean corpus. Once again it concerns the logic of eventful time. There can be no order without an end in the sense of final cause or *telos*, and yet in philosophies where teleology prevails, as in Aristotle, Aquinas and Hegel, determinism holds sway. What emerges into order is that which the being always already was, as Aristotle put it, *to ti ên einai* (*Metaphysics*, 7.4). Teleological development in Aristotle and Aquinas is the unfolding of an inchoate but necessary determination, hidden in the beginning, and to that degree a species of determinism. What Peirce shows Bradley is that *telos* can, and indeed must, be conceived non-deterministically. As Whitehead also makes plain, a relation of ground to consequent is conceivable that does not bind the two together deterministically but frees the consequent and makes possible a non-deterministic emergent order. Non-deterministic teleology, according to Bradley, who follows Peirce closely on this, requires

---

43. See Schelling, *Philosophy of Revelation*, 173–85.
44. Bradley sometimes casually described himself, understatedly to be sure, as a Peircean.

an explicit recognition of the triadic structure of being as such. For in the end it is Peirce, not Schelling or Whitehead, who proves for Bradley that existence as such, from the micro to the macro, from the real to the ideal, from the possible to the actual, is constituted by a triad of principles that mutually imply each other and give rise to an emergent and open-ended order.[45]

Peirce describes the three categories of 'firstness', 'secondness' and 'thirdness' in a bewildering variety of ways. Bradley's preferred Peircean terms are 'spontaneity', 'difference' and 'order'. While the relation of the Christian Trinity to Peirce's logic frequently enough goes uncommented upon by mainstream scholars of Peirce, it is obvious to Bradley, as it is, I think, to most serious scholars of theology. Nathan Houser, for example, never mentions the Christian Trinity in his otherwise superb summary of Peirce's thought, even when he describes Peirce's three categories as follows: 'Firstness is that which is as it is independently of anything else. Secondness is that which is as it is relative to something else. Thirdness is that which is as it is as mediate between two others.'[46] Few trinitarian theologians will fail to see this as an expression of what Scholastic theology calls 'subsistent relations', that is, essential differentiae, which are distinguished from one another not in terms of substance or essence but in terms of the relations of terms to one another.[47] Indeed the Peircean categories so described apply

---

45. Bradley draws an important distinction between triads and triunities (above all in the seminal essay, 'Triads, Trinities and Rationality', Chapter 5 below). Both triads and triunities make opposition and synthesis of opposites basic to order. But where triads represent a *hierarchical* order, in which one of the three principles has primacy over the other two, triunities are non-hierarchical, and posit a co-equality of three principles, in which the third principle is not a mixture of the first and the second but the principle of connectivity or relation between the two. Plato's limited, unlimited and mixed is a triad, because the relations are hierarchical – the limited is superior to the unlimited, which is subordinated to it and dependent upon it as matter is to form in Aristotle; the third is clearly defined as a mix rather than an ordering of the two opposites. Augustine's trinity of 'mind', 'word' and 'love', by contrast, is a triunity for there is no subordination of any one of the three to any other and the third orders the preceding two. See Table 1 in Appendix A below, 'Triadic Theories of the Ultimate Principle of Actualisation.'
46. Nathan Houser, introduction to *The Essential Peirce. Selected Philosophical Writings, Volume 1 (1867–1893)*, ed. Nathan Houser and Christian Kloesel (Bloomington: Indiana University Press, 1992), xix–xli, at xxx.
47. The term 'subsistent relation' is used by Aquinas to explain how the divine persons defined at the councils of Nicaea and Constantinople can be one in being or substance and yet each irreducibly distinct. Aquinas notes that the distinctions between the Father and the Son are first defined at these councils in terms of relations of opposition. The Father is opposite to the Son in being uniquely unbegotten; the Son is opposite to the Father in being uniquely begotten. The Spirit then is 'the bond of love', as Augustine first described him (*vunculum amoris*), not only uniting the Father to the Son but also logically uniting the two opposites. See Aquinas, *Summa Theologica*, 1a, q. 28, 'The Divine Relations', and q. 29, 'The Divine Persons', especially a.

directly and without alteration to the three subsistent relations by which the three divine persons are distinguished from one another in the one divine nature at the councils of Nicaea and Constantinople: the Father is ungenerated, the Son is begotten, and the Spirit (in the Latin reception of the Niceno-Constantinopolitan Creed) proceeds from the Father and the Son, or less controversially, from the Father *through* the Son, as Aquinas puts it (*Summa Theologica*, 1a, q. 36, a. 3). The Father is God insofar as he is unoriginated and originating, grounded only in Godself, and the ground of all that proceeds from within God, infinite and dependent upon nothing and antecedent to everything. The Son is God insofar as God has generated another to the Father, one who is equal to the Father in everything and distinct only in the relation of being begotten of the Father and hence dependent upon the Father. The Spirit is God insofar as the relationship of the Father and the Son constitutes a distinct third, equal to the divine nature and possessing all that the Father and the Son possess but distinct from both in its uniquely having proceeded from the Father through the Son, the one 'which is as it is as mediate between two others'.[48]

> Once mathematics and natural science had established the intrinsic relationality of the natural world, the relational model could unproblematically be transposed under the rubric of triunity, not only to the analysis of the constitution of the finite subject (as with Kant's plethora of triunities), but also to the whole of reality, defined as an Absolute Subject with three essential modes or operations (Hegel and Schelling).[49]

The development of the trinitarian significance of Peirce's thinking in particular is perhaps Bradley's main contribution to Peirce scholarship.[50] Bradley, however, aims at far more than a contribution to scholarship.

4: 'Therefore a divine person signifies a relation as subsisting' (*Persona igitur divina significat relationem ut subsistentem*). Aquinas is building on Augustine, *De Trinitate*, Book V, ch. 5. Medieval Christianity is thus driven by revelation to articulate a new conceptual understanding of relations as not only accidental but in some cases subsistent, an understanding that is universalised in modern logic and mathematics. On subsistent relations in the Trinity, see Peter Harris, '*Esse*, Procession, Creation: Reinterpreting Aquinas', *Analecta Hermeneutica* 1 (2009), 136–67, at 144–5.

48. This is not the place to open up the *filioque* controversy, the debate concerning the procession of the third person of the Trinity which divides Western and Eastern Christianity to this day. Bradley, like Peirce, adheres to the Latin line wherein the Spirit is held to proceed not directly from the Father, but from the Father and the Son. Peirce agrees. 'By the third, I mean the medium or connecting bond between the absolutely first and last.' C. S. Peirce MS 1.337, cited in Vincent G. Potter, *Charles S. Peirce on Norms and Ideals* (Worcester, MA: University of Massachusetts Press, 1967), 87.

49. 'The Triune Event', Chapter 6 below, 138.

50. See A. J. Robinson, 'A Semiotic Model of the Trinity: God, Evolution and the Philosophy of Charles Sanders Peirce', PhD dissertation, University of Exeter, 2003; Andrew J. Robinson, 'Continuity, Naturalism and Contingency: A Theology of

His philosophy of Trinity has at least three aims in view: first, to think eventful time without surrendering the principle of reason, that is, to think an emergent order of being, non-deterministically, as communication; second, to demonstrate the universality of triune logic and so the unity of philosophical experience and the largely unacknowledged reasonableness of Christian dogma; and third, to show the continuity of the history of Western theology and the history of Western philosophy, that is, to think the history of Western thought as a whole (with theology influencing philosophy at decisive points, and philosophy influencing theology from the beginning). Bradley's philosophy of Trinity is as dependent upon his theological training and his wide-ranging reading of the history of theology as it is upon his relatively late discovery of Peirce.

Having said that, the following qualification is necessary. Bradley does not presume a theological perspective on philosophy, but rather endeavours to draw on theology with the same neutrality with which he draws on logic and the sciences. If he advocates a notion of divinity in the end, which he does, it is arrived at through purely philosophical arguments. That Bradley's notion of divinity happens to coincide with the Trinitarian God of the Niceno-Constantinopolitan tradition is a result of his philosophical investigations, not a presupposition of his research. At least that was how he understood himself. It may be that with his late Collingwood research Bradley re-examined the whole business and reconsidered to what degree an ahistorical approach to triunity is even possible. Certainly he wanted to believe that in principle, anyone at any point in history ought to have been able to discern the triune structure of the real. But in fact, this discernment does not seem to have occurred outside of the orbit of the influence of revealed Christianity. I must say, in my all discussions with Bradley, I never remember him discussing faith or arguments from faith. He appeared to have suspended his theological voice, quite likely for very good reasons.

That said, at the centre of Bradley's mature expression of the philosophy of Trinity is the Johannine notion of the self-explanatory principle of the divine as 'love', a concept that Bradley most sublimely defines in 'the tenth thesis' of 'Philosophy and Trinity':

> Being or activity is not here primarily analysed as substance or as subject but as communication, the unconditional communication of freedom by the triune principle of actualisation. Unconditional communication is thus the actualising condition of substance and of subjectivity, of all determination. At this point we cannot avoid the question: just what is unconditional communication? There is only one answer, and this is my tenth and final thesis: being as communication is love as unconditional giving or donation, un- conditional concern (*agape*). Only

---

Evolution Drawing on the Semiotics of C. S. Peirce and Trinitarian Thought', *Zygon: Journal of Religion and Science* 39.1 (2004), 111–36.

in this way can the spontaneity and individuality of things and, in particular, the contingent evolution of physical nature, be properly secured. And the reason is that unconditional concern is open to what it does not control or determine. It does not stand in opposition to contingency, nor does it treat contingency as a lower moment of some absolute completeness, for unconditional concern *surrenders* itself to contingency.[51]

This one passage could easily stand as the fundamental thought of Bradley's speculative philosophy. A book could, and indeed should, be written on it alone. Bradley's use of the term 'love' here is drawn from the Johannine Gospels and Epistles. But he also references Peirce's famous and somewhat inscrutable essay, 'Evolutionary Love', and it might be useful here to remember Peirce's argument in that piece, if for no other reason than to avoid a sentimental or Romantic misinterpretation of what work the concept of love is doing for the later Bradley.

Peirce distinguishes three different models of evolution: evolution by chance or 'tychasm' (from *Tyche*, the Greek goddess of fortune), which is the theory espoused by Darwin; evolution by necessity or 'anancasm' (from the Greek *ananke* or necessity), which according to Peirce is Hegel's model; and evolution by creative love or 'agapasm' (from *agape* or selfless love), which is Peirce's theory. The three models of evolution are plainly rooted in the three categories, with tychasm emphasising the element of spontaneity or fortuitous variation in evolution, anancasm stressing the mechanical necessity (external or internal) determining evolutionary processes, and agapasm emphasising the creative love that guides natural and human history. What Peirce means by the last is not obvious. He writes: 'The movement of love is circular, at one and the same impulse projecting creations into interdependency and drawing them into harmony.'[52] What Bradley understands by this is fairly clear from the last pages of 'Philosophy and Trinity'. Love is a synthesis of spontaneity and necessity: it sets individuals free on a course of creative self-development by granting to them that creative power of origination which is also their origin. And yet love ordains that out of

---

51. 'Philosophy and Trinity', Chapter 10 below, 261. In *Philosophy After F.H. Bradley*, edited by James Bradley (the only book Bradley published in his lifetime), Bradley's former colleague at the University of Ottawa, the late Canadian philosopher Leslie Armour, writes: 'Only goodness can explain the whole. For if we try to explain everything by some thing then it itself needs explanation. Only values have a kind of necessary ontological status without being things, and only goodness, perhaps, could logically be self-explanatory.' Leslie Armour, 'F. H. Bradley and Later Idealism: From Disarray to Reconstruction', in James Bradley (ed.), *Philosophy After F.H. Bradley* (Bristol: Thoemmes Press, 1996), 1–30, at 26. See also Leslie Armour, 'Values, God, and the Problem About Why There is Anything at All', *Journal of Speculative Philosophy* 1.2 (1987), 147–62.
52. Peirce, 'Evolutionary Love', 362, cited by Bradley in 'Triads, Trinities and Rationality', Chapter 5 below, 128.

that creativity, harmony rather than chaos shall ensue. Love brings about harmony not coercively but by the power of attraction. In a universe whose origin is love, one finds oneself in synch with one's neighbours by remaining true to one's own call. Understood on a cosmic scale, a lawfully ordered universe is brought into being through the unconscious collaboration of an infinity of diverse agents.

This triune logic was the best way out of the speculative descriptivist bind (presuming a rich notion of being as activity but finding nothing but disordered difference as a result) and the most articulate spokesman for it was Peirce:

> In my view, the best way out of these strange formulations [of Deleuze, Badiou and Harman], which still preserves some of the radical emphases, is to be found in Peirce's triunity. As noted, his firstness or theory of origin is the concept of a dynamical free indeterminacy that as such has no specific nature of its own, and in communicating itself to all things, is necessarily never the same. Moreover, because it communicates itself to all things, it follows that all difference or individuals, and all specific structures or laws, carry free or inexhaustible indeterminacy in their nature. That is, all individuals and all laws are essentially vague: they are inexhaustibly determinable determinations, and in this respect they do not obey the law of excluded middle. In consequence, individuals are more than any of their properties or qualities and they can never be reduced to fixed determinations. Equally, structures are always more than any of their individual instances and they are the subjects of evolution. There are, in short, no complete or completable wholes or totalities. The theory of vagueness constitutes in my view one of the great revolutions in the theory both of individuals and of forms or universals, and succeeds in completely dissolving any correlation between the concept of a necessary being as ground and an unacceptable necessitarian view of the world.[53]

Let us take note of the theological point at the end, Bradley's almost casual reference to 'the concept of a necessary being as ground'. Here Bradley is at his most Schellingian, for it is the theme of the whole of Schelling's positive philosophy that God understood as necessary being can be the ground of a freely emergent order. God does not determine the world in a necessitarian way, God determines the world to be free, that is, to evolve, to develop, to become what it will be. Bradley, with Peirce, goes further than Schelling, however, and leaves the future radically open, not prophetically oriented towards an eschaton. The degree to which Bradley breaks with Christianity here, which is essentially directed towards an eschaton (1 Cor. 15:28), is worth thinking about.

Peirce's three categories are never given in isolation, for they mutually imply one another. Any account of reality that fails to recognise all three will be abstract and one-sided. One can see the unavoidability of the three principles in their recurring appearance in one form or another of

---

53. Bradley, 'The Semiotic Object', 7.

philosophy, each of which compensates for what is lacking in the other, but with equal one-sidedness. The adequate philosophy will be generous enough to recognise all three categories in all of their diverse manifestations and applications: the spontaneous or non-conceptual ground of the real; the determinations and differences to which the ground gives rise; and the ordered relations which render those differences not a chaos of mutually incompatible realities, nor a deterministic system, but a complex and variegated emergence of being from non-being. For Bradley, Peirce's firstness means above all indeterminate being, the *me on* of possibility, which might be anything because it is actually nothing.[54] Firstness is in this sense free, and since it is preceded by nothing, it can be described as spontaneous, pure or self-moving. The Nicene tradition calls it 'the Father'. Firstness gives rise to secondness and self-differentiation, but only for the sake of thirdness or ordination. The Father begets a Son so as to send the Spirit.

Caution must be exercised on this very point. To stress thirdness at the expense of firstness is a perennial temptation of rationalists, who find order everywhere and freedom nowhere. What Hegel calls contingency is merely the negative side of the genuine necessity that guides all becoming. On the other hand, to stress firstness at the expense of secondness is the more pedestrian idealist mistake, which explains the tendency among idealists such as FHB and the early Schelling towards monism. Those who stay with being as possibility or spontaneity become pantheists of one stripe or another, and just as much enemies of individual freedom as rationalists. Finally, the more familiar error today is to stress secondness at the expense of firstness and thirdness: to assert freedom on purely negative terms and refuse any doctrine of positive freedom, that is, to refuse any notion of the good. This is the mistake most characteristic of our age, which sees difference everywhere and finds order nowhere, indeed, which refuses all ordering principles as totalising and violent. Secondness abstracted from firstness and thirdness prevails in academic meetings, where scholarship is wholly dedicated to decolonising, endlessly differentiating and negating all explanatory schema, all 'meta-narratives', because it sees in all metaphysical theories nothing more than generalisations at the expense of the irreducible

---

54. *Me on* means 'non-being', as distinct from *ouk on*, which means 'nothingness', a distinction that is traceable to Plato and is developed in a modern key by philosophers such as Schelling and Berdyaev, and in a theological key by figures such as Tillich and Moltmann. It is important to situate Bradley, if not Peirce, in this meontological tradition. See Schelling, *Philosophy of Revelation*, 48–9. For a tidy summary of the distinction, see Paul Tillich, *Systematic Theology* (Chicago: University of Chicago Press, 1951), I, 187–9. On the history of the distinction and its significance for the philosophy of religion, see Emil L. Fackenheim, *The God Within: Kant, Schelling, and Historicity* (Toronto: University of Toronto Press, 1996), 128–30.

and essentially un-orderable and undefinable singularities of history. Such scholarship takes Derrida, Deleuze, Foucault and Butler as its guide, and anathematises the great metaphysicians, Aristotle, Plotinus, Augustine, Aquinas, just as much as Fichte, Hegel and Schelling, because it suspects domination and systemic racism, sexism and Eurocentrism behind any and every explanatory schema, including the tentative and fallibilist late modern efforts to discern order emerging from the new.

Bradley's speculative move is to allow the singularities of history their irreducibility and spontaneity, and to acknowledge their power to disrupt the hegemonic systems of domination inherited from the past, while remaining open to, and on the lookout for, the new intelligibility which they are grounding. In his wide-ranging reading of philosophy, old and new, he sees traces in every discourse of a procession from the identity of possibility without determination, through the difference of determination, to the ordering of possibility and actuality, identity and difference. Hence he is simultaneously interested in and sceptical of all so-called 'postmodern' efforts to absolutise difference.

Where many theologians have argued that the universe is trinitarian in its structure because it was created by the Trinity, Bradley's innovation is to maintain the Trinity as a fully philosophical position, that is, the Trinity offers the best possible explanation for the existence of an emergent, ordered universe. What is remarkable about the Trinity according to Bradley is that it not only explains the constitutive elements of order, it also explains why order emerges at all. 'An order that is self-explanatory is in the nature of the case an active order [by distinction from a merely given order], an order that can be explained in terms of its own activity of ordination.'[55] Bradley's speculative Trinity is self-explanatory and open to the new, for it not only explains itself and the emergence of principles from identity for the sake of love, it also explains why that emergent order cannot be closed but must be open to the new: because it emerges out of spontaneity or freedom, what it grounds, since it is a likeness of it, is also capable of spontaneity and free production.

In the end, all the basic questions of philosophy converge for Bradley on the theorem of self-actualising or triune order: the logical question concerning universal and particulars, the one and the many, which eventuates in the dispute between realists and nominalists; the ontological question concerning being and nothingness, which divides philosophers into two camps, theorists of being in its weak sense as quantification, or in its strong sense as activity; the epistemological question concerning the relation of

---

55. 'Triads, Trinities and Rationality', Chapter 5 below, 117.

the knowing subject to the known object, which fractures philosophy into mutually exclusive camps of sceptics, naturalist, empiricists, rationalists and idealists; and the cosmological question concerning the closed versus the open universe, which divides the history of philosophy into two halves. On the one side are ancient determinists, from Plato to Aquinas, on the other side are modern thinkers of eventful time, who are constantly endangering the philosophical enterprise itself by falling prey to the irrationalism of chaotic and endlessly self-dissipating historical time. All these questions for Bradley can only be adequately addressed through a triune conceptualisation of self-actualising order, even if such a conceptualisation requires nothing short of the entire history of philosophy and theology if it is to get off the ground.

When he died, Bradley was only beginning to work out the relation between his concept of self-actualising order and historical Christian Trinitarian theology. In the end Bradley argues, on well-reasoned rather than confessional grounds, that the universe originates in a triune ordering activity that is best characterised as love, in the Johannine sense of *agape* (1 John 4:8). It has also been called 'the Good', which gives or diffuses itself in the universe that emanates from it, without need or motivation; it gives solely because it is its nature to do so.[56] The self-explanatory origin gives itself unconditionally. To name it 'love' is not merely to poeticise, but neither is it to precisely define it. Love is a vague term, in Peirce's sense, a symbol; it is richly, productively underdetermined. As the activity of actualisation, as distinct from any of the actualities to which it gives rise, the origin will by definition elude predication. But this qualification should not be understood in some obscurantist sense. One cannot define the undetermined in terms of the determinations to which it gives rise. The origin is not a determination but the ground of determination. The question, 'Why does self-actualising order exist?' is indeed answerable, if still mysterious and in need of a clarification that is not possible in the present, but points ahead towards a fullness of knowledge still to come. Love exists so that others might be. It exists to give or communicate being as widely as possible. That this is a conception of divinity, Bradley admits openly. Most importantly for the breakthrough to historical consciousness, the self-ordering universe produced by love is not finished; the love that produces everything does not do so externally or deterministically; rather it creates possibilities for new forms of self-ordering, the pinnacle of which is the free moral subject, or better, the society of free subjects.

This was James Bradley's path to the Trinity, and if he was not granted the time he needed to develop a systematic philosophy of the Trinity, he

---

56. See Plato, *Republic*, 509b8–10.

communicated the broad outlines of what such a philosophy would be, clearly and indefatigably, in his lecturing and teaching, and to those who knew him personally, in the way he lived and died.

Sean J. McGrath
Holyrood, NL
All Hallows' Eve, 2020

Chapter 1

F. H. Bradley's Metaphysics of Feeling and its Place in the History of Philosophy[1]

Monism as the Theory of Feeling

I want to present a simple and strictly historical thesis: that neither Bradley's position in the history of philosophy, nor any important aspect of his metaphysics, can properly be understood without reference to the theory of immediate experience.

More often than not Bradley calls immediate experience 'feeling'. And I shall follow him in this. For while he has been variously cast as a Hegelian, as a rationalist, as a Platonist, as essentially a British empiricist, as a critic of empiricism, and as a mere aberration in an otherwise unspoiled philosophical culture, the term 'feeling' usefully conveys what is in fact the central thrust of his metaphysics. He attempts, that is, to secure and guarantee the monism of the German post-Kantians, yet not through Schellingian intuition or Hegelian dialectic, but by means of a transformed account of the native Lockean theory of sensation – an account which would establish his own work as the legitimate issue both of British empiricism and German idealism.

Unlike others, then, I will not be interpreting Bradley's philosophy in terms of logical form, as paradox, metaphor or analogy; nor psychoanalytically, as a symptom of infantile or linguistic neurosis. My claim is that if Bradley is to be understood, he must be understood in terms of the substantive content of his thought and of the theoretical problematic in which it was developed.[2] The central factor in Bradley's problematic is, I

---

1. This essay owes much to the teaching and inspiration of Professor D. M. MacKinnon and Mr Gerd Buchdahl.
2. See Matthew Arnold, 'The Function of Criticism at the Present Time' (1885), in *Essays in Criticism*, First Series (London: Macmillan, 1886), 7, 17, 39; and E. Caird, 'The

believe, that the thinkers of his generation perceived the radical intellectual and social changes which took place in their time as a series of dislocations or disunities – above all, in terms of a dichotomy between nature and spirit. On the one hand, the new scientific discoveries were being philosophically elaborated in mechanistic, epistemologically dualist and agnostic terms,[3] while on the other hand, the available alternatives lacked cogency – as the critique of Matthew Arnold mounted by both Green and Bradley indicates. Arnold himself had in fact perceived that a 'time of criticism' was needed, during which 'the ideas of Europe' could penetrate the national culture; but, as Edward Caird insisted, the real 'age of criticism' could be inaugurated only by philosophers who had actually studied those ideas.

Now the German post-Kantians had directly addressed the nature–spirit problem. In this regard, as against the reductive, mechanistic materialism of the French Enlightenment, their achievement is the qualitative differentiation of nature and society. They did not, however, abandon the Enlightenment ideal of a fundamental unity of both, and in line with this ideal they set out to resolve what they saw as Kant's dualism between consciousness and things-in-themselves. Thus, for the early Schelling, nature and spirit are the equivalent expressions of an identical subject-object which is their eternally present, pre-given source and origin, and which as such is at any time accessible by means of an esoteric intellectual intuition. In contrast, Hegel, in the *Phenomenology of Spirit*, develops a historical dialectic which manifests the exoteric realisation of reason in the social order. Consequently, the identical subject-object is not for Hegel a given but a product; only now, in the epoch consequent upon the French Revolution, can it be retrospectively recognised to have been *an sich* from the start.

As is evident everywhere in their work, it is the reconciling identical subject-object of the post-Kantians which constitutes the connection between the British idealists and their German predecessors. Yet this connection, properly understood, does not turn them into 'Anglo-Hegelians'. For all abandon the dialectic of history as the road to monism.

Briefly, the difficulty was that even nature had a history now. The vast dimensions of cosmological and evolutionary time were perceived as eroding the significance of human development, and, from the early 1870s onwards, the new astrophysics lent increasing support to the view that the universe was moving towards a final state of quiescence.[4] In consequence,

---

Problem of Philosophy at the Present Time' (1889), in *Essays in Literature and Philosophy*, 2 vols (Glasgow, 1892), I, 179ff.
3. See James Ward, *Naturalism and Agnosticism*, 2 vols (London, 1899).
4. For the effect of astrophysics, see David Masson, *Recent British Philosophy*, 3rd edn (London, 1877 [1865]), 141–7; see also, of course, Tennyson's 'Locksley Hall Sixty Years After' (1886), and H. G. Wells, *The Time Machine* (1895).

the qualitative differentiation of nature and society no longer needed to be made; the problem was their reconciliation. And in this situation it was hardly likely that socio-historical experience would be seen as offering an adequate ground or basis for the identical subject-object. Even Caird's evolutionary Absolute was first of all established and defended as the necessary outcome of the German tradition, while Green's monism was arrived at by way of a critique of empiricism and Kantianism, and Bosanquet's derived from a logical criterion of coherence or wholeness. In order, however, to understand Bradley's account of the identical subject-object as grounded on the theory of feeling – which is his *ratio cognoscendi* as the guaranteeing foundation of his thought (and my sole concern in this paper) – it is necessary to specify more closely the problematic in which it was developed.

Context of *ratio cognoscendi*

T. H. Green is of course a crucial influence. To overcome that 'heavy burden on the human spirit'[5] which he sees as a consequence of the empiricist antithesis between spirit and nature, Green criticises Locke and Hume in terms of a disjunction: either the real is nothing more than a flow of discrete sensations, in which case knowledge of relations, as the work of the mind, cannot be knowledge of reality; or the order of sensations is determined by relations, and the real is thus in the last resort the work of the mind.

Green's disjunction owes a great deal to his immediate native predecessors, especially James Mill. His interpretation of British philosophy – Hume as sceptic rather than naturalist – is a retrospective account of the consequences of Mill's view of the world as the structureless abode of pure, particular feelings. And his theory of Eternal Reason is exactly the converse of that view: if feeling is structureless, mind alone must constitute the ordering structure of the world.

Now Bradley endorses Green's critique of the dualism of mind and matter inherent in empiricism and Kantianism.[6] But he rejects Green's version of the identical subject-object as Eternal Reason. Green indeed asserts that the Eternal Reason may be indifferently viewed as feeling or thought.[7] Yet because he assumes with the empiricists that sensations or feelings are structureless, discrete particulars, he either treats them as an unintelligible *surd*, and thus loses his unity, or he asserts that the order of experience can only be the product of relating reason, and thus, in order to

---

5. T. H. Green, *Works* (London, 1885), I, 142.
6. See F. H. Bradley, *Essays on Truth and Reality* (Oxford: Clarendon Press, 1914), 199.
7. T. H. Green, *Prolegomena to Ethics* (Oxford: Oxford University Press, 1883), 51.

preserve the unity, abolishes the feeling. Against Green's dualism, Bradley will interpret feeling, not as a series of discrete sensations which requires a structuring mind, but as a continuous whole of content constituting a non-relational unity of subject and object. And against Green's rationalism, Bradley will uphold the Reidian 'instinct' of his well-known epigram on metaphysics[8] – he will try with this theory of feeling to preserve the distinction between thought and existence.

In discussing the origins of his theory of feeling, Bradley himself refers to the psychology of Aristotle and of Hegel as his sources.[9] And this, though usually ignored, is of some significance. First – hardly surprising in the Oxford of his day[10] – he mentions Aristotle, not Plato. And the reference is to Aristotle's denial of psychological atomism; his view of sense-content as a kind of continuum which persists through and in change and is the ever-present basis of every stage of experience. Secondly, Bradley cites Hegel's *Philosophy of Mind* (paras 399ff.), where Aristotle's view is presented in terms of immediate feeling and goes hand in hand with a genetic or developmental theory of the individual and the race: feeling as the first stage of mental evolution. Bradley starts, then, neither with Hegel's *Phenomenology*, nor with his logic, but with his psychology.[11] And supported by Wundt's theory of 'total feeling', psychology always remains an integral element in the presentation and defence of Bradley's own account of feeling.[12]

But what of course transforms the psychological theory of feeling into the core and basis of Bradley's thought are the specific metaphysical functions which that theory has to perform. And here he owes a great deal to his nineteenth-century predecessors in the empiricist tradition – particularly J. S. Mill. For Mill set out to replace Hamilton's doctrine of the relativity of mind and matter, ego and non-ego, as the basic data of consciousness, with his own neutral stuff of discrete feelings. Of course, Mill himself admits that the continuity of feeling is as real as the sequence, but confesses that

---

8. F. H. Bradley, *Appearance and Reality* (New York: Macmillan, 1893), x; F. H. Bradley, *The Principles of Logic* (London: Oxford University Press, 1922), 591; Bradley, *Essays on Truth and Reality*, 268.
9. Bradley, *Principles of Logic*, 515.
10. See G. R. G. Mure, 'Oxford and Philosophy', *Philosophy* XII (1937), 291–301.
11. See also Bradley, *Appearance and Reality*, 508; *Essays on Truth and Reality*, 153.
12. See Wilhelm Wundt, *Human and Animal Psychology*, 3rd edn (1863), trans. E. Creighton and E. B Titchener (London, 1908), 218; compare Bradley, *Appearance and Reality*, 80n. *Essays on Truth and Reality*, 161–71, owes a great deal to Wundt's analysis of oscillatory and discordant feelings (*Human and Animal Psychology*, 219). For a historically accurate but critically dubious account of the German psychological background to Bradley's feeling, see James Ward, *Psychological Principles* (Cambridge: Cambridge University Press, 1920), 42n.

this is unaccountable, a 'final inexplicability'.[13] What conclusions Green drew from this we know. But to Bradley, reading Green and Mill together, a different conclusion could be drawn. After Mill's confession, the ground is ready for feeling to be defined, with Hegel, as a continuous whole; and, with that, it is only a short step from Mill's position to feeling taken, in Mill's manner, as both psychologically and logically primary – a creature at once mental and metaphysical. Bradley's all-too-evident ambiguity here is a result of grafting Mill's sensationalism on to the original unity of the post-Kantians.[14] And it is these two sources which account for the subjective language in which he will always elaborate his monism, even though feeling is in fact held to be neither subjective nor objective in nature.[15] Yet, so understood, Bradley's feeling will at least allow him to avoid the difficulties presented both by Green's rationalism and Hegel's dialectic in establishing the ultimate unity of nature and spirit.

Sensationalist Ground of Non-Relational Unity

The use to which Bradley puts feeling conceived as a given non-relational unity can be simply stated: from *The Principles of Logic* onwards his main doctrines have that theory as their premise.[16] Of course, Bradley is usually regarded as an intellectualist, at least to the extent that while it is admitted that he maintains a supra-rational conception of reality, the doctrines which entail that conception are held to rest on purely logical or internal analyses of our concepts. His account of relations, for instance, is universally presented as if it were modelled on Hegel's critique of the understanding. But it is then difficult to know why he refuses to follow Hegel's dialectical logic into the realm of reason. And this refusal only becomes intelligible when it is recognised that Bradley's own critique of thought is prosecuted from the start on a thoroughly sensationalist, if anti-atomistic, basis.

Such a view does not, however, carry the unlikely implication that every one of his arguments is premised on the theory of feeling. When, for example, in chapter 2 of *Appearance and Reality* he is considering the Spencer–Huxley account of relations as independent term-like entities which are given as separate impressions or feelings alongside the terms they relate, Bradley can hardly reply merely by invoking his own alternative

---

13. J. S. Mill, *An Examination of Sir William Hamilton's Philosophy* (1865), 6th edn (London: Macmillan, 1889), 248.
14. The Scottish professor Masson had already perceived how easily Mill could be taken to a post-Kantian conclusion; see David Masson, *Recent British Philosophy*, 2nd edn (London: Macmillan, 1867), 219–60.
15. Bradley, *Appearance and Reality*, 128; *Essays on Truth and Reality*, 159.
16. See Bradley, *Appearance and Reality*, 494.

theory of feeling. Instead, he convicts his opponents of incoherence, that is, of offering an account of relations which fails to explain their relatedness. And this done, he can then go on to argue[17] that relations are the work of the mind, that is, that the objects of cognition are constituted in and by our cognitive activity itself.

Now it is here that we meet the idealist dimension of Bradley's thought – the most significant register of his debt to Hegel and of his kinship with Green and Bosanquet. For all agree that there is no such thing as the direct apprehension of particulars, whether ideas, sense-data, physical objects or anything else. And this position renders especially significant the otherwise unexceptionable point that all our ideas or concepts are essentially contrastive in nature, that is, that they cannot be introduced on their own but are necessarily bound up with one another. For, once granted that there are no directly apprehended particulars, this essential character of ideas also becomes the essential character of ideally constituted objects. Because all the property-terms by which we can characterise determinate objects are essentially contrasted with others, and because we have no knowledge of objects otherwise, then the characterisation of an object as possessing a quality is at the same time its characterisation negatively as not possessing others. The red object is thus essentially not-blue; its contradictory is its contrary and all its relations are internal or essential to it. In short, its identity is an identity-in-difference.

So far Bradley and the idealists concur. But the ground on which he advocates these doctrines is markedly different from theirs. Bosanquet, for instance, following Hegel, regards what is given as no more than the indeterminate 'this' of present perception. And he maintains that, as such, it is completely assimilated in the process of cognition; the sensible particular is nothing outside the mediating system of universal concepts. Now Bradley agrees that sensation or feeling – as non-relational – fulfils none of the conditions of knowledge or of objects qua known – hence the areas of accord already mentioned. Nevertheless, he maintains that the specific 'this' comes always as continuous with or embedded in a non-relational whole of feeling.[18] And it is on account of its holistic character that Bradley denies that feeling is reducible to ideas or relations. Explicitly insisting that if there were no given whole the relational form would be unquestionable,[19] he argues that in fact our knowledge of objects both depends upon, and is condemned as incoherent by, feeling so understood. In consequence, reality cannot be identified with the system of thought.

---

17. Bradley, *Appearance and Reality*, ch. 3, para. 1.
18. See Bradley, *Principles of Logic*, 51–6, 94–8, 659; *Essays on Truth and Reality*, 174–6.
19. See Bradley, *Essays on Truth and Reality*, 190; F. H. Bradley, *Collected Essays* (Oxford: Clarendon Press, 1935), 674.

This is all clearly evident in Bradley's account of relations in chapter 3, paragraphs 2 and 3 of *Appearance and Reality*. Usually, of course, his position there is held to rest on a logical or internal incoherence in the concept of terms and relations as such. But that is Hegel's view,[20] not Bradley's. Bradley's argument, rather, is that while on the one side a term is known only as it is differentiated in virtue of its relations, on the other side it is given as an element in the whole of feeling – and so 'cannot wholly be made by', but 'must come to', its relational differentiation.[21] As such, a term has a 'double nature'[22] as both 'given' and 'made'. And while no hard-and-fast line can be drawn between these two aspects, neither can they be reconciled in any higher synthesis of dialectical logic. For in the nature of the case, the term qua given cannot be assimilated to or identified with its relational differentiation, that is, it cannot be rendered intelligible. And on account again of the sensible nature of a term[23] – the argument here does not work equally from both sides like Hegel's, but depends on the term qua given – relations cannot 'bear a relation'[24] to their terms in the proper sense, that is, relations do not, as they claim, constitute the natures of their terms. Thus the relational form is condemned to incoherence in any attempt to explain fully the nature of the connections we find in the world.

It is of course often suggested that in chapter 3 of *Appearance and Reality*, Bradley is either assuming or implying the ridiculous view that relations do not relate, that is, that they are not relations. But in fact his point is that while relations indeed approximate to, or 'inadequately express',[25] actual connections, these connections are not relational in nature. So relations do relate for Bradley, but not because they themselves have any relating power. Rather, relations relate only in virtue of the non-relational unity given in feeling. Far from constituting the connections we find in the world, it is upon the given unity that the relational form depends.[26]

Bradley's account of relations is, then, premised upon the theory of feeling (whatever may be thought of that). Yet I cannot adequately defend such an interpretation of all his main doctrines here. It would require too much space, for instance, to show how, far from upholding the rationalist

---

20. See G. W. F. Hegel, *Science of Logic*, trans. W. H. Johnston and L. G. Struthers (London: Allen and Unwin, 1929), 143ff.; and *Encyclopaedia of the Philosophical Sciences: Logic*, trans. W. Wallace (Oxford: Oxford University Press, 1892), 245ff.
21. Bradley, *Appearance and Reality*, 25; see also 159, 501, and *Essays on Truth and Reality*, 193.
22. Bradley, *Appearance and Reality*, 26.
23. Ibid., 26
24. Ibid., 27.
25. Ibid., 125.
26. See ibid., 125, 512; *Essays on Truth and Reality*, 200, 231n., 239; *Principles of Logic*, 695–6.

view that, as an absolute necessity of thought, the law of non-contradiction is also an apprehension of logical necessity in the being of things, Bradley's definition of consistency in fact rests on the given unity of feeling.[27] Or, again, that when in chapter 14 of *Appearance and Reality* he defines reality as experience, 'the very ground on which [he] stand[s]', as he says, that experience is given as 'a whole'.[28] But even though assertion is no substitute for argument, I hope I have at least said enough to suggest that, once recognised as premised upon the theory of feeling, Bradley's doctrines are quite distinct from those with which they are normally identified.

Such a view must not, however, be taken to imply that the theory of feeling itself remains fixed and unchanging from *The Principles of Logic* to *Essays on Truth and Reality*, despite the difficulties all too obviously attached to it. Admittedly, Bradley's thought is usually regarded as having been presented in its completest form in *Appearance and Reality*, *Essays on Truth and Reality* being treated as a collection of supplementary essays. But this is far from being the case; the theory of feeling in fact undergoes radical development in the course of Bradley's career. And so it had to.

In *The Principles of Logic* the whole of feeling is little more than an anti-atomistic device – Mill with the continuity put in, so to speak. As such, it is described as a 'congeries of related phenomena',[29] which is said both to contain relations[30] and to be non-relational in nature.[31] Yet its main purpose is already clear: to secure the conditional nature of judgements as abstractions from 'the presented whole'[32] and so guarantee the distinction of thought and existence against a 'cheap and easy Monism'.[33] In line with this intention, feeling had more or less become an unreservedly non-relational whole by the time of *Appearance and Reality*. Yet nowhere in that work does Bradley make any attempt to secure or defend it as such. In fact he is guilty there of treating the theory of feeling as self-evident and unquestionable, no doubt encouraged by the confluence of varied sources which, as we have seen, impelled him towards it. And it is precisely this confluence of sources which in *Appearance and Reality* leads Bradley to present feeling in so confused a fashion as merely subjective and psychological in nature, as a genetically prior 'stage' of development and, more properly, as a logically prior ground. But even though he never quite gives up Hegel's

---

27. See Bradley, *Appearance and Reality*, 123–6, 461–2, 504, 508; *Essays on Truth and Reality*, 312–14.
28. Bradley, *Appearance and Reality*, 128.
29. Bradley, *Principles of Logic*, 8n.
30. Ibid., 94.
31. Ibid., 96.
32. Ibid., 97.
33. Ibid., 591.

genetic theory, nevertheless Bradley's mentalist tendencies in *Appearance and Reality* are more a matter of his debts to Hegel's psychology and Mill's sensationalism reinforcing each other than of any significant element in the theory of feeling itself. For by the time of *Essays on Truth and Reality*, Bradley had developed an account of feeling which is not only purged of the earlier obfuscations, but also shifts the post-Kantian concern with the demonstration of the identical subject-object on to a wholly new basis. And here his greatest debt is to his critics.

Non-Relational Continuum

Not surprisingly, the theory of feeling had to face serious challenge from philosophical psychologists such as Ward and James.[34] They concur with Bradley in rejecting an atomistic, in favour of a continuum, theory of sensation. But they maintain in different ways that the presentational continuum is relational in nature. Such a view Bradley cannot of course accept: the given non-relational unity is the premise of his metaphysics. And this makes the question of non-relationality doubly difficult for him. For Bradley is claiming, not (as is usually thought) that there is, impossibly, an 'experience' of unity without an experiencing subject, but that the non-relational unity of subject and object is given and manifest as such within the subject-object relation of knowledge. And he attempts to secure this crucial claim in his well-known but none too well understood essay *On Our Knowledge of Immediate Experience*.[35]

Bradley's starting point here is a remark made in criticism of him by G. F. Stout. And this, though usually ignored, is of some importance in specifying his exact intentions. Stout says: 'Immediate experience is in no sense knowledge of itself. It does not characterise itself either as being mere feeling or as being this or that sort of feeling.'[36]

Now Bradley of course agrees that there is no such thing as immediate knowledge. But he puts Stout's statement in the form of a question: 'How can immediate experience make an object of itself . . . know about itself?'[37] And here he is not asking how, impossibly, feeling can 'know itself' in the

---

34. See James Ward, 'Bradley's Doctrine of Experience', *Mind* 34 (1925), 13–38; and William James, *A Pluralistic Universe* (New York: Longmans, Green, 1909), Lecture VII, and *Essays in Radical Empiricism* (New York: Longmans, Green, 1912), chs I and II.
35. Bradley, *Essays on Truth and Reality*, ch. 6.
36. G. F. Stout, 'Bradley's Theory of Judgment' (1902), in *Studies in Philosophy and Psychology* (London, 1930), 208.
37. Bradley, *Essays on Truth and Reality*, x; see 160, 181.

sense of become self-conscious, or be anything more than immediate and unknowable, outside of the subject–object relation of knowledge. Rather, the problem at issue is the epistemic status of feeling. In asking how feeling can have 'knowledge of itself', Bradley is referring to and taking up Stout's definition of that phrase and turning his critic's assertion into a question: Does the non-relational unity of feeling 'characterise itself' as such at the cognitive level?

Now as non-objective and non-relational, feeling cannot be a presentation in any usual sense,[38] nor can it properly be said to stand in any relation to the objective world.[39] Consequently Bradley argues in chapter 6 of *Essays on Truth and Reality* that the unity of feeling manifests itself at the level of subject and object by means of the role it plays in the cognitive determination of both terms. And it is by means of that role that the given unity characterises itself as such, that is, as the non-objective 'condition' and 'background' of the subject–object world, which is 'verified by its working'[40] in the processes of objectification.

Bradley is thus presenting in this chapter what, since Dewey, we would call a 'functional' account of the role of feeling. And he arrives at that account by means of an analysis of what, since Dewey, we would call individual problematic situations. The situations that Bradley analyses are indeed almost trivial in what the Deweyites would call their 'normality' and 'concreteness'. But while there is no space to examine them here, their import is clear enough: in chapter 6 of *Essays on Truth and Reality*, Bradley's treatment of feeling has moved from the confused anti-atomism of *The Principles of Logic*, through the mentalism and dogmatism of *Appearance and Reality*, to a theory that is grounded in the nature of our investigative experience and that finds there the basis and justification for metaphysical philosophy. Bradley has anchored the identical subject-object of the post-Kantians, not in intuition, or dialectic, or 'reason', but in what his opponents too confidently call the 'empirical' world.

Chapter 6 cannot, then, be regarded as such a watershed in Bradley's thought as his Deweyite commentators naturally claim, using it as a lever with which to include him in the already over-populated pantheon of

---

38. See Bradley, *Principles of Logic*, 109, n. 19, 517 n. 8; *Collected Essays*, 377n.
39. Bradley, *Essays on Truth and Reality*, 177. In this respect, as also with the doctrine of finite centres (not touched on here as belonging to his *ratio essendi*), Bradley's feeling operates in much the same way as Kant's Transcendental Ego – a register both of the extent of the 'shift' and of the problems involved in his sensationalist treatment of German idealism. See E. E. Harris's superb article, 'The Problem of Self Constitution for Idealism and Phenomenology', *Idealistic Studies* 7 (1977), 1–27.
40. Bradley, *Essays on Truth and Reality*, 182, 188.

proto-pragmatists.[41] Nevertheless, as their enthusiasm for the essay suggests, it has a significance in modern philosophy which British commentary has notably failed to appreciate. This can, I think, best be shown through a brief comparison with Deweyite pragmatism.

An enlightened Deweyite steeped in Dewey's *Logic*[42] and unusually well-informed about Bradley would be readily prepared to admit that his colleagues, even Dewey himself, have made mistakes in interpreting Bradley's development. After all, he could equally well point out that Bradley systematically misunderstood Dewey's concept of 'practice'. But scoring exegetical points would not be to his purpose. Rather, he would want to acknowledge both the historical importance of, and pragmatist debt to, Bradley's transformation of the empiricist doctrine of sensation: his shift from atomistic particulars to the whole of feeling or 'total field',[43] his treatment of that whole as a logical ground, without lapsing into any kind of foundationalism in which the given is regarded as the 'really Real', or as the source of indubitable knowledge; and, above all perhaps, his move from the ocular imagery and causal model of perception or representation, to 'function'. Moreover, he would admire the originality of Bradley's method in chapter 6: examination of the individual problematic situation or specific 'inquiry' in which the total field or situation is, in Bradley's words, 'grouped round and centred in the object' of investigation.[44]

Beyond this point, however, our enlightened pragmatist would not go. He would indeed agree with Bradley that immediate experience itself is non-relational – but[45] he would hold it to be purely a matter of investigative practice whether we regard it as plural, that is, as a matter of given 'existences',[46] or as a total field. Again, he would agree that in the 'inquiry-situation', feeling functions as materials-source and critical corrective. But he would see it as no more than that, that is, as no more than a phase of empirical method. For while he would grant that Bradley has escaped the Kantian fallacy of unification – locating the unity of the sensory manifold in a Transcendental Ego – he would see him as still enmeshed in the post-Kantian fallacy of unification: locating unity in an

---

41. See F. C. S. Schiller, 'The New Developments of Mr. Bradley's Philosophy', *Mind* 34 (1915), 345–66; R. Kagey, *The Growth of Bradley's Logic* (New York, 1931); R. D. Mack, *The Appeal to Immediate Experience* (New York: King's Crown Press, 1945); and J. H. Randall Jr, *The Career of Philosophy in Modern Times*, vol. II: *The Hundred Years Since Darwin* (New York, 1969), ch. 8.
42. John Dewey, *Logic: The Theory of Inquiry* (New York: Henry Holt, 1938).
43. Dewey, *Logic*, 124; see William James, 'Bradley or Bergson?' (1910), in *Collected Essays and Reviews* (London, 1920).
44. Bradley, *Essays on Truth and Reality*, 180; see Dewey, *Logic*, 124.
45. See Dewey, *Logic*, 124.
46. Ibid., 522.

identical subject-object. And these are fallacies because, for the pragmatist, the problem of unification is solved by the nature of inquiry itself: the unification that our experience requires is constituted precisely by the consummatory outcome of inquiry. Thus, with his theory of feeling, Bradley is guilty of generalising and hypostatising the character that properly belongs to the resolution of individual problematic situations.[47] To be sure, the pragmatist would readily admit that in divesting himself of the cumbersome machinery of transcendentals, intuition and dialectic, and in resting his theory of unification on the nature of 'inquiry', Bradley has placed the traditions in which he works on a new basis. But he would maintain that in doing so Bradley has also unwittingly shown the bankruptcy of those traditions, for it is precisely the nature of inquiry that renders a metaphysics of experience and reality otiose. In other words, Bradley's transformation of the theory of the given, and his inquiry-based regeneration of metaphysics, lead him – and with him both British empiricism and German idealism – straight into Deweyite pragmatism.

There is no denying the sweep and power of such a reading of Bradley. Its legitimacy cannot of course be debated here, but at least it indicates something of Bradley's significance for contemporary philosophy: he keeps his old wine in new bottles.

It does not, however, rest easily there. Indeed, Bradley himself is always disarmingly ready to admit that his theory of feeling, and the doctrines premised on that, are not without severe difficulties. What, then, does he regard as the ultimate rationale for such a confessedly intractable metaphysics?

Historical-Critical Rationale

Throughout all his writings, Bradley's tactic is to impale us on the available alternatives, recapitulating the relative advantages of his own position as he does so. He relies, in other words, on what might be called historical-critical considerations; the theory of feeling and its consequences are established neither deductively nor inductively, but in terms of their coherence and comprehensiveness in relation to the extensive range of questions and difficulties in British and German philosophy which constituted his problematic. Bradley's reasoning is formed, to use Wisdom's words, 'not like the links of a chain but like the legs of a chair'.[48]

---

47. Ibid., 533–4.
48. Quoted by Renford Bambrough, *Reason, Truth and God* (London: Methuen, 1969), 58.

Thus the theory of feeling provides a basis for reality conceived in the post-Kantian manner as an identical subject-object. Nevertheless, in Bradley's view the theory of feeling allows him, not only to avoid what he regards as the abstract Ego and dualism of Kant, but also to dispense with Hegel's dialectical logic.[49] And while for Bradley as for Hegel the reality is not as such a given, at least Schelling's insistence on the need for some kind of given remains, though without his guaranteeing mechanism of intuition.[50] This is replaced by Mill's feeling, which itself is transformed into a non-atomistic and functional doctrine of sensation.

The theory of feeling further preserves the distinction between thought and existence, while knowledge and truth (not discussed here) can be regarded both with Hegel as expressions of the one reality, and with the empiricists as a matter of practical efficacy. Similarly, the doctrine that reality is experience is not the assertion of some strange world-stuff or hidden essence, but an indication of positions rejected and a complex register of the Lockean and post-Kantian traditions in which Bradley stands. And as he himself says, his metaphysics breaks down the barriers between nature and spirit, 'poetry and fact'.[51]

Now it is, I suggest, this historical-critical rationale that Bradley would have us weigh and which sustains him through all his turnings and windings. And it is on this basis that, alongside his ready acknowledgement of the difficulties involved, he can also maintain of his doctrine of reality, 'to doubt it logically is impossible'.[52] Bradley is not here claiming that his metaphysic has the status of a body of logically necessary truths, nor is he endowing it with a spurious finality – he does not remove philosophy from history in the manner of post-Hegelians such as Schopenhauer or Kierkegaard.[53] Rather, the logical indubitableness of a metaphysic is for Bradley a matter of its coherence and comprehensiveness in relation to the range of issues and alternative positions in philosophy.[54] And the point is, it can only be met in those terms. The formal logician's disjunction 'true or false?' is as inappropriate to the complex historical-critical structure that constitutes a metaphysic as is either the claim to atemporal necessity or a mere historicist reductionism.

I conclude, then, that Bradley is engaged upon the transformation of empiricist and post-Kantian philosophy into a metaphysics of feeling. So understood, he is not an aberration, nor a surrogate for less digestible

---

49. See Bradley, *Essays on Truth and Reality*, 278.
50. See Bradley, *Principles of Logic*, 654.
51. Bradley, *Essays on Truth and Reality*, 444; *Appearance and Reality*, 434–9.
52. Bradley, *Appearance and Reality*, 459.
53. See ibid., 5.
54. See Bradley, *Essays on Truth and Reality*, 17–18.

thinkers; his elaboration of the theory of feeling and its implications gives him the status of an original. Indeed, unless the theory of feeling is recognised as the core and centre of his thought, he will continue to haunt Anglo-Saxon philosophising like an unlaid ghost. And, where it is recognised, he will be seen to be a much more considerable figure in twentieth-century philosophy than is usually held to be the case. Certainly, the theory of feeling shows him to be something other than a perpetrator of instructive confusions who did all that could be expected of him in generating the realist and pluralist reactions. Even if his metaphysics is to be regarded largely as a transitional form, preparatory to Russellian logical atomism, Deweyite pragmatism or Whiteheadian cosmology, it nevertheless relates to those developments not merely as their remote source or occasion, but also as a standing comparison and critique. In developing a theory of the given that is anti-foundational,[55] a theory of knowledge that is anti-epistemological,[56] and all the while elaborating a monistic doctrine of reality upon the basis of a functional analysis of inquiry, his metaphysics of feeling holds together 'traditional' and 'modern' concerns in a unique fashion.

---

55. See ibid., 210.
56. See Bradley, *Appearance and Reality*, 65.

Chapter 2

Whitehead, Heidegger and the Paradoxes of the New[1]

Much philosophical thinking in the twentieth century is characterised, on the negative side, by a critique of philosophy as inextricably entangled with the concept of 'ground'. On the positive side, this is matched by an extensive elaboration of what may be called 'self-realisation' as the principle of analysis, where whatever is taken to be the proper subject matter of philosophy is understood as reflexive in nature, that is, as in some sense subject and object of itself, immanently constituting its own order and character. This spectrum of concerns has been expressed in a variety of ways, of which perhaps the best-known are the self-creating, rebellious individual of Sartrean existentialism and the problem-solving, tool-wielding subject of Deweyan pragmatism.

From the point of view of the later Wittgenstein, however, the concept of a world-producing subject, existential or pragmatic, is itself just another secularising expression of the metaphysical concept of ground. The human subject for the later Wittgenstein is a 'decentred' subject: it is understood as constituted by the structures of languages it inhabits, structures that have the self-organising, groundless character of 'play' (*Sprachspiel*) as the site where language and world coextensively open up or unfold each other.

Similar considerations have been developed in the theory of interpretation. Gadamer, for example, drawing on the aesthetics of the

---

1. I would like gratefully to acknowledge the generous support of the Alexander von Humboldt Foundation while doing much of the research for this essay. I am also indebted to numerous invaluable discussions with Gerd Buchdahl and Dorothy Emmet, and to the many telling comments and criticisms made by colleagues and students at the Colloquium of the Department of Philosophy, the Memorial University of Newfoundland.

German idealist tradition, finds his primary models for the self-expanding question-and-answer structure of dialogue both in the substrateless character of play and in the work of art, understood as immanently unfolding and enacting its own meanings.[2] But the twin themes of groundlessness and self-realisation find perhaps their most radical specification in thinkers such as Whitehead and the later Heidegger, who may be regarded as making these concepts themselves the proper subject matter of philosophy. This they can be said to do by universalising self-realisation, so that, in one way or another, all things are understood as self-realising in nature – a position that they express by characterising self-realisation in terms of the realisation or 'temporalisation' of time.

These two moves are intimately related. Where self-realisation is the universal principle of analysis, the self-realising natures of things are necessarily also a matter of the realisation of time, that is, temporal form and particular content have to be understood as reflecting into each other perfectly. In consequence, where self-realisation is the universal principle of analysis, time cannot be treated in traditional fashion as a prior structure in which things happen. Rather, time has itself to be characterised in terms of its realisation – a requirement that has significant consequences.

First, in virtue of the ultimate irreducibility of time – that is, the fact that time cannot be broken down into non-temporal elements of which it is a construct or synthesis – the realisation of time can only be described in temporal terms. Whitehead and the later Heidegger therefore give time-concepts a privileged position in respect of the concept of self-realisation: because self-realisation is a matter of the realisation of time, and time is irreducible, self-realisation is characterised in terms of temporal entities – by the concept of 'occasions' in Whitehead and by that of 'event' (*Ereignis*) in the later Heidegger.[3]

Secondly, these event-concepts or event-analyses (as they may be called) have a specific rationale. On the ground that, where self-realisation is the

---

2. On play, see H.-G. Gadamer, *Truth and Method*, trans. Joel Weinsheimer and Donald G. Marshall (New York: Continuum, 1976), 91ff., esp. 93, 97, 101. On the connection of play and temporality, see 108ff. On language as 'eventual', see 386–7. On hermeneutics as 'eventual', see 442ff.
3. The English word 'event' is, of course, wholly inadequate in conveying the complex of meanings and associations of Heidegger's term *Ereignis*; see here Werner Marx, *Heidegger and the Tradition* (Evanston, IL: Northwestern University Press, 1971), xxxvi–xli, and Joan Stambaugh's Introduction to her translation of Martin Heidegger, *On Time and Being* (New York: Harper and Row, 1972), vii–xi. The present essay makes no claim to offer an exhaustive analysis of *Ereignis*, but is concerned only with certain aspects of that term that it attempts to show are central to any final consideration of its nature and significance.

universal principle of analysis, time is not a prior structure in which things happen, Whitehead and the later Heidegger maintain that time cannot be understood as infinite time, that is, as a continuous series of nows, infinitely divisible and stretching endlessly into the future. Instead, in attempting to characterise time in terms of its realisation, they treat it as a matter of discrete, indivisible and finite elements which are unique and unrepeatable and in that sense radically new. This position is represented by their respective event-concepts. Their work can be taken as expressing the claim that, where self-realisation is the universal principle of analysis, both self-realisation and time require to be described in terms of event-concepts.

These concepts are the subject of the present essay. The set of concerns they represent will for brevity be referred to in what follows as the theme of radical novelty, or the self-realising new, as is convenient.

In part, the theme of radical novelty is inspired by developments in modern physics, which from the early 1900s treats matter not as a substance occupying the infinite receptacles of space and time, but as the immanently unfolding order and passage of space-time events. Nevertheless, the theme has its own philosophical anticipations: for example, in Marx's identification of humanity with its history; in the unique moment or now in which Kierkegaard's believer leaps anew into faith, thereby conferring reality on past and future as the history of redemption; in the utterly discrete, underived moment when Nietzsche's artists of the future create their own freedom; and in the temporalising constitution of the early Heidegger's Dasein. There are of course significant differences between these positions. Marx does not deal with time other than as history, which he understands as a linear and teleological continuum constituted by the actions of communal subjects. For Kierkegaard and Nietzsche, in contrast, time – and thus history – is a matter of a discrete series of breaks or ruptures engendered by the free acts of individual subjects. And while the early Heidegger shares this view, unlike Kierkegaard and Nietzsche he does not treat time mainly as a metaphor or expression of the human condition. Rather, the realisation of time in the early Heidegger is a necessary dimension of the human subject understood as a self-realising, reflexive unity of form and content.

For all their differences, however, what clearly unites these positions is that time is analysed in the context of human subjectivity. Yet where self-realisation is the universal principle of analysis, time cannot be defined merely in terms of human subjects – or forms of language. Because the realisation of time is a matter of the self-realising natures of all things, the theme of radical novelty implies the abandonment of philosophical anthropocentrism in all of its guises. This implication is already to some extent present both in Nietzsche's posthumously published argument for the eternal recurrence of the moment, and in Bergson's concept of real duration.[4] But Nietzsche's position is notoriously problematic, while Bergson opposes duration to the object-world. Indeed, because Bergson treats the object-world, not as a matter of self-realising unities of form and content, but as a pragmatic distortion of real duration, his thought is to that extent still fractured by a non-reflexive division between the underlying reality and its appearances. In continental European philosophy it is only from the 1930s onwards, with the highly influential analyses of the event undertaken by the later Heidegger, that the theme of radical novelty receives its most uncompromising statement.

Clearly enough, Whitehead's 'one genus' theory of 'actual occasions' – variously characterised as 'self-realising', 'self-forming', 'self-creating', 'self-producing' – belongs squarely within the same thematic. Nevertheless, Whitehead is a philosopher who is sometimes quoted but rarely considered. In contemporary discussions he occupies at best a marginal place, despite the fact that his analysis of the concept of occasions had been fully elaborated in *Process and Reality* as early as 1929. Yet the reason for this neglect is obvious enough. Despite all their differences, what unites the other exponents of self-realisation is their common critique of 'metaphysics', understood as a narcissistic attempt by reason to transcend the limits of language, or to evacuate the plenitude of time and history, by the elaboration of an eternally complete principle of ground or order or totality. Heidegger is the strongest voice here: as is well known, he regards his 'event' as constituting a wholesale repudiation and destruction of the entire enterprise of philosophy.

Whitehead, however, presents himself as a metaphysician in the grand tradition, whose work has the character of 'a recurrence to pre-Kantian modes of thought'.[5] The inevitable result is that his writings from *Process and Reality* onwards are generally regarded as naive anachronisms. It has gone unnoticed that his theory of occasions is part and parcel of a self-conscious and thoroughgoing redefinition of the nature of metaphysics in the context of the theme of radical novelty. Perhaps the best way of indicating what is at issue here is by means of a comparison between Whitehead and the later Heidegger.

---

4. See especially Friedrich Nietzsche, *The Will to Power*, trans. Walter Kaufmann and R. J. Hollingdale (New York: Vintage, 1967), para. 1053–67; and Henri Bergson, *Introduction to Metaphysics*, trans. T. E. Hulme (Indianapolis: Bobbs Merrill, Library of Liberal Arts, 1955).
5. A. N. Whitehead, *Process and Reality: An Essay in Cosmology* (corrected edn, New York: The Free Press, 1978), xi.

I

To both Whitehead and the later Heidegger one main significance of their event-concepts is that they represent particularly well the requirement laid upon thought by the theme of the self-realising new. For if all things are to be described as self-realising, then their natures as such can only be defined in terms of themselves. They cannot be understood as arising from certain fundamental 'productive' structures, whether these be defined as the procession of forms, or the procession of divine being, or immaterial monadic reals, or principles of possible experience, or the all-containing whole. Rather, the self-realising new requires a mode of discourse which stands in what can be called a content-reflexive relation to its subject matter, that is, which does not refer its subject matter away from itself to something else as its 'cause' or 'ground' or 'condition' or 'productive' principle, however conceptually extended the sense of these terms may be. Hence the aptness of event-concepts. Not only do they carry the appropriate connotative links with history, physics and aesthetics, but they are also exhaustively translatable into their subject matter without any aetiological remainder.

The point can perhaps be illustrated (and this is no more than an illustration)[6] by reference to the phrases 'the event of . . .' and 'the occasion of . . .', where the 'of' can be regarded as having the character both of a subjective and objective genitive, that is, the concepts of 'occasion' and 'what occurs', of 'event' and its 'content' can be taken as coextensive elements with no status of any kind apart from each other, registering the unique and unrepeatable differences, or acts of self-differentiation, by which things make themselves what they are. So understood, the concepts of event and occasion are intended to indicate that the 'cause' or 'constitution' or 'principle' of what occurs is nothing else than the difference of its own self-realising occurrence. Thereby the concept of the subject is, so to speak, returned to the object – where it used to be – and, with that, the distinctions of knowing subject and object known, of real and ideal, of nature and spirit, lose their status as the fundamental polarities of philosophical analysis.

As with the German post-Kantian idealists, the specific target here is Kant's threefold division of experience into cognition, morality and aesthetics, at least (in Whitehead's case) so far as that is taken as the baseline of the analysis. Yet Whitehead and the later Heidegger attempt to fuse the realms of nature, history and art, not by any resort to monism, but by severally developing unitary modes of discourse where such historically laden notions as 'subject', 'synthesis' and 'constitution' are either completely

---

6. Martin Heidegger, 'The Origin of the Work of Art', in *Poetry, Language, Thought*, trans. A. Hofstadter (New York: Harper and Row, 1975), 86.

transformed and redefined, as in Whitehead, or are completely repudiated, as by the later Heidegger.

What unites Whitehead and the later Heidegger here is their common recognition that the theme of the self-realising new requires the abandonment of the metaphor of ground and all its works. What divides them is their views on the enterprise of philosophical analysis in that context. Once granted that the traditional models of philosophical self-understanding – represented by such notions as cause, ground, realised totality, etc. – need to be laid aside in the context of the self-realising new, the key question is: how is the status of event-concepts to be understood? At issue here are what might be called the paradoxes of the new. These arise from the fact that, under the rubric of the self-realising new, the question of the nature of concepts or universals – a question that has defined the domain of philosophy since Plato – now rebounds upon philosophy itself, threatening to leave it with nothing to do but dismantle itself.

For consider: the concepts of event and occasions represent truth-claims of the largest kind. That is, these concepts are intended to indicate that the principle of what occurs is nothing else than the self-realising occurrence itself. As such, they are truth-claims that define the status of truth-claims as historically situated happenings. But what then is their own status? Do they not represent strong, or unrestricted and non-revisable, truth-claims of the kind that traditionally characterise metaphysics? Do they not state 'what truly is'? And yet have they not undercut their own claim to truth-as-validity by redefining truth as historical occurrence?

The first and most obvious paradox of the new is thus the familiar paradox of self-reference, now become, in the context of the theme of radical novelty, a question of the nature of philosophy itself.[7] It can here be summarily stated as: what is the relation of the proposition 'All is relative' to itself?

This paradox is, however, compounded by another, which represents a different way of specifying the difficulties inherent in the theme of radical novelty. The paradox of self-reference arises when the theme of radical novelty is looked at from the point of view of its implications with respect to the relation of philosophical analysis to its own propositions. The second paradox arises when the theme of radical novelty is looked at from the point of view of its implications with respect to the relation of philosophical analysis to its subject matter, understood as a self-realising or reflexive unity of form and content. This second paradox is the paradox of content reflexivity. It may be expressed by the question: how do the propositions 'All is self-realising' or 'All is new' stand to their subject matter?

---

7. For a discussion of the problem of self-reference in the framework of philosophy of language, see Hilary Lawson, *Reflexivity* (LaSalle, IL: Open Court, 1985).

On their own terms, the subject matter of event-concepts is nothing else than the unique and unrepeatable difference of the self-realising new. But the unique and unrepeatable is, as such, unintelligible or incomprehensible in its own nature. Is it therefore the case that event-concepts cannot claim any positive meaning or content, but are no more than strictly negative elaborations of that which cannot be philosophically analysed? Are they concepts of an 'other' from which reason has to recognise its complete exclusion? Do they have no other task than ironically to efface themselves before their object?

Another way of expressing the paradox of content-reflexivity would be in terms of the concept of 'philosophical necessity', that is, the kind of necessity attributed to the concepts of philosophical analysis. Now philosophical necessity – the claim that things are and not otherwise than as laid out in the analysis – is a necessity of its own kind, for it is the character belonging to those concepts that defines the nature of the contrasts we ordinarily make between necessity and possibility or necessity and contingency. Nevertheless, philosophically necessary concepts represent what is held in some sense or other to be an invariant or permanent structure of things, which is why they are called necessary and why they have often been understood on the models of logical or causal necessity. The question therefore is: how can event-analyses make any such claims for themselves if the only kind of 'intrinsic nature' things have is the essential variability of the self-realising new? How can event-analyses represent that which is in any sense invariant or permanent if their subject matter is unique and unrepeatable difference? In the context of the theme of radical novelty, the price of theoretical abstraction would seem to be the essential vacuity of theory.

To be sure, it is a truism that analysis can proceed only by way of abstraction. But what is involved here is no illegitimate stipulation that meaning be what it intends, nor can the issue be negotiated merely by acknowledging the need for some kind of distinction between thought and existence. Rather, the difficulties hitherto presented by particular kinds of concepts, such as that of God in Aquinas or freedom in Kant – difficulties that were rendered tractable precisely by their contrast with what were taken to be the conceptually determinable realms of 'world' or of reliable cognition – now present themselves with any subject matter viewed as self-realising. Indeed, event-concepts may be said to universalise and thereby radicalise the paradoxicality of traditional analyses of the divine nature and creation. The question is now, not how the character of a self-realising entity wholly different from the world could be a possible subject of analysis, but how the self-realising differences of entities in the world could be. Were event-concepts to designate anything more than that which is theoretically indeterminable, they would apparently be, not concepts of the self-realising new, but descriptions of a fixed, invariant pattern, whereby the perpetual novelty of self-realisation is obliterated under a conceptually determinate order, with the event or occasions becoming mere passages suspended between origin and end. As Whitehead puts the difficulty to himself, in terms of his analysis of the structures of process:

> Process and individuality require each other. In separation all meaning evaporates. The form of process . . . derives its character from the individuals involved, and the characters of the individuals can only be understood in terms of the process in which they are implicated. A difficult problem arises from this doctrine. How can the notion of any generality of reasoning be justified? For if the process depends on individuals, then with different individuals the form of process differs. Accordingly, what has been said of one process cannot be said of another process . . . Our doctrine seems to have destroyed the very basis of rationality.[8]

Once the self-realising new moves to the centre of philosophical concern, the relation of thought and existence is so redefined as to render philosophy problematic from within. In this situation, the later Heidegger does not hesitate to draw the conclusion that, as from its beginnings a matter of conceptual determination, the enterprise of philosophical analysis which began with Plato has to be repudiated *tout court*. In effect retrojecting Lukacs's analysis of reification back across the entire history of Western thought, he sees philosophy from Plato onwards as essentially anthropocentric in nature, implicitly intent from the start on reducing the world to a conceptually determinable, and therefore manipulable, object-for-use. While acknowledging that the event is the achievement of Western metaphysics, which he submits to a massive, retrospective analysis in that light[9] – he also sees the event as in the nature of the case the final outcome of that tradition, and thus announces the 'completion' or 'end (*Vollendung*) of philosophy', that is, the closure of any attempt to determine what cannot be determined. As components of the apparatus of 'representation', notions such as 'category', 'concept' and 'method' are to be abandoned in favour of a mode of discourse or 'poetry of thinking', the language and style of which consistently enacts the negation of its own propositional status, and by thus pointing away from itself, opens up that which cannot be 'communicated' or 'mediated cognitively' but 'must be experienced'[10] – namely, the event.

In the work of the later Heidegger the critique of philosophy, which has always gone hand-in-hand with modern versions of self-realisation, receives its fullest elaboration. The intractable, self-negating character of his texts is the final completion of what is implied for philosophy in Kierkegaard's

---

8. A. N. Whitehead, *Modes of Thought* (New York: The Free Press, 1968), 133.
9. See, for example, Martin Heidegger, *Der Satz von Grund* (Pfullingen: Neske, 1957).
10. Heidegger, *On Time and Being*, 25–6. As the title suggests, this is a key work for the understanding of the later Heidegger.

preaching, in Nietzsche's telegraphic calls to the artists of the future, and in Bergson's appeal to intuition. The thought-project of the (significantly titled) *Philosophical Fragments*, the aphorisms of Zarathustra and the 'images' of Bergson's prose are all so many admissions that the self-realising new cannot be the subject of philosophy. There is only literature now.

Perhaps the best way to characterise what is at issue here is in terms of a contrast between the theme of radical novelty and Hegel's position. Hegel maintains the ultimate unity of concept and object in absolute reason, which is understood as a totality that includes or encompasses subjective reason and its other. The absolute thereby transcends the subject–predicate division of language; but as systematically representable, the unity of the whole can be rendered intelligible beyond the mere form of language in the speculative proposition. It may thus be said that Hegel sees the relation of concept and object, rational and real as a univocal relation in that these terms have an ultimately identical meaning. With that, however, the fate of the new is sealed.[11]

To be sure, Hegel does not treat the movement from identity to difference and back to identity in an Aristotelian fashion as a matter of the 'return' of the 'same' identity. Instead, the movement proceeds to an identity that is enriched through the progress of the thesis via the antithesis. Here, it would seem, there is the possibility of the arrival of the new; out of the immediate actuality there comes what Hegel calls 'quite another shape of things' from which a 'new' actuality emerges.

However, Hegel's 'new' is already contained in its beginning. 'Immediate actuality' already has within itself, as the 'inner', the possibility of the 'new' reality as its 'other'. As such, immediate actuality is the 'condition' and 'germ of the other'. In consequence, the 'new' that emerges from this process is not a new in the sense of what has never been there before. As Hegel says: 'Thus there comes into being quite another shape of things, and yet it is not another; for the first actuality is only put as what it in essence was.' He can thus ultimately conceive the movement of the absolute, all-containing totality as a 'return' to itself and regard it as the revolving of a circle after the fashion of Aristotle.

In this context it is not surprising that the later Heidegger insists on the rational inaccessibility of the other of reason conceived as the new. Reason is here regarded by Heidegger as purely subjective reason, intent on the subjugation of the world for use, over against which the task of thinking is to deconstruct the conceptualising impulse from within so that the alterity

---

11. I am here following Marx, *Heidegger and the Tradition*, 59ff. For the quotations from Hegel given in the text, see his *Encyclopedia: The Logic*, trans. W. Wallace and A. V. Miller (Oxford: Clarendon Press, 1976), para. 146 add.

of the other can properly manifest itself. In contrast to Hegel, it may be said that the later Heidegger sees the relation of concept and object, rational and real, as an equivocal relation in that these terms have different and even mutually exclusive meanings.

In this context, not a little of the significance of Whitehead's position arises from the fact that, while addressing the issues involved in the fundamental conflicts of European thought, he writes out of a different philosophical tradition and consequently is not caught in the internal polarisations of an intellectual history otherwise too massive and entangling to be escaped. Hence Whitehead's response to the paradoxes of the new is quite different from that of other thinkers of radical novelty. As a glance at *Process and Reality* indicates, Whitehead is prepared to elaborate a complex 'categoreal scheme' for the purpose of analysing the self-realising new as a process of occasions – a scheme which as unhesitatingly helps itself to traditional concepts as it introduces new ones, and unashamedly involves an account of 'Philosophic Method'.[12] Programmatically announcing that 'the task of philosophy is . . . to exhibit the fusion of analysis and actuality',[13] Whitehead would dissolve the paradoxes of the new in a mode of thought which has the capacity to be at once 'the expression of necessity'[14] and the articulation of 'the creative advance into novelty'.[15] As he puts it: 'The crux of philosophy is to retain the balance between the individuality of existence and the relativity of existence.'[16] In addressing this crux, it will become evident that over against the univocity of Hegel and the equivocity of the later Heidegger, Whitehead develops what can be called an analogical analysis – or, more precisely, an analogical algebra – of the new.

2

As might be expected from one of the authors of *Principia Mathematica*, Whitehead constantly reiterates that what he refers to as 'the algebraic method' is the rubric under which he elaborates his position.[17] In his own words: 'Logic prescribes the shapes of metaphysical thought';[18] or

---

12. A. N. Whitehead, *Adventures of Ideas* (New York: The Free Press, 1967), ch. 15. See Whitehead, *Process and Reality*, ch. 1.
13. A. N. Whitehead, *Essays in Science and Philosophy* (New York: Philosophical Library, 1947), 113.
14. Whitehead, *Essays*, 128.
15. Whitehead, *Process and Reality*, 349.
16. Whitehead, *Essays*, 111.
17. See ibid., 109ff., 127ff.
18. Whitehead's Foreword to W. V. O. Quine, *A System of Logistic* (Cambridge, MA: Harvard University Press, 1934), ix–x.

again, 'Poetry allies itself to metre, philosophy to mathematic pattern.'[19] Nevertheless, he takes a route out of *Principia* radically different from that of Russell, the early Wittgenstein or the logical positivists, for he transforms the algebraic method into a medium of 'speculative philosophy', marrying mathematics with the characteristically anti-rationalist theme of the self-realising new. What he calls the 'generalized mathematics' that results[20] challenges the critique of reason mounted by the thinkers of radical novelty, well-represented in Bergson's remark that 'universal mathematics' is 'the chimera of modern philosophy'.[21] This critique assumes that rational analysis is indissolubly tied to the traditional concept of mathematical system – modelled on Euclidean geometry[22] – with the result that the contingency and particularity of the new is inevitably subsumed to structures of necessity understood as essentially complete and unchanging. In contrast, Whitehead would restore the Platonic vision of a unity of 'mathematics and the good'[23] by way of a transposed algebra rather than a transposed geometry, a position intended to allow the redefinition of that unity in terms of a connection between rationality and creativity. He thus sees himself as opening an epoch which will recover, in new form, 'the logical attitude of the epoch of St. Thomas Aquinas':[24] he would once again attempt to articulate a theory of *actus purus*, albeit now pluralistic and cosmological rather than theocentric, in a rigorous methodological and conceptual framework.

The first clue to what Whitehead means by the 'algebraic method' is provided by the organisation of *Process and Reality*. As the Table of Contents indicates, the entire work is an extended exercise in the elaboration of hypotheses. Part I presents the 'categoreal scheme' or set of 'working hypotheses';[25] Part II, and indeed the rest of the book, is concerned with 'Discussions and Applications'. It would seem likely that it is in terms of his employment of this procedure as a metaphysical method that Whitehead's treatment of the theme of radical novelty can best be understood.

The categorial scheme is referred to as the 'rational side' of the analysis.[26] It can be regarded, on the 'algebraic model' of a modern mathematical or logical system,[27] as a series of postulates, having the form 'Let the working hypothesis be . . .' and based on an initial conditional premise of the sort, 'If

---

19. Whitehead, *Modes of Thought*, 174.
20. Whitehead, *Essays*, 109.
21. Bergson, *Introduction to Metaphysics*, 52.
22. See Whitehead, *Process and Reality*, 209.
23. Whitehead, *Essays*, 97ff.
24. Ibid., 131.
25. Whitehead, *Adventures of Ideas*, 220ff.
26. Whitehead, *Process and Reality*, 3.
27. See Whitehead, *Essays*, 109ff., 127ff.

the real be the new . . .' The entire scheme thus represents a set of concepts intended to express the concept of the new – where the word 'express' is used advisedly, as neutral in respect of the paradoxes of self-reference and content reflexivity. The hypothetical categories of the scheme are oriented towards what Whitehead calls the 'empirical side' of the analysis as the field over which they range.[28] He variously defines the empirical side as 'everything of which we are conscious as enjoyed, perceived, willed or thought',[29] or, again, as 'the ideas and problems which form the complex texture of civilized thought'.[30] So understood, the empirical in Whitehead is not to be conflated with the impressions or sense-data of the empiricists, nor with the indeterminate 'immediate experience' of the idealists, nor with the life-world of the phenomenologists (that is, it is not a complex of primitive meanings that is prior to reflective or scientific conceptualisation), nor with any Quinean ocean of naturalistically conceived objectivity. Rather, Whitehead's concept of the empirical includes (as he says) 'every element of our experience'[31] – God and value, art and politics, science and technology, as well as the observable objects and events which more usually furnish our notions of the empirical.

In this light it is evident that what can for convenience sometimes be referred to as Whitehead's 'empirical world' is not a neutral 'given' which the speculative scheme organises or constructs, and to which it thereby gives us access. The scheme–world distinction, that is, is not in Whitehead based on any epistemological distinction between the 'given' and the 'interpreted' and hence is not involved in any suggestion that there are alternatives to the familiar world we actually inhabit.

We are not thereby restored, however, as Davidson would have it, 'to unmediated touch with the familiar objects and antics which make our sentences and opinions true or false'.[32] For we do not need to leave or step outside the empirical world to find it confusing. The assurance that the world we are familiar with is actually opened up in the language we speak does not make that world any less puzzling than it is familiar. As Whitehead puts it: 'Philosophy does not initiate interpretations. Its search for a rationalistic scheme is the search for more adequate criticism, and for more adequate justification, of the interpretations which we perforce employ.'[33]

---

28. Whitehead, *Process and Reality*, 3.
29. Ibid., 3.
30. Ibid., xi.
31. Ibid., 3.
32. D. Davidson, 'On the Very Idea of a Conceptual Scheme', in *Inquiries into Truth and Interpretation* (Oxford: Clarendon Press, 1984), 198.
33. Whitehead, *Process and Reality*, 14–15.

Now, understood as including our 'interpretations', Whitehead's concept of the empirical world is clearly not that of an uninterpreted element which the scheme confronts as a theory-neutral quantity. Rather, it is an historical concept which designates both the 'oceans of facts' and the 'evaluative interests', 'intrinsic within each historical period', in respect of which the individual philosopher seeks to discover whether there is a 'thread of coordination'.[34] So, of course, does everyone else: artist, critic, social scientist, common man or woman. But this fact cannot be used – as Rorty uses it[35] – to provide an argument for the assimilation of philosophy to general literature. For it is simply an indication of the inescapably philosophical character of the special sciences, and therefore of the need for a science of 'final' or 'ultimate' 'generalities';[36] that is, a science which will attempt 'to coordinate the current expressions of human experience, in common speech, in social institutions, in actions, in the principles of the various special sciences, elucidating harmony and exposing discrepancies'.[37] Regarded in this way, philosophy is not a permanent, or neutral, or ahistorical discovery of some previously hidden dimension of experience – as Rorty would have it[38] – but is an historically located attempt, critical and constructive, 'to promote the most general systematization of civilized thought'.[39] Yet is this anything more than a matter of philosophy understood as media for or interpreter among the special sciences?[40] Traditionally, the significance of the enterprise of 'general systematization' may be grasped from the fact that, understood as metaphysics, it lays claim to be concerned with the concept of the 'real' in its widest or ultimate sense. But what meaning, if any, such a claim might have with respect to the historically experienced empirical world is, as Whitehead is aware, itself a philosophical question that awaits examination, at least, of the level of generalities with which the discipline is peculiarly concerned. His concept of the empirical is therefore best understood as a name for the entire ensemble of affairs in historical experience as that which constitutes the *explanandum* of philosophical analysis – with the concept of the 'real' left as an empty, undetermined and questionable logical space, lying, so to

---

34. Whitehead, *Modes of Thought*, 18.
35. See Richard Rorty, 'Philosophy as a Kind of Writing', in *Consequences of Pragmatism* (Minneapolis: University of Minnesota Press, 1982), 90ff. What follows is an outline of what I take to be Whitehead's answer to the question Rorty puts to philosophy in this book, asking 'why we need a discipline at that level of generality' (p. 77).
36. Whitehead, *Process and Reality*, 8.
37. Whitehead, *Adventures of Ideas*, 222.
38. Rorty, *Consequences of Pragmatism*, 74, 80, 87.
39. Whitehead, *Process and Reality*, 17.
40. For a contemporary version of such a position, see Jürgen Habermas, 'Philosophy as Stand-In and Interpreter', in *After Philosophy*, ed. K. Baynes et al. (Cambridge, MA: MIT Press, 1987), 296ff.

speak, between the two sides, categorial and empirical (this is Whitehead's solution to the Meno paradox). The formula under which Whitehead approaches the theme of radical novelty can thus be summarised as: how do the categorial and empirical stand to each other?

3

Whitehead's basic position on the relation of scheme and world can be put like this: the categorial and empirical are related as an equation defining a function is related to the value of its variables. Within the categorial scheme, as Whitehead says, all the elements of the empirical 'are reduced to the ghost-like character of real [that is, free or independent] variables'.[41] In contrast, the categories of the scheme can be said to have the status of polyadic propositional functions; they could be expressed as $R(x\ldots y\ldots z\ldots n)$, where $x\ldots y\ldots z\ldots n$ are the variables representing the empirical elements and R represents the categories of the scheme.[42]

What is the significance of this analogy?

As Whitehead insists, the algebraic method undergoes considerable extension when used beyond its normal provenance as a model for philosophical analysis. Mathematics he defines as 'the study of pattern in abstraction from the particulars which are patterned'.[43] However, whereas mathematics is satisfied with the notion of 'any',[44] philosophy, as noted earlier, is distinguished by its attempt to provide an analysis of the nature of individuality as well as of connection. In the context of the theme of radical novelty, it is clearly of central importance to specify the way in which, on Whitehead's view, such a task can be fulfilled by a speculative scheme constructed on the algebraic model of variable and value.

In this connection, it is important to recognise at the outset that Whitehead sees the construction of a philosophical scheme of categories as an enterprise of 'imaginative generalization'.[45] His point is that when we try

---

41. Whitehead, *Essays*, 128; see *Adventures of Ideas*, 242; *Modes of Thought*, 106–7.
42. The student of Whitehead is permanently indebted to Wolfe Mays, *The Philosophy of Whitehead* (London: Allen and Unwin, 1959), where the centrality of the algebraic method in Whitehead's thought is brilliantly expounded; see especially ch. 5. Unfortunately, however, Mays treats the concept of occasions not as a connective or categorial function, but as identical with accidents or empirical values. He also applies a very restricted concept of 'necessity' to decide which of the categories are properly 'metaphysical' and which are not. As will emerge, the centrality of the algebraic method in Whitehead requires a very different account of his work than that which Mays offers.
43. Whitehead, *Essays*, 111; see Bergson, *Introduction to Metaphysics*, ch. 2.
44. Whitehead, *Essays*, 110.
45. Whitehead, *Process and Reality*, 5.

philosophically to analyse and coordinate the main features of the empirical world, we do so by means of the analogical employment of some or other features of that world. We talk of 'mind', 'matter', 'reason', 'will', 'things', 'events', and so on. In so doing, however, we are not referring to particular features of the empirical world; rather, we are employing particular features of the empirical world as analogues for the coordinating characterisation of its main features. Here the historically located empirical world is related to the scheme, not just as the subject of analysis, but as the source of analogues for the definition of the 'real', where these analogues have the status of heuristic aids in the establishment of theories. In this respect, the procedure of 'schematization'[46] runs, as it were, from the empirical to the rational side of the analysis and gives it the character of 'descriptive generalization';[47] that is, it is 'the utilization of specific notions, applying to a restricted group of facts, for the divinization of the generic notions which apply to all facts'.[48] The categorial scheme thus represents a set or constellation of hypothetical analogues – 'Let the working hypothesis be events in their process of origination'[49] – where each of these analogues expands or qualifies the partiality or excesses of the other. As Whitehead puts it: 'to arrive at the philosophic generalization . . . an apparent redundancy of terms is required. The words correct each other.'[50]

It should be noted here that Whitehead's appropriation and expansion of the algebraic method for the elaboration of a metaphysics of the new is clearly an instance of itself. That is, the employment of the algebraic method as an account of metaphysical method is itself an analogue with hypothetical status in respect of its subject matter – namely, philosophical analysis.

Understood in this fashion as a self-referential schematisation or generalisation, Whitehead's method clearly does not involve him in any kind of metaphysical 'dogmatism'. The point of taking the inclusively defined empirical world as the unreconstructed subject matter and analogue source of the analysis (even with respect to methodology) is to distinguish it from the issue that is addressed by the analysis, that is, to avoid the familiar problems consequent upon any conflation of the notions of the 'world' and 'reality'. Redefined as the empirical, the Leibnizian notion of the world *simpliciter* disappears: the investigation is restricted to the realm of experience,[51] the world is always an interpreted world,[52] and there are no *a*

---

46. Ibid., 16.
47. Ibid., 10; see *Adventures of Ideas*, 234.
48. Whitehead, *Process and Reality*, 5; see 13.
49. Whitehead, *Adventures of Ideas*, 235–6.
50. Ibid., 236.
51. Whitehead, *Process and Reality*, 4.
52. Ibid., 14–15.

priori or self-evident propositions on the basis of which the 'real nature' of things can be determined.[53] In Whitehead, there is no trace of any 'real' to which we have direct access.

The rejection of dogmatism does not mean, however, that Whitehead's analysis takes the form of a theory of knowledge. Among other things, he elaborates a theory of knowledge, and in particular a theory of philosophical knowledge that is the especial concern of this essay. Yet in this connection the distinction of categorial and empirical is not to be conflated with any distinction between 'mind' and 'world', or knowing subject and object known, understood as constituting the final parameters of philosophical analysis. The notion of the schematisation of the empirical dissolves the assumption that there are any such privileged starting points in philosophy; polarities such as 'mind' and 'world' can now be recognised as particular features of the empirical which have been employed as coordinating analogues for the characterisation of its contents. The status of cognition may thus be treated as an open question; experience need no longer be taken to be primarily a matter of the cognition of objects, nor recourse to the knowing subject the inevitable corollary of the abandonment of dogmatism. In this context it is hardly surprising that the problem of scepticism is not for Whitehead a major issue, for scepticism assumes that the mind–world contrast has fundamental metaphysical status.

Whitehead's method of schematisation further emancipates the investigation both from the assumption that there is a 'complete' or 'realised' real, understood as something given in itself, which awaits characterisation, and equally from its twin; namely, that if there is no thing-in-itself, the 'real' can be nothing other than a concatenation of historically changing perspectives which are solely attributable to, or relative to, their centres, and hence are not facts about an objectively independent world in any significant sense of those terms. With the notion of schematisation, the otherwise compelling, mirror-like alternatives of a 'substantial' or 'perspectival' real can be seen for what they are: particular analogues in terms of which the evident givenness and reliability of the world, and the equally evident historical and perspectival character of knowledge, have found philosophical interpretation. As a result, such manifest empirical features can now be considered without conflation with the mesmerising polarity of the thing-in-itself and its subjectivist counterpart; they become something that the categories of the scheme must register and appropriately characterise. The method of descriptive generalisation opens the way for that transformation of philosophy in terms of algebraic method which Whitehead intends.

---

53. Ibid., 8, 12.

4

In defining the character of schematic analysis, Whitehead pushes the analogy between algebraic and categorial scheme as hard as he can, appropriating the so-called method of 'application', 'interpretation', or 'substitution'[54] as a procedural model. He maintains that just as in algebra or symbolic logic we give the variables of the equation defining a function a value, which is known as the 'substitution-instance', 'application', or 'interpretation', so we do also in philosophy with the categorial scheme.[55]

For understood as having the character of propositional functions, the categories of the scheme are as such incomplete or indeterminate. To be completed they must be given empirical application. It is the success with which the scheme can find empirical applications that determines its adequacy as a scheme, that is, as having the level of generality or coordinating power appropriate to metaphysics. On this basis it is possible to define the mode of discourse which Whitehead characteristically employs in *Process and Reality* and elsewhere. For schematic substitution cuts both ways: as propositional functions, the categories remain essentially incomplete or indeterminate without their empirical subject matter, as does the empirical subject matter without its coordinating categorial definition (were it otherwise, there would be no such thing as philosophy). In consequence, the analysis can be said to seek both categorial interpretations for empirical features, and empirical applications for its categories. Schematic substitution, that is, is essentially two-sided: 'rational side' and 'empirical side' are substitutionally related. And if that is the case, we would expect Whitehead's texts to be a constant, mutually illuminating movement back and forth between the two. In other words, we would expect to find that the relation of the two sides of the analysis is essentially reciprocal – that the demonstration of 'the power of the scheme'[56] in respect of its substitution instances is also and at once an elaboration of its significance.

This is exactly what Whitehead tells us we will find. As he explicitly says of all parts of *Process and Reality* at the outset of that work (and the same clearly holds for his later writings): 'the unity of treatment is to be looked for in the gradual development of the scheme in meaning and relevance . . . In each recurrence [to particular topics] these topics throw some new light on the scheme or receive some new elucidation.'[57] To apply or to interpret the categorial scheme is also to develop its 'meaning', that is, the expansion

---

54. Ibid., 116.
55. See A. N. Whitehead, *A Treatise on Universal Algebra. With Applications* (Cambridge: Cambridge University Press, 1898), ch. 1; *Essays*, 128.
56. Whitehead, *Process and Reality*, xi.
57. Ibid., xii; see xi, xiv; *Treatise on Universal Algebra*, 12.

of the scheme's relevance, or range of empirical interpretations, also expands the meaning-content of the categories. Throughout, the analysis follows the twofold path of categorial and empirical determination. It is this double movement, Whitehead is reminding us, that goes on throughout his analysis. His every line has always to be read with bifocals, as a simultaneous elaboration of categorial meaning and empirical relevance.

So understood, the interpretative procedure is clearly circular in nature: each of its 'sides' requires and finds its 'completion of meaning'[58] in the other. Yet this is of course a virtuous and not a vicious circle; it is an integral feature of schematic analysis insofar as that is nothing else than the mutual determination and elucidation of its two sides, categorial and empirical.

5

In contrast to what happens in mathematics or symbolic logic, not only construction but also application or interpretation is for Whitehead analogical in nature. That is, he does not regard analogy merely as a heuristic device in the elaboration of a scheme of categories. Rather, he sees analogy as an essential feature of metaphysics: understood as a descriptive generalisation, the scheme posits a relation of analogy between its categories and the empirical world.[59] In his own words: 'The procedure of rationalism is the discussion of analogy.'[60] How is this relation of analogy to be understood?

---

58. Whitehead, *Essays*, 128.
59. Witness, for example, Whitehead's treatment of physical energy, where he 'substitutes' (*Process and Reality*, 116) various concepts drawn from physics (e.g., 'scalar localisation') for the variables of certain categories of the scheme (e.g., 'quantitative satisfaction') in order to indicate the analogical 'agreement' (*Process and Reality*, 116) of the categories with the notions of modern physics. The 'light' (*Process and Reality*, 116) which Whitehead believes is offered by this particular application is not any kind of contribution to natural science, nor does it involve the discovery of some previously hidden aetiological feature of the world, but is nothing else than an elucidation of the fit of the two 'sides' of the analysis. The point of the application is not to ascribe 'quantitative satisfaction' to nature, nor to endow the claims of modern physics with some kind of metaphysical necessity, but to indicate the analogical 'power of the scheme' in respect of empirical states of affairs presently understood in terms of scalar localisation.
60. Whitehead, *Modes of Thought*, 98. Whitehead is perhaps best seen here as extrapolating and generalising from the philosophy of science developed at Trinity by his contemporary, N. R. Campbell. See N. R. Campbell, *Physics: The Elements* (Cambridge: Cambridge University Press, 1921); reprinted as *The Foundations of Science* (New York: Dover, 1957). On Campbell, see the entry by Gerd Buchdahl in P. Edwards (ed.), *The Encyclopedia of Philosophy* (New York: Macmillan, 1967). On the role of analogy in philosophy, see especially Gerd Buchdahl, *Metaphysics and the Philosophy of Science*, 2nd edn (New York: University Press of America, 1988); and, with particular reference to Whitehead, Dorothy Emmet, *The Nature of Metaphysical*

There are two important points here. First, what the categories of the scheme seek for in the empirical world is interpretation or application; that is, categorial analysis is analogical analysis in the sense that it is a matter of the application of analogies to particular empirical subject matters. This means, secondly, that just as (for example) the analogical term 'good' is an indeterminate or incomplete expression – akin to an algebraic or propositional function – outside of its interpretation in specific contexts ('good film', 'good meal', 'good game', etc.), so an analogical category such as that of occasions is purely formal or lacking in explanatory power ('practically unintelligible'[61] outside of its applications).

The significance of the fact that the scheme–world relation is a matter of the application of analogies cannot be underestimated. For it is the character of the categories as determinable only by means of their analogical application to specific instances which itself represents their content-reflexivity in respect of the new.

What Whitehead does, in other words, is to employ the procedure of analogical application as an analogue for the content-reflexivity of the categories as analyses of the new. Analogical application is that relation of concept and object which analogically articulates the fact that the self-realising acts of something – its occasions – are as such wholly its own. To use Whitehead's own preferred analogue for the significance of analogical application (which cannot be analysed other than analogically): it is the algebraic status of the scheme, as an expression that can be rendered complete only by its interpretations, which expresses its content-reflexivity. As he puts it in one place, the algebraic model of application represents 'the suffusion of the connective by the things connected', that is, it enacts that kind of reflexive 'concurrence of mathematical-formal principles and accidental factors'[62] which alone is adequate to the theme of the self-realising new.

The reason for the significance which, in contrast to the other thinkers of radical novelty,[63] Whitehead attaches to modern mathematics is now apparent: it provides a model for the analysis of radical novelty in that it can be analogically employed as an expression of the reflexive 'fusion of

---

Thinking (New York: St Martin's Press, 1966). Apart, of course, from his concern with mathematics, the significant early influence on Whitehead (see *Treatise on Universal Algebra*, Preface) of F. H. Bradley, *The Principles of Logic*, 2 vols (Oxford: Clarendon Press, 1883), cannot be discounted when considering his method: see Bradley's treatment of the hypothetical judgment, 'working hypothesis' and 'ideal experiment'.

61. Whitehead, *Process and Reality*, xi.
62. Whitehead, *Essays*, 128.
63. It is interesting to note, however, that at one point Kierkegaard describes himself as speaking 'algebraically'; *Philosophical Fragments* (Princeton: Princeton University Press, 1962), 114.

analysis and actuality',[64] necessity and contingency,[65] demanded by the theme of the self-realising new. It can therefore be said that in schematic analysis, philosophical necessity is to be understood as substitutional necessity. That is, the categories of the scheme do not constitute an invariant structure. Rather, it is for Whitehead the analogical elaboration of categorial 'meaning' and empirical 'relevance' which renders the analysis 'necessary';[66] by which he means that it displays or bears 'within itself its own warrant of universality'[67] solely in virtue of its power of analogical interpretation. Schematic necessity, that is, is nothing else than the content-reflexive fit of its two sides, categorial and empirical – anything else would contradictorily refer the self-realising new away from itself for its principle.[68] When, for example, Whitehead refers to the categories of the scheme throughout his writings as 'generic notions', the whole point of his recourse to the Aristotelian notion of the generic concept is to redefine it in terms of the algebraic method. 'Cosmology', that is, is no longer to be tied to a necessary return of the same. The categories of the scheme are not to be regarded as reproducing the procedure by which the real substance unfolds itself in its specific forms of being, nor as in any sense the creative or generative forces or origins from which particular things spring. Instead, like the new physics of his day (a key analogue of construction), 'in the place of the Aristotelian notion of the procession of forms', Whitehead's schematic analysis 'has substituted the notion of the forms of process'.[69]

Here the notion of the 'forms of process' is offered as a redefinition of the concept of 'forms' such that it makes no sense to talk of the 'recurrence' of the categories. Instead, it has to be said that the forms of process neither recur nor do not recur. They are neither the 'same' nor 'different'. Rather, they are analyses of the realisation of recurrence and non-recurrence, sameness and difference, in terms of a vectorial movement of unique and unrepeatable occasions understood as expressing the self-realising natures of things in the only way they can be expressed: namely, analogically.

Perhaps the best way of describing what is at issue in Whitehead's redefinition of the concept of 'forms' as 'forms of process' is to say that it is intended to overcome Aristotle's objection to Plato that his forms do nothing. With its categories understood as structures of self-realisation,

---

64. Whitehead, *Essays*, 113.
65. See ibid., 123.
66. Whitehead, *Process and Reality*, 4.
67. Ibid., 4.
68. A lot more clearly needs to be said at this point about the nature and status of eternal objects. As is implied in what follows, Whitehead's redefinition of the concepts of 'universal' and 'particular' is, I suspect, best apprehended in the context of analogical algebra. But there is no space for further remarks here.
69. Whitehead, *Modes of Thought*, 140; see 82.

schematic analysis does not invoke any principle of production. Yet the abandonment of the traditional mode of philosophical self-understanding does not mean for Whitehead that none but negative statements can be made about the self-realising new, that is, that the enterprise of explanation is also to be abandoned. In that 'fusion of analysis and actuality' represented by the algebraic method of schematic analysis, form and content, necessity and accident, can be understood by way of analogical application as reflecting into each other without remainder in the occasion.[70]

Seen in the context of the algebraic method, Whitehead's own response to the paradox of content-reflexivity should come as no surprise. When considering his own objection to the theme of the self-realising new, quoted earlier, to the effect that 'our doctrine seems to have destroyed the very basis of rationality', his reply is couched in terms of the two-sided, analogical procedure of algebraic interpretation. As he puts it, with characteristically deceptive simplicity and directness: 'We can start our investigation from either end; namely, we can understand the process and then consider the characterization of the individuals; or we can characterize the individuals and conceive them as formative of the relevant process. In truth, the distinction is only one of emphasis.'[71]

Whitehead's claim here is nothing less than that the self-realising new need be conflated neither with reason nor with the non-rational. By means of the analogical algebra, the Hegel–Heidegger disjunction may now be dissolved. The mutual inversions of univocity and equivocity which have fed off each other for so long can be transcended in the true speculative proposition, which is the analogical proposition of schematic analysis.

6

In order to make good this claim, schematic analysis must be considered in relation to the paradox of self-reference. As noted, the categorial scheme has thoroughgoing hypothetical status. At no point in the analysis is there any claim to the achievement of absolute certainty. Indeed, Whitehead is

---

70. I would suggest that it is only in this context that Whitehead's important response to Dewey, 'The Analysis of Meaning' (*Essays*, 122ff.), can properly be understood. Whitehead there denies Dewey's suggestion that his categories constitute an 'aboriginal structure of the world', some 'independent and ready-made forms'; hence he denies that he needs to decide between what Dewey calls the 'mathematical-formal' and 'genetic-functional' approaches. On Whitehead's view, the reflexive 'fusion of the two' (*Essays*, 123) is made possible in philosophy by the analogical algebra. What is happening in this exchange is, of course, quite momentous: it is the clash of the two great concepts of function – the algebraic and the biological.
71. Whitehead, *Modes of Thought*, 98–9.

unusual in laying great stress on the fact that his philosophy is what other philosophies have only retrospectively been recognised to be: namely, a coordination of historical[72] and contemporary experience,[73] in terms of certain historically preferred analogues, which is essentially revisable in character[74] and has the status of just one 'deposition' among others;[75] that is, not claiming any privileged kind of necessity for itself, it can contemplate even the abandonment of its main categories.[76]

Now there can be no doubt that, internally speaking, schematic analysis dissolves the problem that dogs philosophies that are self-conscious enough to recognise their own historical locatedness. Usually such theories are forced either finally to surrender to an absolute conception of the real, giving themselves a privileged position above change on the ground that they represent the culminating form of change; or, in reaction, to embrace an out-and-out historical relativism or perspectivism. But no such disjunction exists for Whitehead, as is indicated by two of his uses of the concept of the 'real'.

In schematic analysis any absolute conception of the realised real is rejected in that, defined as a vectoral process of occasions, the real is essentially incomplete. This does not mean, however, that there is no 'given' reality in the sense of that which is distinct and independent of the subject qua self-unfolding occasion. In this latter sense, understood as a vectorial process, reality is a movement in which the contents of antecedent occasions are objectified ('prehended') in the becoming or 'concrescence' of subsequent occasions.[77] The schematic concept of process thus succeeds in reconciling the fact that reality is not a complete thing-in-itself, and that knowledge is perspectival, with the fact that both knowledge and reality also require to be defined in terms of objects distinct from and independent of the subject or concrescent occasion.

The problem as to how we may 'get out' of our 'perspectives' to some counterpart 'world' no longer arises here. Understood in terms of a vectorial process of occasions, our perspectives are not something which we are ever simply 'in', nor does the world lie 'outside' of them[78] – which is the reason why epistemological concerns are what schematic analysis addresses in the course of its elaboration, not what it sets out from. Admittedly, schematic

---

72. Whitehead, *Process and Reality*, 17; *Modes of Thought*, 18.
73. Whitehead, *Adventures of Ideas*, 222; *Modes of Thought*, 171, 173–4.
74. Whitehead, *Process and Reality*, 7, 8, 10–11; *Adventures of Ideas*, 223.
75. Whitehead, *Process and Reality*, 10–11.
76. Ibid., 9.
77. See Whitehead, *Adventures of Ideas*, 209ff.
78. See A. W. Murphy, 'Relativism in Dewey and Whitehead', *The Philosophical Review* 36 (1927), 132.

analysis has itself the character of a hypothetico-deductive 'intellectual construction';[79] that is, it involves a contrast of mind and world. But the point is that this fact does not endow either the knowing subject or the knowledge-relation with any fundamental status or metaphysical finality. Instead, intellectual constructions are themselves specified and relativised by the analysis as elements in a process of occasions which, far from being defined in terms of a theory of knowledge, itself provides the parameters in terms of which a theory of knowledge is elaborated.

Of course, schematic analysis may be regarded as the best evidence of the knowing subject's ability to define its place in the order of things. But this does not provide any opportunity for the knowing subject to give itself metaphysical airs. On the contrary, one main point of the scheme's character as an intellectual construction is emphatically to register the knowing subject's ability to recognise and define itself as only a single element in a complex movement of which it is neither more nor less than a particularly sophisticated instance. As Whitehead puts it: 'Philosophy is the self-correction by consciousness of its own initial excess of subjectivity.'[80]

Yet the real question still remains: whether or not schematic analysis has the capacity to define or delimit itself in terms of its own analysis of the real, that is, to negotiate the fact of the relativity and locatedness of its own categories. Here it may be objected that the relativising self-referentiality of Whitehead's scheme comes too cheaply: a scheme can obviously be defined as historically relative in terms of the kind of hypotheticity elaborated within the scheme – but there is nothing about that which qualifies the claim to truth made for hypotheticity! After all, as an account of metaphysical reflection, the hypothetical scheme treats all alternative positions as competitor hypotheses – a claim that theories such as Plato's or Hegel's seem to deny. Thus the final limit of the hypothetical method is that method itself. Here, as always, relativism contradicts itself in presupposing one absolute – its own validity. No philosophy has the capacity to carry its own *memento mori* about with it.

What this objection overlooks, however, is the hypothetical character of hypothesis. That is, it confuses the claim that there is no complete or final truth with that claim's own elevation to affirmative rank, regardless of the different status of both.[81] What Whitehead calls the 'suspended judgment' of metaphysics is neither a negative nor an affirmative judgement, but a

---

79. See Whitehead, *Process and Reality*, 5.
80. Ibid., 15; see *Modes of Thought*, 107–8.
81. Theodor W. Adorno, *Negative Dialectics*, trans. J. E. Ashton (New York: Seabury Press, 1973), 35–6, notices this. But always the Marxist counterpart of Heidegger, he thinks that the discovery of history by philosophy requires the abandonment of 'traditional philosophy'.

judgement of compatibility alone,⁸² that is, it represents a claim to empirical or interpretative fit that as such does not exclude alternative accounts. In what specific way does schematic analysis achieve this? By analogy. That is, by the evident analogical character of the analysis. Analogical application is the categorial register of hypotheticity. And it is so, first of all, in the sense that analogies overdetermine their subject matter to the extent that they necessarily carry with them a suggestive surplus of connotative meaning. This surplus has a heuristic function in that it aids in the extension and revision of the theory.

But secondly – and more significantly – analogical application is always partial or approximate or incomplete, that is, there is always an acknowledged looseness of fit or underdetermination between it and its subject matter when it is used as a mode of analysis. Analogy is the form whereby reflection expresses the fact that the *explanandum* is always more than the *explanans*. It is therefore the analogical character of schematic analysis which allows it to say 'what truly is', that is, which holds together its strong compatibility-claims with its self-understanding as historically located and revisable. The hypothetical 'is' of schematic analysis is the 'is' of analogical predication; a claim, it should be remembered, which is an instance of itself in respect of its subject matter – namely, the nature of philosophy.

So understood, schematic analysis is fallibilist in respect of itself, including its own algebraic account of philosophy. Indeed, it is for this reason that schematic analysis has the power to insist upon its own evident historical locatedness: it can specify the hypotheticity of its categorial analogues in terms of their derivation from and relevance to the historical context in which they are elaborated. Schematic analysis thereby sustains the universality that is characteristic of metaphysics without making any claim to the 'pathetic' status of 'final metaphysical truth';⁸³ that is, it makes good its claim to universality precisely because it can take into account its own evident historical locatedness and revisability. And this claim, like all the truth-claims of the analysis, is a claim only to analogical fit. It may be said that the rationale of the algebraic method is that it preserves the difference between scheme and world – a dividing line that can only be crossed (in either direction) by means of analogy.⁸⁴

---

82. See Whitehead, *Process and Reality*, 274.
83. Whitehead, *Essays*, 125.
84. It should be noted that, by preserving the difference between scheme and world, the algebraic method also allows Whitehead to secure his pluralism, that is, to preserve the differences in the world. For example, one purpose of the category of actual occasions is to overcome the traditional dichotomy between humans and nature (see *Adventures of Ideas*, 184–5, 189). So in his elaboration of the scheme, Whitehead attempts to give the notion of occasions sufficient scope to embrace both poles of the dichotomy and to provide 'an analogy between the transference of energy from

7

It is now evident that Whitehead's 'recurrence to pre-Kantian modes of thought'[85] is rendered possible by the analogical character of the categories. It is as analogies that they can represent the extra-linguistic reach and content of language, that is, the capacity of concepts to think that which is other than concepts.

Nowhere is this clearer than in respect of the question of the relation of language and temporality. It is perhaps here, if anywhere, that the twentieth-century linguistic turn meets its limits: the one feature of experience that cannot be assimilated to language is temporality. Consider, for example, Gadamer's 'temporal' account of language as a matter of the infinite possibilities of finite utterance.[86] Here it is not clear if the infinite possibilities of finite utterance are conditions of the temporal character of language as the event of dialogue, or if the temporal character of language as the event of dialogue is an instance of a temporality that is more fundamental than language. It may be said that Gadamer's analysis of language appears to wobble between Hegel's account of temporality in terms of finitude, and Heidegger's account of finitude in terms of temporality.[87] Given that language is for Gadamer the final horizon of hermeneutics, it seems that he must either absorb temporality into language, or tacitly admit that temporality lies beyond the capacity of hermeneutics. However, the first alternative imposes too much strain on the concept of language,

---

particular occasion to particular occasion in physical nature and the transference of affective tone, with its emotional energy, from one occasion to another in any human personality' (*Adventures of Ideas*, 188). The fact, however, that the analysis strictly confines itself to securing an analogy between nature and spirit means that their unity cannot be rendered as an identity – whether materialistic, monistic or panpsychist. The pluralistic character of analogical application resides in the fact that it allows for the differences between its interpretations while maintaining their unity as interpretations of the scheme.

85. Whitehead, *Process and Reality*, xi.
86. See Gadamer, *Truth and Method*, 397ff. Readers of Richard Rorty, 'The Subjectivist Principle and the Linguistic Turn', in George L. Kline (ed.), *A. N. Whitehead: Essays on His Philosophy* (Englewood Cliffs, NJ: Prentice Hall, 1963), 134ff. – the best critique of Whitehead from the linguistic point of view – will recognise that Whitehead would agree with Rorty that there is a difference between objects and facts about objects, and that the 'about' relation is ultimate. However, Whitehead would not agree to take that relation as unanalysable, as Rorty does. It is the 'about' relation that Whitehead analyses in terms of the vectorial process of occasions – in order 'to take time seriously'; an intent Rorty completely ignores.
87. See G. W. F. Hegel, *Encyclopedia: The Philosophy of Nature*, trans. A. V. Miller (Oxford: Clarendon Press, 1970), paras 247 add., 248 add.; and Martin Heidegger, *Being and Time*, trans. J. Macquarrie and E. Robinson (Oxford: Blackwell, 1962), paras 65ff.; Heidegger, *On Time and Being*, 48, 54.

while the second reveals a glaring shortfall in the proclaimed universality of hermeneutic theory.

If the self-realising new is to be retained as a subject of rational analysis, it can be argued that the only possible approach here is Whitehead's, where the movement of language, defined as that component of the vectorial process of occasions which is a matter of the experiences of interlocutors, is an instance of the realisation or 'temporalisation' of time.[88] The movement of language here becomes a model or analogue for that which is also more than language.

Now there are definite hints of such a metaphysic in Gadamer[89] – but they remain just that. If he were to go further, he would have to follow Whitehead, who, in defining the 'temporalisation' or realisation of time in terms of a vectorial process of 'prehending' occasions, also understands the interpretative or hermeneutic phenomenon as universal or cosmological in scope; but it is universal as a feature or character of the temporalising process, not simply as a feature or character of the infinite possibilities of language. In this context, Whitehead can be seen to have the best of reasons for refusing either to identify the hermeneutic phenomenon with language, or to take language as the final horizon of philosophy. Hence his recourse to analogy: analogical application is the mode whereby reflection breaks out of the abstract circle of language without leaving it. Indeed, to speak more accurately, there is no need for that: the analogical power of language is the means whereby it can exhibit or express itself as only one element in a movement of self-realisation that is greater than itself. In this sense, there are for Whitehead no final horizons in philosophy; there is only the rigorous play of the analogical imagination.

The significance of this position can perhaps be expressed by noting that Whitehead's analogical algebra renders redundant the disjunctive notion that the world or the 'real' must be either theory-independent or (to use Putnam's term) theory-internal. For the analogical algebra, theory and world, concept and object, are neither independent nor identical. Rather, they are analogically related, that is, each is in its own way both more and less than the other, for analogies are at once overdetermining in meaning and underdetermining in interpretative application. Hence schematic analysis has the power both to acknowledge that the unfolding world is more than itself, and to specify itself as an element in the unfolding of the world.

So regarded, there can be little doubt that, despite its neglect, Whitehead's schematic analysis has at least the right to do what all significant theories have done: its historicist self-understanding, whereby it locates

---

88. See Whitehead, *Adventures of Ideas*, 181ff.
89. Gadamer, *Truth and Method*, 97 [cf. 443], 387, 395, 432, 442ff.

itself in the horizontal movement of the new as hypothetico-analogical in character, allows it to place its confidence in the irreversibility of its philosophical insight. Like every universal theory, it calls to the future; but it calls to a future that it can understand as its own criticism and revision.

Hegel was the first to recognise that certain kinds of entities – works of art, theories, historical events – are essentially variable in character, that is, that their nature or meaning only fully emerges in their subsequent historical existence. But Hegel did not extend this insight to his own philosophy. Only after and against Hegel does that shift take place, with the result, understandably, that in the German tradition it is generally seen as involving the destruction of metaphysics. In schematic analysis, however, metaphysics now has the capacity to define itself qua metaphysics as an essentially variable object, thereby retaining its ancient claim to universality. Schematic analysis transforms the Liar Paradox, which has threatened to undermine philosophy since Nietzsche, into the site of philosophy's latest triumph and discovery: the categorial scheme weaves about itself its own shroud even as it prepares for its posthumous life. Hence philosophy can now make the claim that previously could properly be made only by works of art: *l'oeuvre, c'est la posterité de l'oeuvre* (Proust).

8

To underline the strength of Whitehead's schematic analysis of the new, it is useful to look briefly at the later Heidegger's position in its light. Like Whitehead, the later Heidegger is explicit about his use of analogues, or what he calls 'ontic models', in the discourse of thinking; he here inherits Nietzsche's rediscovery for German philosophy of the metaphoricity of concepts. As Heidegger puts it: 'a model is that from which thinking must necessarily take off'.[90] But just as Nietzsche's 'mobile army of metaphors' is no more than an instrument for the creation of the moment, so the later Heidegger's ontic models are merely heuristic aids in the self-emptying of thought before the impenetrable otherness of the event. He himself draws attention 'to the fact that, and the manner in which, ontic models given in language are used up and destroyed' in his writing; explicitly in the manner of 'negative theology'.[91] Statements now become apophatic gestures.

The insistent intractability of the later Heidegger's texts is thus much more than a pedagogical device to force the reader to reflect by shocking him or her out of the familiar rhythms and motifs of school philosophy.

---

90. Heidegger, *On Time and Being*, 50.
91. Ibid., 47.

The negation of rational method cannot contradictorily set itself up as a method – even a negative method – in its own right. It can be sustained only in 'Sayings' (*Sagen*), which are line-by-line enactments of the fact that, in the face of the paradoxes of the new, the only statements possible are ones so constructed as to evacuate their own propositional content before the event towards which they mutely point.

However, the price the later Heidegger pays for such a hasty and premature response to the paradoxes of the new is too high. Lacking any recourse to the notion of appropriate analogical application, he has no way of specifying or delimiting the descriptive scope of the models he employs. In consequence, far from being used up or destroyed in the movement of his discourse, his models expand, unchecked and unrestricted, far beyond the limits of careful or attentive application. The result is that the later Heidegger's writings become a strange, inverted mirror-image of all that he would repudiate. This inversion plays itself out in a variety of ways. Thus, for example, placed beyond the realm of reason as the impenetrable other of a secularised *via negativa*, the later Heidegger's event turns into its opposite: it becomes a sacral dispensation that has to be passively received by the initiated listener. This is not the simplistic claim that Heidegger's 'Being' can everywhere be translated as 'God' – it cannot – but rather an explication of why one is tempted to do that: because conceivable only as the negation of method, the self-unfolding event takes on the character of a fateful, unsayable, originating power.[92]

To be sure, the later Heidegger cannot be put aside as a Schellingian; he would redefine 'origin' as 'event'.[93] Note, however, that he carefully avoids any general analysis of the connectedness of events, that is, of the ways in which an event may be 'prepared' in the past.[94] He might have felt the particular threat of Hegel here, precisely where he most needs to confront him. But the negation of method forbids that, with the result that he has to give the notion of self-creation so unrestricted an import that it is conflated with self-origination – the very move that the vectorial structure of Whitehead's process of occasions is designed to render unnecessary.

In this connection, one of the main reasons for the complexity of *Process and Reality* is that – against the monism which goes hand in hand with F. H. Bradley's theory of relations[95] – that work represents a massive

---

92. Jürgen Habermas, *The Philosophical Discourse of Modernity*, trans. F. Lawrence (Cambridge, MA: MIT Press, 1987), chs 6 and 7.
93. On the later Schelling's notion of origin, see Julian Roberts, *German Philosophy: An Introduction* (Englewood Cliffs, NJ: Humanities Press International, 1988), 144ff.
94. See Heidegger, *Poetry, Language, Thought*, 76.
95. For some comments on the theory of relations in F. H. Bradley and Whitehead, see my 'The Critique of Pure Feeling: Bradley, Whitehead and the Anglo-Saxon

attempt to provide an account of the relatedness of things in the context of a theory of the self-realising now understood as an analysis of the realisation of relations.⁹⁶ The alternative, as the later Heidegger's work indicates, is to turn the event into a temporalised, mystical origin which cannot be spoken about – and therefore cannot be spoken against.

What is at stake here emerges in the later Heidegger's treatment of speech or language, which is unrestrictedly given the character of a self-originating subject-event in its own right, and is represented as such in his oracular mode of 'questioning' utterance. In this way, truth-as validity is wholly assimilated to truth-as-occurrence – a strategy by means of which Heidegger intends to avoid entanglement with the paradox of self-reference in that the truth-value of propositions is defined as nothing else than, or as wholly immanent within, the underived event of their utterance.⁹⁷

It here becomes clear why, as has often been remarked, it is difficult to determine the status of the later Heidegger's own propositions: what kind of claim do they make for themselves? The answer is: none. Outside the event of their utterance, their status is radically indeterminate, for they must unfold themselves anew – that is, they can only derive or manifest their meaning – within every such event. Now, in one sense, this is unobjectionable; less dramatically stated as, say, by Gadamer⁹⁸ – it can be taken as an account of what has here been called the essentially variable character

---

Metaphysical Tradition', *Process Studies* 14.4 (1985), 253–64. For a fuller analysis of Bradley's position, see my 'Relations, intelligibilité et noncontradiction dans la métaphysique du sentir de F.H. Bradley: une réinterprétation', *Archives de philosophie* 54.4 (1991), 529–51; 55.1 (1992), 1–20.

96. It should be noted here that Whitehead cannot be criticised on the grounds that, unlike Heidegger, he merely replaces a 'static' concept of substance with an 'active' one, that is, that he is still tied to what Heidegger calls a metaphysics of 'presence'; see Peter B. Manchester, 'Time in Whitehead and Heidegger: A Response', *Process Studies* 5.2 (1975), 106–13. The concept of actual occasions is the concept of 'connectives', not of real substances. That is, occasions are nothing else than a movement towards and beyond themselves; they have no moment of plenitude in their own right. Because the concept of the process of actual occasions is a content-reflexive concept of the connective acts through which things make themselves what they are, actual occasions themselves never 'are'; when in concrescence they do not 'exist', and their completion is their 'perishing'. All that 'exists' is what occurs understood as self-actualising – a situation that, as has been argued, can only be analysed analogically. Whitehead's anti-Bradleyan title, *Process and Reality*, should be taken for what it is: a critique of the metaphysics of presence, of which Bradley was the last, self-consciously problematic exemplar in the British tradition. See my 'Process and Historical Crisis in F. H. Bradley's Ethics of Feeling', in P. MacEwan (ed.), *Ethics, Religion and Philosophy in the Thought of F. H. Bradley* (Lewiston, NY: Edwin Mellen Press, 1996). I develop the notion of 'actualisation' with respect to Whitehead in my 'Transcendental or Schematic Analysis?', in P. Mazzarella and E. Wolf-Gazo (eds), *Kant and Whitehead* (forthcoming).
97. See again Habermas, *Philosophical Discourse of Modernity*.
98. See Gadamer, *Truth and Method*, 442ff.

of propositions, which in Heidegger is represented by the 'questioning' or interrogative style of his prose.

The problem is, however, that the notion of questioning utterance is never sufficiently elaborated by Heidegger to avoid the consequences of its metamorphosis into self-originating subject-event. As the expression of nothing but itself, the questioning utterance becomes autistically immured, beyond interrogation, in the irreducible finality of its own autopoesis or self-manifestation; it thus takes on all the privileges of the philosophical subject it was originally intended to replace. What is here lacking in the later Heidegger is that strict and crucial distinction between propositions and occasions or events which Whitehead makes, defining propositions, not as subject-events, but as components of events, having that character in philosophy that has been analysed in this essay. Thus, perhaps uniquely in recent philosophy, the possibility of critical discourse is preserved in the context of a theory of the new.

Nowhere is the importance of this more evident than in respect of the later Heidegger's event-theory of politics, where the indefinite and uncontrolled character of his models brings with it disastrous consequences. In the first place, the tacit conflation of the models of the work of art and the event, always present in his writings, here becomes fully explicit, for the freedom of the self-unfolding event is in Heidegger the freedom only of aesthetic spontaneity; lacking the notion of analogical application, there is no place in the analysis for freedom as free will, that is, for the appropriate distinctions between nature, art and history which are the achievements of critical Enlightenment. Secondly, because the aesthetic event is given unrestricted application to any entity or state of affairs, great cultural or political transformations can be treated as its paradigms; regarded as spontaneous acts, they can be seen, like great works of art, as having an originality such that they themselves create the principles in terms of which they can be assessed.[99]

In the political sphere, as is well known, Heidegger drew the appropriate conclusions for the Germany of the 1930s. Moreover, in the cultural sphere, as has already been noted, Heidegger sees his own thinking of the event in a similar light, as a fundamental break with the history of Western philosophy.

On a Whiteheadian analysis, however, such an unrestricted application of event-analysis to the cultural sphere merely represents a mirror-like inversion of the monolithic continuities of nineteenth-century histories of philosophy. Cultural history is to be thought of, not in terms either of

---

99. See Heidegger, *Poetry, Language, Thought*, 77–8.

continuities or of ruptures, but as 'adventures of ideas' in which there are no final completions or final closures but only the constant, shifting movement of the loss or reinterpretation or rediscovery of significances.[100]

In the political sphere, similarly, Heidegger's event-analysis retains key features of the nineteenth-century concept of the social organism it purportedly repudiates, in that it treats supra-individual entities such as 'nations', 'peoples', or historical epochs as agent-subjects as well as causal influences.[101] Here lies the *rationale* for Whitehead's careful distinction between occasions and events: the notion of the self-unfolding new he locates wholly in the category of occasions, which alone possess agency as well as causal efficacy, while events are defined as what he calls 'societies' of occasions with causal efficacy alone. In other words, the application of the category of occasions – and thus the employment of the notion of agency – is strictly scaled or delimited by the analysis; summarily, it could be said that there are no higher or more complex instances of occasions than the occasions of experience of the human individual. Interpreted socio-historically, the categorial scheme is so clearly intended as a corrective to collectivism in its various forms[102] that it could be said to represent a metaphysics of radical or reformist liberalism.[103]

It is thus only the 'rational analysis' made possible by the analogical scheme that saves the concept of the self-realising new from the promiscuity all too characteristic of the Heideggerian event. If Nietzsche's critique of reason exposed the metaphoricity of concepts, Whitehead's schematic analysis has rediscovered the conceptual power of metaphors.

On a Whiteheadian view, therefore, the later Heidegger is guilty of 'the fallacy of discarding method'. As Whitehead himself says – explicitly naming one of the figures who intimately affected Heidegger's later thought and still dominates the cult of post-philosophy – the assumption is 'that if there can be any intellectual analysis it must proceed according to some one discarded method, and thence to deduce that intellect is intrinsically tied

---

100. See Whitehead, *Adventures of Ideas*, passim, and Richard Rorty's telling comments in *Contingency, Irony, and Solidarity* (Cambridge: Cambridge University Press, 1989), 119n. R. G. Collingwood's claim in *The Idea of Nature* (Oxford: Clarendon Press, 1945), 177, that 'no-one can answer the question what nature is unless he knows what history is. This is a question which . . . Whitehead [has] not asked', simply ignores *Adventures of Ideas*, *Modes of Thought* and *The Function of Reason*.
101. See Heidegger, *Poetry, Language, Thought*, 42, 48, 74. For a telling analysis of Heidegger's treatment of historical institutions and periods, see Roberts, *German Philosophy*, ch. 9. See also Adorno, *Negative Dialectics*, 128–31, and *The Jargon of Authenticity*, trans. K. Tardowski (New York: Seabury Press, 1973).
102. See Whitehead, *Process and Reality*, 91, 108.
103. In a verbal communication, Dorothy Emmet tells me that she heard Whitehead say, a propos of *Process and Reality*: 'It's a defence of liberalism!'

to erroneous fictions. This type is illustrated by the anti-intellectualism of Nietzsche and Bergson, and tinges American pragmatism.'[104]

In the light of such a remark, it is not unfair to say that Whitehead is a thinker unique in the twentieth century. He may also be one of the greatest of its philosophers. Yet up till now the position he elaborates has hardly been noticed, least of all by those who most often invoke his name. As the metaphysician of the new, it is time he was given the consideration, and the criticism, that he deserves.

---

104. Whitehead, *Adventures of Ideas*, 223.

Chapter 3

From Presence to Process: Bradley and Whitehead

It is obvious that the title of Whitehead's major work explicitly refers to that of Bradley's: Bradley's *Appearance and Reality: A Metaphysical Essay* (1893) becomes Whitehead's *Process and Reality: An Essay in Cosmology* (1929). But while the importance of Bradley's thought for Whitehead is now well established, what needs further attention is the larger significance of their relation. For inscribed in these differences of title is nothing less than a transformation in the nature of metaphysical analysis – a transformation in which neither the role of Bradley's work nor the nature of Whitehead's achievement has yet been properly appreciated. To analyse some of the main connections between these two thinkers is to see both in a way quite different from conventional accounts.

I

Bradley and Whitehead are both engaged in metaphysical analysis in the sense that what unites them is that both maintain a metaphysical or positive theory of being or existence. That is to say, in contrast to empiricist-oriented accounts of being or existence, they do not regard being or existence merely as (in one form or another) an underivable 'given', about which nothing else can be said. Rather, they maintain that being or existence has a specific or 'positive'[1] nature of its own which is describable,[2] although statements

---

1. F. H. Bradley, *Appearance and Reality: A Metaphysical Essay* (Oxford: Clarendon Press, 1930), 215.
2. Cf. A. N. Whitehead, *Process and Reality: An Essay in Cosmology* (corrected edn, New York: The Free Press, 1978), 20.

about the positive nature of existence cannot be treated as having the status of qualities or attributes or predicates in any usual sense. In this context, the best way to understand both the unusual character of Bradley's absolutism and its historical role in relation to Whitehead's thought is in terms of the close relation between two distinctive features of Bradley's work – the concept of philosophical method and the theory of immediate experience or 'feeling'.

Too often Bradley's work is seen as a typical piece of Victoriana, a curio eccentrically and over-confidently cast in the 'high priori' style of an alien rationalism. In other words, his account of the nature of philosophical inquiry is commonly held to be intellectualist in character; that is, to rest on some form of the principle of non-contradiction, or, more usually, on a purely logical analysis of the concept of relations. Bradley's own ironic protests on the issue go unnoticed: 'There is an idea', he says, 'that we start . . . with certain axioms, and from these reason downwards. This idea to my mind is baseless.'[3]

In his *Principles of Logic*, Bradley characterises all theoretical inquiry as a matter of what he calls 'ideal experiment', the elaboration, as he puts it, of 'working hypotheses'. That position is more fully developed in *Essays on Truth and Reality* where, in response to critics such as Russell, Bradley says that the 'method' he employs is not axiomatic but 'experimental': 'we experiment ideally on the nature of things'.

The starting point of philosophical inquiry for Bradley is not any kind of metaphysical presupposition but what he calls 'a principle of action'; namely, the search for what he terms 'intellectual satisfaction'.[4] In seeking for intellectual satisfaction, Bradley holds that 'philosophy . . . in the end rests on what may fairly be termed faith'.[5] That is to say, philosophical inquiry presupposes that intellectual satisfaction can be achieved. As he describes his approach in *Appearance and Reality*: 'I have assumed that the object of metaphysics is to find a general view which will satisfy the intellect, and I have assumed that whatever succeeds in doing this is real and true, and whatever fails is neither.'[6] In other words, the assumption of inquiry is that it is the world which we are trying to understand, and that in some sense this world is intelligible.[7]

Bradley says two things about the nature of this faith or assumption. First, he remarks that it 'can neither be proved nor questioned'.[8] Secondly,

---

3. F. H. Bradley, *Essays on Truth and Reality* (Oxford: Clarendon Press, 1914), 311.
4. Ibid., 26.
5. Ibid., 15.
6. Bradley, *Appearance and Reality*, 491.
7. Cf. F. H. Bradley, *Ethical Studies*, 2nd edn (Oxford: Clarendon Press, 1927), 73.
8. Bradley, *Appearance and Reality*, 491.

he points out: 'But as to what will satisfy I have of course no knowledge in advance . . . the way and means are to be discovered only by trial and rejection. The method is clearly experimental.'[9] These remarks make quite clear that we are not here being provided with an 'intellectualist' criterion of reality. In all respects open-ended, the principle of satisfaction – the search for intelligible order of some kind[10] – does not embody a metaphysical premise of any kind, but is offered as nothing else than a procedural rule to which any participant in philosophical inquiry subscribes. Everything clearly depends on how Bradley goes on to determine the content of the concepts of 'satisfaction' and 'reality'.

The central text for Bradley's account of the nature and relation of the concepts of 'satisfaction' and 'reality' is chapter 13 of *Appearance and Reality*. Here it emerges that it is the 'non-contradictory' or 'consistent' which satisfies the intellect as true and real. But as Bradley now observes: 'The question is solely as to the meaning to be given to consistency.'[11]

The real problems begin at this point. For Bradley is clearly maintaining both that non-contradiction or consistency cannot be understood in metaphysics as a merely formal criterion – either in the sense that it is absolutely independent of any subject matter or in the sense that it is relatively independent of any subject matter – and that it cannot be understood as a report of linguistic usage, a convention with no reference to the world. As a result, it is usually claimed that Bradley's theory of non-contradiction is rationalist in nature – that, like Bosanquet or Joachim, he maintains the law of non-contradiction, as an absolute necessity of thought, to be also an apprehension of necessity in the being of things.

But what has always been overlooked here is the way in which Bradley derives the nature of 'inconsistency' in chapter 13. For having stated there the unavoidability of taking the principle of consistency (in some indeterminate sense) as the criterion of the real (in some indeterminate sense), he then goes on to show that the consistent or the real could not be plural in nature, that is, that it could not be a collection of independent or externally related reals. And why not? Both because 'a mode of togetherness such as we can verify in feeling' – which Bradley defines as non-relational in character – 'destroys the independence of the reals', and also because 'Relations . . . are unmeaning except within and on the basis of a substantial whole [of feeling].'[12]

---

9. Bradley, *Essays on Truth and Reality*, 311.
10. Cf. Bradley, *Ethical Studies*, 209.
11. Bradley, *Appearance and Reality*, 23; cf. 506; *Essays on Truth and Reality*, 315; F. H. Bradley, *The Principles of Logic* (London: Oxford University Press, 1922), 165, 145–6.
12. Bradley, *Appearance and Reality*, 125; cf. *Essays on Truth and Reality*, 313–14.

For Bradley, therefore, it is feeling or immediate experience that defines the metaphysical account of contradiction. The contradictory is that which fails to include the non-relational unity or substantial whole of feeling. In Bradley, non-contradiction is not a matter of some *a priori* demand of the intellect, but is a demand of the object as experienced in non-relational feeling.[13]

2

The concept of non-relational feeling has more than one important role in Bradley's work. Besides defining the nature of intellectual satisfaction – a topic which will be further considered below – non-relational feeling also provides Bradley with an account of the pre-cognitive content of our system of beliefs in terms of an adverbial theory of sensory acquaintance, as David Crossley shows.[14] Two further roles should also be briefly explained.

In the first place, the concept of non-relational feeling means for Bradley that there is no such thing as direct knowledge of immediate experience. This is what puts him among the idealists: all knowledge is held to be a matter of ideal or relational activity, and consequently any identifiable term or quality is what he calls an 'ideal construction', that is, all identifiability or particularity is a matter of the ideal or relational differentiation of non-relational feeling. It is thus hardly surprising that, like the idealists, Bradley prefers the doctrine of internal to that of external relations. Neither an axiom which he takes for granted, nor the result of some metaphysically presuppositionless analysis of the nature of concepts, the doctrine of internal relations is for him a consequence of the claim that, as ideal products, terms are nothing apart from their relational differentiation.[15]

In the second place, however, unlike other idealists such as Bosanquet, Bradley does not regard non-relational feeling as a privative concept. That is to say, as his use of the term 'substantial whole of feeling' suggests, he does not regard feeling as the merely indeterminate starting point of thought which as such is assimilable in the process of cognition. Rather, Bradley maintains the irreducibility of the distinction between thought and

---

13. Cf. Bradley, *Appearance and Reality*, 504; *Essays on Truth and Reality*, 313–14.
14. David Crossley, 'Justification and the Foundations of Empirical Knowledge', in James Bradley (ed.), *Philosophy After F.H. Bradley* (Bristol: Thoemmes Press, 1996), 307–30. See also David Crossley, 'The Multiple Contents of Immediacy', in Guy Stock (ed.), *Appearance versus Reality: New Essays on Bradley's Metaphysics* (Oxford: Clarendon Press, 1995), 181–92.
15. See Bradley, *Appearance and Reality*, ch. 3; on which, see my article 'Relations, intelligibilité et non-contradiction dans la métaphysique du sentir de F.H. Bradley: une réinterpretation', Part I, *Archives de philosophie* 54.4 (1991), 529–51.

sensation, concept and object. This is not, however, held to be a matter of some distinction between knowing subject and object of knowledge, nor of any surd-like particulars. It is instead a matter of the difference between the non-relational unity of feeling and the relational form of thought.

For unlike other idealists, Bradley maintains that thought is inadequate to the nature of things on account of the fact that the non-relational unity of feeling, as such, cannot be ideally or relationally comprehended or 'reconstituted'.[16] On this analysis, even internal relations are regarded as contradictory in that, as relations, they necessarily fail to provide an intelligible or satisfactory account of the connectedness of things as experienced in the non-relational unity of feeling.[17] Thus, in contrast to the rationalist idealisms of Bosanquet or Joachim or Blanshard, the realm of ideality or relations is graphically described by Bradley as a tragic realm of 'endless', 'hopeless' 'process'.[18] This is his realm of 'appearance', or contradiction, in which relational thought fruitlessly searches to render intelligible or to reunite ideally the connectedness of things as experienced in the non-relational unity of feeling. He therefore argues that the feeling-based principle of non-contradiction or intellectual satisfaction can be met only if we 'postulate a higher form of unity'[19] which includes both the unity of feeling and the differentiations of relationality. Such a non-contradictory, supra-rational unity is, of course, Bradley's Absolute: the real is understood as eternally and completely present, and defined as the perfect infinite, the all-inclusive, self-subsistent unity of all things. The search for an intelligible account of the non-relational unity of feeling ironically takes reflection beyond both thought and feeling.

3

This brief summary of some of the roles of non-relational feeling in Bradley's work indicates that it is the main premise and driving principle of his thought. Its larger significance remains to be considered.

It is already evident that Bradley's non-relational feeling is an account of the nature of sensory acquaintance. Feeling is non-cognitive, a matter of the sensory apprehension of a plurality of features or 'felt mass'[20] without distinction of subject and object. Sensory apprehension is thus a non-relational state in the sense that there is no distinction between feeler and felt, between

---

16. Bradley, *Essays on Truth and Reality*, 231.
17. Cf. ibid., 190.
18. Bradley, *Appearance and Reality*, 28, 157.
19. Bradley, *Essays on Truth and Reality*, 190.
20. Bradley, *Appearance and Reality*, 155.

what he calls the 'finite centre' of experience and the experience; there is only the experience of their unity.

But that is not all Bradley means by non-relational feeling. For the non-relational feeling-whole is held to be the permanent ground or 'present foundation'[21] of all ideal construction or differentiation. It is this peculiar metaphysical status accorded to non-relational feeling which makes it much more than an account of sensory experience. There are at least four points to be considered here.

1. In the first place, defined as the ground of all differentiation, the concept of non-relational feeling means that Bradley's metaphysics has the character of a theory of affirmative or 'positive' 'being'.[22] That is to say, Bradley denies both that negation is based on opposition or privation – the abstract negation of the empiricist tradition – and that negation is equivalent to affirmation – which in his view is Hegel's position. In contrast, under the slogan 'no ideas float', Bradley maintains that all negation has its basis in the 'positive' diversities of feeling.[23] Where all ideal content belongs to the real, for all ideal content is a differentiation of the real as it is experienced in feeling, it makes as little sense to call Bradley a metaphysical idealist as it does to call him a metaphysical realist[24] – as will emerge even more clearly in the next point.

2. In the second place, as the 'foundation' or 'vital condition' of the objective world,[25] which is neither subjective nor objective but the condition that makes such distinctions possible, non-relational feeling has the status of a logical ground of possibility in the strong transcendental sense of that term. That is to say, first, there is nothing in the objective world which the concept of non-relational feeling as logical ground denotes, nor to which it refers, nor which corresponds to it, for it is an account of the conditions of denotation, reference and correspondence.[26] Secondly, there is therefore nothing 'out there' in the world that makes statements about permanent feeling determinately true or false, either independently of, or in terms of, our capacity for knowledge. Thirdly, there is nothing in the objective

---

21. Bradley, *Essays on Truth and Reality*, 159–60.
22. Bradley, *Appearance and Reality*, 215.
23. Bradley, *Principles of Logic*, 122, 150, 410, 662ff.
24. Cf. Bradley, *Appearance and Reality*, 485.
25. Bradley, *Essays on Truth and Reality*, 159–60, 161, 176.
26. There is no space here to deal with the tensions and ambivalences introduced into Bradley's thought by his treatment of non-relational feeling as at once a strong non-relational condition and an account of actual experience. On this, see my 'The Transcendental Turn in Bradley's Theory of Feeling: Being, Presence, Immanence', in W. J. Mander (ed.), *Perspectives on the Logic and Metaphysics of F.H. Bradley* (Bristol: Thoemmes Press, 1996), 39–60. As will emerge, there is no ambiguity of this kind in Whitehead.

world that stands to permanent feeling in any relation of resemblance or actualisation; that is, permanent feeling does not stand to anything in any of the causal or productive relations in terms of which the connection of the possible to the actual has usually been understood.

In its role as transcendental principle Bradley endows permanent feeling with structural complexity. To be sure, in order to express this structural complexity, relational concepts have to be employed. Hence, as Bradley emphasises, any description of permanent feeling is analogical; that is, that which is non-relational in nature can only be analysed on analogy with the relational order.[27] But this is of course strictly a matter of analogy of method, not of any analogy of (eminent) being.[28]

The concept of 'finite centres of experience' constitutes Bradley's analysis of the structure of which permanent feeling is the non-relational unity. That is to say, Bradley analogically analyses the structure of permanent feeling in terms of the difference between feeler and felt, between finite centre of experience and what is experienced. This difference of finite centre and experience is, of course, a difference of a special kind: it is a non-relational difference, in which the finite centre 'is the immediate experience of itself and the Universe in one';[29] or, as Bradley also puts it, it is the non-temporal 'presence' of all that is.[30]

Perhaps the first point to note here is that Bradley is quite explicit about the transcendental status of finite centres. He describes them as 'that which lies behind objects' – 'the basis on and from which the world of objects is made'[31] – which have the status of 'necessary ideas'.[32] That is to say, finite centres are 'ideal constructions'[33] of a particular kind: they are not themselves given or presented but are the way in which the conditions of experience have to be conceived. Hence Bradley calls them 'special appearances'[34] in order to indicate their purely conceptual status as transcendental conditions in the strong sense.[35]

---

27. Bradley, *Essays on Truth and Reality*, 177, 196, 411.
28. I take the use of the analogy of method, as opposed to the analogy of being, to be characteristic of transcendental analysis from Kant onwards. See Gerd Buchdahl, *Metaphysics and the Philosophy of Science*, 2nd edn (New York: University Presses of America, 1988), and *Kant and the Dynamics of Reason* (Oxford: Blackwell, 1992).
29. Bradley, *Essays on Truth and Reality*, 410.
30. Ibid., 410 and n. 2.
31. Ibid., 411.
32. Ibid., 412.
33. Ibid., 412.
34. Ibid., 412.
35. On the difficult question of what kind of distinction the concept of finite centres might be, and the relation of ideal distinction in general to Bradley's monistic concept of the Real, see my article cited in note 15 above.

The second point that needs to be made is that a finite centre of experience is not to be understood as a cognitive self or subject, nor as merely a condition of the cognitive self, but as a condition of any kind of difference whatsoever. That is to say, although in *Appearance and Reality* Bradley often talks of finite centres and selves in one breath, both in that work and even more clearly in *Essays on Truth and Reality* he defines finite centres as conditions of differentiation *simpliciter*, quite independently of the activity of ideal or cognitive differentiation.[36] It is of course tempting to describe Bradley's use of feeling here to move beyond the idealist view of differentiation as ideal or cognitive differentiation in terms of panpsychism. But he himself refuses to draw any such conclusion, for the obvious reason that the concept of finite centres of experience is an analogical and transcendental concept which, as prior to the distinction of subject and object, renders that distinction relative – hence the point from which we elaborate their relativity is a matter of indifference.[37]

3. Besides being a theory of affirmative being with transcendental status, Bradley's non-relational feeling has a special and problematic connection to his concept of the complete real – a connection which allows him to employ feeling as the premise of his absolutism. As initially introduced in *Ethical Studies*, Bradley's real is 'the unity of finite and infinite' where 'you can distinguish without dividing'.[38] But while he suggests there that such a familiar concept of the real must be established 'on a fresh basis'[39] – a basis already hinted at by his claim that 'the felt contradiction [of moral experience] implies, and is only possible through, a unity above discord'[40] – *Ethical Studies* is not a metaphysical work[41] and he does not offer his account of the real as 'positive doctrine'.[42] The same is true of *Principles of Logic*. Here, again, the real is the perfect infinite and, in tandem with a variety of accounts of feeling, that concept is appealed to throughout.[43] But no direct defence of it is offered.

Appearance and Reality and *Essays on Truth and Reality* represent Bradley's attempt to develop a full-scale defence of the real understood as the supra-rational perfect infinite. In this respect, as has been indicated, non-relational feeling plays a crucial role: being in the nature of the case incomprehensible to relational thought, the non-relational unity of feeling

---

36. Bradley, *Appearance and Reality*, 464n., 468–9; *Essays on Truth and Reality*, 350n.
37. See T. S. Eliot, *Knowledge and Experience in the Philosophy of F.H. Bradley* (London: Faber and Faber, 1964), 30.
38. Bradley, *Ethical Studies*, 77.
39. Ibid., 324n.
40. Ibid., 324.
41. Ibid., 5, 60–1, 249.
42. Ibid., 249.
43. Cf. Bradley, *Principles of Logic*, 46, 52, 71, 187ff.

means that intellectual satisfaction is to be found only in an absolute unity which includes both feeling and thought. Non-relational unity is thus the ground or foundation of Bradley's 'deduction' of the perfect infinite. As he says in repudiation of what he takes to be Hegel's dialectic:[44]

> I do not believe in any operation which falls out of the blue upon a mere object . . . the series of reflection is generated by and through the unity of immediate experience . . . the principle of the process therefore does not reside in pure thought, but on the contrary must be said to imply a mere conjunction [that is, it entails that mere conjunction is the character of thought].[45]

The question that Bradley obviously has to face here is whether or not the concept of feeling can carry the metaphysical weight he attaches to it. In this connection, it is noteworthy that in *Appearance and Reality* he constantly reiterates that the non-relational unity of feeling is an 'imperfect appearance' or 'incomplete form' of the perfect unity of the real.[46] That is to say, the non-relational unity of feeling is throughout interpreted in terms of the concept of the perfect infinite. It is that concept which confers on feeling its special significance as 'substantial whole' for Bradley.

If, however, the concept of the real as perfect infinite were to be rejected, while much that Bradley says about non-relational feeling may well be cogent, it would not possess the metaphysically foundational importance he attaches to it. And that this is indeed the case is indicated not only by the obvious fact that Bradley's theory of feeling can be maintained as an adverbial analysis of perception quite independently of the concept of the perfect infinite, but also – as will emerge – by the account Whitehead offers of what Bradley calls non-relational unity. So while non-relational feeling certainly defines the nature of non-contradiction or intellectual satisfaction for Bradley, it does so only because it is viewed in the light of the concept of the perfect infinite. In providing Bradley with what he believes to be an anchor-point in actual experience for the concept of the perfect infinite, feeling takes on a momentous metaphysical significance it would not otherwise have. There would be no Bradleyan Absolute without the correlation of non-relational feeling and the concept of the perfect infinite.

4. In this connection, finally, it should be noted that Bradley's correlation of non-relational feeling and the perfect infinite not only leads him to define the latter as supra-rational, but also means that he deprives it of any productive relation to its appearances. To be sure, he retains the concept of limitation to define finite appearances. But limitation is not the limitation qua realisation of a prior order of infinite possibility. Because no (relational)

---

44. Bradley, *Essays on Truth and Reality*, 278; cf. *Principles of Logic*, 515.
45. Cf. F. H. Bradley, *Collected Essays* (Oxford: Clarendon Press, 1935), 655.
46. Bradley, *Appearance and Reality*, 141, 156, 159, 199, 203, 215, 509.

analysis can be given of how appearances appear, limitation for Bradley is in effect equivalent to difference or differentiation, that is, the real is no longer conceived as a causal or productive principle. However, it is but a short step from this to defining limitation wholly in terms of differentiation, that is, as nothing else than a matter of the self-differentiation of the finite without reference to the complete real. As will become evident, Bradley's abandonment of the real as a principle of production opens the door to a concept of the real quite different from his own.

4

Perhaps the shortest route to understanding the relation of Whitehead to Bradley is to see Whitehead's metaphysics as the development and transformation of some of the central features of Bradley's theories of feeling and ideal construction. Whitehead is explicit about his debt to Bradley in both cases[47] – which allows his early concept of 'logical construction' to be seen as an elaboration of Bradleyan themes[48] – and he takes up both Bradley's affirmative account of feeling and his transcendentalism in order to elaborate a positive theory of being or existence. However, the primary motive for his redefinition of these theories is not difficult to see: he abandons the concept of the real as the perfect infinite[49] – which he sees as the consequence of the subject–predicate model of analysis[50] – and, taking the step Bradley's work invites, attempts an analysis of the real in terms of the principle of difference or differentiation, understood as a matter of the pluralistic self-differentiating or self-actualising natures of things without reference to any principle of cause or production.

In this context, Whitehead's concept of self-actualising 'occasions' can be seen as developing Bradley's concept of finite centres by universalising the concept of construction. As Whitehead himself points out, because he understands all things as self-actualising, construction becomes a concept of

---

47. A. N. Whitehead, *A Treatise on Universal Algebra. With Applications* (Cambridge: Cambridge University Press, 1898), ch. 1; A. N. Whitehead, *Adventures of Ideas* (New York: The Free Press, 1967), ch. 15.
48. On Whitehead's origination of the theory of logical construction, see Bertrand Russell, *Portraits from Memory* (London: Allen and Unwin, 1956), 39; *Our Knowledge of the External World* (London: Allen and Unwin, 2nd rev. edn, 1926), 7–8, 70ff. For Whitehead's own early version, see *Treatise on Universal Algebra*, ch. 1; *Adventures of Ideas*, chs 9, 10. For the purposes of this essay, the reader need only keep in mind the usual Russellian version of the theory.
49. Whitehead, *Adventures of Ideas*, 330.
50. Cf. Whitehead, *Process and Reality*, 157, 190; *Adventures of Ideas*, 133, 157.

the real,[51] not primarily a concept of cognition as in Kant or Russell. To this end, he redefines construction in terms of 'process', that is, as the serial or, more precisely, vectorial[52] connections or transitions between occasions of self-actualisation. Indeed, it can be said that a great deal of the complexity of Whitehead's work arises from his attempt to undertake an exhaustive analysis of 'ideal' or 'logical' construction in terms of the 'genetic process' or vectorial connections of occasions. For this enterprise he appropriates Bradley's theory of the unity of feeling, but he redefines it as a matter of horizontal, vectorial connection.

In the present context only one aspect of Whitehead's detailed vectorial account of feeling needs to be considered: his concept of 'physical feelings', in particular 'simple physical feelings', defined as the 'initial data' in the process of becoming or 'concrescence' of an occasion out of antecedent occasions. A simple physical feeling is the relation between the objective datum – that is, the feeling of an antecedent occasion – and its feeling or 'prehension' by a subsequent, concrescing occasion.[53]

Now it will immediately be evident that Whitehead thinks of physical feelings in terms of an 'object–subject' relation.[54] Here the object is the antecedent occasion and the subject is the concrescing occasion – or, as he also puts it, explicitly indicating his departure from Bradley, the object-occasion is the completed, antecedent 'reality', and the concrescent subject-occasion is 'appearance'.[55]

Despite the fundamental, vectorial difference, however, Whitehead agrees with Bradley that experience is not primarily a matter of the cognition of objects, insisting that 'the subject–object relation is the fundamental structural pattern of experience . . . but not in the sense in which subject–object is identified with knower–known'.[56] That is to say, the vectorial relation of object–subject in physical feeling is not for Whitehead a cognitive relation. Moreover, it cannot be said that there is in physical feeling any kind of distinct object–subject relation; for in genetic process the concrescent subject-occasion is not yet itself, but in process of becoming, that is, genetic process is (in a sense to be explained) an account of the conditions that make possible the differentiation of object and subject. Hence Whitehead regards physical feeling as the direct experience of antecedent occasions by subsequent occasions – a position which Dorothy Emmet interprets as an adverbial theory of perception. In this light, it may be said that Whitehead's

---

51. Whitehead, *Process and Reality*, 156.
52. Cf. ibid., 19, 164, 231, 237.
53. Ibid., 236.
54. Whitehead, *Adventures of Ideas*, ch. 11.
55. Ibid., 269.
56. Ibid., 225.

vectorial analysis of feeling perfectly preserves the unities of finite centre and experience, and of content and existence, which for Bradley constitute the non-relationality of feeling understood as an account of sensory awareness.

Yet nothing alters the fact that Whitehead is engaged in what he calls 'a critique of pure feeling'.[57] In redefining the real as the becoming of occasions, the unity of feeler and felt no longer has for Whitehead the significance as criterion of the real it had for Bradley. Further, by analysing feeling as a matter of vectorial connection, Whitehead is able to combine the empiricist notion of the objective datum – of an object independent of the subject – with the idealist notion of constructive activity by placing them on a horizontal plane as different 'phases' or 'stages' in the becoming of occasions.

Something of the critical power of this transformation is indicated by what it allows Whitehead to do with the doctrine of internal relations. For Bradley, as for other idealists, the doctrine of internal relations is inseparable from some form of monism. For Russell, as for other empiricists, the asymmetry of serial relations destroys the doctrine of internal relations and any concomitant monism.[58] For Whitehead, however, the vector character of feeling means that any subsequent occasion is internally related to its antecedent occasions, but its antecedent occasions (as completed or 'perished') are not internally related to it. That is to say, the internal relations of occasions are serial or asymmetrical in character. In contrast to both Bradleyan idealism and Russellian empiricism, Whitehead's vector-analysis of feeling maintains the doctrine of internal relations in the context of a pluralist theory of serial or asymmetrical difference. His concept of the vectorial process of occasions is a concept of the nature of things as a matter of moving, interacting lines of force, which are rationally analysable as such.

5

For all the power of Whitehead's analysis, however, it obviously presents serious problems of interpretation. First, there is the obvious question as to whether or not Whitehead's theory of process, understood as universalising the principle of self-actualisation, constitutes a metaphysical realism which dogmatically assumes direct access to the real, blithely ignoring any critical analysis of the powers and limits of reasoning or language. This is certainly

---

57. Whitehead, *Process and Reality*, 113.
58. See Bertrand Russell, *Principles of Mathematics* (Cambridge: Cambridge University Press, 1903), paras. 212–16; and 'The Monistic Theory of Truth', in *Philosophical Essays*, rev. edn (London: Allen and Unwin, 1966), 131–46.

how many 'Whiteheadians' see him, even maintaining that his employment of the concept of feeling commits him to panpsychism.

Secondly, Whitehead is like Bradley in abjuring any principle of ground or production. But while (as has been noted) he analyses the real, not in terms of presence or the complete real, but in terms of the process of self-actualising occasions, this is a strategy that presents as many difficulties as does Bradley's monism. Just as Bradley faces the question of the relation of a plurality of appearances to the one real – a question that always threatens the status and possibility of his own analysis – Whitehead faces the difficulty as to whether or not the analysis of self-actualisation is possible; that is, how can metaphysical reason analyse that which in the nature of the case is unique and unrepeatable or genuinely new? How is a metaphysics of the new possible?[59] It is surely no accident that other twentieth-century critics of the principle of ground have, in attempting to think the self-realising new, taken their cue from the later Heidegger and announced the end of philosophy.

6

Whitehead clearly shares with Bradley a recognition of the role of analogy in philosophical construction. But he also shares much more. For I would suggest that the purpose of Whitehead's rigorous distinction between the categorial and empirical sides of his analysis is to underline the transcendental status of his categorial scheme. The categorial scheme, that is to say, does not constitute a metaphysical realism but is an analysis of the conditions of possibility of the empirical world understood as conditions of self-actualisation. So regarded, Whitehead's transcendental analysis has three key features.

First, Whitehead's categories are transcendentals in the full, medieval sense that they refer, not only to the nature of cognitive representation, but to the nature of everything that is.[60] No transcendental subreption is involved here on account of the self-referentially inclusive character of the categories as historically situated, analogical concepts. It is thus possible unproblematically to replace the transcendental concept of 'being' with the more inclusive concept of 'creativity' – something which, with his explicit references to the traditional medieval transcendentals, Whitehead quite clearly indicates to be his intention. In my view, Whitehead's response to these difficulties is best understood in terms of his elaboration of the

---

59. Cf. A. N. Whitehead, *Modes of Thought* (New York: The Free Press, 1968), 133.
60. Whitehead, *Process and Reality*, 20.

concept of construction as that is self-referentially applied by philosophical analysis to itself. Here the full significance of his self-description as engaged in 'a critique of pure feeling' becomes evident. For apart from the obvious and direct influence of Kant,[61] Whitehead takes up and develops certain transcendental themes that characterise Bradley's analysis, and, under the inspiration of his own early concept of logical construction, transforms them into a philosophical method which he calls the 'intellectual construction' of a 'speculative scheme' of categories.[62]

In order to understand the nature and status of Whitehead's speculative scheme, it is essential to note that he makes a distinction between 'immediate experience' and 'feeling'. Feeling is a concept or category of the scheme; immediate experience, however, is his term for the 'topic' or subject matter of the scheme – what he calls its 'empirical side'.[63] The significance of this designation cannot be underestimated.

As he states at the beginning of *Process and Reality*, chapter 1, a speculative construction has for Whitehead two 'sides' – the 'rational side' and the 'empirical side'.[64] The rational side is constituted by the 'categoreal scheme'.[65] In contrast, the empirical side is defined as 'everything of which we are conscious as enjoyed, perceived, willed, or thought';[66] or again as 'the ideas and problems which form the complex texture of civilized thought'.[67] That is to say, the subject matter of a categorial scheme is immediate experience,[68] defined as the problematic welter of naturalistically conceived objects and past and present interpretations or beliefs. For clarity, in what follows I will refer to immediate experience so understood as the 'empirical world'.

Now clearly, in the first place, such a concept of the empirical world is not to be conflated with the indubitable sense-data of empiricists such as Russell, nor with the immediate experience of the idealists, nor with the life-world of the phenomenologists (that is, it is not a complex of primitive meanings prior to any reflective or scientific conceptualisation). Rather, the concept of the empirical world refers to everything of which we are conscious – doctrines and ditties as much as cabbages, sealing wax and

---

61. See Russell's remark in his *Autobiography*, one-volume edn (London: Allen and Unwin, 1975), 129. See also my article, 'La cosmologie transcendentale de Whitehead', *Archives de philosophie* 56.1 (1993), 3–228.
62. Cf. Whitehead, *Process and Reality*, ch. 1.
63. Ibid., 4.
64. Ibid., 3.
65. Ibid., xi, 3–4.
66. Ibid., 3.
67. Ibid., xi.
68. Ibid., 4.

physics. It is with 'assemblage' in this inclusive sense that philosophical construction begins.[69]

In the second place, understood as including our past and present beliefs, the concept of the empirical world is an historical concept, designating both the 'oceans of facts' and the 'evaluative interests' which are 'intrinsic within each historical period'.[70] What the philosopher works within, that is, is an historically situated assemblage of interests, orientations and attitudes characteristic of a given epoch. And what the philosopher seeks in respect of that assemblage is some 'thread of coordination'[71] in order to 'coordinate the current expressions of human experience, in common speech, in social institutions, in actions, in the principles of the various special sciences, elucidating harmony and exposing discrepancies'.[72]

The coordinating generality of philosophy should not, however, be confused with any kind of ahistorical neutrality or permanence. For, in the third place, if the empirical world is an historically situated assemblage, so also is the categorial scheme that analyses it. That is to say, Whitehead sees the construction of a philosophical scheme of categories as an enterprise of 'imaginative generalisation', involving 'the utilisation of specific notions, applying to a restricted group of facts, for the divination of the generic notions which apply to all facts'.[73] His point here is that the empirical world is historically related to the categorial scheme as a source of analogues for the definition of the nature of the real. In other words, when the main features of the empirical world are analysed or coordinated philosophically, this is done by means of the analogical employment of some or other features of that world – features to which the strains and tensions, the discoveries and difficulties, of a specific historical period give an especial relevance or appropriateness. Hence our use of terms such as 'mind', 'matter', 'will', 'feeling', 'events', 'occasions', and so on. These terms do not refer to particular features of the world; rather, culturally saturated and historically significant features of the world, representing routes of convergence in mathematics, art, politics, physics and technology, are generalised as analogues for the coordinating characterisation of its main features. The construction of a categorial scheme, the creation of concepts,[74] is primarily a matter of the construction of coordinating analogies out of the singularities of historical experience.

---

69. Whitehead, *Modes of Thought*, 2–3.
70. Ibid., 25.
71. Ibid., 25.
72. Whitehead, *Adventures of Ideas*, 286.
73. Whitehead, *Process and Reality*, 5; cf. 13.
74. A. N. Whitehead, *The Function of Reason* (Princeton: Princeton University Press, 1929), 15, 27.

Secondly, however, the choice of creativity over being as the ultimate category indicates that the categories of the scheme are transcendentals in the Kant-derived sense that they are transcendental conditions. That is to say, transcendental analysis is here explicitly linked to the concept of construction, the categories of the scheme being given the status of principles of constructive activity.[75] Transcendental analysis is not now a matter of the basic properties of all things (*consequens omne ens*), but of the conditions of things and their properties.[76]

Thirdly, however, the categories of the scheme are conditions of the self-constructing natures of things. In contrast to medieval transcendentals, this means that the schematic categories are not structures of being (*ens*) but structures of the self-actualisation of being (*esse*). In contrast to Kant, it means that the schematic categories are conditions, not of cognition, but of the natures of all things, understood as self-actualising. As such, the schematic categories are not metaphysically causal or productive principles; that is, they do not refer their empirical subject matters away from themselves to something else as their ground, cognitive or otherwise. It can thus be said that whereas medieval transcendentalism thinks being in terms of its representable conditions, and Kantian transcendentalism thinks being in terms of the conditions of its representation, Whitehead's transcendentalism thinks being in terms of its immanent, vectorial conditions of self-actualisation. In this context, it is hardly surprising that Whitehead disliked being called a panpsychist.[77]

7

Even if a transcendental interpretation of Whitehead has some cogency, however,[78] the question as to how a transcendental analysis of self-actualisation is possible remains to be answered. How can the transcendental structures of the categorial scheme be defined in such a way as to be 'structures' of the new?

Here, Whitehead exploits the character of his categories as analogical terms to the full. He defines what he calls the relation of 'application' that holds between the categories of the scheme and the empirical world as an

---

75. Whitehead, *Process and Reality*, 156.
76. Cf. Kant, *Critique of Pure Reason*, B114.
77. See Victor Lowe, 'The Concept of Experience in Whitehead's Metaphysics', in G. Kline (ed.), *A. N. Whitehead: Essays on His Philosophy* (Englewood Cliffs, NJ: Prentice-Hall, 1963), 124–33, esp. 126.
78. For an extended defence of such an interpretation of Whitehead, see my article 'Whitehead's Transcendental Analysis', *Process Studies* 23 (1994), 140–72.

analogical relation. Application is not an analogical relation of attribution, however, but of proportionality; that is, it is a matter of the correspondence of relations (as *a* is to *b*, so *c* is to *d*), not of terms, as Whitehead indicates throughout.[79] So understood, this 'substitutive' relation of scheme and world, as he also calls it,[80] is a strictly equivalent or (so to speak) reflexive relation, such that the categories of the scheme are exhaustively translatable into their subject matter without any kind of etiological remainder. In Whitehead's hands, that is to say, the analogy of proportionality is nothing else than a particular principle of translation which allows the empirical subject matter of the analysis to be translated into a set of categorial statements that say equivalent things, but not the same things, about their subject matter as can be empirically stated. In contrast to the subject–predicate logic in which he sees Bradley as embroiled, Whitehead's model for the status of his categories is that of the propositional function.[81] Being or existence can now be understood as having a positive nature of its own which is intelligible in terms of the vectorial structure of relations, and is free of the noumenal content of Bradley's reality.

It should now be evident that on account of his elaboration and transformation of certain themes in Bradley, Whitehead can be accused neither of dogmatism, nor of ignoring the problems presented by the project of a metaphysics of the new. It is the status of the speculative scheme as a set of proportionally translatable categorial functions and their variables which makes possible a structural analysis of the unique and unrepeatable, ensuring that the transcendental conditions of self-actualisation do not refer things away from themselves to anything else as their grounding principle. And so understood, Whitehead's categorial analysis does not represent a naive pre-Kantian metaphysical realism. The strong anti-idealist language of the philosophy of process is not the discourse of traditional metaphysical realism, but of a transcendental theory of self-actualisation where, necessarily, conceptual analysis and empirical description disappear into each other in the reflexive relation of proportional translatability. Whitehead's analysis has always to be read with bifocals, as a simultaneous elaboration of transcendental meaning and empirical application.[82]

Seen in this light, it can be said that the Bradley–Whitehead relation is one main strand in the movement from nineteenth- to twentieth-century philosophy. It involves a complete transformation of metaphysics – but

---

79. Cf. Whitehead, *Process and Reality*, 116, 117, 177, 212, 246; *Modes of Thought*, 231; *Adventures of Ideas*, 242.
80. Cf. Whitehead, *Treatise on Universal Algebra*, Introduction; *Process and Reality*, 116.
81. Cf. A. N. Whitehead, *Essays in Science and Philosophy* (New York: Philosophical Library, 1947), 127ff.
82. Cf. Whitehead, *Process and Reality*, xiii; cf. xi, xiv; *Treatise on Universal Algebra*, 12.

one carried out from within metaphysics and on behalf of metaphysics. Its significance resides in the fact that it represents the history of the Anglo-American transition from a traditional metaphysics of presence to a metaphysics of the new, the different – a metaphysics of process. To forget Bradley's role in this transition is seriously to misunderstand what comes after him.

Chapter 4

The Speculative Generalisation of the Function: A Key to Whitehead[1]

Speculative as opposed to analytical philosophy is centrally concerned with the concept of activity, understood as the activity of actualisation that makes things what they are. Moreover, speculative philosophy has characteristically maintained that the activity of actualisation is self-explanatory in the sense that it is defined in terms of a distinct kind of entity (substance, God, the Absolute) which has necessary existence or whose existence is not derived from anything except itself. It will be argued here that the hitherto unrecognised significance of A. N. Whitehead resides in the fact that he fuses together a speculative philosophy of activity and logical analysis by drastically reinterpreting the nature of the mathematical function and redefining the self-explanatory in terms of the applicability or descriptive adequacy of his functional analysis to the nature of things.

The Generalisation of the Function

It is no accident that Whitehead describes philosophy as 'imaginative generalization'[2] and sees his thought as a 'generalized mathematics'.[3] He states that 'the algebraic method' – the 'examination of pattern with the

---

1. For discussions on various topics in this essay, I am deeply indebted to Andre Cloots, Guy Debrock, J.-C. Dumoncel, the late Dorothy Emmet, Roland Farber, Lewis Ford, Stephen Gardner, Peter Harris, Charles Lewis, Ilie Parvu, Julian Roberts, Philip Rose, David Scott, Johan Siebers, Peter Trnka, Jan van der Veken, Luca Vanzago and Michel Weber.
2. A. N. Whitehead, *Process and Reality: An Essay in Cosmology* (corrected edn, New York: The Free Press, 1978), 5.
3. A. N. Whitehead, *Essays in Science and Philosophy* (New York: Philosophical Library, 1947), 109.

use of real [free or unquantified] variables'[4] – is the rubric under which he elaborates his speculative philosophy, and he insists that 'Logic prescribes the shapes of metaphysical thought.'[5] What he means by this is evident throughout *Process and Reality* (1929), which is the revision and culmination of his earlier mathematical and philosophical work, in particular his collaboration with Russell in *Principia Mathematica* (1910–12). For in *Process and Reality* and subsequent writings, Whitehead builds on the brilliant success of the Frege–Russell generalisation of the mathematical function and develops his philosophy on that basis. Moreover, like other Cambridge figures such as Ramsey in his last writings and Wittgenstein after 1929, the position Whitehead develops from around the middle of the 1920s is markedly constructivist in character.[6] The difference resides in the way Whitehead generalises functional structure, which he does in two distinguishable senses.

First, Whitehead generalises the meaning of the function. That is, he seeks the highest or most general description of the nature of the function in order to provide a meta-functional analysis of the nature and conditions of any function at all. As strictly descriptive,[7] the analysis is not guilty of dogmatically assuming, or making an *a priori* appeal to, the principles of necessary or sufficient reason. Secondly, on the basis of his general description of the function, Whitehead is able to generalise the range of the function over any entity, so that his analysis of the function is intended to provide an account of the nature of all that is.

Whitehead's generalisation of the function makes the claim that the generalised function has 'ultimate' status. This means in part that, with Frege, Russell and the early Wittgenstein, he regards the generalised function as irreducible (as not further definable or derivable from any higher principle) and as transcendental (as universal in range or application). However, Whitehead's transcendental theory of the function is a theory, not of cognition, but of the constitution of all order. Moreover, the claim to the irreducibility of the generalised function rests not on an appeal to any kind

---

4. Ibid., 130–1.
5. Whitehead's Foreword to W. V. O. Quine, *A System of Logistic* (Cambridge, MA: Harvard University Press, 1934), ix–x. See also A. N. Whitehead, *Modes of Thought* (New York: The Free Press, 1968), 174. To my knowledge, the first writer to recognise the importance of algebraic method in Whitehead's metaphysics is Wolfe Mays, *The Philosophy of Whitehead* (London: Allen and Unwin, 1959), esp. ch. 5. See also his *Whitehead's Philosophy of Science and Metaphysics* (The Hague: Nijhoff, 1977).
6. See F. P. Ramsey, *Notes on Philosophy, Probability, and Mathematics*, ed. M.-C. Galvotti (Naples: Bibliopolis, 1990). On Wittgenstein's constructivism, see Mathieu Marion, *Wittgenstein, Finitism, and the Foundations of Mathematics* (Oxford: Oxford University Press, 1998).
7. A. N. Whitehead, *Science and the Modern World* (New York: The Free Press, 1967), 92.

of *a priori* rational intuition, nor is it a matter of its logical 'primitivity', for in Whitehead the ultimacy of the generalised function is not such that it could be held to be inexplicably given. Rather, his generalised description is intended to establish the function as irreducible by showing it to be a particular kind of self-explanatory ultimate, which he terms 'process' or 'creative process'. The way he sets about establishing this extraordinary claim is best explained in a series of three steps. The first step considers the concept of creativity in its own right as 'the category of the ultimate'.

The First Step: The Function as Mapping Activity

In *Process and Reality*, Whitehead develops his position by the elaboration of a 'speculative scheme'[8] or 'matrix'[9] of categories, which, after the style of *Principia Mathematica*, he presents and defines at the start of the work. There, he defines his 'category of the ultimate'[10] as a matter of 'creativity, many, one'. Creativity is said to be 'the ultimate principle', whereby 'the many become one and are increased by one'.

In defining the ultimate by reference to the relation of many and one, plurality and unity, Whitehead is taking up a theme which has been basic to speculative philosophy since the Greeks. In his view, however, this theme can be more adequately treated than hitherto on account of the modern mathematical discovery of the function.[11] That is, when Whitehead defines the ultimate by reference to the relation of many and one, he is defining it in terms of the set-theoretical definition of the function as the class of many-to-one relations.

A mathematical function, matrix or schema is a rule of 'mapping' in which the elements from one set or 'domain' are matched to elements of another set or 'co-domain'. Take the function 'is the square of' symbolised as $(x)^2$, where x is the variable of the argument of the function. The square function is a rule under which the numbers 2 or –2, the values of the variable in the domain, can be mapped on to or matched with the value 4 of the variables in the co-domain. Hence the definition of the function as the class of many-to-one relations or mappings.[12] However, a function or mapping rule can also be defined as an infinite set of ordered pairs $<x, y>$, with x belonging to the domain and y to the co-domain, where a

---

8. Whitehead, *Process and Reality*, 3.
9. Ibid., 7–8.
10. Ibid., 21–2.
11. Whitehead, *Essays*, 97–113, 127–31.
12. On this definition of the function, both one-to-many relations and one-to-one relations are analysed as special cases of many-to-one relations.

correspondence is mapped between the member of the domain and the member of the co-domain (so for $(x)^2$ we could have the ordered-pair values <2, 4>, <3, 9>, and so on). By the time Whitehead was writing *Process and Reality*, this had become, and still is, the generally preferred definition of the function.[13] Yet although mathematically respectable, it is not a definition that he could accept as philosophically fundamental.

First, the definition of the function as the class of many-to-one relations aligns the analysis of the function with the philosophical question as to the nature of plurality and unity, thereby lifting the concept of the function to the highest level of metaphysical generality. When Whitehead defines the ultimate by reference to many-to-one relations, he is at once laying out the fundamental issue that a philosophical account of the nature of the function must address, and defining the concept of the ultimate as the concept of the function in general.

The significance of this basic strategy cannot be underestimated. For, secondly, in distinguishing 'creativity' from 'many, one', Whitehead's point is that the function in general is the mapping of the relation between a domain and a co-domain. The function in general is the concept of mapping in general, and mapping in general establishes or maps to structure or order.

Whitehead is here rejecting the view that the concept of set is the basic concept, and that the function is to be defined in terms of sets of ordered pairs of a certain sort. His claim is that the generalised concept of mapping as the mapping of order is distinguishable from that of any specific order, for it is the process whereby order is generated. Mapping is not any set of ordered pairs, but the concept of the ordination of order, of the ordering of pairs into sets. It is not any specific relation or rule, but the concept of the configuration of any specific relation or rule. It is not any specific difference or form, but the concept of the differentiation of difference, the formation of forms. In consequence, as the very term suggests, the concept of mapping in general is the concept of an activity. Because mapping is distinguishable from the domain out of which it proceeds, from the co-domain to which it proceeds, and from any relation or rule which it establishes as such, the concept of mapping is the concept of the activity of actualisation as the actualisation of relations or rules. The concept of mapping is the concept of mapping activity, and it is not reducible to, explicable by, or exhaustively analysable in terms of any of its components. It is the ultimate, underivable condition of transformation or composition, the universal principle of construction or actualisation, understood as the activity of establishing a relation between the structure of a result and its bases.

---

13. See, for example, W. V. O. Quine, *Word and Object* (Boston: MIT Press, 1960), Section 53, 'The ordered pair as philosophical paradigm.'

What Whitehead has done here is to begin the generalisation of the meaning of the function exactly where Frege does: with the concept of mapping.[14] But he does not follow the extrinsic neo-Kantian limitation Frege lays upon his generalisation, which defines mapping as the 'thought' or concept in general and thus restricts it to a theory of cognition. Instead, Whitehead develops the dynamical aspect of the concept of the function, which in Frege makes it the principle of cognition and in Russell makes it the principle of logical construction out of sense-data, and he unrestrictedly generalises it over any relation or order. The claim is that, just as there is a distinction between a mapping rule and its particular applications, so also there is a distinction between the activity of mapping and a particular mapping rule, and it is this all-important distinction that is lacking in the tradition of logical analysis. In other words, the Frege–Russell generalisation of mapping is an insufficient or improper generalisation of the meaning of the function in that it treats functional mapping as nothing other than a matter of particular mapping rules. Mapping is indeed absolutely inseparable from particular rules, as will become apparent. But the point is that the proper generalisation of the meaning of the function as the activity of mapping in general discloses at the very heart of functional analysis the ineradicability and irreducibility of the concept of the activity of actualisation, now defined as the mapping activity of differentiation. The concept of the ultimate or the function in general is equivalent to the mapping of a domain, and Whitehead's speculative generalisation is intended to ensure that no term in this commonplace formulation of the nature of the function is tacitly suppressed or ignored.

Activity as Mapping Activity

Defined as mapping, the concept of activity in Whitehead 'means the origination of patterns of assemblage'.[15] The way he understands the nature of ultimate creativity so defined can be stated as follows.

First, from the nature of mapping as an activity that is the universal principle of construction and is ultimate in that it is not derivable from any higher concepts, it follows that it is a particular kind of ultimate principle: as the universal principle of the structuration of structure, 'all characters

---

14. See Gustav Bergmann, 'Frege's Hidden Nominalism', in E. D. Klemke (ed.), *Essays on Frege* (Urbana, IL: University of Illinois Press, 1968), 42–67, esp. 49–52.
15. Whitehead, *Essays*, 106. 'Assemblage' is a coinage of Whitehead and Russell to describe the mapping of sets. See, for example, Bertrand Russell, *Our Knowledge of the External World* (London: Allen and Unwin, 1914), Lecture IV.

are more special than itself'.[16] This means that, as the highest description possible of the nature of the function, the concept of universal mapping activity is not a generic property or universal but a supra-generic property or universal. In other words, it is 'characterless' in the positive sense that it is a non-determining property or predicate, and the claim is that it is universally applicable to any specific determination.[17] Universal mapping activity is thus properly to be described as a transcendental property in the Kantian sense, for it is that activity of actualisation that is a ground or condition of any determination. More precisely, it is a condition of any other transcendental predicates there may be, as well as of all real or generically determining properties or predicates. In short: universal mapping activity is 'the universal of universals'.[18]

We must be careful about the concept of a 'universal', however. For, secondly, the universal mapping activity of actualisation is a non-determining transcendental condition in a further, radical sense: as the principle of ordination or differentiation, it is prior to logic and is a condition of logical order. More precisely: since differentiation is the basic condition of inconsistency, exclusion or negation, in the concept of universal mapping activity 'the whole movement of logic is provided for',[19] since difference, inconsistency or negation is the fundamental definition of determination of any kind. In consequence, while mapping activity is universal, it is not a universal form but a universal activity. That is, the concept of universal mapping activity is not to be understood as a unity of essence and existence, nor of logic and ontology, for the activity of differentiation is the ground or condition of the principle of non-contradiction. It does not follow, however, that the claim to the primordiality of activity collapses into non-rationality or ineffability. Yet before considering the question of the rationality of the concept of universal mapping activity, another, equally crucial feature of that concept must be introduced: infinity.

By definition, thirdly, the concept of universal mapping activity cannot be exhaustively analysed in terms of any instance of mapping, for it is a condition of there being any instance of mapping at all. Now, the generalised

---

16. Whitehead, *Process and Reality*, 31.
17. Because it is characterless, Whitehead likens mapping activity both to Aristotelian matter (except that it is not passive), and to the neutral stuff or neutral monism of the later William James and Russell, in that it is not a subject–object relation considered in its own right, but is the condition of subject–object relations (*Process and Reality*, 31). Whitehead points out, however, that the many-to-one connectivity of mapping activity means that, unlike neutral stuff, it is not to be conceived as standing in external relations, for it is intrinsically relational. What this means will be spelled out in the course of this essay.
18. Whitehead, *Process and Reality*, 21.
19. Whitehead, *Modes of Thought*, 52.

concept of mapping is the concept of a universal activity, and the concept of a universal activity that is inexhaustible by any of its instances is the concept of an infinite activity. What kind of infinity is this?

Considered in itself or in complete abstraction from its instances, the concept of infinite mapping activity is the concept of a merely negative infinite in that it is indeterminate, or lacking determination of any kind. As a merely limitlessly determinable *apeiron*, it would be characterless, not in the positive, but in the negative sense that it is utterly empty or vacuous, simply a nonentity. However, that would not be activity at all. For activity is a relative term: 'there is no entity which is merely "any"',[20] no such thing as activity (or power, agency or causality) in general, nothing which in its own right is *a priori*. And what that means is that there is infinite mapping activity only relative to its instances.[21] The concept of universal mapping activity is thus the concept of an infinite activity in the sense that it is the concept of an activity that is transcendent relative to any of its instances. That is, universal mapping activity is the concept, not of a complete, but of a syncategorematic, potential or relative infinite activity. To begin to see what such a notion of the infinite might imply, we need to consider the second step in Whitehead's speculative analysis of the function. It will emerge that Whitehead's analysis of the function does not merely conform to the definition of the function as the mapping of many-to-one relations, but constitutes a constructivist metaphysical proof of that definition carried out in the realm of ontology or the theory of actualisation.

The Second Step: The Activity that Maps to Structure

The ultimate reason[22] of any instance of mapping is universal and infinite mapping activity. However, universal and infinite mapping activity, as the formation of form, maps to structure itself. Mapping to structure constitutes for Whitehead the primary instance of universal and infinite many-to-one mapping, and he defines it in an unusual and controversial way.

Whitehead's interpretation of mapping to structure is conceptualist in respect of universals or what he calls 'eternal objects', and stands in the Cambridge tradition of speculative theology along with the work of his friends and contemporaries.[23] Thus mapping from many eternal objects to one structure is defined as the operation of the 'primordial nature' of God,

---

20. Whitehead, *Essays*, 110.
21. Ibid., 105–6.
22. A. N. Whitehead, *Adventures of Ideas* (New York: The Free Press, 1967), 179.
23. See James Ward, *The Realm of Ends or Pluralism and Theism* (Cambridge: Cambridge University Press, 1911); J. E. McTaggart, *The Nature of Existence*, 2 vols (Cambridge:

on the Aristotelian principle that there must be something in act to realise form or potency.[24] God maps from 'the many eternal objects conceived in their bare, isolated multiplicity'[25] to their unity in an ordered infinity of possible mutual relations which is all-embracing, non-exclusive and non-selective. This unity is not a fixed, necessary ideal order to which all things must approximate,[26] but is a matrix of all possible orders or relations which, in a late essay, Whitehead describes under Brouwer's concept of a 'spread involving an infinitude of dimensions' relative to any finite determination.[27] Whitehead's conceptualism holds at the same time that universals are reals and that they need to be ordered by a constructive act of divine mapping.

Divine mapping or 'valuation'[28] is held to be 'infinite' in that it is not limited by any determinate actuality, and in this respect is also 'free':[29] that is, it is a *causa sui* in respect of how it maps to structure.[30] Here Whitehead stands close to the British voluntarist tradition: 'no reason can be given for just that limitation which it stands in [God's] nature to impose'.[31] However, there is no subscription to the voluntarist notion of an ineffable divine act of will. Divine mapping involves no conscious act on the part of God: it is a necessity of his nature to impose structure upon possibilities as an instance of universal mapping.[32] Whitehead's intention here is to avoid both the anti-rationalist tendencies of voluntarism and the problem of impredication which Russell's Paradox might raise for the concept of a divine mind – or any mind – which surveys all orders of possibility.

In this connection, it would be a mistake to think that Whitehead's theory of 'general potentiality', as he calls it,[33] is a theory of the real infinite.[34] For he describes the divine mapping of the realm of eternal objects as 'deficiently actual',[35] both in the sense that there are other

---

Cambridge University Press, 1921, 1927); F. R. Tennant, *Philosophical Theology*, 2 vols (Cambridge: Cambridge University Press, 1928).
24. Whitehead, *Process and Reality*, 32.
25. Ibid., 349; see *Science and the Modern World*, ch. 10.
26. Whitehead, *Process and Reality*, 84.
27. Whitehead, *Essays*, 88.
28. Whitehead, *Process and Reality*, 31.
29. Ibid., 345.
30. Ibid., 88, 222.
31. Whitehead, *Science and the Modern World*, 178.
32. Whitehead, *Process and Reality*, 345.
33. Ibid., 65.
34. This is clearly not the case with Whitehead's account of extension as the 'extensive continuum', which he defines in constructivist fashion as potential and not real (*Process and Reality*, 35, 61, 283). In his late writing, he also defines the mathematical concept of infinite series in constructivist terms (*Modes of Thought*, 54, 82, 91–2, 97).
35. Whitehead, *Process and Reality*, 345.

essential features of the divine nature (as will emerge), and in the sense that the realm of eternal objects is not self-existent or independent of its finite realisations. On the contrary: not only, in contrast to Platonism, is there is no such thing as general potentiality in its own right, but also, in contrast to Aristotle, eternal objects are not active but wholly passive. This has the effect of completely reversing the notion of participation: the participation of eternal objects in the actual depends wholly on their finite determinations. Like universal mapping activity, general potentiality is thus to be conceived, not as a categorematic, but as a syncategorematic or potential infinity which 'presupposes',[36] or is essentially relative to, its finite determinations. It is here that general potentiality takes on the character of 'real potentiality'[37] without which it would be 'mere vacancy'.[38]

The Third Step: Finite Occasions of Mapping Activity

Infinite mapping is essentially relative to its instances, and its primary instance is divine mapping to general potentiality. General potentiality is in its turn essentially relative to its finite instances, which Whitehead calls 'actual occasions' of mapping (where 'actual' is the adjectival form of 'act'). On account of the essentially incomplete, interdependent and correlative nature of these three basic elements in his ontological generalisation of the function, Whitehead can say that 'Finitude is the condition of activity.'[39]

Whitehead's account of occasions of mapping has close structural similarities to what the Wittgenstein of the *Tractatus* calls an 'operation', which is the condition of particular functions. Although the distinction between the set-theoretic concept of the function and the concept of an operation was still being developed in mathematics at the time they wrote, both Whitehead's occasions and Wittgenstein's operation are concepts of mapping as a 'process' (the term is also Wittgenstein's) which takes its own results as its domain or input.[40] That is, although its content is otherwise undefined, the basis of an occasion or operation is the result of an antecedent occasion or operation. A Whiteheadian occasion of mapping, like a Wittgensteinian

---

36. Ibid., 349, 225, 257.
37. Ibid., 65.
38. Whitehead, *Essays*, 106.
39. Ibid., 105–6.
40. On Wittgenstein's concept of operation, see Marion, *Wittgenstein, Finitism, and the Foundations of Mathematics*; and G. Sundholm, 'The General Form of the Operation in Wittgenstein's *Tractatus*', *Grazer Philosophische Studien* 42 (1992), 57–76.

operation, can thus be described as iterative in that it takes the results of an antecedent occasion of mapping as its basis.

As iterative, occasions of mapping are for Whitehead intrinsically serial or ordered in nature. In principle, this means no more than that any occasion of mapping stands in a single iterative series of occasions, and inherits the entire contents of that series as iterated in each successive occasion. Yet there are good reasons, based on scientific theory[41] and on empirical observation,[42] for maintaining that as a contingent matter of fact there are multiple, contemporary or parallel series of occasions. On the multiple series hypothesis, any given occasion includes in its domain the iterative series of preceding occasions that constitute its environment as much as it includes the iterative series of predecessor occasions in the particular series of mappings in which it stands. Any occasion of mapping is thus intrinsically serial in nature in that it is necessarily a member of a single series of occasions, which in fact is one of a multiplicity of series that constitute its environment. These are the multiple and intrinsically complex routes of inheritance of any occasion of mapping and constitute its genealogical conditions. In consequence, all occasions necessarily have at least the following characters: they are asymmetrical as many-to-one constructions; they are transitive, in that the relations between them are many-to-one relations; they are connected, in that they have predecessors; they are consecutive in that their immediate predecessors are occasions; and they stand in a 'cumulative' relation to their predecessors,[43] for, as iterative, they 'contain' their predecessors in their domains.[44] In the nature of the case, there is no such thing as a single, solitary occasion,[45] and because any occasion stands in a cumulative route of iterations, it necessarily has a complex domain. In other words, it is akin to what mathematicians call a 'functional', at least in the sense that its domain (and thus its co-domain as well) is constituted by sets of functions or mappings. The concept of series of occasions can thus be regarded as an ontological generalisation and constructivist reinterpretation of the Plato–Frege theory of numbers as serial relations, for it installs serial relationality as an intrinsic feature of the nature of things by defining both an occasion and its *relata* as many-to-one

---

41. Whitehead, *Science and the Modern World*, 121.
42. Ibid., 124.
43. Whitehead, *Process and Reality*, 237.
44. Whitehead analyses the notion of containment in terms of a direct realist and singular-causal ontology of 'perception' or information in what he calls his theory of 'feeling'. His account of the domain or genealogical conditions of any occasion means that every occasion iterates and inherits or 'prehends' (which is not primarily a matter of consciousness) the entire previous history of the universe. Thus there is only one universe for Whitehead (*Process and Reality*, 4).
45. Whitehead, *Science and the Modern World*, 174.

configurations or connectives in series.⁴⁶ In the iterative series, that is, occasions switch roles from being a successor mapping, or synthetic subject, to being the predecessor, object or basis, and thus the subject or argument, of a consequent successor mapping. The result is that subject and object, as well as subject and predicate, are not here fixed ontological opposites.⁴⁷ They are not fundamentally different in nature or kind. Rather, they are the basic states or sequential relations of occasions of iterative mapping.

Another aspect of the significance of Whitehead's theory of occasions, as of Wittgenstein's operation, is that it sidesteps Russell's Paradox, the paradox of the class of all those classes that are not members of themselves. For, defined iteratively, no occasion includes itself; it includes in its arguments only the results of antecedent occasions and its own results are included only by its successors. In other words, an occasion is intrinsically a matter of iterative activity, so there is in serial analysis no completely realised real to generate reflexive paradoxes.

There are, however, fundamental differences between Whitehead's and Wittgenstein's theories of functional process. One difference is that, whereas in Wittgenstein the base of an operation is an elementary proposition which is not generated by the application of the operation, in Whitehead's account of finite mapping there are no irreducible logical atoms: there are only complex occasions of mapping. The crucial difference, however, is between Whitehead's theory of functional process as essentially a matter of activity and what Wittgenstein graphically calls an 'automatic' (algorithmic) process, understood as describable independently of any appeal to a principle of activity in the speculative sense.⁴⁸

On Whitehead's account, an occasion of mapping is not exhaustively traceable to infinite mapping activity, for it requires a domain or input. Moreover, infinite mapping activity is a non-determining predicate, which means that it does not determine how an occasion maps from its domain or given content. Equally, how an occasion maps is not exhaustively determined by its domain, for it maps from that domain as its given content. Nor is how an occasion maps exhaustively determined by the structure or rule that it maps, for it is the act of mapping of that structure or rule. It follows that the way any occasion maps is free or spontaneous relative to infinite

---

46. On Plato and Frege, see A. E. Taylor, *Plato* (London: Methuen, 1926), ch. 19. Whitehead regularly cites Taylor's work on Plato, and his interest in the late Plato's theory of mathematics is explicit (*Essays*, 97–113).
47. Whitehead, *Process and Reality*, 157–9; *Adventures of Ideas*, 175–7.
48. For Wittgenstein's view of 'process', see his *Remarks on the Foundations of Mathematics*, ed. G. H. von Wright, R. Rhees and G. E. M. Anscombe (Cambridge, MA: MIT Press, 1983), esp. 68, 69, 95, 246. I leave open the complex question as to the nature of Wittgenstein's treatment of activity, and to what extent he regards activity as lying outside the range of functional analysis.

mapping activity, its domain, and its rule. It is free or spontaneous both in the negative sense that how it maps is not exhaustively traceable to any or all of its conditions, and in the converse, positive sense that it is to this extent irreducibly self-actualising or self-causing. No occasion is sole cause of itself, for it derives from infinite mapping activity and a given domain. As Whitehead puts it, 'there is no such fact as absolute freedom'.[49] But every occasion is a *causa sui* in respect of how it maps from its given domain.[50] So it is not universal and infinite mapping activity which is self-actualising here, but its occasion as relative to a given domain. There are no ways of mapping as such, only instances of ways.

In consequence, any occasion of the infinite mapping activity of differentiation is not merely a transitive configuration but an intransitive difference or singularity. That is, any finite instance of infinite mapping activity is irreducible to any or all of its conditions and is qualitatively different from any other instance because it is, to the extent defined, self-actualising; it is novel because it is a 'never before'; and it is unique in the sense that its activity is unrepeatable – it is a 'never again' as well as a 'never before'. Whitehead's ontological generalisation of the function here provides a way of elaborating a theory of difference, singularity or *haecceitas* from within functional structure itself, independent of the problems of reference presented by standard functional analysis (as in Peirce or Russell).[51]

The Significance of Whitehead's Generalisation

The basic structure of Whitehead's metaphysics is now evident. It includes three types of syncategorematic and correlative infinity: the characterless infinity of universal many-to-one mapping, which is primarily instantiated and characterised by the divine mapping of structure, which in its turn is instantiated and actualised by the iterative mapping of series of occasions. Moreover, each of these three interdependent elements is itself threefold in nature. The ultimate is a matter of 'creativity, many, one', or mapping,

---

49. Whitehead, *Process and Reality*, 133. This is a fundamental difference between the theories of activity of Peirce and Whitehead. Compare C. S. Peirce, *Collected Papers*, vols 1–6, ed. Charles Hartshorne and Paul Weiss (Cambridge, MA: Harvard University Press, 1931–35), VI, paras 214–20.
50. Whitehead, *Process and Reality*, 222.
51. Because Whitehead's theory of occasions of mapping as synthetic subjects provides a universal account of actualisation, his theory of the subject is not to be conflated with the cognitive or conscious subject of idealism or phenomenology, nor is it vulnerable to the critique of the philosophical subject characteristic of systems theory. Consciousness for Whitehead is a high-level instance of universal many-to-one mapping (*Process and Reality*, 157–67, 308).

'novelty' and synthesis or 'togetherness'.[52] God's primordial nature is held to be inseparable from his 'consequent nature', by which he maps from occasions to their timeless preservation and redemption, and the consequent nature is held to be given to the world as part of the domain of each occasion.[53] Finally, each occasion is triadically analysed in terms of a given domain, its private synthetic act as a *causa sui*, and its public or communal role as an object of a successor occasion.[54] It is by way of this unusual analysis of the complex structure of functional activity that Whitehead would explain what for Frege and logical analysis is indemonstrable: the existence of value-ranges or sets.

One obvious feature of Whitehead's speculative generalisation of the function as mapping activity is that it criticises logical analysis in all its forms for completely taking for granted the 'invariableness' or 'self-identity' both of the connectives and of the variables of the function.[55] In other words, he holds functional analysis to be too closely tied to the view that the connectives and variables of a function in its different instantiations are merely numerically different. This means that there has been no proper consideration of what may be involved in the topic-relativity of the concepts of connective and variable, which is arguably implicit in the fact that the function is meaningless apart from its instances. The claim is that the usual accounts of functional analysis are basically Aristotelian in interpreting the function as merely numerically different in its instances. The only difference is that 'substance' has been neutralised into an instance of a variable. Thus Whitehead's functional analysis is not only a generalisation of the mathematical-logical function; it is also a critique of the standard interpretation of the mathematical-logical function in that it rejects the metaphysically loaded use of the term 'constant', understood as that which is fixed, in contrast to the term 'variable', understood as a mere gap waiting to be filled. For Whitehead, the function as employed and usually understood in mathematics and logic is a highly abstract and by no means fundamental product of conscious occasions of many-to-one mapping.[56]

A second central feature of Whitehead's generalisation of the function is that, perhaps for the first time in the history of speculative metaphysics, the concept of the activity of actualisation is not analysed in terms of any kind of emanation, self-differentiation or divine creation *ex nihilo*. Whitehead is

---

52. Whitehead, *Process and Reality*, 21.
53. Ibid., 87–8, 351.
54. Ibid., 87–8. For examples of one-to-many mappings considered as special cases of many-to-one mappings in Whitehead, see *Process and Reality*, 348–9; *Modes of Thought*, 20, 51.
55. Whitehead, *Essays*, 127–8; *Modes of Thought*, 106–7.
56. Whitehead, *Adventures of Ideas*, 254.

critical of such notions as basically non-relational and thus ineffable.[57] In their place, he puts the notion of many-to-one mapping activity, which is not non-rational but non-conceptual.[58] That is, it is a complex, dynamic correlation of whole and part, an irreducible 'togetherness'[59] which is given as such and is neither derivable from concepts nor a product of the synthetic operations of the mind. Yet it is an intelligible given or 'fact',[60] for all its elements are thoroughly relational in that they can be defined not only as 'that from which another comes' (*quo alius*), but also and necessarily as 'that which comes from another' (*qui ab alio*).[61] It would thus seem that the iterative economy of Whitehead's functional analysis is the proper 'concrete universal', for its unity is generated through the correlativity and topic-saturatedness of the parts that make it up, and not in virtue of 'containing' or being 'contained in' an underlying, identical substance, often thought of as having all the reasons for its existence in itself.

In this respect, thirdly, no instance of mapping activity is necessary in Whitehead. Only the absence of any mapping activity at all is inconceivable. His theory of iterative seriality breaks the traditional link between the speculative notion of the self-explanatory on the one side, and, on the other side, the notion of an independent and completely realised reality with its own fully furnished interior of possibilities. Moreover, the self-explanatory in Whitehead does not depend on an *a priori* appeal to the principle that nothing is without a reason. The functional theory of mapping activity indeed contains in itself all the reasons needed to explain why there is existence. Yet each of its reasons are relational elements which are in their own nature incomplete and partial. Only together, and by way of their descriptive adequacy to experience,[62] do they render the fact of existence self-explanatory. In other words, Whitehead's functional scheme constitutes an ontology of necessary reasons strictly in the sense that, granted the descriptive adequacy of the analysis, it shows no more than why, necessarily, something exists – and why all concrete 'somethings' are contingent. The speculative theory of the function agrees with empiricism and logical analysis on the primacy of the actual. But it stands against them in claiming that reasons can be discovered for the primacy of the actual.[63] And it holds that such reasons can never be anything more than necessary reasons, for

---

57. Ibid., 130, 169, 236.
58. Whitehead, *Process and Reality*, 22.
59. Ibid., 21–2, 189.
60. Ibid., 211.
61. I am here referring to the brilliant analysis of the concept of *innascibilis* (ungenerated or unbegotten) developed in respect of the Father or First Person of the Trinity by Aquinas, *Summa Theologiae*, q. 32, a. 3.
62. Whitehead, *Process and Reality*, 4.
63. Whitehead, *Science and the Modern World*, 92.

the necessitarian view that everything has a sufficient reason is denied, and the different kinds of free activity involved in divine and finite mapping are among the reasons posited to explain the fact of actuality. In line with Whitehead's characteristic method of appropriating empiricist and analytic methods for the derivation of speculative results, metaphysical necessity becomes in his hands wholly a matter of the range and applicability of the speculative description of the function.

It follows, fourthly, that, for Whitehead as for Russell, what is philosophically ultimate is what is ontologically ultimate, without any submerged or noumenal depths. However much they may differ on the nature of the function, they do not disagree that there is absolutely nothing beyond or behind functional structure. Consequently, unlike the Tractarian Wittgenstein, Whitehead does not regard the givenness of the world as an ineffable mystery. As he puts it, explicitly challenging the functional analysis of the *Tractatus*, 'the purpose of philosophy is to rationalize mysticism'.[64]

Finally, Whitehead's speculative theory of the function is self-referentially inclusive and can define itself as a finite, revisable or fallible, and non-exclusive construction. It is real so far as it can be consistently and comprehensively constructed or applied[65] and it is ideal and hypothetical so far as, in the nature of the case, there can be no final construction, application or exclusion of alternatives in an infinitely proceeding, aeviternal reality. Thus Whitehead is a constructivist to the extent that he denies the applicability of the principle of bivalence to speculative descriptions,[66] and he replaces the traditional concept of 'proof' with that of the 'working hypothesis' that does not negate alternative analyses.[67] Yet his fallibilist theory of construction does not lead him to deny the principle of *tertium non datur*, the principle that there can be no circumstances in which a speculative claim can be recognised as being absolutely undecidable or absolutely neither provable nor refutable.[68] As itself a historically situated, finite construction, the speculative theory of functional activity has no 'pretensions to the achievement of final truth', which Whitehead regards as 'pathetic'.[69]

---

64. Whitehead, *Modes of Thought*, 174.
65. A. N. Whitehead, *A Treatise on Universal Algebra. With Applications* (Cambridge: Cambridge University Press, 1898), 5–12; *Process and Reality*, 3–4.
66. Whitehead, *Process and Reality*, 8.
67. Ibid., xiii, 7–9; *Adventures of Ideas*, 222–3.
68. Whitehead, *Process and Reality*, 7–9, 274–5. In this context, it is noteworthy that while Whitehead regards *ex absurdo* arguments as justified in mathematics, he castigates their 'misuse' in philosophy. In philosophy 'it is rashly assumed without further question that the peccant premise can at once be located', in disregard of the fact that 'every premise in a philosophical argument is under suspicion' due to the inherent generality and referential indeterminacy of philosophical concepts (*Process and Reality*, 8).
69. Whitehead, *Essays*, 125.

Chapter 5

Triads, Trinities and Rationality

Rationality, Order and Intelligibility

Rationality is inseparable from order and order is inseparable from relation, for order is minimally a matter of two terms and their relation. Whether one thinks of rationality primarily as a feature of the human mind, or as a feature of objects, the rational is the ordered and the ordered is the rational in that whatever is ordered cannot be less than a complex of two terms and their relation. The rational or ordered is thus a matter of three elements, as in the late Plato's triad of the Limit, the Unlimited and their Mixture. For modern examples, think of Dewey's naturalist ontology of events (with their three irreducible features of immediacy, relation and meaning or interconnection) and Kant's idealist theory of cognition as givenness, understanding (the structure of individual objects) and reason (the system of objects); or, again, his threefold analysis of experience as cognition, morality and the unity of the two in teleology and art or the aesthetic judgement.

This initial definition of rationality as a triad of three elements is wholly neutral in respect of how the order of the three elements is itself to be understood. It leaves open whether or not they are to be interpreted as, for example, the essential manifestations or expressions of one basic principle, or as three basic principles that are in some sense distinct yet interdependent. And it does not determine whether the element of relation is to be interpreted as a mediating link between the terms (neo-Platonism); or as their synthesis (Schelling, Hegel); or as one of three active elements that constitute a unity (Aquinas, Peirce); or if it is to be defined in terms of the mathematical function as a binary relation of the variables of two arguments, where the relation is understood to be prior to the terms and exhaustively to define the nature of the terms (Frege, Russell, Quine).[1] Yet here we face the crucial philosophical question in respect of rationality: How is the triadic order of order to be understood? To what extent is the triadic principle of order itself intelligible? Is it susceptible to explanation?

Everything in philosophy depends on how hard we push this question, the question of the rationality of rationality or the order of order itself. If we hold that rationality is essentially a feature of the human mind, we have to take the triadic nature of order as a mere given. It is just the way the mind works, whether as a result of evolution or whatever, for the human mind does not explain rationality but works by it. Further, such a subjectivist position is open to the objection that we find evidence of rationality or order throughout the world, that it seems to be a constitutive, even definitive, feature of the nature of things. Hence the triumphs of natural science and the attractions of materialism or physicalism. But if we take a materialist or physicalist view of order we once again take rationality as a mere given. Insofar as there is physical order it obeys the triadic principle of order and does not explain it. So everything depends on how hard we push the question: To what extent is the triadic order of order itself intelligible or explicable? Or, to put the same point another way, is the ambiguous word 'relation' to be understood actively or passively, as primarily a process or a product? Is it something active or something fixed and given?

The issue here is this: do we take what is ultimate in the order of analysis, what is incapable of further demonstration, what is not further derivable, do we take the ultimate as merely given or as self-explanatory? Is the triadic order of order a mere given or is it self-explanatory? Either that which is ultimate and irreducible is an inexplicable given, or it is self-explanatory. There is no other option, no third here.

Now if there were a self-explanatory account of rationality or order it would be one that is ultimate in the sense that nothing else would be required to satisfy intellectual inquiry in respect of what order is. Nothing further would be required to answer the general question: 'Why is there rationality?', 'Why is there order?', or, to put the same point in the context of existence, 'Why is there anything at all?' These questions I will call the

---

1. The principle of the priority of relations is the reason that the minimal ordinal proposition is for Russell a triad of three terms: 'y is between x and z'; *Principles of Mathematics* (Cambridge: Cambridge University Press, 1903), para. 207, p. 217. For Russell, an order is a series of relations, so to have serial order requires a minimum of three terms, or at least two asymmetrical, transitive, connected and irreflexive relations. Order is in his view a series of relations because order is based, not on quantity or cardinality, but on logic or the logical relations of ordinality. As already indicated, however, the questions of the nature of ordinality (ordination) and of the relative status of terms and relations are matters of debate and constitute the central issues in the theory of rationality or order.

speculative questions of order, for they are the characteristic questions that drive speculative metaphysics and that generate those critical reactions to it that we know as materialist or physicalist, empiricist, naturalist and logical-analytic metaphysics. I will show that it is the speculative question of order that has been the distinctive feature and driving force of Western philosophy. For this reason, some initial remarks about the nature of that question may be helpful.

What is the Self-Explanatory?

The first and perhaps most important characteristic of speculative inquiries into the self-explanatory nature of rationality or order is that they universally seek to explain order in terms of activity. For an order that is self-explanatory is in the nature of the case an active order, an order that can be explained in terms of its own activity of ordination. In other words, a self-explanatory theory of rationality is a theory in which in some sense order is a matter of activity, for it is a theory of the actualisation of order. So in a self-explanatory theory the triadic order of order is understood as active in the sense that it is in some way self-actualising, as it must be if it is to be self-explanatory.[2] Where order is not a mere given but is self-explanatory, the triadic order of order has to be defined in terms of some kind of primordial, self-actualising order whose activity is the explanatory basis of all specific and otherwise inexplicable instances of order, natural and human. Such a primordial order necessarily possesses or contains all the reasons for its existence in its own nature, though as will emerge it is a matter of debate whether or not it does so independently of anything else.[3]

---

2. It is the attempt to construct a theory of activity as self-explanatory that distinguishes what I am calling 'speculative' from non-speculative accounts of activity. Examples of the latter are to be found in the Greek and Roman materialists, Kant's theory of activity as synthesis (ignoring his final and notably conventional theological account of the noumenal realm), Schopenhauer and Bergson's arationalist accounts of activity as will or duration, Dewey's naturalist theory of events, and Wittgenstein's view of the existence of the world as extralogical, as lying outside the range of what he takes to be the functional structure of form, language or action (*Tractatus Logico-Philosophicus*, *Annalen der Naturphilosophie* 14 [1921], 6, 44–5). Rorty has criticised all such accounts by arguing in essence that once the philosophical search for the self-explanatory is abandoned, the search for any kind of specifically philosophical explanation should be abandoned, in ethics as in ontology.
3. Another way to define the self-explanatory would be to say it is that which possesses all the reasons for its actualisation or realisation in its own nature. Such a formulation

Secondly, the speculative search for a self-explanatory account of the activity of the actualisation of order does not carry with it any unacceptable assumptions about the scope of the principle of reason. This is the principle *nihil est sine ratione*, 'nothing is without a reason': that there is always a reason and a reason can always be found. The principle of reason has its corollary in the postulate of the unity of truth: namely, that all features of experience constitute a rational order in the sense that their interconnection can be rendered intelligible or explicable.

Speculative metaphysics is indeed rationalist to the extent that it rejects what Peirce mockingly calls the 'no hypothesis' hypothesis. That is, it rejects the essentially sceptical theory or hypothesis that there are things that no theory or hypothesis can explain. It rejects the hypothesis that there is anything that is ultimately inexplicable, that there is anything about which no explanatory theory or hypothesis can be entertained. Thus the view that the triadic order of rationality is a mere given is repudiated as inconsistent with the entire enterprise of inquiry. Philosophy, if it is anything, is the search for explanations. Nevertheless, the principle of reason or the rejection of the 'no hypothesis' hypothesis is not a dogma of speculative metaphysics. The speculative project is not justified by the principle of reason, but is an inquiry into the status or range of application of that principle. It is an attempt to determine the scope of explanation in respect of rationality itself. Speculative inquiry thus turns the principle of reason into an experimental, hypothetical principle or postulate, for it investigates just how far reason can go in the analysis of the nature of order. It has the status of an ideal experiment, at the outset of which there is no assumption that there is such a thing as an ultimate reason. The purpose of the speculative project is to elaborate ultimate hypotheses, to test them, and so find out just what 'intellectual satisfaction' may be. Moreover, speculative inquiry does not assume that whatever may be self-explanatory or whatever provides a reason must itself have the nature of a reason, for that which provides reasons is not necessarily itself a reason. Whether there is ultimate explicability and what it might be can only be determined in the course of inquiry.

It follows, thirdly, that speculative inquiry into a self-explanatory account of the activity of the actualisation of order is not to be conflated with a common construal of such questions as 'Why is there order?', 'Why is there anything at all?', or 'Why is there something rather than nothing?' That is, speculative inquiry does not depend upon the debatable claim that mere nothingness or vacuity is conceivable, nor upon the even more contentious claim that mere nothingness or vacuity is in some sense prior

---

helps to register the ethical dimension of the notion of the self-explanatory that will briefly be considered in what follows.

to the fact that there is something, so the fact that there is something is held to need a special kind of explanation. Speculative inquiry does not deny the priority of the actual in respect of the possible, and as the starting point of all inquiry. After all, the terms 'actuality' or the 'actual' have their grammatical root in the term 'activity'. And as it has been defined here, speculative inquiry is an attempt to see just how far reflection can go in the analysis of the actual, to see if a description of what actuality is can lead to the discovery of any features that might explain why the actual is, or why the actual persists. Thus speculative inquiry does no more in the first instance than investigate the possibility of a self-explanatory description of the nature of things.

The account so far given of the principles of reason and of the unity of truth as postulatory means, fourthly, that the notion of the self-explanatory is not to be in any way confused with the self-evident in the sense of the absolutely certain or indubitable, whether this is understood as the merely tautological, clear and distinct ideas (Descartes), some kind of intuition (Schelling, Bergson), or a method of transcendental deduction (Kant, Hegel). On the contrary, the notion of the self-explanatory presented here is epistemically anti-foundationalist. It is oriented, not to the traditional understanding of mathematics as based on self-evidently true axioms, but to the postulatory method of modern mathematics. More widely, the self-explanatory is defined in terms of the concept of investigative reason – as found in medieval philosophy, often under the rubric of 'natural theology', and as explicitly elaborated in modern philosophy by the mathematical logicians Charles Sanders Peirce and Alfred North Whitehead under the rubric of 'fallibilism'.[4]

In this context, speculative philosophy, understood as the search for a self-explanatory account of the actualisation of order, is 'speculative' in the following sense. Without claiming any privileged starting point, *a priori* or phenomenological, and based like any inquiry on faith (Latin, *fides*: trust) in the hypothesis of reason, it utilises some striking, specific notions held to have wide application in significant areas of experience as models for self-explanatory activity. By generalising such models, it attempts to construct the most inclusive description possible of the nature of things, and as far as possible to provide a self-explanatory account of the actualisation of order. It is 'speculative', not in the German idealist sense as a matter of the realisation of order in and by the mind, cognitive or absolute, but in three

---

4. See A. N. Whitehead, *Process and Reality: An Essay in Cosmology* (corrected edn, New York: The Free Press, 1978), ch. 1, 'Speculative Philosophy', for what is in my view the clearest and most succinct statement of the experimental and fallibilist understanding of speculative metaphysics derived from the postulatory method of modern mathematics.

specific senses. First, it depends for its cogency on its ostensively demonstrable fit with experience. Secondly, in view of the intrinsic historical relativity of its models, it does not claim to be anything but experimental and revisable or fallible. Thus, thirdly, it is self-referentially consistent in that it makes no claims to its own complete or final truth.

In speculative philosophy so understood, the primacy attached to 'mind' in, say, German idealism would be but one example of the generalisation of a model of activity among many, which would include will, feeling, events, production, art, evolution, information exchange, and so on. Such speculative generalisations proceed according to a specific method: the method of analogy of proportionality. This is not a matter of the similarity, in the sense of the direct comparison, of terms or attributes (the so-called analogy of attribution). It is a matter of the comparison or similarity of terms in relation, of the similarities of role or function that terms such as 'good' play in different contexts (the so-called analogy of relation). In Whitehead's words: 'The procedure of rationalism is the discussion of analogy.'[5] The methodological or procedural criteria used in the determination of specific cases of 'fit' and in the general definition of truth include correspondence, comprehensiveness (both in respect of subject matter and of historical-critical address to alternative accounts), as well as pragmatic success or fruitfulness. These criteria are not understood to be mutually exclusive. The whole range is characteristically employed by a constructivist or developmental theory of the real, in tandem with a repudiation of any disjunctive account of truth and falsity.[6]

The consequence of such an account of speculative philosophy is that self-explanation is not the same as proof – and both are subject to historical change.[7] Not only have a great variety of self-explanatory accounts of the actualisation of order been offered in the speculative tradition, but

---

5. A. N. Whitehead, *Modes of Thought* (New York: The Free Press, 1968), 134.
6. See Whitehead, *Process and Reality*, 7–9, 190–3; A. N. Whitehead, *The Function of Reason* (Princeton: Princeton University Press, 1929), 53. As will emerge, the various tests or criteria of truth listed in the text are accompanied in speculative philosophies by an ontological account of the nature of truth. Speculative philosophy does not primarily define truth as a relation between propositions and the real, which is the usual practice in empiricist and analytical philosophy. For speculative philosophy, truth is fundamentally an intrinsic feature of the real, as will be explained below. To those who do not recognise this, speculative philosophy is a closed book. For an excellent account of ontological theories of truth, see Richard Campbell, *Truth and Historicity* (Oxford: Clarendon Press, 1992).
7. There is a close connection between speculative philosophy as defined here and mathematical constructivism, as the earlier references to Whitehead indicate. On the historicality of proof in mathematical constructivism, see Michael Dummett, *The Elements of Intuitionism* (Oxford: Oxford University Press, 1977), Introductory Remarks, chs 1 and 7.

the question of what constitutes a self-explanatory theory is itself part of what is at issue among them. Indeed, as will emerge, the development of a self-explanatory theory of order can be said to have occupied Western thinkers for some 2,500 years.

At this point, before things get too vague due to lack of examples, I will just mention a fifth basic characteristic of any self-explanatory theory of active order. It is this: if the connections between the three elements of a primordial, actualising order are at all intelligible, then it is likely that these three elements will stand in a serial relation to one another, for serial order is intelligible order and allows of very precise definition. So where the elements of a primordial order are to any degree self-explanatory, they will constitute a series or serial structure of some kind. But to see what this may be, and to recognise what is at stake in this central notion of a primordial, self-actualising triadic order of order, it is necessary to consider some aspects of the history of the analysis of triadic order in Western philosophy. I will begin with the late Plato, for the problems he bequeaths largely determine future developments.

The Late Plato's Triad

The late Plato defines rationality or order as form and form as number (measure or *ratio*). Developing Pythagorean notions, he argues that all order has three constituents: the Limit, One or Monad; the Unlimited or Indefinite Dyad; and their Mixture, which is specific order. The Limit is that which introduces determination into the merely indeterminate or indefinite, which is how Plato understands the Unlimited or the nature of infinity. The Unlimited is called a dyad, duality or doubling and is described as 'the great and small' and 'the less and more' because it can be varied infinitely in the sense of indefinitely in either direction. It is boundless or indefinite because, for example, anything can be hotter or colder than it is. There is no maximum or minimum in either direction, and between any given degrees there can be an endless number of degrees. It seems that Plato understood the Unlimited as the material constituent. Specific order is thus the combination of form and matter.[8]

The thing to notice about Plato's triad is that it is not self-explanatory. The Limit and the Unlimited constitute a duality of form and matter and do not of their own nature explain either themselves – why they are what they are – or their combination. Taken on their own, their combination

---

8. On late Plato, I have here followed A. E. Taylor, *Plato* (London: Methuen, 1926), ch. 19, 'Plato in the Academy – Forms and Numbers'.

would simply constitute an automatic operation that as such does not explain the reasons for itself. Hence Plato posits a fourth element that is the reason for their combination. This is the Demiurge, or the God, who is described not as the good itself but as the perfectly good soul and as mind or intelligence. Plato thereby introduces three crucial considerations into the theory of order.

First, Plato's thinking here indicates the inseparable connection between the self-explanatory and goodness. An activity of actualisation which is merely such is not self-explanatory, for there is nothing about it that explains why it is active. You can posit any kind of activity you like – Schopenhauer's blind will, Bergson's duration, or Derrida and Deleuze's differentiation might be good examples – and you can even describe it as the inexhaustible, unconditioned, originating source of all things. But while it can provide an explanation of all specific determinations, it cannot provide an explanation of its own nature as originating. It does not explain why it operates or why it is an activity of actualisation. It's just a very grandiose automaton, a mere given. By contrast, if you can say that the originating principle is in some sense good you have a reason for its activity: the actualisation of order has its ground in goodness itself. (In Aquinas's neat formulation, *bonum est diffusivum sui*: goodness is essentially active or self-diffusive).[9] Hence Plato's God is perfectly good and it is out of the God's goodness that the Limit and the Unlimited are combined. If you ask what goodness itself is, Plato's answer is that the good itself or perfection is indefinable: it is beyond all being or determination, for it is the ultimate reason for all being or determination, the active basis of the 'justice' or order of all things. Because it is central to self-explanatory theories of activity, the nature of the good itself or perfection will become a fundamental theme in subsequent philosophy.

Secondly, Plato's analysis indicates the inseparable connection between the self-explanatory principle of goodness and mind or intelligence. You may ask why Plato inserts God as an intelligent agent between goodness itself and the triadic order of order. This is a matter of debate, but one reason is clear: for there to be an individual entity that is good out of its own nature, it must direct its own acts and so must apprehend the nature of its acts. An agent of goodness can be good in its own independent nature only if it *recognises* its acts as good. Only an agent that has mind contains in its own nature the explanation for why it is good: it is good because it is itself the reason for its goodness. Once again, automata will not do here, so God's activity of combination is good because God is mind or *nous*. The question of the relation of activity, goodness and mind is here moved to centre-stage, as we will see.

---

9. Aquinas, *De Veritate*, q. 21, a. 1.

In this connection, thirdly, there is obviously another problem that Plato leaves his successors: namely, the relation of God and the good itself, understood as the transcendent source beyond being of the reality and intelligibility of anything other than itself, including the God who is on a lower level of reality as a determinate being or soul. Further, neither Plato's good nor his God are creative in the sense that either one or both is the exclusive origin of all that is. Form and matter are given to God, and while the good holds all things together, the good is not their cause in the sense of maker. There is a multiplicity of entities here – the good, God, and the dualism of the Limit and the Unlimited – the relations between which the neo-Platonists will subsequently try to render properly self-explanatory. It is to the still massively influential neo-Platonic accounts of the triadic order of order that I now turn.

The Neo-Platonic Triads

The most obvious feature of the work of neo-Platonists such as Plotinus (Hellenised Egyptian?, 204–270 CE) and Proclus (Greek, 412–485 CE) is that their account of the triadic order of order is a synthesis of the basic features of Plato's analysis under the concept of the supreme One or Monad. The neo-Platonic One is goodness itself or absolute perfection. It is utterly complete in itself, a pure activity in the sense that it is without lack or potentiality. As such, the One is infinite or unlimited, not as the indefinite but as a self-complete activity that is inexhaustible. It is thus beyond determination, beyond being, and no description is adequate to it; it can be only grasped experientially.

Why are there other things besides the complete One? The answer is given in terms of the concept of emanative cause. The One is the single, self-explanatory origin of all things in that out of its inexhaustible completeness it emanates or 'radiates' other realities as fire does heat. This means, first, that it is an activity of 'undiminished giving' in that its emanations cause no diminution of its nature. Secondly, it means that the One is utterly indifferent to its products; they are simply the overflow of its superabundant power, which as inexhaustible it does not limit to itself. The relation of the One to its products is thus non-reciprocal and its emanative activity is not primarily a matter of free activity but of necessity. Thirdly, because the One is perfect, its products are its diremptions; that is, they are inferior to it and are essentially defective.

None of this means, however, that neo-Platonism abandons the triadic interpretation of order. Indeed, there are so many versions of this I will simply mention Plotinus's. For him, the realm of the infinite or inexhaustible is an order of three 'hypostases' or distinct realities: the One, the Intelligible or order of forms (also described as Mind or Intelligence), and the Soul or World-Soul that is the basis of individual life forms. These three elements constitute a vertical triad or hierarchy of emanations 'proceeding' out of each other from the One, and each is infinite and eternal. The Soul 'participates' in the Mind or intelligible realm, giving a triadic ranking order of the Unparticipated, the Participated and Participation. The cosmos proceeds from the emanative activity of the three primordial, infinite hypostases. The different levels of the cosmos are in turn read in terms of numerous vertical, triadic hierarchies, each of which proceeds from its superior and is both upwardly participating and downwardly participated, constituting a great chain of being.

On the significance of neo-Platonism I will merely say this. First, Plato's theory is here tidied up and developed: God and the good are identified and the dualism of form and matter is replaced by a single causal origin, the processions from which constitute an ordered hierarchical series that is asymmetrical, transitive, irreflexive, connected, consecutive and intransitive.[10]

Secondly, the strategy of defining all things in terms of a vertical triadic order or hierarchical series persists through to our day: for example, in Spinoza's substance, attributes, modes; in Whitehead's creativity, eternal objects or universals, and occasions; and in Deleuze's differentiation, virtualities or ideas, and differences. These sorts of triads I shall call 'holistic' triads. The basic model here is still Plato's triad of the Unlimited, Limit and their Mixture.[11]

Thirdly, however, the neo-Platonists develop a different notion of triadicity that lies at the heart of speculative debate from around the second or third century CE onwards, and has been enormously influential right up to our own time. For besides holistic triads or universal threefold divisions of reality, they introduce the notion of horizontal triads, originally understood as the constitutive relations of a single reality or hypostasis. The horizontal triad or actualising order of a single reality is that of abiding or immanence in one's cause; procession from that cause; and reversion upon it, in that the inferior loves or desires the perfection of its superior cause.

---

10. For the definition of these characteristics of series, see Bertrand Russell, *Introduction to Mathematical Philosophy* (London: Allen and Unwin, 1919), ch. 4, 'The Definition of Order'.
11. Whitehead clearly acknowledges his debt to late Plato when he gives one of his own late lectures the same title as Plato's last lecture; see 'On Mathematics and the Good', in A. N. Whitehead, *Essays in Science and Philosophy* (New York: Philosophical Library, 1947), 97–113. Deleuze's philosophy is best read as a synthesis of Spinoza and Whitehead.

Here it is noteworthy that for the Greeks love is *eros*, or desire arising out of need or lack. The horizontal triad comes to be universally applied and is seen as a law inherent in the structure of all that is. Such horizontal triads I shall call 'internal' triads in that they define the internal process of actualisation or ordering of any differentiable entity. The notion of a horizontal and internal serial threefold, the active elements of which are essentially interdependent or correlative and inseparable, plays a key role in the movement from the neo-Platonic theory of triads to the distinctive Christian doctrine of the Trinity – the triunity or triune nature of the self-explanatory principle of order.

One of the most significant features of this concept of triune order is that the traditional notion that the causal origin must be greater in power than, or at least as powerful as, its effect is here almost given up. It is replaced by the idea of a self-differentiating primordial subject whose power is realised only in and through its differentiations.[12] However, one main problem with Schelling's and Hegel's primordial subject is that they define it as a unity of necessity and freedom. The first principle is necessarily self-differentiating when it is conceived either as essentially communicative will or as an abstract idea that unfolds according to the necessary relations of logical entailment. It is free in that the activity of the godhead is unlimited or unconditioned; that is, it contains all the causes or conditions of action in its own nature and in that sense is wholly self-determining. The neo-Platonic idea of perfection as all-containing and self-sufficient is here decisive in limiting freedom to self-determination in Hegel's case. Creation is eternal, so there is no freedom as the freedom of choice. By contrast, Schelling's original principle of spontaneity allows free choice. In neither case is freedom defined in terms of love, as an activity in which there can in the nature of the case be no compulsion of any kind.

Schelling and Hegel wrote before Darwin's *On the Origin of the Species* (1859). Nature for them was fixed or 'frozen intelligence' in Schelling's phrase. Hence their self-explanatory trinitarian God, while it is essentially and so eternally creative, nevertheless resolves its own basic nature independently of the natural order. With the advent of the theory of natural evolution, the possibility of a whole new theory of self-explanatory order opens up. It is developed by the founder of American pragmatism, C. S. Peirce, who in the view of many is the most original philosopher since Hegel, perhaps even since Kant.

---

12. I am grateful to Peter Harris for pointing out to me this crucial development in the theory of the original or sustaining cause.

The Christian Trinity: The Logic of Events

Peirce's theory of the actualisation of order is uncompromisingly rationalist in that he holds nothing to be inexplicable. It is uncompromisingly empiricist in that he holds that everything is experienced, including the triune order of order. He maintains that we experience all differentiable entities of any kind as having the three intrinsic features of firstness, secondness and thirdness.

These three features are 1) being or presence: the spontaneity (Latin, *spons*: 'of its own accord'), intensity, unique quality or singularity of all things. This is the monadic, eternal 'it' that characterises any differentiable entity. 2) The differentiation of all things as individuals or haecceities by their relation or reaction to other differences or individuals. This is dyadic alterity, the 'I' or existence of a thing (Latin, *ex-sistentia*: 'standing outside of', a term coined by Victorinus to express the nature of the trinitarian relations). 3) The meaning or significance of all things, which is their character as embodying laws or rules or habits governing future reactions or existence. This is the dimension of the 'Thou', of interpretation, or what Peirce famously calls 'semiotics', involving the triune relation of object, sign and interpretant.

Peirce follows both Victorinus and the Franciscan voluntarists (especially Scotus) in making being (*esse*) prior to mind. He follows Schelling and Hegel in coming close to abandoning the notion that the causal origin must be greater in power or at least as powerful as its effect. And he follows Victorinus in viewing each member of the threefold as itself a threefold.[13] Thus Peirce has three types of firstness: firstness itself (which is pure spontaneity), the firstness of secondness (which is existence) and the firstness of thirdness (which is idea). Secondness is analysed as existence, as cause, and as effect. Thirdness is analysed as idea, as the exchange of information, and as interpretation, a threefold more precisely spelled out in the triune relation of semiotics. The fertility of this uncompromising pursuit of triunity in the analysis of all areas of experience is striking and has born considerable fruit in both logic and semiotics. On its basis, Peirce reverses the traditional order of the three transcendental predicates of relation. Being or aesthetic intensity is primary; goodness is a matter of the formulation of practical rules for achieving intensity; and truth or logical order is a matter of the rules of thinking that govern the formation of practical rules.[14] In this Peirce follows a similar reversal in Hegel, though for

---

13. C. S. Peirce, *Collected Papers*, vols 1–6, ed. Charles Hartshorne and Paul Weiss (Cambridge, MA: Harvard University Press, 1931–35), I, paras 530–8.
14. Peirce, *Collected Papers*, V, paras 120–50.

Hegel the triad of art, religion and philosophy is an account of the ascent of experience to the absolute mind. The difference here is obviously based on Peirce's Victorinian and voluntarist-derived pragmatist orientation to the primacy of action over mind.

In common with the trinitarian tradition, Peirce regards his three primordial 'categories' as self-explanatory in nature. They are primordial subsistent relations understood in Kantian terms as 'operations' and unproblematically regarded in the wake of modern developments in mathematics and natural science as the constitutive characteristics of the natural order. They are not 'persons' nor the components of a completely realised subject; hence they are not defined in terms of synthetic activity, either of mind or will, but in terms of freedom or free activity. That is, following the later Schelling, Peirce holds that primordial firstness, intensity or spontaneity is an undifferentiated 'No-thing', a plenitude or continuum which, because it is inexhaustible or unlimited, is completely free or unconditioned. It is intrinsically dynamic in that in the nature of the case it only realises its nature as free activity by its self-differentiation into individual qualities. These qualities or unique, intense singularities are eternal and completely independent of their inherence in anything (including the situation in which they occur) because they are the differentiations of the infinite continuum. Perhaps here Peirce, like Schelling and Hegel, remains to some extent under the mesmerising spell of the neo-Platonic idea of an absolutely all-containing origin, now understood as an undifferentiated totality. The question then arises as to whether or not the created world can give rise to anything that is completely and so genuinely new, something which is a 'never before' in every sense of the term and not merely as the undifferentiated content of an original totality. Hegel explicitly denies this possibility.[15] Yet even though Peirce holds creation to be an eternal differentiation of the same, the fact that his 'same' is the differentiation of spontaneity saves him, like Schelling, from Hegel's conclusion and allows him to go beyond Schelling and fully to exploit the implicit theory of the new contained in the doctrine of divine creation.[16]

Because each individual quality has its own unique firstness or spontaneity, the relations or interactions of individual qualities are always to some degree random. Moreover, there would be a mere chaos of contingently

---

15. G. W. F. Hegel, *Encyclopedia: The Logic*, trans. W. Wallace and A. V. Miller (Oxford: Clarendon Press, 1976), para. 146 add.
16. Perhaps all-containment plays a bigger role in defining Peirce's conception of the final end: Peirce, *Collected Papers*, VI, para. 33. Whitehead's doctrine of serial 'occasions', with their internal triadic structure (*Process and Reality*, 87–8), also constitutes a theory of the new which, in contrast to that of Bergson or Heidegger for example, is rationalist in nature.

interacting differences did individual qualities not develop habits or rules of behaviour. Rules or 'generals' display themselves in the natural order as statistical regularities or probability curves and in the human order as variables or variable structures that are incomplete entities in that they require specification by individuals. Hence they are 'vague' or open to interpretation,[17] and as such they draw individuals together in free community. All laws or regularities – including time and space, for example – are 'generals', not unchanging forms or 'universals', for they are the contingently evolved and so impermanent results of the inexhaustible serial procession of secondness and thirdness out of firstness or infinite spontaneity. Thus any distinguishable entity or actual instance of that process has the character of a triune event.[18] The triune structure of actualisation is evolutionary in that, because it is inexhaustible, it eternally evolves towards its *telos*, which is the establishment of community out of the primordial freedom. This is why Peirce can define the triune structure of events of actualisation as *agape* itself, for 'The movement of love is circular, at one and the same impulse projecting creations into independency and drawing them into harmony.'[19]

In this analysis, theogony is replaced by cosmogony, or, perhaps, the two are identified: the eternal evolution of the order of order is the evolution of the universe. Creation is the realisation of the divine nature, which is perfect as agapeic movement. Because it is a dynamic of open giving, the divine neither contains all the reasons for its existence in itself, nor resolves its own basic nature, in complete independence from anything else. And because it is *agape*, its self-differentiating activity need not be conceived either as fully realised or as an absolutely self-determining unity of freedom and necessity. Where perfection is the openness of love, Peirce's claim is that there is no longer any tension between perfection on one side and, on the other side, the genuine freedom and novelty of evolving creation.[20]

---

17. More precisely, rules or generals are not subject to the principle of the excluded middle. A thoroughgoing 'voluntarist', Peirce maintains that firstness or spontaneity is not subject to the principle of non-contradiction: it is the activity of spontaneity that generates difference or the laws of non-contradiction and excluded middle.
18. It will be evident that Dewey's theory of the triune event, mentioned at the outset, is a naturalist reinterpretation of Peirce's threefold. Habermas's 'life, labour, language' is an exact naturalist mirror of the classical trinity.
19. Peirce, *Collected Papers*, VI, para. 288.
20. In contrast both to the medieval concept of person and the Augustine–Aquinas–Hegel view of the first principle as mind, the problem with the Schelling–Peirce view of the first principle as unlimited freedom (passionate will or spontaneity) is that it is not apparent that the first principle in any sense recognises what it does. Hence while a certain kind of goodness is in each case invoked to explain the reason for initiatory activity – self-communication in Schelling, spontaneous activity in Peirce – it is questionable that such first principles are properly self-explanatory, in contrast to the medievals' notion of person, whether conceived primarily as mind or will. Schelling is obviously ambiguous here (F. W. J. Schelling, *Philosophical Inquiries into the Essence*

The overall originality and significance of Peirce's theory of triune order resides in his replacement of the serial notions of the three persons and the threefold subject with the non-anthropomorphic, serial and operational notion of the threefold event, a strategy also subsequently employed in different ways by Whitehead[21] and the later Heidegger. Peirce's theory of the agapeic event is essentially a theory of the mutual immanence of finite and infinite in the evolution of order. It rescues the notion of intelligibility from any conflation with that of clear and distinct ideas by redefining rational order in terms of vagueness, or the heuristic, experimental character of evolving structures. And it rethinks the notion of a 'personal God' non-anthropomorphically, in terms of the human individual's relation to the openness of agapeic order.[22]

Self-Explanatory Threefolds: Some Reasons Why

For present purposes, I will take Peirce as the furthest point we have got in the search for a self-explanatory account of the triadic order of order,[23]

---

of Human Freedom, trans. James Gutmann [La Salle, IL: Open Court, 1936], 73–4) while Peirce is unhelpful (*Collected Papers*, VI, para. 204). I suspect that the notion of spontaneity Peirce develops out of the later Schelling prevents him from fully recognising the self-explanatory possibilities of his own notion of *agape* when it is taken as the primordial, originating principle, in place of mind, will or freedom.

21. Whitehead, *Process and Reality*, 87–8.
22. Peirce, *Collected Papers*, VI, paras 157, 162.
23. I will not here consider the later Heidegger's influential theory of *das Ereignis* (the Event) with its threefold structure of the *Es gibt* ('It gives'), *die Sendung* ('sending') and *die Gabe* ('the gift'). See his 'Zeit und Sein', in *Die Sache des Denkens* (Tubingen: Max Niemeyer, 1969), 19, translated by Joan Stambaugh as *On Time and Being* (New York: Harper and Row, 1972), 18. In his writings published to date on this trinitarian account of the actualisation of order as event (obviously elaborated with no knowledge of Peirce), the nature of the 'It' in 'It gives' (*Es gibt*) remains unexplicated, as he insists. Consequently, it is not clear what the nature of this giving is and in particular why there is giving, though there are hints of a neo-Platonic, all-containing origin to the extent that the transcendence of the *Es gibt* is described as a matter of its 'hiddenness' 'beyond being', its 'withdrawing' and 'withholding' behind the determinations that it sends. On the trinitarian nature of the later Heidegger's thought, see Peter Harris's indispensable essay, 'Patterns of Triunity in *Time and Being*: Contexts for Interpreting the Later Heidegger', *Analecta Hermeneutica* 3 (2011), available at <www.mun.ca/analecta>. Heidegger's emphasis on giving and gift has received a well-known but generally unhelpful elaboration in some of Derrida's more recent writings. I am grateful to Sheldon Hanlon for pointing out to me that Levinas sees Heidegger's *Es gibt* as abundant 'generosity'; see Emmanuel Levinas, 'Interview with Francis Poirie', in Jill Robbins (ed.), *Is It Righteous To Be?* (Stanford: Stanford University Press, 2001), 45–6. If Levinas is correct, *agape* may have been emerging as a central theme in Heidegger's later work, much of which is still unpublished. This would represent a striking shift from his earlier attachment to Schelling's notion of freedom as the original ground of Being (see Martin Heidegger,

which can now be generally described as the attempt to define the nature of both terms and relations by way of activity. I will conclude by doing two things.

First, I would like to state the fundamental problem I have been dealing with in the following way. Because the late Plato is the common source, there is a close similarity between what may for convenience be called the trinitarian tradition on the one side and, on the other side, the Frege–Russell–Wittgenstein–Quine analysis of the natural number series as an order in which all terms are relations ($n + 1$). Over against logical analysis, the speculative trinitarians hold that activity, not functional form, is the basic principle of explanation, on the ground that only activity can be defined as a self-explanatory principle. This obviously means that the 'is' of existence is not reducible to, and is the basis of, the 'is' of instantiation or quantification: the 'is' of existence is the 'is' of activity or the actual. On both positions, however, *the binary distinction between terms and their relation is not fundamental*. On the speculative side, the distinction is subordinated to activity and leads to a realist analysis of the three elements of order as active powers or subsistent relations of series (as in Aquinas or Peirce). On the analytical side, there is the denial of the distinction of universal and particular by way of the reduction of the particular to the mere instantiation of its predicates (as in F. P. Ramsey).[24] The whole debate is perhaps best understood as a question about the nature of a 'term' in the sense of *any* differentiable or determinable entity. Is a determinate entity the value of a variable (Platonic or logical realism)? Is it an intrinsically threefold relational centre of activity (implying some non-Platonic realism of relations)? Is it an individual substance (nominalism)? Or is it constituted only by the totality of relations that is the active whole (monism)? Just what is the nature of the presence or singularity or actuality that all things have? This question, it seems, lies at the core of the issues discussed in this essay. I presume it is what is called the question of being, properly understood not as a question about the nature of being in the sense of *ens*, entity or given objects, but as a question about the nature of being in the sense of *esse* or

---

The Essence of Reasons, trans. T. Malick [Evanston, IL: Northwestern University Press, 1969], 105), which perhaps lies behind his definition of Being as 'the transcendens pure and simple' (Martin Heidegger, *Being and Time*, trans. John Macquarrie and Edward Robinson [Oxford: Blackwell, 1962], 62). Coupled with some elements of Peirce's trinitarian theory, and freed from neo-Platonic notions of an all-containing origin, the notion of agapeic giving as self-explanatory First could in my view provide a powerful theory of triune actualisation. But that is a subject that will have to be pursued elsewhere.

24. See F. P. Ramsey's classic essay 'Universals' (1925), in his *Foundations: Essays in Philosophy, Logic, Mathematics and Economics*, ed. D. H. Mellor (London: Routledge and Kegan Paul, 1978), 17–39.

the act of being. That is, the question of being is the question of activity, the question of the nature and status of activity in the order of things.

Secondly, I think I have to address the question as to why I have talked about the trinitarian tradition. Why should we take any of this stuff at all seriously? First, there is the objection that any attempts to elaborate self-explanatory theories of order have been inconclusive and it is best to give up on the idea. But this ignores the fact that not only has there been a clear and striking development of thinking here, but it has been and is enormously productive. For it is in this arena that the hugely important, even globally transformative, notions of relations, persons, subjects, events, semiotics and agapeic love as the basis of existence and justice have been elaborated. There has to be something seriously wrong with our education if we are tempted to dismiss it as irrelevant or just silly – which is just what we typically do!

Secondly, there is the objection that a lot of what I have talked about is theology and not philosophy. But my point has been not just that philosophical or fundamental theology is an integral part of the history of philosophy and thus of our cultural self-understanding, but above all that this is what we should expect. For theology, like mathematics and art, is and always has been inseparable from philosophy where philosophy is what it should be – the uncompromising pursuit of explanation. The attempt to shunt theology off into an area we call 'the philosophy of religion' has been a very successful effort to insulate certain dominant anti-speculative philosophies from comparison and criticism and to make the world safe for the philosophical faith-cult of natural science, whose current high priest is Quine and whose acolytes are the so-called 'philosophers of mind'.

Thirdly and more seriously, there is the objection from relations: namely, that any speculative attempt to provide a self-explanatory account of the nature of relations must step outside the realm of relations and thus end up in the realm of the arational or alogical, or even the anti-rational. This may be true of philosophers such as Schopenhauer, Nietzsche or Bergson, and their French successors such as Derrida and the postmodernists. But I have shown it is not true of the trinitarian tradition. That tradition is committed to the hypothesis of reason or explicability and thus to the primordially relational nature of the real. In this respect modern mathematical, scientific and philosophical developments in the theory of relations have rendered intelligible and familiar what for the medievals was a profound mystery that uniquely characterised God: namely, the primacy of relations and the notion of triunity. No one finds that the complex triunities of Kant, the self-explanatory triunity of Peirce, or the naturalist triunity of Dewey present any problems of comprehension, no matter what other difficulties there may be in these positions.

Fourthly and finally, it may be objected that even so, the speculative project does not abide by appropriate rational constraints in that it oversteps the limits of experience and so ends up freewheeling in the realm of the incomprehensible and ineffable. Yet this view is exactly what I have shown is controverted by the speculative concern with the activity of the actualisation of order.

It is indeed the case that speculative metaphysics has never identified activity with concepts. It has always recognised the ineradicable role of *the non-conceptual* in experience (the good, will, love etc.). And it has always maintained that the non-conceptual is intelligible or explicable. This does not mean, however, that we have to deny that the non-conceptual is incomprehensible. It certainly is so – but in the *strict and proper* sense of the term: namely, that in the nature of the case the non-conceptual cannot be exhaustively described or 'encompassed' (*comprehendere*) by concepts, for it is not merely an instance of concepts. This is hardly objectionable, for it is arguably true of most things in our experience – for example, space and time, as Kant held. Again, the non-conceptual is certainly the ineffable. Yet it is so, once more, in the *strict and proper* sense of the term: namely, it is 'that which cannot be told' (*ineffabilis*), that element of actuality in things to which all language, all description, is inadequate. Once more, this is obviously true of most of our experiences – of love, of death, of disaster, even the look, manner or 'presence' of another person. Everything has something irreducible about it, something not exhausted by its predicates, which is its *esse*, or spontaneity, or what empiricists such as Russell call its 'feeling of reality'. We all know that there is an ineradicable gap between thought and existence; the only question is how far we are prepared to go in explaining that gap.

Let me put the general point bluntly. There is no one who does not know what a person is, what self-actualisation is, what the infinite or inexhaustible is, what *agape* is, what a free act is. At no point here have we crossed the limits of experience; on the contrary, we have witnessed the age-old attempt to make connections between, and to construct unified explanations of, these features in accordance with the hypothesis of reason and its correlative, the unity of truth. The only lines we have stepped over are those anti-rational and deeply problematic lines that people draw across experience and call 'the observable', or 'the physical', or 'the scientific'. You may well want to deny that agapeic love is an ultimate feature of reality, or that there is free will. But let's not pretend that we don't know what these things are or what such claims mean. And that is perhaps the best argument for their significance and import and the best place to begin our discussion of 'rationality'.

Chapter 6

The Triune Event: Event Ontology, Reason and Love

My claim is simple and straightforward: that an adequate discussion of event ontology is seriously deficient without consideration of the theory of the triune event. Philosophical debates in contemporary event ontology are dominated primarily by the traditions of thought associated with the names of Whitehead, Deleuze and Badiou. Into these debates, I would like to introduce another and much older tradition: that associated with the doctrine of trinity. I shall argue that, in 'the logic of the events' of Charles Sanders Peirce, even theory finds an original and powerful articulation of the principle of triunity that stands critically over against current formations. In most of the literature, admittedly, Peirce is presented as a naturalist, in line with the prevailing culture of the schools. I shall maintain to the contrary that his theory of the triune event, like the other event ontologies we are discussing, is a speculative metaphysics. That is to say, it is a theory of the condition of the actualisation of the empirical world.

These claims will be developed by way of the presentation and discussion of six theses. At the outset I shall assume, in common with the major contemporary event ontologies, the hypothesis of reality: namely, that reality is that which has a nature of its own in the sense that it is so independently of our minds or independently of whatever or not we think it to be. I shall also assume the hypothesis of universalism, or the reality of universals, which is another familiar feature of event ontology. Nevertheless, claims that support both hypotheses will be advanced in the course of what follows.

The Principle of Reason

My first thesis is that the furnace in which event ontology should be tested is the principle of reason. That is the principle that 'Nothing is without a reason', or 'Everything that is the case must have a reason why it is the case.'[1] It has its corollary in the principle of unity of truth: the claim that all the features of the experience are in some way intelligibly interconnected.[2]

Negatively, the principle of reason requires the rejection of the no hypothesis hypothesis: 'the hypothesis that no hypothesis is possible'.[3] For the principle of reason rejects the essentially sceptical theory of hypothesis that there are things that no theory or hypothesis can explain. It rejects the hypothesis that there is anything about which no explanatory theory can be sought and entertained.

Positively, the principle of reason requires unrestricted commitment to the search for explanation. No appeal is made here to *a priori* rules. We have only the experimental or hypothetical application of the principle of reason to the fact that we live in a puzzling world. Further, the principle of reason requires that we go beyond even the most basic laws and operations of logic, mathematics and physics, for these do not account, nor do they attempt to account, for why there are laws or operations at all. Unrestrictedly applied, the principle of reason requires that we look for an ultimate that is self-justifying or self-explanatory.

A self-explanatory theory of reality is necessarily a theory of the actualisation of the empirical world, and thus in the nature of the case it is a theory of the *activity* of actualisation. Moreover, such a theory would have to meet the stringent requirement that whatever is held to be the ultimate principle of actualisation must possess in its own nature, or provide out of its own nature, all the nature needed to explain its existence or activity.

Self-explanatoriness is not of course the same as proof. Indeed, the question as to what constitutes an adequate self-explanatory theory of the activity of actualisation is hotly debated between the different schools that seek the self-explanatory. For brevity, I shall dub them speculative 'explanatorists'. In that tradition, from Plato on, the principle of reason generally has the form defined by C. S. Peirce: 'The surprising fact *C* is observed/ But if *A* were true, *C* would be a matter of course/ Hence, there

---

1. For this latter formulation, cf. Alexander R. Pruss, *The Principle of Sufficient Reason: A Reassessment* (Cambridge: Cambridge University Press, 2006), 3. I use the term 'principle of reason' and not 'sufficient reason' in order to disassociate the concept from the usual necessitarian interpretations, both of it and of Leibniz. For this mistake, cf. e.g. Alain Badiou, *Infinite Thought: Truth and the Return to Philosophy*, trans. Justin Clemens and Oliver Feltham (London: Continuum, 2003), 138.
2. Whether or not the concept of the unity of truth is inextricably wedded to the notion either that it arises from a primordial unity, or that it is itself a primordial given, is a question that for the present may be left open.
3. Charles Sanders Peirce, Harvard Library MS 956, c. 1980.

is reason to suppose that *A* is true.'[4] The argument is not a deduction, since it does not claim that its conclusion must be true if its premises are true. It is not inductive, since the statement referred to in the conclusion is not tested by sampling. Whereas induction tells us that a statement, true in some cases, is likely to be true in unobserved cases, abduction allows us to conclude to the likelihood of something unlike anything that is observed. It is inference to the best possible explanation. The procedure is fallibilist: repeated application of abductive inference may lead to continued revision of our hypothesis in light of new observations, as has always been the case with speculative theories of actualisation. And the hypothesis is not just tested against experience. Experience is tested against the hypothesis, which has the status of a critical principle: do the putative observations, or our descriptions of the observed, display the characters posited by the hypothesis? Ostensive demonstration cuts both ways. Or, more precisely, it moves in a virtuous circle.

There are two main objections to exceptionalism that need to be considered at the outset. First, there is the objection from contingency, the claim that there is no need for an ultimate principle of actualisation at all. For what is wrong with contingency as the ultimate principle? Why is contingency not enough?

From the Greeks onwards many speculative philosophers have made contingency an essential element in their theory of the self-explanatory nature of reality. But it cannot be the only element. For the question 'Why not just contingency?' answers itself. The contingent is to be in relation to something else, such as the *laws* of logic or physics. The contingent is always relative and so cannot *by itself* be a self-explanatory principle.

Perhaps what is really meant here is 'chance'? Yet if that is the case, chance is something more than an event whose cause is unknown to us, and it is more than a concurrence of two independent causal chains. As definitions of chance, both these notions simply mean 'an order whose operations cannot be predicted by us'. So, we are not talking of chance in any realist or ontologically significant sense.

The notion of 'chaos' cannot help either. In the first place, there can be no such thing as 'pure chaos'.[5] Chance is always relative chaos because, even if there is chaos of some kind, there must be determinate entities (*ens*) that have some sort of unity (*unium*) – that is, irreducibility – about them in order for them to be chaotically related, or related at all. And if there are distinct entities, not only must they stand to one another in a relation of

---

4. C. S. Peirce, *Collected Papers*, vols 1–6, ed. Charles Hartshorne and Paul Weiss (Cambridge, MA: Harvard University Press, 1931–35), V, para. 189.
5. As will become evident, chaos is not to be confused with indeterminacy.

difference (*aliquid*), no matter how minimal, but they must also persist, or display certain characters or behave in a specific way (*res*), no matter how fleeting. To be in chaos, that is, they must possess individual identities or internal order, no matter how simple. The notion of chaos also seems to depend on that of sequence – a sequence of events – which again entails order of some kind. It hardly needs adding that so-called 'chaos theory' is not only thoroughly deterministic but assumes that order is a given, introduced, so to speak, in one dose in the 'initial conditions'.

What contingency and chance might mean in the context of a self-explanatory event ontology will be further considered below. The second main objection to explanatorism is more immediately relevant, for it is in various degrees characteristic of contemporary event theory. It is an historical as much as a conceptual objection and indeed has considerable historical justification. This second objection is the claim that explanatorism necessarily issues in a theory of the All, or Totality, or Absolute, or One, understood as a complete and all-containing presence.[6] Such a theory, because it refers things away from themselves to a self-explanatory principle or ground, has no place for real contingency or the really new and so is inextricably committed to necessitarian ontology. This is clearly a serious claim to make against any attempt unrestrictedly to introduce the principle of reason into event ontology. Much of what follows will attempt to examine its cogency. My second thesis is a step on the way.

A Taxonomy of Principles of Actualisation

My second thesis is that it is historically illuminating and critically significant to assess event ontologies in the context of a taxonomy of the difference principles of actualisation elaborated in a speculative metaphysics. There are five basic types to be considered.

A principle of actualisation could be monadic, as is Nietzsche's theory of the will to power, or, most obviously, the Judaic and Islamic account of the creator God as an absolutely unique, singular being whose nature is defined as completely transcending human powers of reason. A principle of actualisation could be binary or dyadic, as when the foundations of the cosmos are held by Empedocles to be the twin principles of love and strife, by Democritus to be atoms and the void, by Schopenhauer to be will and idea, by Samuel Alexander to be space and time, or by Alain Badiou to be being and event. A principle of actualisation could be triadic, as is Plotinus's

---

6. Cf. Alain Badiou, *Being and Event*, trans. Oliver Feltham (London: Continuum, 2005), 9–10.

hierarchy of the One, Mind and Soul, Spinoza's hierarchy of substance, attributes and modes, and Deleuze's non-hierarchical threefold of difference (or event, or being),[7] virtualities, and specific differences or events. A principle of actualisation could be tetradic, as in Plato's *Timaeus* with its fourfold of the Good, God, Form and Matter, or as with Whitehead's creativity, God, eternal objects and actual occasions.

There can be no question, however, that the tradition that dominates the history of Western speculative thought is that which holds the principle of actualisation to be a triunity of three distinct, inseparable and co-equal elements. Most would acknowledge that this tradition stretches from Plato's *syntrisi* or three-in-one,[8] through the medieval period, to the idealism of Hegel and Schelling. It is not so often noticed, however, that it has been a significant feature of modern developments in event theory over the last one hundred and fifty years. I refer primarily to Peirce's ontology of firstness, secondness and thirdness, but there is also the later Heidegger's *das Ereignis* ('the Event'), with its triunity of *Es gibt* ('It gives'), *die Sendung* ('the sending') and *die Gabe* ('the Gift'), as well as Collingwood's treatment of the Trinity as the fundamental 'absolute presupposition' of natural science.[9]

Two comments may help to dispel any puzzlement there may be at the persistence of the notion of triunity in event theory. First, because the triune theories mentioned are explanatorist, they are elaborated so as to address three basic questions. These are the questions of the nature of origin, difference and order. For in the first place, a theory of the activity of actualisation requires a theory of the origin of difference and order. That is, it requires an account of that activity which is in some sense prior to difference and order because it is the condition of difference of the actualisation of difference or individuality, of the nature of differentiation. And in the third place, such a theory requires an account of the actualisation of order. The primacy attached to these issues is, of course, characteristic of the triune tradition

---

7. Gilles Deleuze, *Logic of Sense*, trans. Mark Lester and Charles Stivale (New York: Columbia University Press, 1990), 179–80. Cf. Robert Piercey's excellent essay, 'The Spinoza-intoxicated Man: Deleuze on Expression', *Man and World* 29 (1996), 269–81.
8. Plato, *Philebus*, 64–5; on which, see H.-G. Gadamer, *The Idea of the Good in the Platonic–Aristotelian Philosophy*, trans. P. Christopher Smith (New Haven: Yale University Press, 1986), 115–16.
9. Cf. R. G. Collingwood, *An Essay on Metaphysics* (Oxford: Clarendon Press, 1940), ch. 21; Martin Heidegger, *On Time and Being*, trans. Joan Stambaugh (New York: Harper Books, 1972), on which see my 'Transformations in Speculative Philosophy', in Tom Baldwin (ed.), *The Cambridge History of Modern Philosophy 1870–1945* (Cambridge: Cambridge University Press, 2003), 438–48. Josiah Royce's theory of the triune structure of interpretation could be added to the names I have given in the text; cf. his *The Problem of Christianity* (New York: Macmillan, 1913), esp. vol. II. This is a book written under the acknowledged influence of Peirce.

itself. But they have a certain obviousness about them that helps to indicate the rationale of the general position.

Secondly, there is a set of considerations connected with the development of mathematics and the rise of natural science. In the medieval period, the doctrine of the triune God, with its 'subsistent relations' of Father, Son and Spirit, was expounded as a supernatural or revealed mystery of faith. This is not to deny that the triune God is employed to provide a self-explanatory account of the activity of actualisation. In Aquinas, for example, all things have their *esse*, or act of being, which is given by the Father; their individual nature (species), which is given by the Son or Logos; and their relation to other things, which is given by the Spirit, the principle of gift or love or community.[10] Nevertheless, the concept of an essentially relational being cuts across the Aristotelian view that finite substances exist independently and that relations are accidents. Hence, it is difficult in this context to develop a trinitarian account of all the features of the created world. By contrast, once mathematics and natural science had established the intrinsic relationality of the natural world,[11] the relational model could unproblematically be transposed, under the rubric of triunity, not only to the analysis of the constitution of the finite subject (as with Kant's plethora of triunities),[12] but also to the whole of reality, defined as an absolute subject with three essential modes or functional operations (Hegel and Schelling).[13] As Collingwood puts it: 'The doctrine of the Trinity, taught as a revelation by early Christianity . . . becomes in Kant and his successors a demonstrable and almost alarmingly fertile logical principle.'[14] Triunity here becomes an immanent principle of actualisation, although it is still apprehended as complete and all-containing. In order to prepare for the sea-change, Peirce works in the theory of triunity, transforming the medieval theory

---

10. Cf. Aquinas, *Summa Theologiae*, q. 45, a. 7, resp.
11. Badiou, *Being and Event*, 142–9. Cf. Ernst Cassirer, *Substance and Function* (1910), trans. W. C. Swabey and M. C. Swabey (New York: Open Court, 1923); and Gerd Buchdhal, *Metaphysics and the Philosophy of Science* (Oxford: Blackwell, 1969), ch. 1.
12. Hegel says of Kant: 'the conception of Trinity has, through the influence of the Kantian philosophy, been brought into notice again in an outward [read: purely formal] way as a type, and, as it were, a ground plan of thought, and this in very definite forms of thought.' G. W. F. Hegel, *Lectures on the Philosophy of Religion*, trans. E. B. Speirs and J. B. Sanderson (New York: Humanities Press, 1974), III, 32–3.
13. That this position is not to be confused with Sabellianism is indicated by the fact that the theologians Karl Barth and Karl Rahner work within its purview. Cf. Karl Barth, *Church Dogmatics*, trans. G. T. Thompson (Edinburgh: T & T Clark, 1936), I, pt 1, ch. 3; and Karl Rahner, *The Trinity*, trans. Joseph Donceel (New York: Crossroad Herder, 1970).
14. R. G. Collingwood, 'Reason is Faith Cultivating Itself' (1927), in *Faith and Reason*, ed. Lionel Rubinoff (Chicago: Quadrangle Books, 1968), 119–20.

of subsistent relations and the German idealist theory of the subject into a logic of events. My third thesis extends the analysis of the principles of actualisation so far offered.[15]

The Activity of Actualisation and the Principle of Reason

My third thesis is that the preceding taxonomy of five types of principle of actualisation can be considered from the point of view of their relation to the principle of reason. The relevance of this to event theory should quickly become apparent.

There are three basic orientations here, and a little reflection will show that they cut across the fivefold taxonomy. At one extreme are the explanatorists, who subscribe to the unrestricted application of the principle of reason. This orientation will be considered at some length below. At the opposite extreme are those who regard the principle of actualisation as in some essential respect irrational. Schopenhauer is I believe one of the few figures who belongs here. Standing in varying degrees between these two extreme of explanatorism and irrationalism are what I shall call the speculative 'descriptivists'. Their theories of actualisation are in one way or another either explicitly opposed to the unrestricted application of the principle of reason – Badiou is one of these – or they stand ambiguously to it. Whitehead and Deleuze belong to the latter group, and because of their central importance in event theory, I will make some remarks on both.

On Deleuze, Badiou had made the essential point: that there is in Deleuze 'no clear position on the question of the One'.[16] Where there is nothing prior to the endless multiplication of differences, what is difference, or the event, or being? A univocal concept, yes; but is it supposed to explain the togetherness and continuity of differences, or is it to be taken as a descriptive posit, an underivable primordial given? Further, if it is an

---

15. It will I hope become evident that it is regrettable that Peirce scholars, Peircean philosophers of religion and theologians generally ignore Peirce's Trinitarianism, no doubt influenced by the predominant naturalism and conceptual-historical amnesia of Anglo-American culture. For the only exceptions to this rule that I know, see Hermann Deuser, *Gott: Geist und Nature. Theologische Consequenzen aus Charles S. Peirce Religionsphilosophie* (Berlin: Konigshausen and Neumann, 1993), 157, 166, 173, where, albeit briefly and cautiously, he points out the correlation of Peirce's categories to the Trinity; and Hermann Deuser and Helmut Maassen (eds), *Charles Sanders Peirce: Religionsphilosophische Schriften* (Hamburg: Felix Meiner, 1995), xli–xlii.
16. Alain Badiou, 'Gilles Deleuze, the fold: Leibniz and the baroque', in Constantin V. Boundas and Dorothea Olkowski (eds), *Gilles Deleuze and the Theater of Philosophy* (London: Routledge, 1994), ch. 4.

infinite in the sense of inexhaustible activity, is it so as a plenitude of some kind or as an iterative movement of synthesis? Presumably the latter; but if so, what is the relation of differentiation to synthesis (order)? Difference or the event is at once a principle of origination, but its nature as such is not clearly explicated. In particular, there is no obvious philosophical reason why differentiation is good, and is treated always in such a sacral, celebratory style. Deleuze's speculative metaphysics definitely looks like a form of speculative descriptivism, though perhaps shot through with a quasi-theological dimension.

Whitehead is, if anything, harder to pin down. On the one hand, his tetrad appears to have some kind of self-explanatory principle in God. On the other hand, there is the ultimate category or creativity, which is defined on the set-theoretical definition of the function as the class of many-to-one-relations. Here, the activity of actualisation is constructivistically construed as the inexhaustible activity of the mapping of relations between a domain and a co-domain.[17] Now, so far as it is inexhaustible activity, creativity is a self-explanatory principle of actualisation. Yet no reason is given as to why this inexhaustible activity is a mapping activity, that is, an activity of differentiation and ordination. Differentiation and ordination are simply posited as components of the ultimate principle, and both God and occasions are held to be instances of that structure. The necessary consequence of attempting to construct a speculative metaphysics of actualisation out of the mathematical-logical function is that functional analysis already has built into it the very features that require explanation under the principle of reason.

These brief comments on Whitehead and Deleuze indicate that the decisive issue for event ontology is the theory of origin. This is, of course, the subject of endless debate as 'beyond being (*ousia*)', which means that that the origin is beyond activity (*einai*) but that it is not a determinate thing (*ousia*) because it is the ground for determination. My next thesis concerns the various ways in which this has been understood.

Theories of Origin

My fourth thesis is that there are three basic theories of origin in the explanatorist tradition. To begin with, as in Plotinus and in the Judaeo-Islamic doctrine of God, the origin can be held to be a complete and all-containing One that is not only beyond specific determination but is for that reason

---

17. See 'The Speculative Generalisation of the Function', Chapter 4 above.

beyond intelligibility. Here the principle of reason leads to the conclusion that the ultimate reason is beyond reason. This supra-rationalist position, as I shall call it, has influenced triune accounts of actualisation. Thus, in Heidegger's writings published to date, the nature of the 'It' in 'It gives' (*Es gibt*) remains unexplained, as he insists.[18] Consequently, it is not clear what the nature of this giving is and in particular why there is giving.[19] Nevertheless, there are hints of a neo-Platonic, all-containing origin to the extent that the transcendence of the *Es gibt* is described as a matter of its 'hiddenness' 'beyond being', its 'withdrawing' and 'withholding' behind the determinations that it sends.

At the opposite pole, secondly, there are the triunities of Augustine, Aquinas and, most recently, Hegel, who at the highest level of his analysis of actualisation defines the first principle of the threefold as 'pure activity in itself... universal activity' whose 'content is no other than the Universal itself'.[20] This is the eternal, self-positing Idea. Hegel stands within what may be called the 'rationalist' tradition of triunity, going back to Augustine, which describes the threefold of actualisation on the analogy of mind itself. Self-ordering mind is held to be the ground of order. The origin is 'thought thinking itself', not as unmoved mover but as all-containing, absolute completeness. It is important to note, however, that there is no single, simple origin here. Summarily: the Father is such only because he unconditionally gives the Spirit or gift (*donum*) of love to the Son.

In contrast to this rationalist triunity, there is thirdly an intermediate position: what might be called the 'explicabilist' view holds that all things are intelligible with mind or rationality. Here the first principle of the threefold is understood not as Idea (Hegel) or as self-consciousness (Augustine, Aquinas) but as activity alone. This activity is held to be unconditioned because it is original. So, it is free or spontaneous in that it is the sole cause of its own activity. But it is activity, so it is essentially relational and teleological; for it is necessarily *ekstatic* in the sense that, whatever else it may be, activity is nothing less than ablative or abductive movement, movement out from itself. The notion of the first principle of the threefold as this kind of unity of the ecstatic and the unconditioned, of necessity and freedom, is the sort of position defended by voluntarists such as Scotus and Schelling (who use the psychological analogy of will rather than mind to define origin) and by pragmatists such as Peirce (who reinterprets will as action). They insist on the priority of activity to mind or thought, in particular to the laws of logic, and they maintain that activity is a perfectly knowable feature of experience.

---

18. Heidegger, *On Time and Being*, 18.
19. Emmanuel Levinas, 'Interview with Francis Poirie', in Jill Robbins (ed.), *Is It Righteous To Be?* (Stanford: Stanford University Press, 2001), 45–6.
20. Hegel, *Lectures on the Philosophy of Religion*, III, 8.

As my reference to Peirce indicated, it is out this explicabilist tradition that I think he weaves his triune of logic and events. His triunity is the subject of my fifth thesis.

Peirce's Triunity

My fifth thesis is that Peirce's is an ostensive trinitarianism, a natural theology, or, more precisely, an empiricist-oriented metaphysics of the trinity: it attempts to make manifest the necessarily creative and radically immanent triune principle of actualisation across the fields of logic, mathematics, phenomenology, semiotics and speculative cosmology. Although there is no space to elaborate this large claim here, I will say something about how I interpret each principle of his triunity, drawing specifically on this cosmology, and I will try to indicate as I proceed something of its significance as an event ontology. Throughout, it is important to keep in mind that for Peirce, any differentiable entity whatsoever is to be analysed in terms of this triune principle of actualisation, which is distinct but inseparable from that which it actualises or creates. This means, as will become evident, that any differentiable entity has the nature of a triune event in the infinitely or inexhaustibly proceeding iterative movement of actualisation.

In the first place, the self-explanatory first principle of actualisation is pure ekstatic or ablative activity, abductive 'movement from. . .' Because it is origin, it is unconditioned. So, it is free or spontaneous in the sense that it acts wholly out of its own nature. Because it is unconditioned or free activity, it is limitless in the sense that it is absolutely indeterminate in its own nature. That is, free *ekstasis*, as such, possesses no 'real' or determining properties or predicates. Its character as free ekstatic activity means that in the nature of the case it is a non-determining power.

This concept of origin follows both Marius Victorinus and the Franciscan voluntarists in making being or activity (*esse, actus essendi*) prior to mind, and it owes a great deal to Schelling's theory of *Abgrund*. However, Peirce abandons the psychological notion of the will, characteristic of voluntarism, as well as the Gnostic and mystical elements in Schelling. Instead, he elaborates the concept of origin in terms of a particular kind of mathematical infinite. His is not the potential infinite of Aristotle and the intuitionists, where however many parts it is divided into, it is possible for there to be more. Nor is it the real categorematic infinite of set theory, involving an infinite multiplicity of sets in which the parts or components are really there and their number is greater than any given. Rather, Peirce's firstness is in my view a particular kind of syncategorematic infinite. That is, his primordial infinite is real in that it is inexhaustible activity, and it is potential in that its absolute indeterminacy means 'it contains no definite parts';[21] it is a continuum of potential parts only.[22] Peirce's infinite is a syncategorematic infinite of real or dynamical potentiality.

The significance of this theory of infinity is that here we have a concept of origin which, in the nature of the case, is not a One, not an All, not a Totality, not even a multiplicity of any kind. As Peirce stresses, this is a mathematical concept of pure chance.[23]

Peirce describes free or indeterminate firstness as no-thing or void.[24] That is, firstness is nothing not as all-containing plenitude (*per excellentiam nihil*), nor as vacuity (*omnino nihil*), nor as negation (*nihil privativum*), but only as infinite indeterminacy (*nihil per infinitatem*).[25] It might be objected that this infinite origin is a 'unity' of free indeterminacy. However, as will be more fully explained in a moment, unity is, in Peirce as in Badiou, an effect, not a property of the origin; in Peirce, unity emerges out of the triune relation as its realisation. The sole kind of unity that the first, considered in its own nature, possesses is the unity of irreducibility (*unum*), for the first is the *principium non de principio* and as such unconditioned freedom. Peirce's firstness is not a unicity in any other sense; rather, it is the univocal concept of a dynamical free indeterminacy that as such has no nature of its own, and, in communicating itself to all things, is necessarily never the same.

This brings us to Peirce's principle of secondness. Because the first principle is ekstatic, self-realising movement, it gives rise out of itself to a second activity or principle of actualisation: the principle of essentially and spontaneously self-differentiating activity, of dative 'movement to . . .' The distinctness of this second principle resides in the fact that it is determination: it constitutes differences or singularities, and it does so by communicating to them the spontaneity that is the positive basis of all determinacy or actuality. Such differentiating activity is also the positive basis of the logical laws of non-contradiction, negation and the excluded middle.

There cannot, however, be any such thing as pure differences, as we noted earlier in connection with chaos. Rather, for ecstatic activity to realise its differentiations as such – and so to realise itself in relation to its differentiations – it articulates its communicative nature as a law or rule of relation itself and its differentiations. That is, because *ekstasis* is essentially

---

21. Peirce, *Collected Papers*, VI, para. 168.
22. Ibid., para. 185, and C. S. Peirce, *The New Elements of Mathematics*, ed. Carolyn Eisele (The Hague: Mouton, 1976), IV, 343.
23. Peirce, *Collected Papers*, VI, para. 201.
24. Ibid., para. 214.
25. These various distinctions in the meaning of the term 'nothing' are made by John Scotus Eriugena; Peirce's version of the *nihil per infinitatem* is not of course Eriugena's, though his Trinitarianism has close relations to Eriugena's. On Eriugena, see Werner Beierwaltes, 'Negati Affirmatio', *Dionysius* 1 (1977), 127–59, esp. 133–4.

communicative and self-realising, it determines itself as a rule or law and communicates that power to its differentiations as their medium. Such power is the potentiality of order, and it is the medium in which differences are constituted. The distinctness of this third element resides in the fact that it is the activity of ordination, the dynamic principle of order or structure.

Peirce's thirdness or power of mediation defines the implications of his theory of origin for specific laws or rules. Like differences, all structures are determinations of free indeterminacy, which is inexhaustible. In consequence, all structures carry free indeterminacy within their nature. So all structures possess an inexhaustible indeterminacy. What this means is that all specific laws or rules are essentially and intrinsically vague: they are infinitely or inexhaustibly determinable determinations. Thus, there are no really complete or completable wholes: as Peirce insists,[26] for any given whole or continuity (e.g. 'All men are mortal'), the universal quantifier is to be interpreted distributively ('For each. . .') not collectively ('For all. . .'). Wholes are infinitive in the distributive wholes because they are intrinsically vague or infinitely indeterminate.

What we have in this *mathesis universalis* is one of the great revolutions in the theory of universals. Forms do not constitute an infinite multiplicity of fixed entities, as for Whitehead and Badiou; rather, they are potentials that are subject to evolution, to development and decay. This is an explanatorist theory of the activity of actualisation in which there is no complete, all-containing Totality or One. Unity – and with it the unity of truth – is an effect, not an origin. All achieved unities – including that of the triune principle of actualisation itself – are dynamical events of spontaneity, difference and order, which as such are essentially incomplete and open to further determination. For Peirce, there are no absolute individuals, for all entities are infinitely determinable determinations.

With Peirce's explanatorist theory of the activity of actualisation now laid out, at least as I understand it, a number of clarificatory points about its nature and implications as an event ontology are in order. First, this *is* a triunity. The three distinct and mutually irreducible principles of activity, differentiation and ordination do not constitute a temporal sequence. There is not *first* activity and *then* difference and order. Rather, the communicative activity of actualisation is only realised in and by spontaneous activity, spontaneous differentiation and spontaneous ordination. Thus in the nature of the case, all three principles are correlative and interdependent as well as irreducible. They are intrinsically relational because each is essential to the realisation of the others, and they can be defined only by way of the opposition of relations that constitutes their trinity.

---

26. Peirce, *Collected Papers*, V, para. 532.

Secondly, the triune theory of events *is* a theory of the radically new. For there is on this ontology not even a pre-given multiplicity of possibilities, however understood. Further, no axiom need be invoked, and the laws of logic themselves are actualisations, infinitely determinable indeterminacies that are subject to development. There is here only the open, eternal dynamic of triune actualisation.

Thirdly, because this triunity constitutes the nature of any differentiable entity, nominalism is completely rejected. In contrast to Whitehead, Deleuze and Badiou, there are no absolute individuals or events, for all individuals or events are unities of singular individuality and vague structure.[27] As in all event ontologies, difference or individuality is both the site of decision or determination, of *haecceitas*, and is also essentially relational in that it is a constitutive component of an iterative series. For Peirce, however, its intrinsic sociality or communality arises from this and from the fact that its infinitude is never complete or closed, never final. Here we approach the subject of my sixth thesis.

The Agapeic Community

My sixth thesis is that the theory of the triune event of actualisation is the basis of a transformative ethics and politics.

For consider. Being or activity is not here primarily analysed as substance or as subjectivity but as communication, the unconditional communication of freedom by the triune principle of actualisation. Unconditional communication is thus the actualising condition of substance and of subjectivity, of all determination. At this point, we cannot avoid the question: just what is unconditioned communication?

There is only one answer: it is love, not as need or desire in the sense of lack (*eros*), but as unconditioned giving or donation, unconditioned concern (*agape*). Hegel always translates 'love' into 'spirit'. The point here is that 'spirit' in the sense of the immanent triune structure of actualisation should always be translated as 'love'. For the ultimate principle is not self-transparent, all-containing mind that comprehends everything in its nature; rather, it is unconditional concern. Only in this way can the spontaneity and individuality of things, and in particular the contingent evolution of physical nature, be properly secured. And the reason is that unconditional concern is open to what it does not control or determine. It

---

27. It should be noted that, even if reality is basically tetradic for Whitehead, he gives both God and actual occasions an internal triune structure; see A. N. Whitehead, *Process and Reality: An Essay in Cosmology* (corrected edn, New York: The Free Press, 1978), 87–8.

does not stand in opposition to contingency, nor does it treat contingency as a lower moment of some all-containing absolute completeness. The completeness of all-containment is not to be confused with the eternally achieved completeness of perfection that is the threefold agapeic principle, for unconditional concern *surrenders* itself to contingency. We see this in parental love, in all genuine love. As Peirce says in his essay on 'Evolutionary Love': 'The movement of love is circular, at one and the same impulse projecting things into independency and drawing them into harmony.'[28]

The significance of this analysis of the triune principle of actualisation should now be apparent. For ancient Greeks as well as for modern philosophers such as Iris Murdoch, love as *eros* is the *medium* by which we come properly to apprehend and to participate in the ultimate reality. For Whitehead, love is one aspect of the divine nature. In contrast, the claim here is that the ultimate reality *is* love as infinite or inexhaustible *agape*. This is the infinity that characterises the three principles of actualisation in their unity of co-realisation. And it is this infinite love that is the active condition of order in the universe, the ultimate ground of actuality, that which provided out of its own nature all the reasons needed to explain the existence of its ordering activity. In consequence, love is the ground of the complications that wherever possible accompany ordination. It is the ground of that synthetic developmental tendency to inclusiveness or community of structure without which there could not be evolution as we mean the term, either generally or with particular reference to what has happened on this planet over the last few billion years. All specific complications or communities – not just the human mind, but mathematical order, time and space, possibly even extensity – *are* contingent. Yet ordination itself, as complication or inclusive community, is not. For these reasons, the real is not only the true; the real is essentially good.

I should perhaps add that in the context of the history of our philosophy and culture I do not think this claim is anything unusual or bizarre. This is an ancient claim, and I have tried to indicate that, in the context of the philosophical principle of reason, it is a powerful claim. And here is a further reason why: it is a claim that in fact tacitly informs all our attitudes, a claim by which in fact we tacitly measure all our actions. For what it implies is that the ultimate, the highest ethical and hence political principle, is that which is the ground of reality; namely, the impossibly demanding principle of universal unconditional concern. On this point, I challenge any of the schools of contemporary ethics among us to explain why we do or should act in the way they say without at some point (as Kant thinks is essential) appealing to the principle of unconditional concern. Put it like

---

28. Peirce, *Collected Papers*, VI, para. 288.

this: do you value or have high regard for that principle? If so, note that it cannot be derived or based on any lesser principle. As I will try to show, it is irreducible. And its irreducibility (as Kant saw) constitutes an ethical clue to the ultimate nature of reality.

So, let me ask a question of the various schools of event ontology. How would one go about analysing the proposition 'Jane loves John'? For purposes of comparison, I will offer a triune analysis.

In the first instance, a triune analysis of 'Jane loves John' would go something like this. We mean there is intense, spontaneous feeling towards another and in that respect Jane is that which Peirce calls an 'emotional interpretant'. We mean also that there are actions and effort involved, and in this respect Jane is an 'energetic interpretant'. And we mean further that this is an adopted rule, habit of behaviour or ideal, in which respect Jane is an ideal or 'logical interpretant'.[29] It is the *unity* of all three that is meant by 'loves'. The interpretative power of triune analysis is I think well demonstrated here.

Yet it may be asked if we could not leave it at that. In other words, why not settle for some kind of descriptivist or naturalist theory of the triune event, as so many influenced by Peirce do? Does an explanatorist theory of reality have any role here? Just what does it add to the description?

However, experience demands that we go beyond descriptivism. For the hallmark of all genuine love is some element of unconditional concern. And as Kant puts it, unconditional love is not a matter of affection or 'pathological love' but 'practical love'. It is not a feeling or a disposition, for we can and should show unconditional concern for those we might be disposed to dislike, even hate. We have here an alignment of feeling and action with an ideal, where feeling is no longer erotic, nor merely an affective sentiment of sympathy, but a matter of self-surrender.

How else can this be understood except as a spiritual act, in the sense of a total orientation of our natures that transcends natural impulse? It is something more than just 'mind', something more than ordinary 'feeling', and usually involves extraordinary action. Moreover, not only does unconditional concern extend beyond people to other things – so it is not an instance of species-centrism – but also it obviously cannot be explained as enlightened egoism. Least of all can it be explained by some kind of consequentialism, for consequences are what it ignores, often to the point of sacrifice of life itself. In short, it is irreducible, even to the imperatives of biological self-interest or evolutionary survival.

What has to be said, I think, is that where there is such love – and we can find it manifest in artworks as well as people – we have a glimpse of the

---

29. Ibid., V, paras 473–6.

perfect unity of feeling, exertion and rule. *Either* this is a perfection, an ideal, that is utterly without reason, is quite irrational and even self-destructive (as Nietzsche claimed, holding 'life' to be the *summum bonum*); *or* this is a perfection that has its reason – its only reason – in the ultimate order of things. So, it is here that the self-explanatory theory of agapeic triunity finds its final and decisive vindication. It is in the *mathesis amoris* of the triune logic of events that justice and freedom have their only adequate basis. Anything less, anything besides the impossible demand of *agape*, is open to compromise and will betray us into a lack of faithfulness. For that reason, along with the others I have given, I have faith or trust (*fides*) in the self-explanatory hypothesis of the triune event.

Chapter 7

What is Existence?

Weak Theories of Existence

At the heart of every metaphysics there lies a theory of existence, an account of what it is for anything at all to exist. Such theories, which decisively shape the claims made in all other areas of philosophy, come in two basic versions that we shall call 'strong' and 'weak' theories. What is usually termed 'speculative metaphysics' characteristically defends a strong theory of existence. Other kinds of philosophy, such as materialism or physicalism, naturalism and analytical philosophy, strenuously maintain a weak theory. The differences between strong and weak theories, as also between various versions of strong theory, are so fundamental to any views we might have of the nature of reality that the debates between them are the driving force of Western philosophy. Indeed, these debates are at the centre of the conflicts and oppositions, the arguments and alternatives, that characterise not only Western philosophy but Western culture as a whole. Without some understanding of what is at stake here, the nature and significance of the enterprise of metaphysics, and in particular of speculative metaphysics, will forever remain mysterious, as will the import of most of the views about reality we are likely to encounter.

The claim that existence is central to philosophical and cultural debate except as merely a matter of historical record is highly contentious. Weak theorists characteristically regard existence as a notion about which there is little that can or should be said except as a corrective to strong theories. In general, weak theorists follow David Hume in treating existence as an ultimate given that is not further derivable or explicable. This is basically the position that Immanuel Kant articulates in his theory of cognition when he makes existence a modality of empirical judgements. In the context of cognition, Kant maintains that '-exists' is not a real but a non-determining predicate: affirmations of existence add nothing to the content of a concept, but simply posit an object corresponding to a concept.

Both materialists and pragmatic naturalists such as John Dewey agree with the Hume–Kant view of existence to the extent that they treat existence as an ultimate given that is not further derivable or explicable. Traditionally, however, they have taken '-exists' to be a very general kind of predicate. It is not a real or determining predicate, for it does not add any determinate feature or content to the concept of an object. Rather, '-exists' is a non-determining predicate: it designates that activity which is a condition of things having any determining predicates at all. Existence is here understood as 'active' existence or 'actualisation': the ultimate givenness of existence is a matter of the ultimate givenness of some kind of activity of actualisation that is an essential constituent in the nature of things.

Materialism defines all that exists in terms of matter and energy and looks to the natural sciences for an account of what matter and energy are. The activity of existence is nothing other than what is given in the dynamics of the material world, and no further explanations are to be sought because to do so would be to step outside that world. By contrast, naturalists such as John Dewey take a broader view of what exists than materialists. They usually include in their account of what exists non-material properties or relations, various kinds of abstract entities such as numbers, sets and propositions, and also human enterprises such as art. Moreover, Dewey defines all the different things there are as 'events' or components of the dynamic interaction of 'events'. To exist is to occur, to be an event. Yet, like materialists, Dewey holds existence to be an ultimate, underivable given. The rich and diverse world of nature must be studied on its own terms. As he strikingly states of the inexplicable givenness of active events:

> Immediacy of existence is ineffable. But there is nothing mystical about such ineffability; it expresses the fact that of direct existence it is futile to say anything to one's self and impossible to say anything to another . . . Things in their immediacy are unknown and unknowable, not because they are remote or behind some impenetrable veil of ideas, but because knowledge has no concern with them.[1]

In the context of such a minimalist view of active existence, it is not surprising that the Hume–Kant view of existence becomes central in contemporary metaphysics. It finds its most influential elaboration in the work of Gottlob Frege, who, in a series of publications from 1879 onwards, founded what has become known as the school of 'logical analysis' or 'analytical

---

1. John Dewey, *Experience and Nature* (La Salle, IL: Open Court, 1929), 85–6.

philosophy'.[2] To this school A. N. Whitehead and Bertrand Russell made a decisive contribution in their *Principia Mathematica* (1910–13), and partly as a result, logical analysis has become the dominant philosophical movement in the English-speaking world. Because logical analysis and its implications are a central if often unrecognised concern of strong as well as weak theorists in modern metaphysics, a brief account of some of the basic features of Frege's position is relevant here.

Frege's fundamental idea is to generalise the mathematical function beyond mathematics and to use it as a model or analogue for the analysis of the logical structure of propositions. In a function such as $fx = x^2$ the variable or sign of the argument is x, whereas the full formula, function or schema specifies a rule, 'is the number whose square is', by which to determine fx. Thus we might construct a variable sentence $f(x) = 4$, which, given $fx = x^2$, is true if $x = 2$ or -2, and false if otherwise. The function or schema explains what is going to be done; but nothing is done until something is put in the slot marked x, that is, until the variable or sign of the argument is given its value. Before that is done, the function, schema or rule is, Frege says, 'incomplete' or 'unsatisfied' or 'unsaturated'. When the variable is given its value, the function is 'complete', 'satisfied' or 'saturated', producing a determinate sign.

Frege's analysis of propositions follows the structure of the mathematical function. The subject in subject–predicate propositions has the status of the variable, while the predicate has the status of the function-schema. This analysis gives rise to the so-called modern predicate. Subject–predicate sentences such as 'Socrates is human' are not to be analysed in the triadic fashion of traditional logic as subject: Socrates, copula: is, predicate: human. Rather, such sentences are to be analysed as having the structure, subject: Socrates, modern predicate: is human. Even a one-place predicate such as '- is human' is elucidated in terms of the dyadic relation 'x is a member of y', symbolised as xEy, which is the mathematical counterpart of the relation 'x has (as one of its properties) y'. Propositions, in short, are to be analysed in terms of the binary structure of the function.

This approach to the nature of propositions is thus called 'logical analysis' or 'analytical philosophy'. As will emerge, the term 'analysis' also indicates that Frege and his followers hold that their interpretation of the function allows them to dispense with any notion of activity, in particular the Kantian and idealist notion of cognition as an activity of synthesis. So great are the advantages offered by the functional analysis of propositions in the

---

2. Most of Frege's main writings are available in *The Frege Reader*, trans. and ed. Michael Beaney (Oxford: Blackwell, 1997).

field of logic that there can be little doubt that Frege's work is revolutionary, as Whitehead and Russell were among the first to recognise. The enormous metaphysical significance it has often been credited with is most clearly registered in the way it can be used to analyse existence statements.

The basic point is that propositions can be hierarchically ordered according to the range of values of the variables of their arguments. First-order propositions are those whose arguments are individual objects. That is, they are propositions whose arguments are individual objects and that contain predicates such as '. . . is a horse'. Second-order propositions are those whose arguments are not individual objects but first-order functions. Now, existence statements are statements that contain, explicitly or implicitly, either an 'existential quantifier' of the form 'there is. . .' or 'something is. . .', or a 'universal quantifier' of the form 'everything is. . .' Frege's claim is that statements such as 'There is (there exists) a horse' are second-order propositions that state of first-order concepts that they have actual objects falling under them; that is, that certain first-order propositions have a reference.

On this analysis, statements of the form 'x exists' are not, as one might ordinarily suppose, statements about x in the sense that they predicate the existence of x. Existence is not a predicate of x, for x is not an individual object but a first-order class or kind. Indeed, on this analysis, existence-statements do not ascribe any predicate or property to individual objects at all. Instead, as has been shown, statements of the form 'x exists' are second-order statements that refer to a property or class p that x falls under. That is, such statements say of a class or kind p that there are objects falling under it; or, to put it otherwise, they say about a certain kind of object that there are objects of that kind. Statements of the form 'x exists' are thus to be interpreted as quantificational or extensional statements about a class, to the effect that the class is not empty but has instances or examples.

Existence is thus exhaustively definable as the satisfaction or instantiation of the quantified variables of the proposition. To exist is to answer a description. Whether one is talking about prime numbers or about concrete entities such as stones and people, statements of existence are defined in the same way: as saying that something satisfies a description. In this respect, logical analysis can be regarded as putting a premium on rationality; for the existent is now through and through describable in terms of its predicates, with no mysterious residues. The logical subject of a proposition is drained of any independent features of its own outside those defined by the schema of functional predicates. The schema alone determines the content of the logical subject of a proposition, so the subject is divested of any elements not imported by the modern predicate. Hence the subject is philosophically minimalised: it has no nature or activity of its own in virtue of which it is what it is. The existence of Socrates, for example, is not an opportunity for abstruse reflections on the nature of 'being' as in traditional metaphysics, but is nothing other than the substitution or instantiation of a variable. It is not surprising that the development of analytic philosophy is marked by 'the linguistic turn':[3] the focus of interest shifts from questions about what it is to exist to questions about the nature of the meaning of propositions and what it is to make true or false assertions.

There can be no doubt that the weak, quantificational or extensional theory of existence has some very significant features. First, weak theory gives a meaning to 'x exists' such that a precisely corresponding meaning can be given to 'x does not exist'; for statements of existence and non-existence alike can be analysed as a matter of the quantification of the variable of the function. Thus, for example, the statement 'mermaids do not exist' can be understood as a quantificational or extensional statement about the term or class 'mermaids', to the effect that such a term or class has no instances or objects falling under it. There is no danger on this analysis of construing statements such as 'mermaids do not exist' as having the contradictory form 'Something has being which does not belong to the class of being' or 'Something has being which is not.'

A second and more important feature of quantificational or extensional existence is that it accounts for the distinction between concept and existence in a clear and straightforward fashion. Questions such as 'What is added to the possible when existence is asserted?', 'What is it about the object of a concept that is more than its definition?' or 'What is being as opposed to non-being?' are answered by the conceptually primitive notion of instantiation. Once again, there is no place for abstruse metaphysical analyses of 'being' here. Indeed, it is evident that a quantificational analysis of existence is not properly a *theory* of existence at all. Existence is simply removed from the realm of reflection and replaced by an analysis of the logical structure of propositions.

Because the logical analysis of existence defines all things in terms of the function, the function takes on the status of a theory of reality or ontology in the Frege–Russell tradition. It becomes the fundamental, irreducible ontological principle beyond or behind which it is not possible to go. Functional relations are interpreted as ultimate logical objects that are given, not constructed. They are found, not made. The world is a given world of forms (Frege) or given relational complexes of facts (Russell), and no further principle of unity is needed. The order of things is complete, eternal and fixed, and individual instances of order have no special features

---

3. See Richard Rorty (ed.), *The Linguistic Turn: Recent Essays in Philosophical Method* (Chicago: University of Chicago Press, 1967).

of their own other than those defined by the possibilities of the function. This position is usually called 'logical realism'.

Some indication of the power and range of the logical analysis of the function is given by the fact that, including Frege's, at least four basic types of generalisation of the mathematical function have been developed in modern philosophy. In all versions, the basic model is mathematics, where, given a particular function or rule, such as the successor operator $n + 1$, it is possible to derive any series of natural numbers simply by following the rule. The crucial claim is that in mathematics, rule following requires no reference to any special activity of synthesis or decision making on the part of a directing subject, cognitive or otherwise, for the connectivity of functional order is an ultimate and irreducible given. The logical structure of the function is thus held to define a set of 'operations' that, because they are independent of any appeal to a distinct actualising activity, constitute an 'automatic process'.[4]

The four types of generalisation of the mathematical function characteristic of analytical philosophy are different versions of what we shall generically call a theory of 'algorithmic process', a theory of the 'algorithmic function', or 'algorism' for short. We use these terms in the largest and loosest sense, in complete independence from the variety of meanings they have in mathematics and computer science, to indicate that all reference to existence as involving any special kind of activity of actualisation is dispensed with.[5] In one way or another, the relational structure of the function is held to provide an exhaustive account of its nature and to constitute an automatic process or operation. The point is that the analytical generalisation of the mathematical function is always at bottom a generalisation of the mathematical function understood in one way or another as an automaton, even though this fact is nowadays so much taken for granted as to be almost invisible and has even been claimed to be 'the natural ontological attitude'.[6]

The first type of generalisation of the mathematical function is Frege's neo-Kantian version, where the mathematical function defines the logical structure of the concept and is the primitive and underivable principle of 'thought'. The logical structure of the concept replaces all the complex

---

4. The terms are Wittgenstein's. For his own view of 'process', see his *Remarks on the Foundations of Mathematics*, ed. G. H. von Wright, R. Rhees and G. E. M. Anscombe (Cambridge, MA: MIT Press, 1983), esp. 68, 69, 95, 246.
5. In employing the term 'algorithm' and its cognates, we would stress that we dispense with any connotations relating this term to some principle of finitude or constructivity, and that we retain only its connotation of law-likeness.
6. See Arthur Fine, 'The Natural Ontological Attitude', in his *The Shaky Game* (Chicago: University of Chicago Press, 1986), 112–35.

machinery of Kant's analysis of the conditions of cognition, and, in particular, Kant's theory of the synthetic subject is relegated to the realm of psychology: meanings are intuitively grasped, determinate 'senses', and identity of reference is held to be accounted for by functional-logical structure. Secondly, Russell generalises the mathematical function in an empiricist context as the 'propositional function'. Although, as in Frege, functional-logical structure is taken as primitive, reference or instantiation is not, and the propositional function is held to require a theory of reference based on the subject's sensory acquaintance with the world. The propositional function is here the cognitive rule whereby the objects of ordinary experience are logically constructed out of 'sense-data'. Thirdly, the later Wittgenstein extends the model of the mathematical function beyond cognition (to which it was limited in his *Tractatus*) and generalises it as a theory of the nature of language and social practice or action. Just as following the rules of a game is what constitutes a game, so by following the rules of a language or social practice we constitute ourselves and our world. The Fregean dissolution of the cognitive, synthesising subject – which goes hand-in-hand with the dissolution of the logical subject of a proposition and its reduction to the mere instantiation of a predicate – is here extended to the realm of discourse and action. Once it is recognised that to understand a rule is to operate with it, and that the rule itself constitutes a decision-making procedure, there is no need to appeal to a principle of connection over and above the rule itself. Human subjects or persons are thus nothing more than the effects of those functional structures that define their behaviour. Finally, there is the most recent type of generalisation of the mathematical function, which extends it to the realm of physical nature. All natural entities, including human beings, are exhaustively interpreted as the products of complex automatic or algorithmic processes. It is the business of natural science to define these algorithmic processes in terms of the laws of physics and of evolution, and they are presumably contingent in that they have themselves evolved out of antecedent algorithmic processes in the past history of the cosmos. In contrast to the traditional kind of naturalism defended by philosophers such as John Dewey, this fourth type of functional generalisation can be called 'algorithmic naturalism'. It attempts wholly to assimilate activity to automatic process – generally understood as the inexplicably given, law-like regularity of the natural order – yet it does not necessarily involve the materialist claim that all automatic processes are purely physical in nature, and it can even hold (coherently or not) that there are 'choice machines' which are programmed to be variable and unpredictable. What nevertheless seems to be agreed upon both by contemporary materialists and by naturalists (even those like Richard Rorty who analyse human nature in terms of some given kind of creative activity) is that at least physical nature is exhaustively definable by what they take to be the algorithmic processes uncovered by natural science.[7]

Strong Theories of Existence and the Principle of Reason

The claims of logical analysis do not, however, impress the strong theorists of existence, the speculative philosophers. For speculative philosophy holds that existence is much more than the silent, featureless pendant to ontological-functional structure. Speculative philosophy denies the primitivity of the function, at least as that is usually understood, and thus it refuses to assimilate the 'is' of existence to the 'is' of mere quantification. The reason for this resides in the three key differences between speculative and other kinds of philosophy. The first and most basic difference can be stated as follows.

All philosophical accounts of the nature of existence attempt to define it in terms of that which is incapable of further demonstration, that which is not further derivable, that which is ultimate in the order of analysis, over against which anything else can be shown to be derivable, partial or abstract. In contrast to other kinds of philosophy, however, speculative metaphysics is characterised first and foremost by the fact that it pushes philosophy's commitment to intellectual inquiry to its limits. That is, speculative metaphysics is uncompromising in its commitment to the principle of reason.

This is the principle *nihil est sine ratione*, 'nothing is (or exists) without a reason': there is always a reason and a reason can always be found. The principle of reason has its corollary in the principle of the unity of truth: namely, that all features of experience constitute a rational order in the sense that their nature and interconnection can be rendered intelligible or explicable. The entire enterprise of speculative metaphysics is an attempt to discover reasons for that which is given in experience. What this means can only be understood by means of a 'definition-in-use'; that is, by looking at the way the principle is actually employed in speculative metaphysics. It is in relation to a theory of existence that the role of the principle of reason in defining the specific character of speculative metaphysics is clearest.

---

7. A well-known representative of algorithmic naturalism is Daniel Dennett; see especially his *Elbow Room* (Cambridge, MA: MIT Press, 1984) and *Freedom Evolves* (New York: Viking, 2003). However, some kind of algorithmic naturalism seems to lie at the back of the work of many North American philosophers, such as Donald Davidson and Arthur Fine as well as Richard Rorty. It is the most up-to-date version of that kind of 'scientism', dominant in North America, which leaves to an algorithmically interpreted natural science the explanation of most things.

In bringing the principle of reason to bear on the question of the nature of existence, speculative metaphysics puts to logical analysis what might be called the strong question of existence: 'Why is there that which answers a description?', 'Why is there instantiation?' This a question about the nature of givenness, about what it means for something to be given. Thus, as will emerge, speculative metaphysics examines the concept of what it is to be given, or the givenness of the given, very closely indeed. At its most general level the strong question is usually put in the following way: 'Why is there that which exists?', 'Why does anything at all exist?', or (in Leibniz's formulation) 'Why is there something rather than nothing?'[8] It can be summarised as 'Why is there existence?', understood as a shorthand for the speculative inquiry into whether or not there is a common feature or features shared by anything that answers a description that explains the fact that it does so.

The strong question of existence is at first sight an odd kind of question, and one that weak theorists do not think it is possible to answer. It is completely intelligible, nevertheless, and as we shall see, Hume, Kant and Frege readily grant its intelligibility. Whether it is either legitimate or fruitful to ask such a question is of course another matter. But at least the peculiarity of the strong question helps to indicate the specific enterprise that speculative metaphysics is.

For what speculative metaphysics is looking for under the rubric of the principle of reason is a self-explanatory theory of existence. The principle of reason does not allow speculative metaphysics to accept an infinite regress of reasons in respect of existence, for in the nature of the case such a regress does not answer the strong question. By contrast, a self-explanatory theory of existence would be one that is ultimate in that nothing further is required to answer the strong question. Such a theory would completely satisfy intellectual inquiry into the reasons why anything at all exists. Thus a self-explanatory theory of existence, if there can be such, is definable as one that is not further derivable or demonstrable because it provides all the reasons required to explain why there is existence. There are, admittedly, many existent things that we do not know of, and there is a great deal about the existent things we know of that we do not understand. Yet that is not what is at issue here. The only claim of a self-explanatory account of existence is that any failure of knowledge or understanding on our part is not a failure in our knowledge or understanding of the reasons why there is existence.

---

8. G. W. Leibniz, 'The Principles of Nature and Grace, Based on Reason' (1714), in *Leibniz: Philosophical Papers and Letters*, trans. and ed. Leroy E. Loemker (Dordrecht: Reidel, 2nd edn, 1976), 639.

This is not to suggest that self-explanatoriness is the same as proof. Not only have a great variety of self-explanatory theories of existence been offered in the speculative tradition, from Plato in the fourth century BCE through to C. S. Peirce, A. N. Whitehead and Martin Heidegger in the twentieth century, but the question of what constitutes a self-explanatory theory is itself part of what is at issue among them. For these reasons among others, the very idea of a self-explanatory theory of existence is nowadays usually met by weak theorists with puzzlement, hostility, even mockery. An initial account of the way in which the present writer understands some of the considerations involved in the search for a self-explanatory theory of existence will help to indicate what is at issue here.

As already mentioned, what a self-explanatory theory of existence is has been understood in various ways in the speculative tradition. Most typically, it has been identified with the self-evident in the sense of the absolutely certain, whether this is understood, for example, as the *anhypotheton* or indubitable that is the final achievement of metaphysical inquiry (Plato); as the *a priori* necessities of thought that provide clear and distinct ideas (Descartes, Leibniz); as some kind of intuition that can only be arrived at by reflective struggle (Bergson); or as a special method of deduction (Kant, Hegel). The overconfidence characteristic of these sorts of approaches has given speculative inquiry a bad name, for in the last resort such approaches fail to take into account the fact that what is understood by a self-explanatory theory of existence undergoes constant revision in the speculative tradition. There is, however, an alternative view of self-explanatory theories that has been developed in the speculative tradition, particularly in the work of Schelling, Peirce and Whitehead. It has had a huge influence in philosophy generally over the last two hundred years.

This alternative approach involves a specific methodology. It abandons the idea that there are any special starting points or foundations for metaphysical reflection. In consequence, it is epistemically anti-foundationalist. Unlike self-evidential approaches such as that of Plato or rationalists such as Descartes and Leibniz, it is oriented, not to the traditional understanding of mathematics as based on self-evidently true axioms, but to the postulatory method of modern mathematics. More widely, it defines what a self-explanatory theory of existence is in the context of the concept of investigative reason – as found in medieval philosophy, often under the rubric of 'natural theology', and as explicitly elaborated in modern philosophy by the mathematical logicians Peirce and Whitehead under the rubric of 'fallibilism'.[9] This position has a number of significant features that should

---

9. See A. N. Whitehead, *Process and Reality: An Essay in Cosmology* (corrected edn, New York: The Free Press, 1978), ch. 1, 'Speculative Philosophy', for a clear and succinct

go some way towards allaying the unease and suspicion that strong theories of existence so often encounter.

First, the speculative search for a self-explanatory theory of existence does not carry with it any unacceptable assumptions about the scope of the principle of reason. There can be no doubt that speculative metaphysics is rationalist to the extent that it rejects what Peirce mockingly calls the 'no hypothesis' hypothesis.[10] That is, it rejects the essentially sceptical theory or hypothesis that there are things that no theory or hypothesis can explain. It rejects the hypothesis that there is anything that is ultimately inexplicable, that there is anything about which no explanatory theory or hypothesis can be entertained. Thus the view that existence is a mere given is repudiated as inconsistent with the entire enterprise of inquiry. Philosophy, if it is anything, is the search for explanations. Nevertheless, the principle of reason or the rejection of the 'no hypothesis' hypothesis is not a dogma of speculative metaphysics. There is no assumption here that the way we think is identical with the real, or accurately reflects the real. The speculative project is not justified by the principle of reason, but is an inquiry into the status or range of application of that principle. Indeed, it is an attempt to determine the very scope of inquiry. Speculative philosophy thus turns the principle of reason into an experimental, hypothetical principle or postulate, for it investigates just how far reason can go in the analysis of the nature of existence. The purpose of the speculative project is to elaborate ultimate hypotheses out of experience and to test them in relation to experience. The principle or postulate of reason has the status of an ideal experiment, at the outset of which there is no assumption that there is such a thing as an ultimate reason, nor, if there is, that it is self-explanatory. Hence speculative inquiry does not assume that whatever might be self-explanatory or whatever provides a reason must itself have the nature of a reason, for that which provides reasons is not necessarily itself a reason. Whether there is ultimate explicability and what it might be can only be determined in the course of inquiry. But at least the speculative project keeps on the table the strong question about what it is to exist, which weak theorists are content to ignore.

It follows, secondly, that speculative inquiry into a self-explanatory account of existence is not inextricably tied to the kind of claims critics have sometimes read into strong questions such as 'Why is there anything at all?',

---

statement of the experimental and fallibilist understanding of speculative metaphysics derived from the postulatory method of modern mathematics.
10. See C. S. Peirce, MS 950, c. 1890, Harvard University Library, quoted in Helmut Pape, *The Irreducibility of Chance and the Openness of the Future: The Logical Function of Idealism in Peirce's Philosophy of Nature* (Roskilde: Roskilde Universitetscenter, 1996), 2.

or 'Why is there something rather than nothing?' Such questions, it is suggested, depend not just upon the debatable claim that absolute nothingness or vacuity is conceivable but upon the false claim that absolute nothingness or vacuity is in some sense prior to the fact that there is something, so the fact that there is something is held to need a special kind of explanation.[11] Such questions thus appear to ignore the fact that all reflection is based on the givenness of the real. As will emerge, however, the speculative tradition distinguishes between 'nothing' as absolute vacuity (*omnino nihil*, whether conceivable or not), 'nothing' as negation (*nihil negativum*), and 'nothing' as 'no-thing', understood either as an unlimited power and plenitude that is not itself a 'thing' but the ground of all specific 'things' (*nihil per excellentiam*) or as an unconditioned potentiality. Moreover, we shall see that the speculative tradition is divided between the so-called 'ontological tradition' which maintains the principle of the priority of the actual to the potential, and the 'meontological tradition' which maintains the priority of the potential to the actual.[12] It will become evident that in both traditions, it is various versions of 'nothing', not as vacuity but as 'no-thing', which have played a significant role in the elaboration of a self-explanatory principle of existence. These two different traditions do not depend upon arguments about the conceivability of absolute nothingness, nor upon any childish assumption about the priority of absolute nothingness. Rather, what unites them is the attempt to see just how far reflection can go in the analysis of the actual. They begin, as we all do, *in medias res*. Speculative inquiry attempts to discover if a description of what actuality is can lead to the discovery of any features of experience that might explain why the actual is, or (to put it another way) why the actual persists. Thus speculative inquiry does no more in the first instance than investigate the possibility of a self-explanatory theory of existence, without any prior entanglements in doctrines of absolute nothingness.

In this context, thirdly, speculative metaphysics is 'speculative' in the following sense. Without claiming any privileged starting point, *a priori* or

---

11. For the view that absolute nothingness is inconceivable, see Henri Bergson, *Creative Evolution* (1907), trans. A. Mitchell (London: Macmillan, 1911), ch. 4. For the view that absolute nothing is conceived by speculative philosophers as prior to anything, see, for example, Robert Nozick, *Philosophical Explanations* (Cambridge, MA: Harvard University Press, 1981), ch. 2. For an excellent critique of the sophisticated but largely irrelevant treatments of the speculative concept of the self-explanatory perpetrated by some contemporary analytical philosophers, see Arthur Witherall, *The Problem of Existence* (Aldershot: Ashgate, 2002), chs 1 and 2.
12. See Emil Fackenheim, *Metaphysics and Historicity* (Milwaukee, WI: Marquette University Press, 1961), 28–34. Fackenheim constructs the term 'meontological' from the Greek *me on*, meaning indeterminate being or activity, as opposed to *ouk on* or non-being.

phenomenological, and based like any inquiry on faith (Latin, *fides:* trust) in the principle of reason, it utilises some striking, specific notions held to have wide application in significant areas of experience as models or analogies for self-explanatory activity. By generalising such models or analogies, it attempts to construct the most inclusive description possible of the nature of things, and as far as possible to provide a self-explanatory account of existence. The primacy attached to 'mind' in, say, Hegel, would be but one example of the generalisation of a model or analogy among many; other examples have been will, events, time, and so on. Such a metaphysics is 'speculative', not in the German idealist sense as a matter of the realisation of the real in and by the mind, cognitive or absolute, but in three specific senses. First, it depends for its cogency on its ostensively demonstrable fit with experience. Secondly, in view of the intrinsic historical relativity of its models, it does not claim to be anything but experimental and revisable or fallible. Thus, thirdly, it is self-referentially consistent in that it makes no claims to its own complete or final truth.

What specific methods of generalisation or analogy are employed here, and what criteria are used in the determination of specific cases of 'fit', can be considered later. In the meantime, one great advantage of this non-dogmatic, experimental, generalising and fallibilist view of the speculative enterprise is that it enables speculative metaphysics reflexively to acknowledge not only that self-explanation is not the same as proof, but also that both are subject to historical change. Further, it helps to bring out that the fundamental concepts employed by speculative metaphysics are not, as they are so often mistakenly taken to be, clear and distinct ideas that accurately reflect the real and provide us with absolute certainties. Rather, they are essentially and virtuously vague: they are experimental, open to development and revision, and await coordination and assignment to their proper spheres. As will emerge, it is matter of considerable debate in the speculative tradition just how precise or determinate self-explanatory concepts of existence can be. Finally, the method of experimental generalisation indicates that the speculative project does not primarily rest on any appeal to the logical analysis of existence-statements. This is one of the chief ways in which, since Frege, those sympathetic to speculative metaphysics have defended a strong theory of existence, arguing that the proper logical analysis of the 'is' of existence demonstrates that it is irreducible to the 'is' of instantiation – a claim that has been strongly resisted by weak theorists.[13] Yet whatever the merits of

---

13. See Gottlob Frege, 'Dialogue with Pünjer', in *Posthumous Writings*, ed. Hans Hermes et al. (Oxford: Blackwell, 1979), 53–67; W.V.O. Quine, 'On What There Is', in *From A Logical Point of View* (Cambridge, MA: Harvard University Press, 1951), 1–25; C. F. J. Williams, *What is Existence?* (Oxford: Clarendon Press, 1981); Michael Dummett, 'Existence', in *The Seas of Language* (Oxford: Clarendon Press, 1993),

the arguments presented on both sides, speculative metaphysics elaborates strong theories of existence that are usually established and defended on quite different grounds. The first is the concern with the self-explanatory. The second arises out of that concern: it is the concept of activity.

Activity

Like traditional (non-algorithmic) forms of materialism and naturalism, speculative metaphysics regards existence as essentially involving activity of some kind. Existence is understood as 'active' existence or 'actualisation', and '-exists' is taken as a very general predicate that refers to that activity of actualisation without which there cannot be anything at all. It is in this context that the use of the term 'being' for the subject matter both of speculative metaphysics and of traditional forms of materialism and naturalism should be understood. 'Being' is the English translation of the Greek terms *einai* and *ousia* and the Latin terms *esse* and *ens*. *Einai* and *esse* are the infinitive form of the verb 'to be'. *Ousia* and *ens* designate a determinate entity of any kind (the word 'entity' is derived from *ens*). The verbal noun 'being' is used for both pairs of terms,[14] and, like them, it can be variously interpreted as designating the sheer presence of something; as designating the impact or efficacy of something in respect of the world around it; or as designating that activity in virtue of which things are what they are.[15] The crucial thing is to recognise that, contrary to the popular view, 'being' does not denote a mysterious, impalpable abstraction. As a verbal noun, it is intended to capture the active existence of things. Thus a good general rule for the modern English speaker is to understand 'being' as denoting activity of some sort. The only exception to this rule is Parmenides, who held that all being is utterly fixed presence without any kind of movement at all. Indeed, despite popular claims to the contrary, there is in the history of Western speculative philosophy no such thing as a static or non-dynamical theory of *actualisation* on account of the very nature of that concept.

In contemporary usage, the term 'philosophies of being' is generally reserved for speculative theories of existence as an activity of actualisation.

277–307. For a brilliant critical treatment of weak theory from the viewpoint of modern logic, see Peter Geach, 'Form and Existence', in *God and the Soul* (London: Routledge, 1969), 42–64; also Julian Roberts, *The Logic of Reflection* (New Haven: Yale University Press, 1992), chs 1 and 2.

14. For an indispensable account of the complexities surrounding the philosophical use of the Greek term *ousia*, see C. C. J. Webb, *God and Personality* (London: Allen and Unwin, 1918), Lecture II, 34–60

15. See the excellent discussion of 'The Notion of Being' in Christopher Stead's remarkable book, *Divine Substance* (Oxford: Clarendon Press, 1977), 7–19.

For speculative metaphysics is distinguished from all forms of materialism and naturalism on account of its search for a self- explanatory theory of active existence under the rule of the principle of reason. It is primarily on account of the search for the intelligible that speculative metaphysics holds existence to be an activity of actualisation.

The general line of thought here goes something like this. It is evident that the weak theory of existence as quantification, because it takes instantiation to be an underivable given, does not and cannot answer the questions: 'Why is there instantiation?', 'Why is there that which answers a description?', 'Why are our concepts or predicates satisfied?' Now, on account of the gap between the conceptual and the actual, concepts or predicates are not enough to answer the question of instantiation. To cross that gap, something more than concepts or predicates is required, something that provides an account of instantiation in terms of the actualisation of concepts. Yet actualisation, if it is anything, is an activity in some sense of the term. It follows that, beyond concepts, some account of existence as activity, as active existence or actualisation, is needed to explain the difference between the conceptual and the actual. Questions about existence cannot stop at questions about concepts or predicates, because concepts or predicates can never be primary. To use the traditional formulation, 'existence precedes essence', so questions about the intelligibility of the world of experience cannot stop at questions about essences, concepts or predicates.

In asking the strong question of existence, therefore, speculative metaphysics asks whether or not the quest for intelligibility can be carried beyond questions of given essence or structure. Either the activity that is existence is unintelligible or it is intelligible. If it is intelligible, existence must in some way be self-explanatory: there must be some identifiable feature or features of existence, besides instantiation, that explain why there is instantiation. Whatever they might be, such a feature or features would be the constitutive elements of what for convenience can be labelled the ultimate or actualising principle of existence.

Admittedly, the concept of an ultimate, actualising principle of existence or activity is often objected to on the grounds that questions such as 'Why is there activity at all?', or 'Why is there actualisation?', are nonsense. For how could there be an account of activity or actualisation that does not itself appeal to a prior activity for its intelligibility? Yet such an objection is far too hasty. It ignores the requirement that the speculative search for the self-explanatory lays upon philosophical inquiry. This is the requirement that whatever is held to be an ultimate or primordial principle *must possess in its nature the reasons needed to explain its own existence or activity and that of anything else.* In other words, a primordial principle that is self-explanatory, if there be such, is an activity of a kind that is intelligible because it contains the conditions of existence in its own nature. Thus an ultimate, self-explanatory principle, if there be such, is a 'necessary' principle: its existence would be 'necessary' in the sense that its nature is such that it exists necessarily. This is not to say that 'Necessarily, a self-explanatory principle exists.' Rather, it is to say that 'If there is a self-explanatory principle of existence, it exists necessarily on account of its nature.' There is nothing nonsensical or dogmatic here. There is only the speculative rejection of the 'no hypothesis' hypothesis and the search for some feature or features in the primordial principle of activity that provides the reasons for why it is primordial.

This account of a self-explanatory actualising principle leaves completely open what the nature of such a principle might be, and we shall see that there are numerous versions in speculative metaphysics. This account does not prejudice the question as to whether the actualising principle is simple or complex, nor the question as to what its relation is to that which is actualised: whether the actualising principle (or set of principles) is completely independent of that which is actualised, or completely inseparable from it, or even in some way identical with it. Yet this account does mean, first, that the actualising principle must be active, at least in the sense that it is the principle of the actualisation of all things, the origin of their existence, without which there would be nothing at all. Secondly, this account means that the actualising principle must be rational or intelligible, at least to the extent that it provides the reason or reasons for why there is existence (even if it need not itself be a reason, and so may be held to transcend the limited range of human reason). In speculative metaphysics, the reason that there is anything that answers a description resides in the activity of actualisation of the self-explanatory principle, however that is understood.

A number of caveats need to be entered here. First, in analysing the self-explanatory principle of actualisation, many speculative metaphysicians – Peirce is an example – distinguish 'being' from 'existence'. They maintain that existence is only one aspect of the real, whether existence is understood either as instantiation or in its original Latin sense as *ex-sistere*, as denoting that which 'stands outside of itself' and so is essentially related to others by the relation of difference. They employ the active verbal noun 'being' as a wider term to denote anything that 'has an effect' in the sense that it plays a role in, or is a factor in, or manifests itself as a feature of, the real. Thus, as we shall see, Peirce holds that being in the sense of unconditioned activity is prior to existence as difference, for in his view unconditioned activity is the origin of differentiation. Others hold that, while God is a reality in the sense of the actualising principle of all existence, God is not an existent; for they hold that the actualising principle is not dependent on, and so not essentially related to, anything else. Again, some speculative metaphysicians maintain that, while universals or forms such as 'human nature' have being or are active features of reality, they are not existents; for although they are essential, formative constituents of the nature of determinate individuals, they are not themselves determinate individuals. For these reasons, we will use the term 'being' and 'beings' rather than 'existence' and 'existent' whenever those terms are appropriate to the type of entity under consideration.

Secondly, we would reiterate that the concept of an actualising principle does not at all mean that there is one unique kind of being that contains all the reasons for its existence in its own nature, and that does so quite independently of anything else. This is the traditional philosophical concept of 'God' that was fully articulated in the medieval period and is characteristic of the Judaic, Islamic and Christian philosophical traditions. As we shall see, however, it is by no means the only concept of God available in these traditions, nor is it the only concept of a self-explanatory actualising principle elaborated in Western speculative philosophy. For example, some speculative metaphysicians from Plato and Plotinus to the present have maintained that an ultimate, actualising principle exists in the sense that there is that which answers such a description, but that it exists 'beyond being'. In their view, that is to say, the ultimate, actualising principle of being is not itself a distinct entity (as in some accounts of God), but exists on an altogether higher level of reality. Again, whether or not the actualising principle is independent of anything else is, we shall emphasise, a matter of intense debate in the speculative tradition, for it involves the whole, long-debated question as to the relation of the actualising principle to that which is actualised.

Thirdly, the concept of an actualising principle of existence is not to be assumed primarily to be a causal principle, efficient (physical) or final. Although we shall see that many speculative metaphysicians have good reasons for employing the concept of causality to elucidate the role of the actualising principle, others such as Heidegger have denied that it is to be understood causally. Either way, within speculative philosophy it is the account given of the actualising principle that defines the nature of reasons, causes and their relation. This is why the active principle of existence is often termed, not a cause, but a 'principle' in the scholastic tradition, and a 'ground' in the German idealist tradition. The concept of cause is a specific variety of the genus 'principle' (*principium*; the Latin translation of the Greek *arche*, origin or beginning) or the genus 'ground' (*Grund*). 'Cause' implies a greater degree of dependence on the part of the effect than do the concepts of 'principle'[16] or 'ground'. We have chosen to use the term 'principle' to

---

16. See Aquinas, *Summa Theologiae*, 1a, q. 33, a. 1, ad 1.

designate whatever is taken to be the primordial activity of actualisation because it is more familiar to English readers. Also, it leaves completely open the question of the degree of dependence that things have in relation to the primordial activity of actualisation, whatever that might be.

The many different ways in which the self-explanatory actualising principle can be understood will be the subject of discussion throughout this book[17] and so may for the moment be postponed. The crucial point here is that the whole enterprise of speculative metaphysics will remain unintelligible unless it is recognised that the concepts of self-explanatoriness and of the activity of actualisation are inseparable, and that at its core Western philosophy is a history of the relation between, and the development of, those concepts. The strong theories of existence characteristic of speculative philosophy are essentially theories about the self-explanatory nature of the activity of actualisation.

This at least makes evident why speculative philosophers are unembarrassed by the fact that they cannot claim the convenience of giving to statements of existence and non-existence a precisely corresponding meaning. Whatever may suffice in more limited contexts of analysis, in the context of the strong view that existence is primarily a self-explanatory activity of actualisation (however that might be defined), affirmative existential statements are only possible where there is such activity. It follows that negative existential statements register the lack, absence or privation of active existence in some respect. Active existence is held to be their ultimate basis, to be prior to existential quantification, and to make existential quantification possible. There must be that which is, has been, or will be active for the instantiation of predicates to be possible. Thus speculative philosophers do not regard the weak or quantificational analysis of existence as offering an adequate theory of the nature of the real. What a self-explanatory theory seeks in respect of quantification is an account of what makes it possible.

Nevertheless, active existence is one of the features of the concern with the self-explanatory which in the eyes of some weak theorists vitiates the speculative enterprise *tout court*. A striking argument in support of this view has been strenuously developed in analytical philosophy. It is based on the claim that the logic of the function renders redundant any theories of active existence, speculative or otherwise.

This argument may be called the objection from relations. It is aimed at the view that the distinction between a thing and its qualities or properties, or in more traditional terminology, between particulars and universals, is a fundamental distinction. Such a view gives rise to those questions that

---

17. The book Bradley planned to write but never did (see Acknowledgements, p. ix). – ed.

have for so long fuelled speculative and other kinds of metaphysics, such as 'What is the relation that holds between a particular and a universal?', or 'What is the bond that unites a particular to its various properties?' The kind of answer speculative philosophers have usually given to these questions is best explained by reference to traditional or pre-Fregean logic, which reinforces the distinction between things and properties, universals and particulars, by taking the copula 'is' in a sentence such as 'Socrates is mortal' to be a distinct part of the sentence that binds together subject and predicate in a judgement. The copula is treated as a third additional item. But taken as an additional item along with its relata, there is nothing about the relation as stated by the copula that explains its connectivity or relating power. Thus is generated the strong question 'Why (or how) do relations relate?' This is a question that speculative philosophers have usually answered by appeal to a connective principle or activity of actualisation that is more than any specific relation because it is the principle of all specific relations. As such, it lies outside the usual scope of logical analysis.

To the speculative appeal to activity the weak theorist has a ready reply: that the concept of a mathematical function is a concept of the intrinsic connectivity of relations in virtue of the very nature of a functional rule. For one of the fundamental features of the Fregean generalisation of the function is that the distinction between things and their properties, between particulars and universals, or between terms and relations, is no longer a fundamental ontological distinction. Because a particular is nothing else than the mere instantiation of its predicates, what is designated as a particular is simply a matter of practical convenience.[18] Functional rules or modern predicates are intrinsically relational in that, as noted earlier, they connect one variable to another, and they are now the fundamental category in terms of which all entities are to be described. In consequence, questions such as 'What is the relation that holds between a particular and a universal?', 'What is the bond that unites a particular to its various properties?', or 'How do relations relate?' become redundant. To ask such questions is mistakenly to view the concept of a relation as the concept of an abstract object or third term over and above its relata, which is the way traditional logic treats the copula 'is'. By contrast, logical analysis treats predication in terms of the concept of a functional rule or modern predicate such as in 'is human'. Defined in terms of functional rules or modern predicates, relations are structurally incomplete, partial objects that cannot occur without relata to complete them. They are, as such, intrinsically connective. Once relations are defined

---

18. See F. P. Ramsey's classic essay 'Universals' (1925), in his *Foundations: Essays in Philosophy, Logic, Mathematics and Economics*, ed. D. H. Mellor (London: Routledge and Kegan Paul, 1978), 17–39. See also D. H. Mellor, *Matters of Metaphysics* (Cambridge: Cambridge University Press, 1991), 153.

as functional or incomplete objects, there is no need to invoke any other principle as a glue that holds together relations and relata, functions and values. That it is the very nature of a function to have values is expressed by its variables.

What is immediately striking about the argument from relation, however, is that it completely misses its target. Because the term 'relation', like other such words in English ('composition', 'construction', 'configuration'), is ambiguous as between the process of relating and the product that is the relation, there is nothing about the intrinsic connectivity that characterises relationality that rules out of court either the speculative or the traditional (non-algorithmic) naturalist concern with activity as the process of establishing relations. Moreover, the concept of the intrinsic connectivity of relations obviously does not decide between, for example, a logical-realist or some kind of constructivist account of the nature of connectivity. Hence, little of philosophical interest is decided by the given fact that there are relations, or partial, incomplete, intrinsically connective objects. Speculative philosophy and traditional naturalism do not deny, nor need they deny, that relations relate. Nor (as will emerge) need speculative philosophy deny that there is something ultimate and irreducible about unity as connectivity. What the speculative philosopher asks is: 'Why are there instantiations of relations or connectivity?', 'Is it possible to establish any reasons for the fact of connectivity?' The speculative philosopher's interest is in the fact that there are relations, and whether or not any account can be given of them over and above the fact that they are partial, incomplete, intrinsically connective objects. In asking 'Why are there relations?', or 'Why do relations relate?', speculative philosophers are not overlooking the intrinsic connectivity of relations. Rather, they are inquiring into the possibility of a self-explanatory account of connectivity in terms of actualising activity. Hence the strong question speculative philosophy puts to relations remains open and is perfectly intelligible. Indeed, it is the strong question as put to relations that gives rise to the third main feature of speculative metaphysics.

Order

The third main distinguishing feature of speculative metaphysics is its concern with the concept of order. There are two main questions here. The first is the correlate of the strong question of existence. It applies the principle of reason to the fact that we live in an ordered world, a world full of law-like relations between things, mathematical, physical, temporal, spatial, and so on. Yet even the most basic laws of mathematics or physics do not attempt to account for why there are laws at all. Hence speculative metaphysics raises the strong question of order: Why is there order? Secondly, arising from the strong question of order, there is the question of the nature of ordination itself: What is ordination? That is, what is the nature of the ordination or actualisation of order? What is the order of order in speculative metaphysics?

In addressing the strong question of existence, speculative theories are centrally concerned with the nature and status of order, for existence is logically inconceivable and so impossible without order of some kind, however minimal. There can be no such thing as 'pure chaos': chaos is always relative chaos, because even if there is chaos of some kind there must be entities that are identifiable or distinguishable in some way. Now, anything that is identifiable must minimally possess what medieval philosophers call 'the transcendental predicates of being'. These are *ens* or active being itself, *unum* or unity, *aliquid* or difference, and *res*, thinghood or efficacy. 'Transcendental' is here to be understood in its basic sense as 'universally applicable': the 'transcendentals' transcend all more special categories and are applicable to anything that is. The claim is that any identifiable entity must have a unity or identity of its own; that it must be differentiable, or stand in a relation of difference to other entities; and that it must have efficacy of some kind in respect of other entities. So if there are identifiable entities, these entities possess individual identities or internal order, no matter how simple or primitive; they stand in relations of difference, no matter how minimal; and they behave in a certain way, no matter how fleeting. Such entities are ordered or related, even if that order or relation is, for example, only one of mutual exclusion, resistance or destruction. Due to the inseparability of existence and order, to ask 'Why is there existence?' is to ask 'Why is there order?' Although the concepts of 'existence' and 'order' are not logically identical, logically equivalent, nor logically interchangeable, they are interdependent concepts or what medieval philosophers usefully call 'convertible' concepts. That is, they 'turn' or 'hang' together, for in relation to the concept of active existence the concept of order introduces something that is not directly or explicitly expressed by the concept of active existence itself but is essentially connected to it. The concept of order thus introduces the basic task that any self-explanatory theory of the activity of actualisation must address: it must provide some explanation of how order of any kind is possible.

With order as with existence, then, everything in philosophy depends on how hard we push the strong question. If we hold that order is essentially a product of cognition or the human mind, we have to take order as a mere given. It is just the way the mind works, whether as a result of evolution or whatever, for the human mind does not explain order but works by it. Further, such a subjectivist position is open to the objection that we find empirical evidence of order throughout the world, that order seems to be a constitutive, mind-independent feature of the nature of things. Hence the triumphs of natural science and the attractions of materialism or physicalism. But if we take a materialist or physicalist view of order, we once again take order as a mere given, for physical order is not self-explanatory. So once again, with order as with existence, the issue in speculative philosophy is: Do we take what is ultimate in the order of analysis, what is incapable of further demonstration, what is not further derivable – do we take the ultimate as merely given or as self-explanatory? Is order a mere given or is it self-explanatory?

It is the strong question of order, however, that gives rise among weak theorists to a number of objections. The first is the objection that the strong question of order is nonsense because any account of order must appeal to a prior order for its intelligibility. However, as in the case of the same objection raised against the notion of existence as activity and considered earlier, this claim ignores the requirement that the speculative search for the self-explanatory lays upon philosophical inquiry. This is the requirement that whatever is held to be an ultimate principle must possess in its own nature all the reasons needed to explain its own activity and that of anything else. It follows that a self-explanatory principle of order, if there be such, would be one that possesses the condition of its order in its own nature. In that sense it would in some way be self-ordering.

Secondly, there is the objection that there is no need for an ultimate principle of order at all. The issue here is: What is wrong with contingency as an ultimate principle? Why is contingency not enough? Now, as will emerge, many speculative philosophers from the Greeks onwards have given contingency a key role in their theory of the self-explanatory nature of existence. Nevertheless, one of the consequences of the above discussion of the notion of 'pure chaos' is that there never is such a thing as absolute, complete or total contingency. Contingency is always relative, because for anything to be contingent it must at least be differentiable or identifiable and thus its nature or behaviour must be ordered in some way, however minimal. Contingency necessarily requires order of some kind, no matter how simple, so there can be no such thing as absolute contingency. A theory of contingency always requires a theory of order, and in the context of the speculative search for the self-explanatory it must be part of a self-explanatory theory of order.

Thirdly, there is the much more serious argument from the nature of reasons. As presented by analytical philosophers, and all weak theorists in one form or another, this argument can be called the objection from irrelativity. It is based on the fact that strong theorists have traditionally regarded any given order or relation as requiring a further principle of ordination or connection. To formulate the objection in functional-logical terms: if there is a reason apart from the relation of instantiation that is the reason for instantiation, such a reason must apparently be irrelative, for the relation of instantiation includes the instantiation of any relational expression. Thus, if there is a reason for instantiation apart from the relation of instantiation, either it is the non-relational contrary of the relation of instantiation; or it is supra-relational in that it contains, but is much more than, any relation, The upshot of strong theory thus seems to be that whatever might be the reason for the connectivity of relations, it cannot itself merely be a relation and so must be irrelative in one or other sense.

This is why Hume, Kant, Frege and their followers object to any attempt to define existence as more than merely given. They readily grant the intelligibility of questions such as 'Why are there impressions?', 'Why are there transcendental conditions of cognition?', 'Why is there sometimes that which answers a description?'[19] Yet they hold that any attempt to answer these questions is pointless. Reason or reflection operates in terms of relations, so irrelativity is beyond the grasp of reason or reflection. It would therefore seem that the speculative search for the self-explanatory inevitably ends up in the realm of the irrelative.

The irrelative is whatever cannot be brought under a rule or a relation of any kind. It follows that even if the irrelative is claimed to be in some sense irreducibly given in experience, its nature is such that it is knowable only as that which lies beyond the scope of rationality. Consequently, even if there were a peculiar feature of experience that might be claimed to be irrelative, to overstep the limits of reflection as defined by the function or some other theory of relation is to take reflection into realms where, apparently, it has no business to be.

This conclusion is often thought to be borne out by the fact that, in the history of speculative metaphysics, many thinkers have regarded the ground of connectivity either as essentially non-relational, and so in its own nature as utterly inaccessible to description of any kind; or they regard it as supra-relational, and so as constituting in its own nature an order of a kind that is beyond the grasp of our limited minds. While they strenuously maintain that we can recognise that there is such a ground, and that we can understand our own relation to it, they often deny that we have any understanding of its nature as it is in itself. Thus it is not surprising that, as a glance at the writings of many speculative metaphysicians confirms all too

---

19. See David Hume, *A Treatise of Human Nature*, ed. L. A. Selby-Bigge (Oxford: Clarendon Press, 1968), Book I, part III, section V. On Kant, see Gerd Buchdahl, *Metaphysics and the Philosophy of Science* (Oxford: Blackwell, 1969), ch. 8. On Frege, see Peter Geach, *God and the Soul* (London: Routledge and Kegan Paul, 1969), ch. 5; and Leila Haaparanta, 'On Frege's Concept of Being', in S. Knuuttila and J. Hintikka (eds), *The Logic of Being* (Dordrecht: Reidel, 1986), 269–89.

well, strong theory is obliged by the nature of its subject matter to employ language in very unusual ways. Because strong theory concerns itself with the actualisation of the world and its contents, strong theory treats of that which is not an obvious, given the content of experience in any usual sense. Yet what kind of rational and evidential constraints can be placed on such a mode of discourse? What criteria of application are relevant to the irrelative? It is surely no accident that, from the outset, weak theorists such as Hume and Kant have characteristically been motivated by fear of unconstrainable and so fanatical claims about the nature of the real – which Hume calls 'enthusiasm', Kant *Schwarmerei* – a fear that remains as justified as it ever was. If mathematics, natural science and technology are perhaps the most strikingly successful enterprises humanity has ever engaged in, is it not wisest to take them as demarcating the limits of reflection and, with Hume, Kant and their followers, to leave behind for good the chequered and inconclusive history of attempts to inquire beyond those limits? Is it surprising that so many modern philosophers, and even some recent strong theorists, see rationality and the search for the self-explanatory as distinct and even opposed to one another?

Whether or not this objection is as damaging to the entire speculative enterprise as it seems to be depends on how speculative metaphysics deals with the second question mentioned earlier: 'What is the ordination of order?' For it is the kind of answer given to this question that in speculative metaphysics defines the nature and status of relations in respect of existence. Here as elsewhere what can be called the fallacy of irreformability must be avoided: it must not be assumed that speculative metaphysics is irrevocably tied to one particular kind of theory of the real, either conceptually or as a matter of historical fact. Moreover, despite the fact that the strong question of ordination is rarely discussed explicitly and is nowadays little understood, it nevertheless plays a crucial role in speculative metaphysics.[20]

---

20. The original, unpublished version of this essay, which was intended as the first chapter of Bradley's book on speculative philosophy, concluded with the following: 'The next chapter will be devoted to considering the basic characteristics or properties that a principle of actualisation must possess. This will prepare the way to the very core and heartland of speculative metaphysics: the main features of speculative theories of ordination and the heated debates they involve.' This chapter, along with the book itself, was never written.

Chapter 8

Beyond Hermeneutics: Peirce's Semiology as a Trinitarian Metaphysics of Communication

The semiology of Charles Sanders Peirce, the founder of pragmatism, is a standing challenge as much to Gadamerian hermeneutics as to Saussure's structuralism and its deconstructionist progeny. Peirce's semiology constitutes a rejection of Saussure: because Saussure's structuralism operates only in terms of a binary or dyadic relation of signifier (words) and signified (concepts), his account of communication is nominalist (concepts say nothing about the world) and subjective-idealist (communication is a matter of linguistic structures alone). Deconstruction takes this subjective idealism to its extreme limit by treating communication as nothing more than the differential plurality of signifiers – a paradoxical form of monism. Peirce's semiology equally rejects the hermeneutical restriction of communication to human interaction with the world; even if Gadamer occasionally hints at a larger metaphysics,[1] he is unable to realise it on account of his subjective-idealist entanglements. Now Peirce is indeed an idealist, but his is an ontological or objective idealism in the sense that he sees the cosmos as an information exchange system, a communication system that is constituted by the interpretation of signs.[2] For Peirce, physical matter itself is

---

1. See H.-G. Gadamer, *Truth and Method*, trans. J. Weinsheimer and D. G. Marshall (New York: Continuum, 1994), 105, 108, 475.
2. Apart from unpublished manuscripts (in the Harvard University Library), references to Peirce's published works in what follows are mainly to his *Collected Papers*, vols 1–6, ed. Charles Hartshorne and Paul Weiss (Cambridge, MA: Harvard University Press, 1931–35); vols 7–8, ed. Arthur E. Burks (Cambridge, MA: Harvard University Press, 1958); *The New Elements of Mathematics by Charles Sanders Peirce*, 4 vols, ed. Carolyn Eisele (The Hague: Mouton, 1976); and *Reason and the Logic of Things*, ed. Kenneth Lane Ketner (Cambridge, MA: Harvard University Press, 1992). Where required, reference will also be made to the *Writings of C. S. Peirce: A Chronological Edition*, vols 1–6, Peirce Edition Project (Bloomington: Indiana University Press, 1982). There are

one specific mode of the activity of semiosis or sign interpretation.³ Briefly to indicate something of the power, originality and historical depth of this extraordinary position, I will first of all outline what I take to be the central point and purpose of Peirce's general metaphysics, for that is in my view the context in which his semiology, or any other aspect of his thinking, is always to be understood. I will then go on to describe the basic features of his theory of signs.

Peirce's Metaphysical Method

Peirce's metaphysics is quite distinct from that of his continental counterparts in that it is elaborated in close relation to modern developments in mathematics and the logic of relations (to both of which he made signal contributions), and it is marked by an insistence on the intelligibility of things. He sees himself as the inheritor of the metaphysical tradition (he was an expert in medieval philosophy) and as bringing about a renaissance of metaphysics: his work has the empiricist intent of rescuing rationality from the absolute necessities of mind or pure reason, characteristic of European rationalism and idealism, and the rationalist intent of restoring intelligible order to those structures of experience which both rationalists and empiricists alike have often consigned to the realm of the non-rational, typically under the rubrics of 'ineffability', 'feeling' or 'action'. Peirce's metaphysical method is oriented, not to the traditional understanding of mathematics as based on self-evidently true axioms, but to the postulatory procedures of modern mathematics and the experimentalism of natural science. In this context, his metaphysics is based, like any inquiry, on faith (Latin, *fides*: trust) in the hypothesis of reason. This hypothesis is for Peirce articulated by the principle of reason, the principle that 'Nothing is without a reason', or 'Everything that is the case must have a reason why it is the case.'⁴ Negatively, the principle of reason requires the rejection of the no

---

no references in the present essay to *Semiotic and Significs: The Correspondence Between Charles S. Peirce and Victoria Lady Welby*, ed. C. Hardwick and J. Cook (Bloomington: Indiana University Press, 1977), but it should be consulted by any student of Peirce's semiology.

3. Unlike Berkeley, as will become evident, Peirce does not reduce material entities to signs. For Peirce's view of Berkeley, see *Collected Papers*, VIII, paras 7–38, or *Writings*, II, 462–87.

4. For this latter formulation, see Alexander R. Pruss, *The Principle of Sufficient Reason: A Reassessment* (Cambridge: Cambridge University Press, 2006), 3. I use the term 'principle of reason' and not 'sufficient reason' in order to disassociate the principle from the usual necessitarian interpretations, both of it and of Leibniz. For Peirce on the principle of reason or 'first law of inquiry', see *Collected Papers*, I, paras 135, 139,

hypothesis hypothesis: 'the hypothesis that no hypothesis is possible', as Peirce puts it.[5] For the principle of reason rejects the essentially sceptical theory or hypothesis that there are things that no theory or hypothesis can explain. It rejects the hypothesis that there is anything that is ultimately inexplicable in the sense that there is anything about which no explanatory theory can be sought and entertained.

Positively, the principle of reason requires unrestricted commitment to the search for explanation. No appeal is made here to an *a priori* rule. We have only the experimental or hypothetical application of the principle of reason to the fact that we live in a puzzling world. Further, the principle of reason requires that we go beyond even the most basic laws and operations of logic, mathematics and physics, for these do not account, nor do they attempt to account, for why there are laws or operations at all. Unrestrictedly applied, the principle of reason requires that we look for an ultimate that is self-justifying or self-explanatory. Peirce's metaphysics is thus a 'speculative' metaphysics in the sense that it is a theory of the actualisation of the empirical world, a theory of the *activity* of actualisation. Moreover, such a metaphysics would have to meet the stringent requirement that whatever is held to be the ultimate or self-explanatory principle of actualisation must possess in its own nature, or provide out of its own nature, all the reasons needed to explain its existence or activity.

Self-explanatoriness is not of course the same as proof. Indeed, the question as to what constitutes an adequate self-explanatory theory of the activity of actualisation is hotly debated between the different speculative schools that seek the self-explanatory. For brevity, I shall call them speculative 'explanatorists', in contrast to speculative 'descriptivists' such as, say, Schopenhauer, Nietzsche, Bergson or Deleuze, who take the principle of reason far enough to offer anti-empiricist theories of the activity of actualisation, but refuse to press it any further and so abandon the concern with the self-explanatory. In the 'explanatorist' tradition from Plato onwards, the principle of reason generally operates in the way that Peirce is the first to define as 'abduction'. In his words: 'The surprising fact C is observed/ But if A were true, C would be a matter of course/ Hence, there is reason to suppose that A is true.'[6] The argument is not a deduction, since it does not claim that its conclusion must be true if its premises are true. It is not inductive, since the statement referred to in the conclusion is not tested by sampling. Whereas induction tells us that a statement, true in

---

150, 405, 170; VI, para. 171; VII, para. 480; VIII, para. 168; and *Reason and the Logic of Things*, 180.
5. Peirce, MS 956, c. 1890.
6. Peirce, *Collected Papers*, VI, para. 528.

some cases, is likely to be true in unobserved cases, abduction allows us to conclude to the likelihood of something unlike anything that is observed. It is inference to the best possible explanation. The procedure is fallibilist: repeated application of abductive inference may lead to continued revision of our hypothesis in the light of new observations, as has always been the case with explanatorist theories of actualisation. And the hypothesis is not just tested against experience. Experience is tested against the hypothesis, which has the status of a critical principle: do the putative observations, or our descriptions of the observed, display the characters posited by the hypothesis? Ostensive demonstration cuts both ways. Or, more precisely, it moves in a virtuous circle.

There are two further hypotheses that are basic to Peirce's metaphysics. There is the hypothesis of reality: namely, that reality is that which has a nature of its own, in the sense that it is so independently of our minds or independently of whether or not we think it to be so. There is also the hypothesis of universalism, or the reality of universals. The hypotheses of reason, reality and universalism are taken up, elaborated and defended by Peirce by way of his speculative metaphysics of actualisation.

The Metaphysics of Triunity

Speculative theories of the principle of actualisation, whether explanatorist or descriptivist, come in five different forms. A principle of actualisation could be monadic, as is Nietzsche's theory of the will to power, or, most obviously, the Judaic and Islamic account of the creator God as an absolutely unique, singular being whose nature is defined as completely transcending human powers of reason. A principle of actualisation could be binary or dyadic, as when the foundations of the cosmos are held by Empedocles to be the twin principles of love and strife, by Democritus to be atoms and the void, by Schopenhauer to be will and idea, by Samuel Alexander to be space and time, or by Alain Badiou to be being and event. A principle of actualisation could be triadic, as is Plotinus's hierarchy of the One, Mind and Soul, Spinoza's hierarchy of substance, attributes and modes, and Deleuze's non-hierarchical threefold of difference (or event, or being),[7] virtualities, and specific differences or events. A principle of actualisation could be tetradic, as in Plato's *Timaeus* with its fourfold of the Good, God,

---

7. See Gilles Deleuze, *The Logic of Sense*, trans. Mark Lester and Charles Stivale, ed. Constantin V. Boundas (New York: Columbia University Press, 1990), 179–80; see also Robert Piercey's excellent essay, 'The Spinoza-intoxicated Man: Deleuze on Expression', *Man and World* 29 (1996), 269–81.

Form and Matter, or in Whitehead's 'categoreal scheme' of creativity, God, eternal objects and actual occasions.

There can be no question, however, that the tradition that dominates the history of Western speculative thought is that which holds the principle of actualisation to be a triunity of three distinct, irreducible, but inseparable and co-equal elements. Most would acknowledge that this tradition stretches from Plato's *syntrisi* or three-in-one,[8] through the medieval period, to the idealism of Hegel and Schelling. It is not so often noticed, however, that it has been a significant feature of modern philosophy over the last one hundred and fifty years. I refer primarily to Peirce's ontology of 'firstness', 'secondness' and 'thirdness', but there is also the later Heidegger's *das Ereignis* ('the Event'), with its triunity of *Es gibt* ('It gives'), *die Sendung* ('the sending') and *die Gabe* ('the gift'), as well as Collingwood's treatment of the Trinity as the fundamental 'absolute presupposition' of natural science.[9]

Two comments may help to dispel any puzzlement there might be at the persistence of the notion of triunity as a theory of the activity of actualisation. First, because the triune theories mentioned are explanatorist, they are elaborated so as to address three basic questions. These are the questions of the nature of origin, difference and order. For in the first place an explanatorist theory of the activity of actualisation requires a theory of the origin of difference and order. That is, it requires an account of that activity that is in some sense prior to difference and order because it is the condition of difference and order. In the second place, an explanatorist theory requires an account of the actualisation of difference or individuality, of the nature of differentiation. And in the third place, such a theory requires an account of the actualisation of order. The primacy attached to these issues is of course characteristic of the triune tradition itself. But they have a certain obviousness about them that helps to indicate the rationale of the general position.

---

8. Plato, *Philebus*, 64–5; see H.-G. Gadamer, *The Idea of the Good in the Platonic–Aristotelian Philosophy*, trans. P. Christopher Smith (New Haven: Yale University Press, 1986), 115–16.
9. See R. G. Collingwood, *An Essay on Metaphysics* (Oxford: Clarendon Press, 1940), ch. 21; Martin Heidegger, *On Time and Being*, trans Joan Stambaugh (New York: Harper Books, 1972); see also James Bradley, 'Transformations in Speculative Philosophy', in Tom Baldwin (ed.), *The Cambridge History of Modern Philosophy 1870–1945* (Cambridge: Cambridge University Press, 2003), 438–48. Josiah Royce's theory of the triune structure of interpretation could be added to the names I have given in the text; see his *The Problem of Christianity* (New York: Macmillan, 1913), especially vol. II. This is a book written under the acknowledged influence of Peirce. The triunity of existence, relation and meaning expounded in John Dewey's *Experience and Nature* (New York: Dover, 1958 [1929]) is a naturalisation of Peirce's threefold.

Secondly, there is a set of considerations connected with the development of mathematics and the rise of natural science. In the medieval period, the doctrine of the triune God, with its theory of the 'persons' of Father, Son and Spirit, was expounded as a supernatural or revealed mystery of faith. This is not to deny that the triune God is employed to provide a self-explanatory account of the activity of actualisation. In Aquinas, for example, all things have their *esse*, or act of being, which is given by the Father; their individual nature (species), which is given by the Son or Logos; and their relation to other things, which is given by the Spirit, the principle or gift of love or community.[10] Nevertheless, the concept of an essentially relational being cuts across the Aristotelian view that finite substances exist independently and that relations are accidents. Hence it is difficult in the context of Aristotelian metaphysics to develop a trinitarian account of all the features of the created world. By contrast, once mathematics and natural science had established the intrinsic relationality of the natural world,[11] the relational model could unproblematically be transposed, under the rubric of triunity, not only to the analysis of the constitution of the finite subject (as with Kant's plethora of triunities),[12] but also to the whole of reality, defined as an absolute subject with three essential modes or functional operations (Hegel and Schelling).[13] As Collingwood puts it: 'The doctrine of the Trinity, taught as a revelation by early Christianity . . . becomes in Kant and his successors a demonstrable and almost alarmingly fertile logical principle.'[14] In a relational world, there is no longer anything unintelligible about the triune principle, which thus becomes an immanent ground of actualisation, even though it is still apprehended as complete and all-containing (Hegel) or as resolving its own nature independently of its creation (Schelling). I now turn to the sea-change that Peirce brings about

---

10. Aquinas, *Summa Theologica*, 1a, q. 45, a. 7.
11. See Ernst Cassirer, *Substance and Function* (1910), trans. W. C. Swabey and M. C. Swabey (New York: Open Court, 1923). See also Gerd Buchdahl, *Metaphysics and the Philosophy of Science* (Oxford: Blackwell, 1969), ch. 1.
12. Hegel says of Kant: 'The conception of the Trinity has, through the influence of the Kantian philosophy, been brought into notice again in an outward [read: purely formal] way as a type, and, as it were, a ground plan of thought, and this in very definite forms of thought'. G. W. F. Hegel, *Lectures on the Philosophy of Religion*, trans. E. B. Speirs and J. B. Sanderson (New York: Humanities Press, 1974), III, 32–3.
13. That this position is not to be confused with Sabellianism is indicated by the fact that theologians as different as Karl Barth and Karl Rahner work within its purview. See Karl Barth, *Church Dogmatics*, trans. G. T. Thomson (Edinburgh: T & T Clark, 1936), I, pt 1, ch. 3; and Karl Rahner, *The Trinity*, trans. Joseph Donceel (New York: Crossroad Herder, 1970).
14. R. G. Collingwood, 'Reason Is Faith Cultivating Itself' (1927), in *Faith and Reason*, ed. Lionel Rubinoff (Chicago: Quadrangle Books, 1968), 119–20.

in the theory of triunity, transforming the medieval theory of persons and the German idealist theory of the absolute subject into a radically immanent logic of events.[15]

Peirce's Metaphysics of Triunity

Peirce's trinitarianism is a natural theology, or, more precisely, an empiricist-oriented metaphysics, of the Trinity: it attempts to make manifest the necessarily creative and radically immanent triune principle of actualisation across the fields of logic, mathematics, phenomenology, semiotics and speculative cosmology. Although there is no space to elaborate this large claim here, I will say something about how I interpret each principle of his triunity, drawing specifically on his cosmology, and I will try to indicate as I proceed something of its significance as an event ontology. Throughout, it is important to keep in mind that for Peirce, any identifiable entity whatsoever is to be analysed in terms of his triune principle of actualisation, which is distinct but inseparable from that which it actualises or creates. This means, as will become evident, that any identifiable entity has the nature of a triune event in the infinitely or inexhaustibly proceeding movement of actualisation.

In the first place, the self-explanatory first principle of actualisation, which Peirce calls 'firstness', is pure ecstatic or ablative activity, abductive 'movement from . . .' Because it is origin, it is unconditioned. So it is free or spontaneous in the sense that it acts wholly out of its own nature. Because it is unconditioned or free activity, it is limitless in the sense that it is absolutely indeterminate in its own nature. It is a free *ekstasis* which, as such, possesses

---

15. It will I hope become evident that it is regrettable that Peirce scholars, Peircean philosophers of religion and theologians generally ignore Peirce's trinitarianism, no doubt influenced by the predominant naturalism and conceptual-historical amnesia of Anglo-American culture. For the only exceptions to this rule that I know, see Hermann Deuser, *Gott: Geist und Nature. Theologische Consequenzen aus Charles S. Peirce' Religionsphilosophie* (Berlin: Königshausen and Neumann, 1993), 157, 166, 173, where, albeit briefly and cautiously, he points out the correlation of Peirce's categories to the Trinity; and Hermann Deuser and Helmut Maassen (eds), *Charles Sanders Peirce: Religionsphilosophische Schriften* (Hamburg: Felix Meiner, 1995), xli–xlii. For strictly biographical treatments of the topic, see Joseph Brent, *Charles Sanders Peirce: A Life* (Bloomington: Indiana University Press, 2nd rev. edn, 1998 [1993]), esp. 54, 62–5, 71, 333; and Max Fisch, 'Introduction', in Peirce, *Writings*, I, pp. xxx–xxxii. Gerard Deledalle, *Charles S. Peirce's Philosophy of Signs: Essays in Comparative Semiotics* (Bloomington: Indiana University Press, 2001), chs 16 and 17, is exceptional in taking Peirce's trinitarianism seriously. Very oddly, however, he interprets Peirce's triunities hierarchically, not co-equally, and conflates this interpretation with the trinitarianism of the Eastern Church.

no 'real' or determining properties or predicates. Its character as free ecstatic activity means that in the nature of the case it is a non-determining power. This concept of origin follows both Marius Victorinus and the Franciscan voluntarists in making being or activity (*esse, actus essendi*) prior to mind, and it owes a great deal to Schelling's theory of *Abgrund*. However, Peirce abandons the psychological notion of will, characteristic of voluntarism, as well as the Gnostic and mystical elements in Schelling. Instead, he elaborates the concept of origin in terms of a particular kind of mathematical infinite. His is not the potential infinite of Aristotle and the intuitionists, where however many parts it is divided into, it is possible for there to be more. Nor is it the real categorematic infinite of set theory, involving an infinite multiplicity of sets in which the parts or components are really there and their number is greater than any given. Rather, Peirce's firstness is a particular kind of syncategorematic infinite. That is, his primordial infinite is real in that it is inexhaustible activity, and it is potential in that its absolute indeterminacy means 'it contains no definite parts';[16] it is a continuum of potential parts only.[17] Peirce's infinite is a syncategorematic infinite of real or dynamical potentiality. One main feature of this theory of infinity is that here we have a concept of origin which in the nature of the case is not a One, not an All, not a Totality, not even a multiplicity of any kind. As Peirce stresses, this is a mathematical concept of pure chance.[18] Peirce describes free or indeterminate firstness as a no-thing or void.[19] That is, firstness is nothing, not as all-containing plenitude (*per excellentiam nihil*), nor as vacuity (*omnino nihil*), nor as negation (*nihil privativum*), but only as infinite free indeterminacy (*nihil per infinitatem*).[20] It may be objected that this infinite origin is a 'unity' of free Indeterminacy. However, as will be more fully explained in a moment, unity is in Peirce an effect, not a property of the origin; in Peirce, unity emerges out of the triune relation as its realisation. The sole kind of unity that the first considered in its own nature possesses is the unity of irreducibility (*unum*), for the first is the *principium non de principio* and as such is unconditioned freedom. Peirce's firstness is not a unicity in any other sense; rather, it is the univocal concept of a dynamical free indeterminacy that as such has no nature of its own, and, in communicating itself to all things, is necessarily never the same.

---

16. Peirce, *Collected Papers*, VI, para. 168.
17. Ibid., para. 185; Peirce, *New Elements of Mathematics*, IV, 343.
18. Peirce, *Collected Papers*, VI, para. 201.
19. Ibid., paras 214ff.
20. These various distinctions in the meaning of the term 'nothing' are made by John Scotus Eriugena; Peirce's version of the *nihil per infinitatem* is not of course Eriugena's, though his Trinitarianism has close relations to Eriugena's. On Eriugena, see Werner Beierwaltes, 'Negati Affirmatio', *Dionysius* 1 (1977), 127–59, esp. 133–4.

This brings us to Peirce's principle of 'secondness'. Because the first principle is ecstatic, self-realising movement, it gives rise out of itself to a second activity or principle of actualisation: the principle of essentially and spontaneously self-differentiating activity, of dative 'movement to . . .' The distinctness and irreducibility of this second principle resides in the fact that it is not in its own nature indeterminate activity, but is the activity of determination: it constitutes differences or individuals, *haecceities*, and it does so by communicating to them the irreducible spontaneity that is the positive basis of all determinacy or actuality. Such differentiating activity is also the positive basis of the logical laws of non-contradiction, negation and the excluded middle. Because everything is itself and not another thing, a key phenomenological character of individuals for Peirce is reaction or resistance to that which is different. There cannot, however, be any such thing as pure differences, for all difference (*aliquid*) involves not just irreducibility (*unum*) but difference of character or behaviour (*res*), however minimal. It follows that, for ecstatic activity to realise its differentiations as such – and so to realise itself in relation to its differentiations – it articulates its communicative nature as a law or rule of relation for itself and for its differentiations. That is, because *ekstasis* is essentially communicative and self-realising, it determines itself as a law or rule and communicates that power to its differentiations as their medium. Such power is the potentiality of order, and it is by way of the medium of order that differences are constituted. The distinctness and irreducibility of this third element resides in the fact that it is the activity of ordination, the actualising principle of order or structure.

Peirce's 'thirdness' or power of mediation defines the implications of his theory of origin for specific laws or rules. Like differences, all structures are determinations of free indeterminacy, which is inexhaustible. In consequence, all structures carry free indeterminacy within their nature. So all structures possess an inexhaustible indeterminacy, which is always more than any of their individual instances. What this means is that all specific laws or rules are essentially and intrinsically vague: they are infinitely or inexhaustibly determinable determinations. Thus there are no really complete or completable wholes; as Peirce insists,[21] for any given whole or continuity (e.g. 'All men are mortal'), the universal quantifier is to be interpreted distributively ('For each . . .') not collectively ('For all . . .'). Wholes are infinite in the distributive, not the collective, mode; and they are distributive wholes because they are intrinsically vague or infinitely indeterminate. What we have in this *mathesis universalis* is one of the great revolutions in the theory of universals. Forms do not constitute an infinite

---

21. Peirce, *Collected Papers*, V, para. 532.

multiplicity of fixed entities; rather, they are potentials that are subject to evolution, to development and decay. This is an explanatorist theory of the activity of actualisation in which there is no complete, all-containing Totality or One. Unity – and with it the unity of truth – is an effect, not an origin. All achieved unities – including that of the triune principle of actualisation itself – are dynamical events of spontaneity, difference and order, which as such are essentially incomplete and open to further determination. For Peirce, there are no absolute individuals, for all entities are infinitely determinable determinations.

Peirce's Semiology

It is evident that in Peirce, being or activity is not primarily analysed as substance or subjectivity but as communication, the self-communication of the triune principle. Because what the triune principle communicates is itself, it communicates communicativity, and on a Peircean analysis communicativity is, in the nature of the case, triune in nature. We are here at the core of Peirce's semiology, the whole point and purpose of which is to make manifest the role of the Trinity in the actualisation of the real.[22] Indeed, it will become evident that his semiology is an evidential or phenomenological argument for the triune theory of evolutionary actualisation. There is no appeal to 'hidden' causes here, only the task of ostensive demonstration, the task of bringing to light that which is most evident, most obvious and familiar, that which is so close to us that we can miss it on account of its universal presence.

Within the fundamental speculative triunity of activity, difference and order, or firstness, secondness and thirdness, semiology is an analysis of order or thirdness. Before turning to this analysis, however, it is helpful to place it in a larger context by noting that, following Victorinus, Peirce views each of the members of his speculative threefold as themselves threefolds, on account of their intrinsically co-relational nature.[23] Thus Peirce has three types of firstness: firstness itself (which is pure spontaneity), the firstness of secondness (which is difference, individuality or existence, *ex-sistere*, to stand outside, a term coined by Victorinus to describe the members of the Trinity) and the firstness of thirdness (which is idea). Secondness is analysed as existence, as cause, and as effect. Thirdness is analysed as idea or sign, as the exchange of information between individual entities, and as

---

22. For an early and explicit indication by Peirce of the trinitarian orientation of his semiology, see his *Writings*, I, 503
23. Peirce, *Collected Papers*, I, paras 530–8.

interpretation; in other words, thirdness is itself a threefold of sign, object and interpretant. Here, sign occupies the position of firstness because it is the potentiality for interpretation; object occupies that of secondness because it is determinate; and the interpretant occupies that of thirdness because the interpretant has the sign-interpreting or sign-ordering role, and so has the status of a third.[24] Thus, for Peirce, semiology is the analysis of the triune relation of sign, object and interpretant. This will be further explained as we proceed. I will begin by giving an initial definition of the three semiological elements, presenting them in an order I find convenient.

The Semiological Threefold

Peirce says: 'A sign is a *representamen* with a mental intepretant.'[25] To use his example, the sunflower is a *representamen* or medium of the sun for its offspring. Its offspring is its interpretant. There is no mental representation here, but a serial information exchange or semiological event in which one entity (the sunflower) is a sign of an object (the sun) to another (the seed). The sign stands in relation to an object. The object need not, however, be a cognised object: think of the sun as object in relation to the sunflower as sign. The object is the independent factor in semiological process, the factor that guides and constrains both sign and interpretant. Here, Peirce distinguishes between the 'immediate' and the 'dynamical' object. The immediate object is the individual object as it appears in a specific interpretative process. The dynamical object is the potentialities that an individual object has beyond any specific interpretative process.

Signs constrain and guide the interpretant. That is, they contain their own developmental conditions that contribute to semiological events consequent upon them. Signs are intrinsically vague and hence can evolve in the semiological process. What kind of process this is I will state in a moment. Peirce uses the term 'interpretant' rather than 'interpretation' to get away from any cognitive connotations. Interpretants need not be existent minds, mental acts, cognitive entities, or even 'experiencing' entities of any kind.[26] It is not even necessary that an interpretant should actually exist: a being *in futuro* will suffice.[27] Whether an object has been interpreted is to be decided not by inspecting the contents of a mind or an experience but by seeing what behaviour follows from the contact in question.

---

24. Peirce, *Collected Papers*, II, paras 228, 274. See also Carl Hausman, *Charles S. Peirce's Evolutionary Philosophy* (Cambridge: Cambridge University Press, 1993), 70–1.
25. Peirce, *Collected Papers*, II, para. 274.
26. Peirce, *Collected Papers*, I, para. 537.
27. Peirce, *Collected Papers*, II, para. 92.

The semiological threefold of sign, object and interpretant constitutes an endless, infinitely proliferating, iterative semiotic series. The sign is what the object becomes for an interpretant, the interpretant is what the sign becomes, and in turn that interpretant becomes an object for a successor interpretant. Peirce's semiology is thus a theory of active causation that rejects regularity and entailment theories: signs, objects and interpretants are each agent-causes that have their own spontaneity, and they are genuinely efficacious in that they are active in the production or determination of their effects. The semiological movement of actualisation – the immanence of the threefold principle of actualisation in all things – is through and through a theory of evolutionary process.

Relations and Applications of the Semiological Threefold

Peirce analyses the relations of the three semiological elements in terms of their inseparability and co-relationality. Given the general principle of Peirce's trinitarian metaphysics that any identifiable entity is analysable as a threefold, it is no surprise that he defines the nature of signs accordingly. Here, I will simply state his basic, interdependent, trichotomous sign-schema and indicate the meaning of his technical terms:

Sign as object: qualisign (quality, intensity); sinsign (individual event/object, 'replica' or token); legisign (general type). Note that no one element in this trichotomy can be what it is without the others.

Sign in relation to object: icon (similarity); index (causal relation); symbol (rule, natural or convention). Note that this second trichotomy has as its condition the first trichotomy.

Sign in relation to interpretant: rheme (predicate, possibility); dicisign (propositions, facts); argument (law for interpretant). This trichotomy is an analysis of the way icons, indices and symbols function for an interpretant.

A further feature of the intrinsic co-relationality characteristic of Peirce's sign analysis is that each member of his semiological threefold mediates the others. First, there is the mediatory role of the sign: the sign mediates object and interpretant. The object is the antecedent, the interpretant the consequence of the sign. For example: 'President Lincoln' as object; 'liberator' as sign; 'President Lincoln as liberator' as interpretant.[28] Secondly, there is the

---

28. On the President Lincoln example, see Hausman, *Peirce's Evolutionary Philosophy*, 67ff.

mediating role of the object, where the object mediates between sign and interpretant in that it constrains and guides both. Thirdly, the interpretant mediates sign and object. That is, it links them in the thought 'President Lincoln as liberator'. Note here, however, that in the infinite proliferation of the semiotic series the intepretant itself can become a sign mediating the object, President Lincoln, to a further interpretant, such as Lincoln's statue in Washington DC. Again, what in our example was the object, President Lincoln, can become the sign that interprets an object, liberator. For Peirce, any referent of the semiological threefold can switch its roles, depending on its position in a specific semiological process

Let me summarise this last point with some basic applications or examples, in order to bring out the extraordinary flexibility of Peirce's conception of the threefold semiological process. The relation of object and interpretant is the sign; for example, the text of *King Lear* as object; audience as interpretant; performance as sign. The sign is what the object becomes in interpretation and each interpretation is an event of truth. The relation is serial: the sign itself becomes another object for a subsequent interpretant. Moreover, any referent, because of its intrinsically threefold nature, can be analysed trivalently. For example, each element equally applies to the division of artist, artwork and audience, for each of the latter can be treated as sign, object or interpretant, depending on the context or perspective. Again, we can treat experience as object, artwork as sign, and artist or audience as interpretants. With respect to the artist or audience, it is noteworthy that the notion of the interpretant implies a semiological theory of the self as a continuous, unified series of self-interpreting events; something more than a Humean bundle and other than a fixed, enduringly identical substance.[29] Above all, no one element in the triunity of object, interpretant, sign can be prioritised over another. So there is space in this analysis for the critical freedom of the interpretant; the sign is defined neither as a differential engine, nor as a destined unfolding of being that operates over the heads of subjects. Thus Peirce can say: 'The word or sign which man uses *is* the man himself . . . Thus my language is the sum total of myself.'[30] Or more graphically: 'A *mind* may, with advantage, be roughly defined as a *sign-creator in connection with a reaction-machine.*'[31] Meaning is use, but it is the use of signs. This is a realist and social practice theory of meaning that never allows the ethical surrender of the individual interpretant.

---

29. For a superb analysis of Peirce's theory of the self, see Vincent M. Colapietro, *Peirce's Approach to the Self: A Semiotic Perspective on Human Subjectivity* (Albany, NY: SUNY Press, 1989).
30. Peirce, *Collected Papers*, V, para. 314, emphasis mine.
31. Peirce, MS 318, p. 18.

Semiology and Teleology

To get a better grip on Peirce's theory of semiological process, we need to ask: what kind of active order is posited here? The first thing to notice is that semiological order or a semiological event is intrinsically triune order. This means it cannot be defined as an order of two dyads: A : B and B : C. Smoke is a sign of fire, but not without an intepretant. There are only signs where there are objects *and* interpretants; that is, all semiological relations are relations that are *directed* to an intepretant. Hence all semiological relations are essentially teleological. Teleology is activity, the goal or end of which is the realisation or actualisation of something. There are three types of teleology that Peirce distinguishes, and all are present to some degree in any semiological event.[32] This analysis cannot, I believe, be ignored in any account of Peirce's semiology.

First, there is random teleology, where the interpretant spontaneously departs from the direction indicated by the sign or rule. Such departures are usually completely insignificant, though universal. They are purposeless, playful and unconstrained either by external circumstance or by any internal logical consequences. The activity of actualisation involved here is teleological in that it is self-realising activity, free self-determination unconstrained by circumstance or rule. It is the teleology of play, purposiveness without (specific) purpose. So this is one type of purposeless teleology that arises from the presence in the realm of order of the ecstatic activity that is firstness or spontaneity.

Secondly, there is another type of purposeless teleology. This is mechanical teleology. Here the end is given and predetermined. External and logical conditions largely determine the outcome that is realised. The sunflower seed is a good example (always remembering that each sunflower seed is an individual or a centre of spontaneity, and so an active, if infinitesimal, departure from the general law). This type of purposeless teleology arises from the differential power of order in respect of individuals.

Thirdly, there is purposive teleology. Here the end is not predetermined and the outcome is not more or less exhaustively determined by external or logical conditions. There is no pre-given result: the sign or rule only vaguely determines or mediates the general character of the outcome. So within specific constraints the result is freely determined by the synthetic, organising activity of the intepretant, which is always as inclusive or self-expansive as it can be. The semiological process here is purposive in that it is self-directed by the interpretant and is directed towards the

---

32. Peirce, *Collected Papers*, VI, paras 287–317.

interpretant. The interpretant, or the realisation of the interpretant, is the object or end of its own activity. A good example might be the vagueness or indeterminate potentialities of a human personality.

On this account, given the universality of the semiological phenomenon, reality itself is essentially vague or incomplete. More precisely: the logical laws of non-contradiction and the excluded middle, as well as the semantic principle of bivalence, are inapplicable or irrelevant to the domain of the first principle of the threefold but hold in that of the second principle, which is their actualising condition. Such rules, that is, are not universal, as on the standard interpretation, but necessary features of individuality and its semantics. It follows that in respect of rules or generals, of which the third principle is the actualising condition, the law of non-contradiction holds of them, but the law of excluded middle and the principle of bivalence do not. For Peirce, therefore, vagueness is an ontological condition of all things, which means that in thinking we enjoy a relatively precise grasp of vague content. To put it another way: the incompleteness and indeterminacy of any identifiable entity, its infinite potentiality, entails the vagueness of all specific content.

Looked at in an historical perspective, Peirce is here appropriating Scotus's theory of the 'imperfection' of metaphysical concepts and Kant's notion of the indeterminacy of regulative ideas. He transforms them into a realist theory of 'vague' universals, or what he likes to call 'generals'. In this way he dissolves the Scotist opposition of logic and metaphysics. Further, he overcomes the Kantian tension between mechanism and teleology by holding them to be (as noted above) experienced and essentially interdependent modes of the realm of thirdness or ordination. Given Peirce's strong realism in respect of universals, it is no surprise that he regards Kant as a nominalist in that 1) Kant treats rules, unlike particulars, as purely constructs of the mind and so gives primacy to particulars; and 2) Kant assumes that the law of the excluded middle applies universally to the real, with the result that the indeterminate has a lesser status; hence 3) Kant problematically treats the noumenal realm of the *Ding an sich* as a realm of determinate individual entities that are nevertheless held to be unknowable. It is thus to be expected that subjective idealism holds no terrors for Peirce: 'experience' is not a restrictive limit, but essentially and dynamically relational. In this context, the crucial implication of Peirce's theories of infinity and vagueness should now be clear: there is no opposition between realism and constructivism, for the real is itself a movement of constructive activity. This is a theory of evolutionary process in which the cosmos is understood as a sign that awaits its realisation as a community by the activity of interpretation. The ultimate *telos* is not the all-containing self-completeness of transparent mind, but the mutuality of shared and perfect community.

A Final Question

In conclusion, given current attitudes, it is necessary to ask whether or not Peirce's semiology can be divorced from its speculative-metaphysical context of trinitarianism. In one sense, this is obviously so: the triune semiological process can be treated as a naturalist cosmology of communication, or merely as a useful interpretative tool. Yet these are dodges: they simply avoid carrying out the kind of metaphysical analysis that the theory of infinity, which underpins the semiology, requires. The same is true of any attempt idealistically to delimit semiology as the interpretative structure of the human sciences and to 'universalise' it on that basis, tacitly acquiescing in the no hypothesis hypothesis. To do that, after Peirce, is merely to lapse back into hermeneutics.

Chapter 9

A Key to Collingwood's Metaphysics of Absolute Presuppositions: The Trinitarian Creed

It is my contention that R. G. Collingwood's *An Essay on Metaphysics*[1] is a major, highly original work in modern philosophy and represents the culmination of his lifelong reflection on the nature of metaphysics. To justify these claims, I will argue that the hitherto unrecognised key to Collingwood's mature thought is clearly and emphatically stated in chapter 21 of that work. Chapter 21 bears the title 'Quicunque Vult'. This is taken from the opening words of the Athanasian Creed, which is commonly known as the 'Quicunque vult . . .' and is so referred to in the Book of Common Prayer. The Athanasian Creed is one of the three main Christian creeds, the others being the Apostles' and the Nicene, and although traditionally named after St Athanasius of Alexandria (c. 293–373 CE), modern scholars agree it was probably composed in the fifth or sixth century CE. Because of its status as a fundamental statement of doctrine concerning the Trinity, Collingwood and his contemporaries would have heard the Athanasian Creed recited in Anglican church services at the end of Evensong on important feast days such as Christmas, Easter, Pentecost and Trinity Sunday. The full opening phrase is: '*Quicunque vult salvus esse, ante omnia opus est, ut teneat catholicam fidem . . .*', 'Whosoever will be saved must, above all, keep the Catholic faith . . .' This is part of the preamble that precedes the Creed's lengthy exposition of the doctrine of the Trinity, belief in which 'Catholic faith' is expounded as necessary for salvation.

Collingwood holds that the Trinitarian Creed (as I will call it) is the 'main or fundamental', 'absolute presupposition' of Western 'science and civilization', 'a background that has remained unchanged' since the Patristic

---

1. R. G. Collingwood, *An Essay on Metaphysics* (Oxford: Oxford University Press, 1940), 227.

age.[2] The Trinitarian Creed thus plays a central role in his much-debated account of metaphysics as the science of absolute presuppositions. This science he understands (in a sense to be determined) as an essentially 'historical' enterprise, and he lays out its logical character in the context of his 'logic of question and answer'.

According to Collingwood's logic of question and answer, all questions are saturated with presuppositions. The presuppositions of a question are the context or frame of reference that defines what constitutes an answer to that question. Questions and answers thus arise from what he calls the 'logical efficacy' of a presupposition,[3] which is the power of a presupposition to give rise to questions and so to answers or propositions that are true or false. Systematic inquiry is a matter of hierarchies of questions and answers. A presupposition that 'stands relatively to one question as its presupposition and to another as its answer', Collingwood calls a 'relative presupposition'.[4] By contrast, a presupposition that 'stands relatively to all questions to which it is related, as a presupposition and never as an answer', Collingwood calls an 'absolute presupposition'.[5] Absolute presuppositions stand at the foundation of the structure of questions and answers that they give rise to, in that they are not relative presuppositions, for they are not answers to questions. Rather, they are the condition of providing true or false answers in propositional form to the questions to which they give rise. So an absolute presupposition is not itself a proposition but something else. The crucial point here is that a proposition is held by Collingwood to be an answer to a question. Thus a relative presupposition can be a proposition, but an absolute presupposition cannot. Precisely what an absolute presupposition is will be a central concern of this essay.

Collingwood's ambition in *An Essay on Metaphysics* is to show, over against A. J. Ayer's justly famous work of 1936, *Language, Truth and Logic*, that the logical positivist or verificationist analysis of meaning and truth as strictly a matter of empirically verifiable propositions simply does not apply to metaphysical claims.[6] Both sides to the dispute are arguing about the extent to which natural science is the right way to see the world. For positivists such as Ayer, metaphysical claims are meaningless because they are empirically unverifiable. Collingwood counters that metaphysical claims are absolute presuppositions: they are not answers to questions, so they are not propositions, and consequently neither empirically true nor false. Rather, they are what make question and answer processes possible, in

---

2. Ibid., 227, 232.
3. Ibid., 39.
4. Ibid., 29.
5. Ibid., 31.
6. Ibid., ch. 16.

that they are the presuppositions of any question and answer process; that is, they are the presuppositions of the relative presuppositions and propositions such question and answer processes involve. Thus, although not empirically true or false, metaphysical claims are held to have their own special kind of meaning and truth as absolute presuppositions. So understood, the theory of absolute presuppositions is intended to defend the cogency and legitimacy of metaphysics, not only against logical positivism, but also against any form of what might be called scientifically oriented naturalism.

As is generally acknowledged, Collingwood's theory of absolute presuppositions is intended to turn the verificationist view of propositions against itself. He accepts the verificationist view of propositions, but holds that it is not applicable to metaphysical doctrines. Indeed, he goes much further: he argues that the purely natural-scientific view of the world espoused by verificationism in fact presupposes metaphysical claims about the Trinity. These are claims of a kind that many besides verificationists regard as the very epitome of meaninglessness, and, not surprisingly, this bold strategy has generated widespread and detailed criticism.[7] Moreover, as he himself states his position, even his defenders generally regard it as seriously flawed and in need of considerable repair and elaboration. It is my contention, however, that Collingwood's supporters and critics alike have more or less completely overlooked the meaning and significance of his treatment of the Trinitarian Creed as the fundamental absolute presupposition of the West. As will emerge, Collingwood's position in *An Essay on Metaphysics* turns on that issue, and it can be regarded as the culmination of his lifelong concern with the relation between metaphysics, faith (*fides*, trust) and theology.

A creed, in the primary meaning of the term, is a formal statement and explication (usually beginning 'I believe in . . .') of faith or trust in a body of fundamental theological doctrines that are held to be given, in the sense of historically revealed to believers. As such, creeds are first-person statements that are explicit performatives, not third-person declaratives or propositions: to state them is to perform an act of trust in, and commitment to, the truth of the expressed statements, and involves taking those statements as rules for thought and action.

Equally, as rules for thought and action, creeds are said to formulate revealed truths in the sense that rules of faith or trust (e.g., 'I believe in God') generate, or can have deduced from them, third-person, rule-interpretative

---

7. See, for example, the excellent and very striking critique of Collingwood by Michael Beaney, 'Collingwood's Conception of Presuppositional Analysis', *Collingwood and British Idealism Studies* 11.2 (2005), 41–114. This article has been a main inspiration for the present essay, and it will be referred to throughout. If Beaney's main strictures cannot be met, *An Essay on Metaphysics* is indeed a mess.

declaratives or propositions (e.g., 'I believe that there is God'). This relation can be stated in the form of a conditional: If you trust or have faith in rule R, then you believe (or ought to believe) that p. Because creedal rules in this way generate, or can have deduced from them, third-person, interpretative declaratives or propositions, any two such rules may be contradictory or inconsistent. That is to say, rules R and Q are logically incompatible, when the following two conditionals are true: 1) If you trust or have faith in rule R, then you believe (or ought to believe) that p; 2) If you trust or have faith in rule Q, then you believe (or ought to believe) that *not p*. The interpretative declaratives or propositions thus generated by creedal rules have always been treated as such by those concerned with correctly formulating and understanding creedal rules, and consequently have always been the subject of different cognitive or 'propositional attitudes' (asserting, questioning, supposing). Belief 'in' statements always generate belief 'that' propositions. Yet a first-person performative rule of faith or trust, because it is a *rule* that is a *first-person performative* and a matter *of faith or trust*, cannot in the nature of the case be reduced to a proposition or set of propositions, or to the relevant cognitive attitudes.[8] Indeed, it is supposed by their adherents that rules of faith and the revealed truths they are interpreted as generating could never have been reached by unaided human reason, and so they are maintained to have developed non-deliberately: that is, they have unfolded or emerged out of the life and circumstances of the community of believers. This is what makes them essentially historical in nature.[9]

The three main Christian creeds are thus traditionally defined as embodying the 'rule of faith' (*regula fidei*). As such, they have a hermeneutical function in the thinking and work of the believing community as both objects and instruments of interpretation. A creed is seen as stating a complex of doctrines, which together constitute the object of a unitary act of faith or trust. This complex has the character of a hierarchically ordered structure, in which some doctrines are the logically necessary presuppositions of others, so that belief in the Trinity presupposes belief in one God, and, in the same way, doctrines concerning God are more fundamental than those concerning the Church. However, creedal doctrines cannot be deduced by logical necessity from one another, for they are held to be, not the products of logical deduction or pure ratiocination, but the results of revelation that has occurred in the historical experience of the community

---

8. See H. H. Price, *Belief* (New York: Humanities Press, 1969), especially Lecture 9, 'Belief "in" and Belief "that"', 426–54. I am very grateful to Stephen Gardner for discussions and indispensable guidance on the pragmatics of the relation between performatives and declaratives, rules and propositions.
9. Collingwood, *Essay on Metaphysics*, 188.

of believers. Thus any doctrine constituent of a creed is, taken separately, an object of faith or trust.

As this partial summary of the complex, sophisticated analysis of creedal statements that is characteristic of the Christian theological tradition perhaps already suggests, I will argue that the theory of absolute presuppositions not only has the nature of creeds as its model, but is a philosophical development of some of the key features of creedal confessions. These features are reinterpreted by Collingwood as foundational conditions of the history of science and civilisation: he uses creedal rules as a model and exemplar of the historicality of beliefs, of the historical situatedness of our basic principles and attitudes. I will try to show that most criticisms of the theory of absolute presuppositions can be met, once the creedal model is recognised as the proper context in which to understand *An Essay on Metaphysics*. Indeed, if the reading I will offer of Collingwood in terms of the creedal model has anything to recommend it, it will emerge that his mature view of the unity of metaphysics and history is best understood in that context. It will, I think, prove necessary finally to abandon the view that he underwent a 'radical conversion' to historicism and relativism late in his career, and instead take a much more developmental view of the relation of his earlier writings on faith and reason to his later work. It will prove necessary to abandon any view that aligns him with the absolutisms of the German or British idealists. It will prove necessary to admit that any attempts to tame and domesticate him in line with the current fashion of the schools as a semanticist or metaphysically neutral monist who has given up on theorising about reality[10] are what they are: historically false. It will also prove necessary to place him in, and to see him as developing, a long but generally ignored philosophical tradition that cuts across the standard historical divisions as much as it puts them in a new light. In short, it will become evident that *An Essay on Metaphysics* is not at all the mess of conceptual confusions that some major commentators have taken it to be, and in fact represents an original and important contribution to metaphysical theory.

This essay is an attempt to recommend such a reading of Collingwood, and is divided into seven sections. The first section explains the philosophical import of the doctrine of the Trinity, in order to show that it is not, as is so often assumed, philosophically silly or unintelligible. This will help to explain why a thinker such as Collingwood, in common with many of the greatest philosophers of the West, ancient and modern, takes the doctrine

---

10. For an uncompromising statement of this view, see Guiseppina D'Oro, 'Robin George Collingwood', *Stanford Encyclopedia of Philosophy*, available at <http://plato.stanford.edu/entries/collingwood>.

of the Trinity as a serious and powerful piece of metaphysics. The second section deals with the specific modern philosophical contexts, conceptual and historical, that shape Collingwood's concern with the Trinitarian Creed. The third section analyses the theory of absolute presuppositions in relation to the creedal paradigm and shows how this resolves many problems in the interpretation of *An Essay on Metaphysics*. The fourth section offers an account of the development of Collingwood's thought on the nature of metaphysics, and in that context the fifth section explores the consequences he draws from his creedal account of absolute presuppositions. The sixth section considers what light the creedal model throws on the vexed question of the relation of truth to the theory of absolute presuppositions. The seventh and final section offers an overall assessment of the theory of absolute presuppositions.

Metaphysics and Triunity

The shortest way to approach the metaphysics of triunity in order to determine its philosophical import is by way of the principle of reason. This is the principle that 'Nothing is without a reason', or 'Everything that is the case must have a reason why it is the case.'[11] As I will show, this principle plays a significant role in Collingwood's thought. In approaching his work, it will become evident that in various ways Peirce provides an excellent foil. For Peirce, the principle of reason requires the rejection of the no hypothesis hypothesis, 'the hypothesis that no hypothesis is possible'.[12] Peirce rejects the essentially sceptical theory or hypothesis that there are things that no theory can explain both as 'an affront to reason and a plain inconsistency'.[13] In other words, Peirce rejects the hypothesis that there is such a thing as absolute unintelligibility, or that there is anything that is ultimately inexplicable in the sense that there is anything about which no explanatory theory or hypothesis can be entertained.

Positively put, Peirce is unrestrictedly committed to the principle of reason, the claim that 'Nothing is without a reason'. No appeal is made

---

11. For this latter formulation, see Alexander R. Pruss, *The Principle of Sufficient Reason: A Reassessment* (Cambridge: Cambridge University Press, 2006), 3. I use the term 'principle of reason' and not 'sufficient reason' in order to disassociate the principle from the usual necessitarian interpretations, both of it and of Leibniz. I should add that, although present in Western philosophy from at least Plato onwards, the principle of reason receives its first explicit formulation in Leibniz because he is forced by the rise of empiricism to articulate what differentiates the methodology of both his own rationalism and previous metaphysics from that of the empiricists.
12. Harvard MS 956, 1890.
13. Harvard MS 956, 1890.

here to an *a priori* rule. We have only the experimental or hypothetical application of the principle of reason to the experienced world. And because even the most basic laws of logic, mathematics and physics do not attempt to account for why there are facts or laws at all, Peirce looks for an ultimate that is self-explanatory.

Theories of a self-explanatory ultimate have two key features. First, such theories reject what may be called 'weak' theories of existence: that is, they reject the view that existence is nothing more than quantification, or the instantiation of predicates, for to treat instantiation as primitive is to treat existence as an underivable given. Instead, they maintain 'strong' or 'speculative' theories of existence, according to which existence is activity, the activity of actualisation, and they often use the verbal noun 'being' to designate such activity. While not denying the power and efficacy of quantificational logic, they hold that it is this activity or being that is the ultimate ground of the instantiation of predicates or the 'givenness' of the given.[14]

Secondly, self-explanatory theories necessarily attempt to elaborate accounts of the activity of actualisation that are ultimate in the sense that they provide all the reasons needed to answer questions such as 'Why is there existence?' For theories that unrestrictedly apply the principle of reason and seek a self-explanatory ultimate have to avoid an infinite regress: that is, they have to meet the stringent requirement that whatever is held to be the ultimate principle of actualisation must possess in its own nature all the reasons needed to explain its existence or its actualising activity, and that of anything else. Such ultimates, therefore, have to possess a nature that completely explains why they are both self-actualising and self-differentiating.

Now, there are of course many philosophies in the modern period that are strong or speculative theories in that they maintain existence to be an activity of actualisation, yet they do not require such an ultimate activity to be self-explanatory. Schopenhauer's will, Nietzsche's will to power, Bergson's *élan vital*, Whitehead's creativity and Deleuze's differentiation would be examples of such speculative theories of being or actualisation. To distinguish the two types of ultimate principles of activity characteristic

---

14. See especially the work of Peirce and Whitehead, both of whom are strong theorists of existence and both of whom made fundamental contributions to quantificational logic: C. S. Peirce, *Collected Papers*, vols 1–6, ed. Charles Hartshorne and Paul Weiss (Cambridge, MA: Harvard University Press, 1931–35); vols 7–8, ed. Arthur E. Burks (Cambridge, MA: Harvard University Press, 1958), esp. III, paras 359–403; A. N. Whitehead, *Process and Reality* (Cambridge: Cambridge University Press, 1929), on which, see 'The Speculative Generalisation of the Function: A Key to Whitehead', Chapter 4 above.

of speculative philosophies of actualisation, I will call them, respectively, 'explanatorist' and 'descriptivist' theories of being or actualisation.

Peirce's is an explanatorist metaphysics, and he finds his ultimate self-explanatory principle in his theory of triunity. What he calls 'firstness' is the origin of all things, considered as unconditioned or undetermined, and so infinite, freedom or spontaneity. Understood as dynamical and ecstatic in nature, the principle of firstness gives rise to the principle of 'secondness', which is held to be the activity of differentiation, difference, or the determination of plurality. The principle of 'thirdness' is the order that is maintained necessarily to characterise, but not to be reducible to, any identifiable difference. Self-explanatoriness is not of course proof, so he demonstrates the applicability of his triunity across a wide range of fields. But the key question here is: why triunity? I offer three comments, all of which are essential background to Collingwood.

First, an historical point concerning speculative principles of actualisation, explanatorist or descriptivist. A principle of actualisation could be monadic, as is Nietzsche's theory of the will to power or, most obviously, the Judaic and Islamic account of the creator God. A principle of actualisation could be binary or dyadic, as when the foundations of the cosmos are held by Empedocles to be the twin principles of love and strife, by Democritus to be atoms and the void, by Schopenhauer to be will and idea, or by Samuel Alexander to be space and time. A principle of actualisation could be triadic, as is Plotinus's hierarchy of the One, Mind and Soul, Spinoza's hierarchy of substance, attributes and modes, and Deleuze's non-hierarchical threefold of difference (or event, or being),[15] virtualities, and specific differences or events. A principle of actualisation could be tetradic, as in Plato's *Timaeus* with its fourfold of the Good, God, Form and Matter, and as with Whitehead's creativity, God, eternal objects and actual occasions.

There can be no question, however, that the tradition that dominates the history of Western metaphysical thought is that which holds the principle of actualisation to be a triunity of three distinct, irreducible yet inseparable and co-equal elements. Most would acknowledge that this tradition stretches from Plato's *syntrisi* or three-in-one,[16] through the medieval period, to the idealism of Hegel and Schelling. It is not so often noticed, however, that it has in fact been a significant feature of modern developments in philosophy

---

15. See Gilles Deleuze, *The Logic of Sense*, trans. Mark Lester and Charles Stivale, ed. Constantin V. Boundas (New York: Columbia University Press, 1990), 179–80; on which, see Robert Peircey's excellent essay, 'The Spinoza-intoxicated Man: Deleuze on Expression', *Man and World* 29 (1996), 269–81.
16. Plato, *Philebus*, 64–5; on which, see H.-G. Gadamer, *The Idea of the Good in the Platonic–Aristotelian Philosophy*, trans. P. Christopher Smith (New Haven: Yale University Press, 1986), 115–16.

over the last one hundred and fifty years. There is not only Peirce's threefold, but also the later Heidegger's *das Ereignis* ('the Event'), with its triunity of *Es gibt* ('It gives'), *die Sendung* ('the sending') and *die Gabe* ('the gift'), as well as Dewey's naturalised or descriptivist triunity of existence, relation and meaning.[17] When you start looking, there is a lot of triunity about.

Secondly, a conceptual point, which may help explain why this is so: namely, that the theory of triunity, in its most representative forms, is elaborated to address three fundamental questions in metaphysics and to provide a self-explanatory answer to them. These are the questions of the nature of origin, difference and order.

In the first place, an explanatorist theory of the activity of actualisation requires a theory of the origin of difference and order. That is, it requires an account of that activity that is in some sense prior to difference and order because it is the condition of difference and order. Such a principle of origination would also provide the ultimate reason for the unity of the real. The principle of origination can be variously analysed as self-differentiating mind, with the trinitarian 'rationalists' or 'intellectualists', Aquinas, Hegel and Collingwood; as self-differentiating will, with the trinitarian 'voluntarists', Scotus, Descartes and Schelling; or as self-differentiating freedom, as with Schelling, once again, and also with the 'pragmatism' of Peirce and of the Heidegger of *Sein und Zeit* (1927), who can both be seen as moving voluntarism away from the psychological analogy of will towards the primacy of action.[18]

---

17. See Martin Heidegger, *On Time and Being*, trans. Joan Stambaugh (New York: Harper Books, 1972); on which, see the indispensable article by Peter Harris, 'Patterns of Triunity in *Time and Being*: Contexts for Interpreting the Later Heidegger', *Analecta Hermeneutica* 3 (2011), available at <www.mun.ca/analecta>; also my essay, 'Transformations in Speculative Philosophy', in Tom Baldwin (ed.), *Cambridge History of Modern Philosophy 1870–1945* (Cambridge: Cambridge University Press, 2003), 438–48. See also Josiah Royce's idealist theory of the triune structure of interpretation in his *The Problem of Christianity* (New York: Macmillan, 1913), esp. vol. II. This is a book written under the acknowledged influence of Peirce, as is Dewey's *Experience and Nature* (La Salle, IL: Open Court, 1929).
18. The debate between the medieval trinitarian 'rationalists' and 'voluntarists' was maintained between the Dominican and Franciscan religious orders respectively. The most famous Franciscan thinkers, Duns Scotus and William of Ockham, are the fathers of empiricism; they taught at Oxford. The Dominican–Franciscan debate continues in the division between mainland European rationalists and British empiricists in the seventeenth and eighteenth centuries, between Hegel and Schelling in the nineteenth century, and, in the twentieth century, between formal-logical philosophers such as Frege and Russell on the one side, and various forms of Peirce-inspired pragmatism on the other. Peirce described himself as a Schellingian. Schelling's enormous influence on most subsequent mainland European thinkers – Schopenhauer, Kierkegaard, Nietzsche, Bergson, Heidegger, Levinas, the modern neo-Bergsonians – is primarily due to his introduction of voluntarism into a predominantly rationalist tradition. Wittgenstein has a complex relation to both sides; in this context, see especially

In the second place, an explanatorist theory requires an account of the actualisation of difference, of the nature of differentiation. This is said to be the realm of individuality or existence. As for example in Peirce, 'existence' is here usually understood in the original sense of the word, first employed by Marius Victorinus in his fourth-century work, *Theological Treatises on the Trinity*. In the *Treatises* he coined the term *ex-sistentia*, meaning 'standing outside of', to define the nature of difference as between the terms of the trinitarian relations.[19]

In the third place, an explanatorist theory requires an account of the actualisation of order, understood as irreducible to, yet inseparable from, individuality. Most trinitarian thinkers – Ockham being the great exception – are realists in respect of universals.

The primacy attached to these three issues is of course characteristic of both the triadic and the triune traditions themselves. But they have a certain obviousness about them that helps to indicate the rationale of the general position.

Now for my third comment: we should keep in mind a set of both conceptual and historical considerations about triunity that are connected with the development of mathematics and the rise of natural science. In the medieval period, the doctrine of the triune God, with its 'subsistent relations' of Father, Son and Spirit, was expounded as a supernatural or revealed mystery of faith. This is not to deny that the triune God is employed to provide a self-explanatory account of the activity of actualisation. Moreover, the creative activity of the Trinity is defined in accordance with its own internal dynamic. In Aquinas, for example, all things have their *esse*, or act of being, which is given from the Father; their individual nature (species), which is given by the Son or Logos; and their relation to other things which is given by the Spirit, the principle or gift of love or community.[20] Nevertheless, the concept of an essentially relational being cuts across the Aristotelian view that finite substances exist independently and that relations are accidents. Hence it is difficult in this context to develop a trinitarian account of all the features of the created world. By contrast, once mathematics and natural science had established the intrinsic relationality of the natural world, the relational model could unproblematically be transposed, under

---

Mathieu Marion, *Wittgenstein, Finitism, and the Foundation of Mathematics* (Oxford: Clarendon Press, 1998).
19. Marius Victorinus, *Theological Treatises on the Trinity*, trans. Mary T. Clark (Washington, DC: The Catholic University of America Press, 1981), esp. 41–2.
20. Aquinas, *Summa Theologiae*, Ia, q. 45, a. 7, resp. See Peter Harris, '*Esse*, Procession, Creation: Reinterpreting Aquinas', *Analecta Hermeneutica* 1 (2009), 136–67, available at <www.mun.ca/analecta>.

the rubric of triunity, to the structure of the world. This is what happens, not only to the analysis of the constitution of the infinite subject, as with Kant's plethora of trinities,[21] but also to accounts of the whole of reality, which is defined in Hegel and Schelling as an absolute subject with three essential modes or relational operations. A little later, with Peirce, trinity becomes a logical, mathematical, cosmological, phenomenological and semiotic principle. As Collingwood puts it in 1927: 'The doctrine of the Trinity, taught as a revelation by early Christianity . . . becomes in Kant and his successors a demonstrable and almost alarmingly fertile logical principle.'[22] He is right, as I have pointed out: in a relational world, there is nothing mysterious or incomprehensible about theories of trinity. It is in this context that his theory of absolute presuppositions and its relation to his account of the Trinity should be approached.

Modern Contexts

If the metaphysics of the Trinity is the first and largest context in which Collingwood's theory of absolute presuppositions should be read, the second is the specific modern influences on his view of the doctrine of the Trinity. There are, I suggest, four main contextual considerations here.

The first modern contextual influence is J. A. (John Alexander) Smith (1863–1939), Collingwood's teacher and friend, and his predecessor in the Waynflete Professorship. Smith wrote little, but he saw metaphysics as the framing of 'suppositions' or 'presuppositions', among which are his view that 'the Real is a (or the) History', and that 'the revealed character of the Real' is realised by mind. On his account, what is thus revealed in history 'are to Mind rather gifts than achievements of its own' and come to mind always 'accompanied or environed by the unselfconscious'.[23] It is not surprising that, according to James Patrick, 'For Smith and Collingwood,

---

21. Hegel says of Kant: 'the conception of the Trinity has, through the influence of the Kantian philosophy, been brought into notice again in an outward [read: purely formal] way as a type, and, as it were, a ground plan of thought, and this in very definite forms of thought.' G. W. F. Hegel, *Lectures on the Philosophy of Religion*, trans E. B. Speirs and J. B. Sanderson (New York: Humanities Press, 1974), III, 32–3.
22. R. G. Collingwood, 'Reason Is Faith Cultivating Itself', *The Hibbert Journal* XXVI (1927). Reprinted in *Faith and Reason: Essays in the Philosophy of Religion by R.G. Collingwood*, ed. Lionel Rubinoff (Chicago: Quadrangle Books, 1968), 119–20.
23. J. A. Smith, 'Philosophy as the Development of the Notion and Reality of Self-Consciousness', in J. H. Muirhead (ed.), *Contemporary British Philosophy: Personal Statements* (London: Allen and Unwin, 1923), 225–44.

the first phrase of the Athanasian Creed was a code word referring to the presuppositions or supposals that made thought possible.'[24]

A second contextual influence is another pupil of Smith's, M. B. Foster (1903–59), a colleague of Collingwood's who was a lecturer and later professor in the Faculty of Philosophy at Oxford. James Connolly has pointed out[25] the significance for Collingwood of Foster's brilliant series of three articles on the relation between the Christian concept of God and the rise of the modern science of nature published in the journal *Mind* between 1934 and 1936. Summarily, Foster claims that the limitations of Greek doctrines of God are the limitations of Greek science. Only with the development in and through history of what he insistently calls the Christian 'revelation', in particular the doctrine of the creator God, did modern science become possible. Indeed, he argues in considerable detail that it is developments in the metaphysics of the Trinity from Aquinas to Ockham that constitute what he terms throughout 'the presuppositions of modern natural science'.[26] As Connolly shows, Collingwood must have known these articles, and I can add that D. M. MacKinnon told me they were much discussed in non-analytical circles in the 1930s at Oxford. The articles demonstrated to Collingwood that the history of natural science itself – the very locus of positivism – was saturated with metaphysics. It is our vaunted scientific practice that, contrary to positivism, is an unexamined body of beliefs, and it is the content of our 'religious faith'[27] that provides modern natural science with 'the conditions of its own possibility'.[28] The study of these conditions Collingwood elaborates on his own terms as the metaphysical science of absolute presuppositions, according to which such conditions are not merely the means by which a particular view of the world, such as that inscribed in the metaphysics of the Trinity, was arrived at *in the past*. The claim is much stronger: that the

---

24. James Patrick, *The Magdalen Metaphysicals: Idealism and Orthodoxy at Oxford, 1901–1945* (Macon, GA: Mercer University Press, 1985), 103, n. 79, and the references to Smith's texts given there; cf. also 90.
25. James Connolly, 'Natural Science, History and Christianity: The Origins of Collingwood's Later Metaphysics', *Collingwood Studies* 4 (1997), 101–32.
26. M. B. Foster, 'The Christian Doctrine of Creation and the Rise of Modern Natural Science', *Mind* 43 (1934), 446–68; 'Christian Theology and Modern Science of Nature (I)', *Mind* 44 (1935), 439–66; 'Christian Theology and Modern Science of Nature (II)', *Mind* 45 (1936), 1–27. These articles, along with a valuable account of Foster's life and thought and a collection of critical essays, are reprinted in Cameron Wybrow (ed.), *Creation, Nature and Political Order in the Philosophy of Michael Foster (1903–1959): The Classic Mind Articles and Others, With Modern Critical Essays* (Lewiston, NY: Edwin Mellen Press, 1993).
27. Collingwood, *Essay on Metaphysics*, 216.
28. Foster, 'The Christian Doctrine of Creation' (1934), 447; Wybrow, *Creation, Nature and Political Order*, 66.

metaphysics of the Trinity as elaborated in the history of the West remains *the real and active fundamental possibility condition* of our scientific practice, whether or not it is ignored, forgotten or repressed by the prejudices of the schools.[29] Whatever questions this claim might raise, it cannot be comfortably put aside as 'historical' in the weak sense, as an account of past developments that have been superseded, for it is a claim that strikes at the heart of logical positivism, and, indeed, any form of naturalism. This view of the significance of the presuppositional status of the metaphysics of the Trinity in Collingwood is borne out if, thirdly, *An Essay on Metaphysics* is seen alongside Charles Norris Cochrane's great work, *Christianity and Classical Culture: A Study of Thought and Action From Augustus to Augustine*.[30] Cochrane (1889–1945), who was a Canadian pupil of both Collingwood and Foster, had his work published by Oxford University's Clarendon Press in 1940, the same year as *An Essay on Metaphysics*, and he acknowledges Collingwood's help in reading and criticising the MS, along with that of the pre-eminent classical scholar Ronald (later Sir Ronald) Syme.[31] The book, which reads like a companion volume to *An Essay on Metaphysics*, is a historically detailed analysis of the strains (sociocultural as well as conceptual) that characterise ancient metaphysics and science. It offers an extended demonstration of the way in which the Patristic writers debated and resolved those strains, and developed a new concept of science and civilisation, by means of the metaphysically and historically 'creative and moving principle' of the Trinity.[32] Throughout, the interaction of fundamental theories and concrete historical contingencies is closely examined. Reading Cochrane, with his strong affirmation of the fundamental and transformative role of the doctrine of the Trinity in the history of the West, one could imagine Collingwood thinking that the year 1940 would, in more propitious circumstances, have marked the emergence of a new

---

29. Foster, it could be argued, remains ambiguous on this matter. Given Foster's strong theological commitments, however, it is likely that Collingwood's is the conclusion he wants his readers to draw.
30. I am very grateful to Professor Rex Martin of the University of Kansas for drawing my attention to the relevance of Cochrane's book, and for the information I have given on him. See the entry on Cochrane in *The Canadian Encyclopedia* (Toronto: McClelland & Stewart, 1999), to which Professor Martin also referred me.
31. Charles Norris Cochrane, *Christianity and Classical Culture: A Study of Thought and Action From Augustus to Augustine* (Oxford: Clarendon Press, 1940). The Clarendon Press edition has the same pagination as the Galaxy Books edition subsequently produced by Oxford University Press. A rather beautiful Liberty Fund edition, edited by Kathleen Alvis and John Alvis, was published in 2003. The Liberty Fund edition provides translations of all the Greek and Latin quotations. In the citations below page references are given first to the Clarendon edition, with citations to the Liberty Fund edition (designated LF) following.
32. Cochrane, *Christianity and Classical Culture*, 409ff.; LF, 443ff.

body of work that would challenge positivism and bring about a revival of metaphysical thought.[33]

Cochrane's work is far too wide-ranging and complex to be summarised here. It is perhaps enough to note that he sees the doctrine of the Trinity as providing 'the basis for a radically new and unclassical account of the structure and content of experience'.[34] In particular, he provides a striking analysis of the role of the Trinity in the treatment of motion in nature, a topic on which Collingwood places great emphasis. Further, as an expert in Greek historiography,[35] he gives a sophisticated account of how the doctrine of the Trinity transforms the understanding of history as 'from beginning to end a continuous and progressive disclosure of the creative and moving principle'.[36] A notion of history as disclosure is, I will argue, a central element in Collingwood's presuppositional analysis. In this respect, by far the most important feature of Cochrane's work in relation to *An Essay on Metaphysics*, and his central theme throughout, is his account of Patristic thinking on the nature of 'presuppositions'.

Using Augustine's contrast between *ratio scientiae* and *ratio sapientiae*, between the Greek method of scientific thinking and the Christian method of wisdom or insight, Cochrane argues that the crucial element in what he sees as the Patristic transformation of classical culture is its treatment of the relation of faith and reason. The theology of Christianity is quite different from that of ancient philosophy, including neo-Platonism, because its truth is understood as dependent on the movement of historical revelation. For Plato, faith is mere opinion, and reason can in ideal conditions rise to knowledge of the ultimate reality that is the divine. On this account, reason is itself divine. For Augustine, in contrast, the ultimate reality that is the divine is given only in and by faith in historical experience. The ultimate reality cannot be uncovered by rational ascent to the highest truth, by neo-Platonic theurgy, or by any kind of purely human effort; rather, its apprehension is a matter of the historical gift of revelation. Only through faith or trust in that which has been revealed in the movement of history can reason achieve what it does. However, this revolt against the Greek view of

---

33. The Foster–Collingwood–Cochrane thesis is also, of course, a challenge and corrective to Edward Gibbon's dismissive treatment of the philosophy and theology of the Patristic period. See Collingwood, *Essay on Metaphysics*, 220 and note; also, 74–5. I am grateful to Jay Foster for pointing out to me their ambitions in this respect. I am also grateful to Michael Tremblay for valuable editorial advice on the present essay.
34. Cochrane, *Christianity and Classical Culture*, 237; LF, 261
35. See Charles Norris Cochrane, *Thucydides and the Science of History* (Oxford: Clarendon Press, 1929). I am grateful to Craig Cramm for helpful comments on the nature of Cochrane's analysis.
36. Cochrane, *Christianity and Classical Culture*, 483; LF, 533.

reason is not for Augustine a return to intuition, or a lapse into blind faith, or an assertion that the intellect is radically corrupt. Rather, in his view, understanding is the reward of faith in historical revelation, and faith and reason 'are in reality correlative and complementary aspects of experience'.[37]

It is in this context that Cochrane employs the notion of presupposition and its cognates. Commenting on the priority of faith to reason consequent upon the Trinitarian revelation, he states that to uphold the latter 'was to alter the entire perspective and maintain that, for all men without exception, the question of primary importance was not so much their capacity for thinking as the presuppositions which governed their thought'.[38] Elsewhere, referring to a passage from Augustine, he says: 'Thus envisaged, the Trinitarian principle presents itself, not as a refinement of scientific intelligence, a tissue of metaphysical abstractions having no existence except in the imagination of theologians, but rather as an attempt to formulate what is "imposed" upon the intelligence as the precondition of science.'[39] It is evident from these remarks that, in what might be called the Oxford–Toronto School of Presuppositional Analysis, the concepts of faith, Trinitarian revelation and presupposition are intimately linked.

In order to grasp the full significance of these interrelations, however, a fourth context is required: Cochrane's work on the ancient world needs to be placed in the modern philosophical and theological framework in which Collingwood himself read it. The conceptual-historical configuration that shapes the theory of absolute presuppositions should thereby become much clearer.

The crucial notion here is that of revelation. Right from the start, the notion of revelation is apprehended in Christianity principally as the activity of God in history rather than the assertion of a body of propositions. As a result of the incarnation, history is seen as the site of divine disclosure, of the manifestation of the fundamental trinitarian structure of reality stated in the creeds. Faith or trust is thus fundamentally a matter of 'belief in' rather than 'belief that'. It is primarily non-propositional: it is not primarily trust in a body of truths, but trust in a particular way of experiencing the world that is unfolded in and by the movement of history and is declared as such in the creeds. This self-disclosure or revelation of the real is not regarded as confined to the Apostolic age, between Christ's birth and the death of the last disciple, but is held to be a continuous feature of the life of the believing community as it learns and works out, in the contingencies of history, the meaning and significance of its beliefs.

---

37. Cochrane, *Christianity and Classical Culture*, 400; LF, 443.
38. Ibid., 238; LF, 261.
39. Ibid., 412; LF, 456.

So understood, the theological concept of revelation history is the context in which the development of the historical sciences in the eighteenth century (which themselves in significant part grew out of debates on the genesis and nature of revealed truths) is taken up and theorised by philosophers of the nineteenth and twentieth centuries. They attempt to render philosophy as historically self-conscious as Christian theology, and to place and determine the role and status of philosophy within the movement of universal history. All follow the Augustinian view of reflective reason as born out of that movement of history which in theology is called revelation and which in its broader signification is the immanent unfolding of reality in and through the conduct of human affairs. This is what Hegel calls 'the cunning of reason', Schelling 'revelation', Peirce 'agapastic development', Whitehead 'adventures of ideas', Heidegger 'the sending of Being', Gadamer 'effective-historical consciousness' and Ricoeur 'tradition'. For all the differences between these thinkers, in every case revelation is generalised as history, and, consequent upon the post-Kantian idealist rejection of a noumenal reality, history itself becomes in various senses the realisation of the real. In every case, theoretical reasoning is seen as historically saturated and embedded, as growing non-deliberately out of concrete historical configurations that are given to reflection and that constitute the material of reflection. The intrinsically historically situated nature of theoretical reasoning works always within the context of given traditions, local, national or international, understood in the largest sense as complexes of established practices, social, cultural, economic, pedagogical, and so on, most of which have not been deliberately or consciously arranged by individuals and of which the practitioners are often in large measure unaware. These constantly shifting, unfolding traditions provide us with most of our beliefs about the world, and it is these traditions that constitute at once the field and horizon of theoretical reasoning, that which it must trust and employ as a guide to its deliberations, no matter how revisionary its conclusions may be. Reviving an old word that has fallen into disuse in English, I shall refer to this general view of the nature of theoretical reasoning, and its articulation in philosophers such as Hegel, Schelling, Peirce and Heidegger, as 'historiology' or 'metaphysical historiology'.

Given Collingwood's connections to German and Italian post-Kantian idealism, to Stewart, Foster and Cochrane, as well as his own work on the relation of faith and reason, it is evident, and will be further argued below, that the theory of absolute presuppositions is a further expression and a self-conscious, original elaboration of the central concern with the relation of history, faith, reason and truth that has always exercised theology and has preoccupied some of the greatest minds in the tradition of metaphysical historiology since the nineteenth century. In this context, Collingwood takes as his clue the non-propositional nature of historical tradition, as epitomised in the creedal formulae, and it is on that basis he makes in *An Essay on Metaphysics* his final attempt to achieve what he describes as his life's work: 'a rapprochement between philosophy and history'.[40] With these considerations in mind, I now turn to examine the theory of absolute presuppositions itself.

The Theory of Absolute Presuppositions

What is the significance of the fact that Collingwood takes the Trinitarian Creed as stating 'the main or fundamental presuppositions of science'?[41] What light does the creedal model throw on the theory of absolute presuppositions? There are, I believe, five main issues here.

1. As noted earlier, it is a theological commonplace that a creed is a 'rule of faith' or *regula fidei*, where *regula* has its original meaning as *that by which statements or propositions are measured*. It is, I contend, the creedal model of a rule, as exemplified by the Athanasian Creed, that provides the definitive clue to the nature of an absolute presupposition.

In the first place, absolute presuppositions are certainly not axioms, for, as Michael Beaney points out, 'while we may treat axioms themselves as unprovable, we do not regard them as neither true nor false'.[42] Nor are they synthetic *a priori* propositions, for, even if they might have the status of historical or quasi-transcendental principles that are demonstrable by a kind of deductive procedure, they are explicitly stated by Collingwood not to be propositions.[43] Again, it hardly needs to be said that absolute presuppositions or creedal rules are not conventions in any of the usual senses of the term. For while, as will emerge, absolute presuppositions are in a significant sense agreed upon, they are neither arbitrary nor optional, as are conventions. As will also emerge, there are intelligible reasons for shifts in the nature of absolute presuppositions or creedal rules, which is not always said to be the case with conventions. Unlike conventions, moreover, absolute presuppositions are fundamental, or not further derivable, conditions of

---

40. R. G. Collingwood, *An Autobiography* (Oxford: Clarendon Press, 1939), 115.
41. Collingwood, *Essay on Metaphysics*, 227.
42. Beaney, 'Collingwood's Conception of Presuppositional Analysis', 51. In Collingwood's early essay, 'Reason Is Faith Cultivating Itself' (1927), he rejects the description of what he there holds to be undemonstrable certainties as 'axioms': 'they are the presupposition of all proof whatsoever, not like the Aristotelian axioms, which enter into particular arguments as their premises, but rather as the conditions of there being any arguments at all' (*Faith and Reason*, 115).
43. For the Kantian reading of absolute presuppositions, see Guiseppina D'Oro, *Collingwood and the Metaphysics of Experience* (London: Routledge, 2002).

thought and practice, and they enjoy a real, albeit historically situated, universality.

By contrast, absolute presuppositions can certainly be regarded, with Rex Martin, as 'basic conceptions'.[44] Yet what needs to be added is that they are basic conceptions of a very specific kind: they are rules. Moreover, they are rules of a very specific kind: they are creedal or first-person performative rules of faith or trust.

Rules are meaningful, but they are not propositions and they are not true or false. Rather, they are meaningful as the constitutive conditions that govern a given system of beliefs or practices. In consequence, rules can be valid or invalid, correct or incorrect. As already noted, the validity of a group of rules depends on the logical compatibility or consistency of the third-person, interpretative declaratives or propositions that those rules generate. Hence one of the main uses of creedal formulae is as a defence against heresies, which are invalid rules of faith. Creedal rules of faith, however, are not algorithms or recipes. Here, as in so many areas of metaphysics, the currently dominant use of the mathematical-logical function as a model for the nature of rules (and, indeed, of transcendental or universally applicable rules in general) is wholly inappropriate. For a creedal rule of faith is a measure, standard or guide for thought and practice. As at once the object and instrument of right thought and practice, it is the condition of its own further development and elaboration, and it is the criterion for testing other forms of thought and practice. It is not, therefore, an automatic operation without any reflexive power, but a formula for theoretical and practical interpretation whose status as such depends upon the place it occupies in the hierarchy of such rules. The notion of absolute presuppositions corresponds exactly with that of creedal rules of faith.[45] Collingwood's reintroduction of the notion of creedal rules into philosophical debate is a challenge and critique of the predominant contemporary view of rules as decision-making, algorithmic procedures or recipes.

---

44. Rex Martin, 'Editor's Introduction', in R. G. Collingwood, *An Essay on Metaphysics*, rev. edn (Oxford: Clarendon Press, 1998), xxiiff. See Beaney's comments, 'Collingwood's Conception of Presuppositional Analysis', 52–3, 101.

45. Beaney, 'Collingwood's Conception of Presuppositional Analysis', 56–9, carefully considers the interpretation of absolute presuppositions as rules. Yet despite pointing out its attractiveness, he rejects it, in part because he overlooks Collingwood's discussion of the Athanasian Creed and so cannot 'find any real textual evidence' for such an interpretation, and in part because he considers the notion of rules only with reference to developments in modern mathematics. He also asks how rules can be legitimately extended from logic to metaphysics. Putting aside the kind of answers Peirce or (following in his footsteps) Wittgenstein might give, the answer Collingwood gives is his theory of absolute presuppositions, as I will try to show. How cogent this answer is will be considered in the course of this essay.

In the second place, however, Collingwood's distinction between relative presuppositions and absolute presuppositions has to be carefully attended to if the precise regulative nature of the latter is to be fully understood. Relative presuppositions need not be, but usually are, rules of one kind or another, as Collingwood's examples tellingly indicate.[46] His main example of a relative presupposition, that of a tape measure, perspicuously shows 1) that a relative rule or presupposition is deliberately constructed and 2) that its correctness or incorrectness is empirically verifiable. By contrast, an absolute rule or presupposition is neither deliberately constructed nor is it empirically verifiable. *What type of rule it is, the creedal model tells us.* For creedal rules are not deliberately constructed at the outset, but grow out of the life of the community. Theologically, creedal rules are historically revealed doctrines that are the objects of faith.[47] Historiologically, the status of creedal rules is taken on by those fundamental principles that have unfolded in the sociocultural movement of traditions and that constitute the largely unthematised structure of basic beliefs that characterise those traditions. Such rules or presuppositions are, for Collingwood, absolute because they cannot be proved, and because in any given historical configuration the question and answer process of proof depends upon them. In this context, it is not in the least surprising, though usually ignored by embarrassed commentators, that Collingwood emphasises his acceptance of Aristotle's identification of metaphysics and theology.[48] In common with most members of the historiological tradition from Hegel and Schelling onwards, Collingwood holds the Trinitarian Creed and the fundamental principles of Western culture to be inseparable.

The upshot is that in treating the Trinitarian Creed as the fundamental absolute presupposition, Collingwood is providing a precise account of the meaning of absolute presuppositions as non-algorithmic, constitutive rules.[49] The Trinitarian Creed is employed not merely as an example, but as a conceptual illustration and an empirical confirmation of the notion of absolute presuppositions. It is intended to illuminate and to bear out the

---

46. Collingwood, *Essay on Metaphysics*, 29–30, 38–40.
47. As the early Collingwood puts it when defining the term 'faith' in respect of its content, 'the word implies the absence of any power of proof or verification' (*Faith and Reason*, 108).
48. Collingwood, *Essay on Metaphysics*, 10, 188, 215, 216.
49. Thus Beaney ('Collingwood's Conception of Presuppositional Analysis', 82-4) and Michael Krausz ('The Logic of Absolute Presuppositions', in Michael Krausz (ed.), *Critical Essays on the Philosophy of R.G. Collingwood* [Oxford: Clarendon Press, 1972], 222–40, esp. 226) are incorrect to claim that Collingwood ignores the question of meaning in relation to absolute presuppositions and that he overlooks or ignores the question of the connection between meaning and verifiability. Collingwood's creedal model of rules does all the work needed here.

nature of absolute presuppositions as rules of a special kind; namely, they are what might be called historically manifested rules that are rules of faith or trust and have the status of first-person performatives.[50] Thus, because they are rules of faith or trust that are first-person performatives, not declaratives or propositions, absolute presuppositions cannot as such be the objects of different propositional attitudes (asserting, questioning, supposing). What in metaphysics can be the object of propositional attitudes will be considered shortly. Yet at least it is now evident that Collingwood's claim that absolute presuppositions are not propositions is much more than merely the result of his acceptance of verificationism, and it is hardly 'counter-intuitive' or 'implausible'.[51] Rather, it is a central component of his contribution to and elaboration of the historiological tradition. When absolute presuppositions are understood on the creedal model, Collingwood has provided clear criteria for their identification.[52]

2. Once the nature of absolute presuppositions is recognised on the creedal model to be that of historically manifested rules, it becomes possible to see the essential relevance of the logic of question and answer to the theory of absolute presuppositions. The strengths and weaknesses of the logic of question and answer as a contextual theory of truth are not at issue here. Even admirers of this logic, such as Gadamer, recognise that much more needs to be done.[53] What is in question is whether or not there is an integral connection between the theory of absolute rules or presuppositions and the logic of question and answer. As Michael Beaney deftly shows, for example, a theory of presuppositions could be derived independently of

---

50. Collingwood, *Essay on Metaphysics*, 216, 256.
51. Beaney, 'Collingwood's Conception of Presuppositional Analysis', 71, 72, 79.
52. Overlooking the creedal model, Krausz denies this ('The Logic of Absolute Presuppositions', 226). It should also be noted here that Beaney claims ('Collingwood's Conception of Presuppositional Analysis', 73–7) that in *Essay on Metaphysics*, Collingwood slides between his own idealist-oriented definition of a proposition as strictly a statement or assertion, and the modern logical conception of a proposition as having a propositional content that can be the object of various propositional attitudes. If there were anywhere such a slide in Collingwood's writings, it would make no difference to his account of absolute presuppositions, once that is understood on the model of creedal rules. In fact, however, Collingwood is nowhere guilty of such a slide, as Beaney points out in respect of all his other work, early and late – with the exception, as he thinks, of *An Essay on Metaphysics*. In *An Essay on Metaphysics*, however, Beaney has simply misread the referent of the pronoun 'it' in the last sentence of Collingwood's Note to Definition 1 (*Essay on Metaphysics*, 25). The 'it' refers, not to the previous sentence of the Note, but to that Note's first sentence and so to the Definition. The creedal model anyway shows that the critical conclusions Beaney draws from this putative ambiguity have no purchase whatsoever on Collingwood's account of absolute presuppositions.
53. See H.-G. Gadamer, *Truth and Method*, 2nd rev. edn, trans. Joel Weinsheimer and Donald G. Marshall (New York: Continuum, 1994), esp. 369ff.

such a logic.⁵⁴ This claim is doubtless true. However, it overlooks the significance of the creedal model. For the crucial feature of revealed doctrines is that they are not in the usual sense answers to questions. What is meant in theology when a doctrine is said to be revealed is that, far from being an answer to questions put by human reason, such a doctrine has been freely communicated by God in the movement of history, and could never have been arrived at by unaided rational inquiry. In the larger, historiological context, the key point is that the development of the basic theoretical principles of a culture could never have been formulated by pure reason alone, and are always the result of a convergence of complex sociocultural conditions. Collingwood is making this historiological point when he defines the nature of presuppositions by way of the logic of question and answer. Absolute presuppositions are not declaratives or propositions that are answers to questions, but first-person performatives of historically manifested rules of faith or trust that make possible complexes of questions and answers. As Collingwood emphasises, the logic of question and answer thus plays an integral and precise definitional role in the formal or 'logical' analysis of the theory of absolute presuppositions out of the model of creedal rules.⁵⁵

3. Another advantage of the model of creedal rules is that it clears up the difficulties and confusions that surround Collingwood's view of the relations that hold among absolute presuppositions. It will be helpful, however, if I first lay out his account of the nature and role of propositions in metaphysics. These Collingwood terms 'metaphysical propositions'. He holds that the true form of a metaphysical proposition is given by what he terms the 'metaphysical rubric': 'in such and such a phase of scientific thought it is (or was) absolutely presupposed that . . .'⁵⁶ Moreover, he explicitly emphasises the correlation of the concept of the metaphysical rubric with creedal formula,⁵⁷ and he uses an example that is indicative of the creedal background to the theory of presuppositions: 'God exists' (if it is a metaphysical proposition) means 'somebody believes that God

---

54. Beaney, 'Collingwood's Conception of Presuppositional Analysis', 46–7, 78–9.
55. Collingwood, *Essay on Metaphysics*, 30, 54. Thus Beaney ('Collingwood's Conception of Presuppositional Analysis', 71, 79) is wrong in thinking that the logic of question and answer is no more than an afterthought, merely employed to make plausible what Beaney believes is the unsupportable claim that absolute rules or presuppositions are not answers or propositions. The same goes for his ironical suggestion (p. 46) that Collingwood's claim that all statements are answers to questions is itself an absolute presupposition of the logic of question and answer. That claim is not a historically manifested absolute presupposition or rule of metaphysics, but, as Collingwood says, part of a logical account of what distinguishes absolute presuppositions or rules from propositions.
56. Collingwood, *Essay on Metaphysics*, 55.
57. Ibid., 187–8.

exists'.⁵⁸ In a metaphysical proposition, that is, an absolute presupposition is interpreted by way of a third-person declarative. What constitutes a metaphysical proposition is a third-person, interpretative declarative or statement or assertion, to the effect that a particular absolute presupposition or rule of faith is operative in a given system or phase of thought. This is why, for Collingwood, metaphysical propositions are essentially 'historical' in nature;⁵⁹ metaphysical propositions are interpretative claims about what functions, or has functioned, as an absolute presupposition or rule in a given doctrine or historical phase. Thus metaphysical propositions are empirically verifiable in the sense that they deal with the question of who absolutely presupposes or presupposed what, when and how.

It is when interpreted by third-person declaratives or metaphysical propositions that absolute presuppositions or performative rules of faith can be the objects of different propositional attitudes. For example, it can be claimed, as Collingwood claims and as any positivist or naturalist would deny, that faith or trust in the doctrine of the Trinity is the real possibility condition of the practice of natural science, whether consciously recognised or not. In other words, this is an interpretative claim that can be asserted, questioned, supposed or denied. Collingwood's point is that the assessment of such a claim essentially involves that historical-conceptual analysis that is a form of close observation and is characteristic of historical investigation into cultural formations. For Collingwood, all metaphysical inquiry is in this sense historical inquiry into the relevant facts of the matter. Against the positivist and naturalist, he would expand the concept of the factual by showing the intrinsic historicity and historically saturated nature of the empirical world.⁶⁰

Returning to the question of the relations between absolute presuppositions, it is evident that Collingwood's account is closely modelled on the nature of creeds. Just as a creed, it will be recalled, constitutes a complex of doctrines that, taken together, is the object of a unitary act of faith, so what Collingwood calls a 'constellation' of absolute presuppositions characterising a particular historical epoch is the object of a unitary act of thought.⁶¹ And just as any individual creedal doctrine, taken separately, is an object of faith, so any individual absolute presupposition is 'a single historical fact' in respect of its presuppositional status.⁶² It will be further recalled that creeds state a hierarchy of doctrines such that, while the fundamental doctrines are such because they are the logically necessary presuppositions of the

---

58. Ibid., 188.
59. Ibid., 55, 188.
60. I am grateful to Evan Simpson for comments on this issue.
61. Collingwood, *Essay on Metaphysics*, 66.
62. Ibid., 67.

less fundamental doctrines, the fundamental doctrines are not sufficient conditions of the less fundamental ones, for the only sufficient condition of a creedal doctrine is revelation. Analogous considerations hold of absolute presuppositions. To say that an absolute presupposition is absolute, not further derivable, or 'presuppositionless'[63] is not to deny that an absolute presupposition has certain logical presuppositions – as is indicated by Collingwood's description of the Trinity as the 'main or fundamental' absolute presupposition of Western science and culture[64] which underlies the non-fundamental or secondary, derivative and in some cases short-term absolute presuppositions of the possibility of applied mathematics,[65] of the conservation of substance, and of universal causation.[66] For Collingwood, to say that an absolute presupposition is absolute, not further derivable, or 'presuppositionless' is to say: 1) that an absolute presupposition cannot be deduced from the absolute presuppositions it logically presupposes;[67] and 2) that what makes an absolute presupposition or rule to be such is not the other rules it may logically presuppose, but the complex contingencies of the historiological configurations that have given rise to it.[68] Like creeds, therefore, constellations of absolute presuppositions are hierarchies or nests of rules that are much more than deductively related to one another. Whatever is held to be the fundamental component of a hierarchy of absolute presuppositions is the necessary, but not historically sufficient, reason for the secondary components.

This creedal reading of the hierarchical nature of absolute presuppositions is borne out by the way Collingwood presents his illustrations

---

63. Ibid., 40.
64. Ibid., 227.
65. Ibid., 253–4.
66. Ibid., 265–8, 324–5.
67. Ibid., 65–6, 76, 248.
68. Thus Krausz ('The Logic of Absolute Presuppositions', 236–40) is correct to point out that Collingwood 'adduces no [logically] presuppositionless example of an absolute presupposition', but he is wrong to view these considerations as fatal flaws in the theory of absolute presuppositions. For the reasons I have given, Collingwood's description of absolute presuppositions as 'presuppositionless' is to be read in the creedal sense of that term: it is the status of absolute presuppositions as rules that are objects of faith which is presuppositionless. Kraus (ibid., 240) also claims that 'All Collingwood's examples of absolute presuppositions presuppose existential statements.' This is true in the cases of the non-fundamental or secondary absolute presuppositions he instances, but, once again, none of them are deducible as rules from their logical presuppositions. It is not true of Collingwood's treatment of God and the Trinity, however. As first person performative of faith or trust, fundamental absolute presuppositions such as 'God exists' are not existential statements or propositions, but perhaps may be understood as existential rules that govern our ontological commitments. Beaney ('Collingwood's Conception of Presuppositional Analysis', 47, n. 6) sees this, but unfortunately does not take up the point in his later discussion of existential statements at pp. 99–100.

of absolute presuppositions. In *An Essay on Metaphysics*, Part IIIA, 'The Existence of God', he moves from the treatment of 'God Exists' in chapter 18, to the creedal 'Quicunque Vult' of chapter 21, treating the latter, not as not logically deducible from, but as logically presupposing the former, in that the former is its necessary but not sufficient condition. Similarly, the account of the absolute presupposition of the Trinity precedes the account given in *An Essay on Metaphysics* of those non-fundamental or secondary, derivative, and in some cases short-term, absolute presuppositions mentioned above. Taking the theory of presuppositions further than Foster or Cochrane, Collingwood holds these secondary presuppositions logically to presuppose, but not to be logically deducible from, the Trinitarian presupposition that is their necessary condition.

4. At this point it is possible to see that an apparently strong and much-cited objection to Collingwood's theory of absolute presuppositions is groundless. This is the objection made by Michael Krausz that Collingwood stands ambiguously between two different positions. Position 1 is the claim that 'If P is an absolute presupposition, then in the *given* systematic inquiry P cannot be an answer to a question.' Position 2 is the claim that 'If P is an absolute presupposition, then in *any* systematic inquiry P cannot be answer to a question.' Krausz argues that on the first position a rational historiography is possible, while on the second it is not. Krausz thinks that Collingwood upholds the first position insofar as he 'adduces examples of presuppositions which may be relative in one systematic inquiry and absolute in another'. At the same time, Krausz maintains that Collingwood also upholds the second position insofar as his theory of the meaning of absolute presuppositions is that they are never propositions. Thus the damaging contradiction.[69]

Now it will be evident from what has been argued in this essay that Collingwood upholds position 2: he maintains that any principle whose logical status is that of a first-person performative that is a rule of faith can, as such, never be propounded.[70] However, this does not make a rational historiography impossible. On the contrary, first of all, this would be the case only if it were mistakenly held that absolute presuppositions must themselves be answers to questions in order to be the subject of inquiry and criticism. In fact, Collingwood's claim is that the subject of metaphysical inquiry is constellations of historically manifested absolute presuppositions or rules interpreted by way of the third-person declaratives or metaphysical propositions that they generate.

---

69. Krausz, 'The Logic of Absolute Presuppositions', 223–4. He is supported by Beaney, 'Collingwood's Conception of Presuppositional Analysis', 75–6.
70. Collingwood, *Essay on Metaphysics*, 32–3.

Secondly, an absolute presupposition, because it is primarily a first-person performative that is a rule of faith, does not normally lose its logical status as a rule in another phase. As will immediately be explained, this can indeed happen, at least with certain non-fundamental, secondary absolute presuppositions. For Collingwood, however, fundamental absolute presuppositions, such as Aristotle's account of God, and secondary presuppositions such as Kant's account of causation, cannot ever become relative presuppositions, for, as noted earlier, there is in the nature of the case nothing about the content of such rules of faith or trust that is exhaustively reducible to a declarative sentence or proposition. However, the place in the hierarchy of rules or constellation of presuppositions of some aspects of such rules may alter, or they may be discarded: that is, their logical efficacy may change or disappear.[71]

Nevertheless, thirdly, there is no doubt that in Collingwood's view there are circumstances in which certain types of secondary absolute presuppositions or rules held by some can, for others, become relative presuppositions. After observing that Locke had conceived nationality 'as a "natural" basis, an absolute presupposition, of all political activity whatever', Collingwood declares that 'Nationality for the modern historian is a relative presupposition; it cannot be an absolute one.'[72] Although no other examples are given in *An Essay on Metaphysics*, what was an absolute presupposition of Locke's natural law theory is here said to have become at a later historical phase a relative presupposition of modern historiography. Such a conversion of status from absolute to relative presupposition is, of course, possible only with a particular kind of secondary absolute presupposition. For that reason, there is clearly no contradiction in Collingwood's position. This is why he is right to hold that absolute presuppositions are as such not propounded, and he is careful not to say that absolute presuppositions can never be propounded.[73]

5. In the context of the creedal model, I will now briefly consider the much-debated question of the relation between different constellations of absolute presuppositions at different historical phases; that is, Collingwood's view of the nature of change in respect of absolute presuppositions. Collingwood claims that changes in absolute presuppositions take place when various elements in a constellation of absolute presuppositions are

---

71. Ibid., 214–18.
72. Ibid., 97–8. This is pointed out by Alan Donagan, *The Later Philosophy of R.G. Collingwood* (Oxford: Clarendon Press, 1962), 76.
73. Beaney ('Collingwood's Conception of Presuppositional Analysis', 75, n. 21) thinks that Collingwood should say that absolute presuppositions could never be propounded.

'logically incompatible'[74] and so give rise to 'strains'. In his words: 'the absolute presuppositions of any given society, at any given phase of its history, form a structure which is subject to "strains" of greater or less intensity, which are "taken up" in various ways, but never annihilated'.[75] Though he says little else about rule transformation, this, I suggest, is in part because Foster's and Cochrane's work offers magnificent and detailed conceptual and empirical-historical accounts of such transformations, with all the strains and debates that gave rise to them. Indeed, their analyses amount to a vindication of Collingwood's claim in *An Essay on Metaphysics* that the most basic 'background' presupposition against which the various subsequent rule transformations can be understood is that of 'God exists'.

The important feature of Collingwood's treatment of strains, for all its perfunctoriness, is that he describes absolute presuppositions in terms of the 'consupponible' and the 'logically incompatible'.[76] Two absolute presuppositions or rules in a given constellation are consupponible when they are performatives, or first-person commitments that are 'logically possible' to hold together,[77] in the sense that there are no logical incompatibilities in the third-person declaratives or propositions that they generate *that are evident to those who believe them.* In other words, consupponibility is an epistemic or cognitive condition that as such is not sufficient for logical compatibility.

By contrast, as noted earlier, two absolute presuppositions or performative rules of faith in a given constellation are logically incompatible when it is the case that one such rule generates, or can have deduced from it, the third-person, interpretative declarative or proposition that p is the case, whereas the other rule generates, or can have deduced from it, the third-person, interpretative declarative or proposition that p is not the case. Yet the actual situation is usually far more complex, as Collingwood's reference to the 'strains' in any given historical constellation indicates. As the term 'strain' implies, there can be varying kinds and degrees of strain in any given historical constellation. The idea that each rule generates one unique class of interpretative propositions is only the limiting case. The fact is, a

---

74. Collingwood, *Essay on Metaphysics*, 331–2.
75. Ibid., 48n., 73–4. It is noteworthy that Collingwood, like Foster and Cochrane, sees shifts and changes in absolute presuppositions in terms of 'strains' and thus as rational and intelligible. In this, his position contrasts markedly with Thomas Kuhn's influential analysis of historical change in science, where 'paradigm shifts' from 'normal' to 'revolutionary' science are not rational or intelligible; see *The Structure of Scientific Revolutions* (Chicago: University of Chicago Press, 2nd edn, 1970). The reason for this is that Kuhn defines 'normal science' in terms of functions or algorithms, and there is no algorithm for historical change. The creedal model of rules imposes no such historiographical limitations.
76. Collingwood, *Essay on Metaphysics*, 66, 331.
77. Ibid., 66.

creedal rule or constellation of rules contains complex and so contestable concepts, and thus is open to a variety of interpretations. In consequence, such a rule or constellation of rules generates, or can have deduced from it, much more than merely one single class of interpretative declaratives or propositions. Each rule gives rise to declaratives or propositions by way of an act of interpretation, and hence different interpretations will generate differing classes of propositions. Thus any creedal rule or constellation of rules generates, or can have deduced from it, a class of classes of interpretative declaratives or propositions. This class of classes of interpretative declaratives or propositions is the range of possible interpretations to which a creedal rule or constellation of rules may give rise, only some of which possible interpretations might be historically actualised.

There can of course be core issues or boundary points on which many interpretants may agree, such as, for example, the third-person, interpretative proposition 'that God is creator', in which case there is no strain in relation to that rule of faith or trust. Obviously, though, the nature of the divine creative act is open to a whole range of possible interpretations, some of which have emerged and unfolded in the contingencies of history. Here, it is these third-person, interpretative declaratives or propositions that may be contradictory or inconsistent, as between, for example, those who interpret the divine creative act in the context of the correlative creedal rules and other absolute presuppositions to mean that the universe was created in six days, and those who interpret it in the context of the correlative creedal rules and other absolute presuppositions to be completely compatible with evolutionary theory, or even to be the fundamental absolute presupposition of evolutionary theory. Strains of this kind need not directly involve the most fundamental absolute presuppositions, but arise elsewhere in a given constellation and concern the interpretative adequacy of a constellation of rules in properly developing its subject matter.

These are the implicit but readily recognised kinds of consideration underlying Collingwood's claim that it is epistemically possible, on good grounds, concurrently to hold together in a single constellation logically incompatible rules, though not without producing strains of some kind and degree in the resulting structure.[78] The basic reason for this claim is that constellations of rules are neither brought nor held together by deductive connections alone, but by historical forces and correlative acts of interpretation of varying degrees of centrality and significance. Different kinds and degrees of strain thereby arise because of logical incompatibilities among the interpretative declaratives or propositions generated by, or deduced from, the constellation of rules that history puts together, and this is a

---

78. Ibid., 331–2.

universal and permanent characteristic of such constellations.[79] Although the logical conflict that results in a strain is necessary, our knowledge of it is on the whole contingent. A strain exists in potential by virtue of purely logical relations, but, before a strain becomes actual, it takes someone to notice it in interpretative thought and action. Thus, when one absolute presupposition or rule in a constellation of absolute presuppositions or rules is identified as logically incompatible with another, this means, not that it is logically impossible for them to be consupponible, but that it has subsequently emerged that they generate, or can have deduced from them, classes of third-person, interpretative declaratives or propositions that are contradictory or inconsistent. To refer to Collingwood's own example, which is yet another permutation on the logical incompatibilities or kinds and degrees of strain that might arise among absolute presuppositions, he argues that the constellation of absolute presuppositions that is Kant's account of causation is to be interpreted as conjoining two different and *independently legitimate* senses or contexts of use of the word 'cause' that are nevertheless logically incompatible or inconsistent *in that constellation*, thus giving rise to change-generating strains in the conception of causation.[80] Hence what is consupponible for Kant emerges as 'not consupponible; or at any rate not consupponible except under a pressure which must produce a somewhat violent strain in the resulting structure'.[81]

In short, consupponibility does not exclude logical incompatibility, for consupponibility is an epistemic condition that is not sufficient for logical compatibility, whereas logical compatibility or incompatibility is a matter of the relations among the intrinsically variable classes of third-person interpretative declaratives or metaphysical propositions generated by, or deducible from, a constellation of first-person performative rules. Logical compatibility implies consupponibility, but consupponibility does not imply logical compatibility.[82]

Faith, Reason and Metaphysics in Collingwood's Writings

With the creedal interpretation of Collingwood's theory of absolute presuppositions laid out, it is now possible to examine the place of *An Essay on*

---

79. Ibid., 48n.
80. Ibid., 331–7.
81. Ibid., 331–2.
82. Thus Collingwood does not use Michael Krausz's term 'inconsupponibility', which conflates consupponibility and logical compatibility; see Krausz, 'The Logic of Absolute Presuppositions', 239. Once again, I am deeply indebted to Stephen Gardner for discussions and indispensable guidance on the whole topic of logical compatibility in *An Essay on Metaphysics*.

Metaphysics in the overall development of his thought on the question of the nature and status of metaphysics, and in particular on the relation of faith and reason, philosophy and religion. Although not acknowledged as such in his *Autobiography*, these are the central themes in his work.[83] In my view there are five interrelated, but clearly distinguishable phases here, which I will try roughly to describe.

The first phase is characterised by what I shall call Collingwood's 'continuum thesis' and is represented by his first work, *Philosophy and Religion* (1916).[84] He thinks of religious faith or trust as the universal medium of life activity; 'all true life is religion',[85] for religious faith is a matter of whatever is believed in or trusted to be of absolute value, and which guides all thought and action.[86] As such, religion is not simply a heterogeneous compound of various activities, but a composite unity of thought and action[87] that he analyses under the idealist rubric of the concrete universal as an all-encompassing unity-in-difference. Because religion is essentially creedal in nature,[88] and creed is 'the intellectual element of . . . religion',[89] religious belief and theology, though distinguishable, are inseparable. As he puts it: 'a creed is a theology'.[90] And because theology and philosophy 'are both views of the same thing, the ultimate nature of the universe, the true religion and true philosophy must coincide, though they may differ in the vocabulary which they use to express the same facts'.[91] As the development of religion and philosophy makes clear, however, these facts are historical in nature.[92] 'History is that which actually exists: fact, as something independent of my own or your knowledge of it.'[93] Thus history 'is philosophical, that is all-embracing, universal . . . because historical fact is the only thing that exists and includes the whole universe . . . history is nothing other than the totality of existence; and this is also the object of philosophy'.[94] It follows that 'history and philosophy are the same thing'.[95] Moreover, this is

---

83. See the excellent critical biography of Collingwood by Fred Inglis, *The History Man: The Life of R.G. Collingwood* (Princeton: Princeton University Press, 2009).
84. R. G. Collingwood, *Philosophy and Religion* (London: Macmillan, 1916; repr. Bristol: Thoemmes Press, 1997). Subsequent citations give the page number of the reprint edition, followed by the page number of the 1916 original.
85. Collingwood, *Philosophy and Religion*, 71; 1916: 35.
86. Ibid., 56–7; 1916: 19–20.
87. Ibid., 68, 71; 1916: 32, 35.
88. Ibid., 46, 48, 50, 74; 1916: 7, 9, 11, 39.
89. Ibid., 51; 1916: 12.
90. Ibid., 51; 1916: 12.
91. Ibid., 55; 1916: 18.
92. Ibid., 73; 1916: 37.
93. Ibid., 83; 1916: 49.
94. Ibid., 84–5; 1916: 51.
95. Ibid., 85; 1916: 51.

a consequence that loops back into theology and religion. In Collingwood's words: 'The value of historical theology, then, consists in the fact that it is already philosophical', and equally 'Religion cannot afford to ignore its historical content, nor can it treat this content as something inessential to the establishment of its speculative doctrines.'[96] On this account, religion, theology, philosophy and history form a continuum of elements constituting the identity-in-difference that is the totality of existence. Of particular relevance here, with reference to *An Essay on Metaphysics*, is Collingwood's statement of the relation of history and philosophy:

> It is incorrect to say that philosophy is theory *based upon* fact; theory is not something else derived, distilled from facts but simply the observation that the facts are what they are. And similarly the philosophical presuppositions of history are not something different from the history itself: they are philosophical truths which the historian finds historically exemplified.[97]

The second phase of Collingwood's thought on the nature and status of metaphysics is characterised by what I shall call his 'hierarchy thesis'. As is generally recognised, this second phase, represented by *Speculum Mentis* (1923),[98] elaborates an account of the relation of religion and philosophy different from that of 1916. Religion is still seen as a basic feature of life, and experience is still treated as a concrete universal or unity-in-difference. But Collingwood now follows the general Hegel–Croce view of experience as constituting a hierarchy of types, in which the higher types correct the deficiencies of the lower types. Collingwood's hierarchy consists, in this order, of art, religion, science, history and philosophy. As he explicitly states, the chief difference between his view of religion in *Speculum Mentis* and that presented in *Religion and Philosophy* is his introduction of 'the distinction between the implicit and the explicit'.[99] That is, following Hegel and Croce, Collingwood in *Speculum Mentis* treats religion, and its essential creedal content,[100] as a matter of pictorial representation: 'it is implicit metaphor, metaphorical assertion mistaking itself for literal assertion'.[101] Theology is now little more than a confused halfway house between religion on the one side and 'the life of thought' (science, history, philosophy) on the other.[102] Indeed, the concrete unity-in-difference that is experience now becomes fully explicit or self-conscious, and so consistent, only in philosophy.

---

96. Ibid., 85; 1916: 52.
97. Ibid., 85; 1916: 51.
98. R. G. Collingwood, *Speculum Mentis or The Map of Knowledge* (Oxford: Clarendon Press, 1923).
99. Collingwood, *Speculum Mentis*, 108n.
100. Ibid., 111, 118.
101. Ibid., 147.
102. Ibid., 146–53.

For Collingwood in this second phase, therefore, the ultimate nature of things emerges by way of a philosophical implicit-to-explicit demonstration procedure that is an *ascent*; for example, from the creedal concept of God as a grounding 'self-differentiating' unity,[103] to the philosophical doctrine of absolute mind as the concrete universal or unity-in-difference. This account of the demonstration procedure of philosophy as an *ascent* from the implicit to the explicit, in which philosophy receives the top ranking, dominates Collingwood's thought for the next decade or more, until *An Essay on Metaphysics*.

The third phase of Collingwood's thought on the nature and status of metaphysics is characterised by what I shall call his 'intuitive certainty thesis', which is clearly stated in his 1927 *Hibbert Journal* article, 'Reason Is Faith Cultivating Itself'.[104] Here, Collingwood no longer sees religion and philosophy as continuous, co-equal aspects of a whole, but neither does he regard religion as merely a matter of pictorial representation. Rather, religion, which had been treated in the earlier writings as a general feature of experience rather than in terms of specific doctrines, now becomes an even more generalised 'faith', understood as 'immediate and indemonstrable certainty'.[105] This faith includes not only religious beliefs, but also, for example, Descartes' *cogito*, which is held to show that 'intuitive certainty is the fundamental source of all knowledge'.[106] Faith as 'immediate, unreasoned and indemonstrable conviction'[107] is now the basis of all knowledge and action, and as such is the 'presupposition' of all reasoning,[108] even though we may not recognise the specific certainties that underpin our activities.[109] In consequence, for all the breadth of this notion of faith, Collingwood's view of the relation of faith to reason is here much more oriented to the Augustinian notion of *ratio sapientiae* than to the Hegelian theory of religion as picture thinking. Indeed, he presents a summary account of the relation of Greek and Christian thought that anticipates the essentials, and is perhaps the germ, of Cochrane's work.[110] For over against the Platonic account of divine reason, Collingwood asserts the Christian view of faith as 'the organ of knowledge'.[111] That is, 'reason is

---

103. That is, a triunity, as the contrastive rejection of the 'mere abstract unity' of the Islamic God makes clear; ibid., 118.
104. Collingwood, *Faith and Reason*, 108–21.
105. Ibid., 114.
106. Ibid., 114; cf. 119.
107. Ibid., 119.
108. Ibid., 115, 118.
109. Ibid., 116.
110. Ibid., 109–12.
111. Ibid., 109.

not the negation of faith, but its development into an articulated system'.[112] Thus philosophy is the essential fulfilment of faith because it articulates faith into a 'self-explanatory system', in the sense defined above in relation to the triune account of the self-differentiating ultimate.[113] As Collingwood puts it: 'Every act is fundamentally an act of faith; but it is not a completed act of faith unless it develops into a rational and self-explanatory system of thought.'[114] It is in this sense that Collingwood concludes, 'reason is nothing but faith cultivating itself'.

The fourth and penultimate phase of Collingwood's thought on the nature and status of metaphysics is stated in *An Essay on Philosophical Method* (1933).[115] Here, philosophy once again moves from the implicit to the explicit; that is, from the lesser to the better known.[116] Thus, in contrast to the universal hypothetical propositions characteristic of natural science, and the categorical propositions about individuals in the world characteristic of history, the propositions of philosophy are categorical (about something existent) and universal (about everything existent). In spelling out the nature of the implicit-to-explicit movement in terms of philosophy's elaboration of categorical and universal propositions, Collingwood develops the notion of a self-explanatory ultimate unity by way of what I shall call the 'ontological proof thesis'.

To understand Collingwood's treatment of the self-explanatory, it is useful to refer once again to the principle of reason. The definition of that principle that Collingwood employs in *An Essay on Philosophical Method* is directly derived from F. H. Bradley. The starting point of philosophical inquiry Bradley calls 'a principle of action': namely the search for what he terms 'intellectual satisfaction'.[117] In seeking intellectual satisfaction, he holds that 'philosophy . . . in the end rests on what may fairly be termed faith'.[118] Of this faith, he says that it 'can neither be proved nor questioned'.[119] That is to say, philosophical inquiry absolutely presupposes the search for intellectual satisfaction. As he describes his approach in *Appearance and Reality*: 'I have assumed that the object of metaphysics is

---

112. Ibid., 118.
113. Cf. ibid., 119–20.
114. Ibid., 118.
115. R. G. Collingwood, *An Essay on Philosophical Method (1933), Revised Edition with The Metaphysics of F. H. Bradley, The Correspondence with Gilbert Ryle, Method and Metaphysics*, ed. James Connolly and Guiseppina D'Oro (Oxford: Clarendon Press, 2005).
116. Ibid., 161.
117. F. H. Bradley, *Essays on Truth and Reality* (Oxford: Clarendon Press, 1914), 26.
118. Ibid., 15.
119. F. H. Bradley, *Appearance and Reality: A Metaphysical Essay* (Oxford: Clarendon Press, 2nd rev. edn, 1930), 491.

to find a general view which will satisfy the intellect, and I have assumed that whatever succeeds in doing this is real and true, and whatever fails is neither.'[120] He adds elsewhere: 'But as to what will satisfy I have of course no knowledge in advance . . . the way and the means are to be discovered only by trial and rejection. The method is clearly experimental.'[121] This Bradleyan version of the principle of reason may be termed the principle of satisfaction. And Collingwood simply paraphrases Bradley's principle of satisfaction when he interprets Anselm's ontological argument in *An Essay on Philosophical Method* as the claim that 'thought, when it follows its own bent most completely . . . sets itself the task of thinking out the idea of an object that shall completely satisfy the demands of reason'.[122]

For Collingwood, only an object that is a complete unity of essence and existence can satisfy the demands of reason. However, the proof that there is an ultimate unity of essence and existence is not for him a result of Bradleyan faith in any hypothetical or experimental principle. Rather, Collingwood asserts that the proof of the ultimate unity of essence and existence resides in Hegel's version of the ontological argument, whereby the finite is analysed as the self-actualisation of the infinite; from which it follows that the infinite is a self-actualising unity of essence and existence. Because there is such an ultimate unity, Collingwood claims that the legitimacy of the otherwise hypothetical principle of reason is demonstrated. Only because philosophy can prove that there is an ultimate unity of essence and existence is intellectual satisfaction possible, for unless that unity can be shown to be real at the outset, thinking alone could never arrive at it.

To summarise: Collingwood 1) reinterprets the ontological argument as asserting the unity of essence and existence; which unity 2) must be philosophically proven, as it is by Hegel's version of the ontological argument; otherwise 3) the principle of reason would be a mere *ens rationis*. The key point is that Collingwood accepts that the mind cannot move from essence or concepts to existence without philosophical proof of their prior unity.

The fifth and final phase of Collingwood's thought on the nature and status of metaphysics is of course characterised by the 'creedal rule thesis' of *An Essay on Metaphysics*, which defines the nature of historically manifested absolute presuppositions that are the subject matter of metaphysics as rules of faith or trust. Enough has perhaps been said to justify this interpretation. What is now required is an account of the place of the creedal rule thesis in the development of Collingwood's thought, and an analysis of the consequences he draws from it. This will be the subject of the next section.

---

120. Ibid.
121. Bradley, *Essays on Truth and Reality*, 311.
122. Collingwood, *An Essay on Philosophical Method*, 125.

Collingwood's Development and his Final Theory of Metaphysics

In considering the final development of Collingwood's thought on metaphysics in *An Essay on Metaphysics*, it is of the utmost importance to note that his historicisation of the notion of presuppositions by way of their status as creedal rules is essentially a return to, and a sophistication of, the 1916 continuum thesis of *Religion and Philosophy*. Faith, creed, theology, philosophy and history once again form a continuum of inseparable elements and a unity of thought and practice. Their relations, now mediated by the constellation of fundamental absolute presuppositions that is the Trinity, are the constitutive conditions of experience. In this respect, *An Essay on Metaphysics* is an immense expansion of the role accorded to faith or trust in 1916. As the Collingwood of *An Essay on Metaphysics* argues in his analyses of various secondary presuppositions, and as he puts it at one point, explicitly referring back to *Religion and Philosophy*: 'The act by which we hold such presuppositions, I have said elsewhere, is religious faith; and God is that in which we believe by faith; therefore all our absolute presuppositions must be presuppositions in holding which we believe something about God.'[123]

By thus making the Trinitarian Creed the fundamental absolute presupposition or rule of Western science and civilisation, Collingwood is completely rejecting the empiricist, positivist and naturalist version of the story of philosophy, everywhere told in the English-speaking world: namely, that philosophy, once the handmaiden of theology, replaced theology in the seventeenth century, only to become in turn the handmaiden of science, a role in which it proudly and properly remains. Over against such claims, Collingwood spells out an alternative and at least equally compelling story. It is one that, as has been noted, is characteristic of the explanatorist and historiological traditions in metaphysics. This is a story in which 'metaphysics and theology are the same'.[124] It is a story in which theology lies at the heart of metaphysics, for theology is the site of the historical unfolding of fundamental absolute presuppositions or objects of faith that it is the business of metaphysics to articulate and develop. To see how Collingwood understands what it means to place faith and theology once again at the core of metaphysics, it is necessary further to examine the place of *An Essay on Metaphysics* in his development.

From *Speculum Mentis* to *An Essay on Metaphysics* Collingwood's demonstration procedure is always a movement from the implicit to the explicit.

---

123. Collingwood, *Essay on Metaphysics*, 216; cf. 253–4, 265–8, 324–5.
124. Ibid., 215; cf. 10, 188, 216, 221.

What alters in *An Essay on Metaphysics* is not the implicit-to-explicit form of the movement, but the type of movement that it is understood to be, which, from *Speculum Mentis* to *An Essay on Philosophical Method*, in one way or another always gives philosophy the top ranking. This alteration is a consequence of a major shift in *An Essay on Metaphysics* in Collingwood's account of the content of the demonstration procedure. The implicit in *Speculum Mentis* is (summarily) picture thinking; in the *Hibbert Journal* article, the implicit is theology; in *An Essay on Philosophical Method*, it is the lesser known, which is replaced by the better known.[125] Correlatively, the explicit in *Speculum Mentis* is philosophy's all-containing absolute; in the *Hibbert Journal* article, it is philosophy's self-explanatory system; in *An Essay on Philosophical Method*, it is, among other things, philosophy's ontological proof of God as the self-explanatory unity of essence and existence. Once one comes to *An Essay on Metaphysics*, however, the implicit is presented, with full critical intent, as philosophy, in the form of positivism, or more generally scientism. The explicit is now the historically manifested absolute presupposition of the Trinity and the secondary presuppositions derived from it. The crucial shifts involved here in the notions of faith, the principle of reason, the self-explanatory, God and history can be considered shortly. Looked at only in terms of Collingwood's demonstration procedure, what has altered is that the ultimate principle is not to be found, as earlier, by way of the ascent *in speculo mentis* through art and religion, nor through such devices as the ontological proof. Rather, the ultimate principle is to be discovered by way of a descent or regress back up a series of conditions from the implicit to the fundamental absolute presupposition or rule of faith. Philosophy, in the form of metaphysics, still has its essential role as that which makes explicit. But metaphysics, in moving from the implicit to the explicit, is now a reductive regress from the inadequate world of philosophical positivism or naturalism to its historiological conditions, understood not as propositions but as rules. Collingwood has here succeeded in reconciling and uniting a Kantian-style regressive analysis of possibility conditions with a Hegelian recognition of their variable, historiological nature.[126] His is a theory of historiological-transcendental, *a priori* rules.

What makes this clear is that, in contrast to the 'intuitive certainty thesis' of the *Hibbert Journal* article, philosophy in *An Essay on Metaphysics* no longer develops the implicit contents of faith into an explicit 'self-explanatory system'.[127] In *An Essay on Metaphysics*, rather, philosophy makes explicit the historical fact that the self-explanatory is a key component of the absolute

---

125. Collingwood, *Essay on Philosophical Method*, 161.
126. I am grateful to Darren Hynes and Peter Trnka for discussions on this topic.
127. Collingwood, *Faith and Reason*, 118.

presuppositions or rules in which we have faith or trust. Faith is still 'the organ of knowledge', but its status as such is no longer a consequence of any prior and overt religious commitments we may have, but of the conceptual-historical investigation that uncovers what our absolute presuppositions or rules are, whether we recognise them as such or not. Faith is still 'immediate, unreasoned and indemonstrable conviction',[128] but these characteristics are not a consequence of any conscious beliefs we may hold, but of the status of those beliefs as absolute presuppositions or rules in a given historical phase.

A similar kind of transformation is undergone by the 'ontological proof thesis' of *An Essay on Philosophical Method* in the context of the theory of absolute presuppositions. First, the reduction procedure of *An Essay on Metaphysics* means that metaphysics does not proceed either by way of the principle of reason or by way of providing an ontological proof of the unity of essence and existence. Rather, the principle of reason, as well as its fulfilment by whatever is held to be the self-explanatory ultimate, have significance only because of the role they play in the constellation of absolute presuppositions. The principle of reason and the concept of a self-explanatory ultimate are now derived by way of a regressive examination of the conditions of our practice. To be sure, the principle of reason is in its own right a hypothetical rule whose range of application is a matter of debate. However, once granted that the doctrine of the Trinity is an absolute presupposition or rule, then there is no need to provide any proof of the principle of reason or of a self-explanatory ultimate. Instead, the claim is that both are historiological givens, for both state features of the nature of the historically manifested absolute presupposition or rule that is the doctrine of the Trinity. That they characterise a fundamental absolute presupposition means for Collingwood that they themselves are among its constellation of absolute presuppositions or rules. If it emerges that our practice has the principle of reason and a self-explanatory unity among its fundamental absolute presuppositions or rules of faith, then we have to acknowledge their role and status as part of the framework conditions or rules to which our practice commits us. Here, indeed, we are face to face with Collingwood's final response to empiricist and Kantian limitations on the range of application of the principle of reason: his claim is that our historiologically constituted faith and practice commits us to the unrestricted application of that principle.

Even if not stated in so many words, this is clearly what Collingwood holds to be the case. For, secondly, Collingwood maintains that the conceptual foundations of modern science are to be found in a self-explanatory

---

128. Ibid., 118.

and so characteristically metaphysical doctrine, namely the Trinity. With Foster and Cochrane, he holds that the doctrine of the Trinity provides the three co-equal principles required for the development of science: a principle of unity, a principle of differentiation or plurality, and a principle of order, which Collingwood (with Aristotle and perhaps Cochrane in mind) terms 'movement'.[129] The defining historical developments of the last 1700 years or so are claimed to have this as their necessary condition. So the concern with the self-explanatory ultimate remains, and the self-explanatory ultimate is still that which possesses in its own nature all the reasons for its existence and that of anything else. Indeed, this is a theme that runs throughout *An Essay on Metaphysics*, where Collingwood is emphatic that the Trinity is a self-explanatory principle. God is the concept of 'the logical ground of everything else',[130] and the concept of a 'logical ground'[131] is the concept of an underived 'activity of self-movement'[132] that is as such a 'self-differentiating unity'[133] – which is the Trinity *par excellence*.[134] The self-explanatory unity of essence and existence that characterises the Trinity is a constituent feature of the 'constellation'[135] that makes up the ultimate absolute presupposition or rule. Thus the principle of reason is still present in *An Essay on Metaphysics* as an integral part of that constellation, and metaphysics is still primarily concerned with categorical universals; however, such universals no longer have the form of propositions, but are the components of absolute presuppositions or rules, and so they are subject to the metaphysical rubric.

It is evident in this context that the Collingwood of *An Essay on Metaphysics* has moved away from the thoroughgoing rationalism of the later Hegel's account of the starting place of philosophy as 'pure being'[136] and of Hegel's account of the ontological *proof*.[137] He is in fact now much closer to the positions of Schelling and Bradley, or, more precisely, to Bradley's anti-Hegelian, Schellingian theory of foundations. For, like both Schelling and Bradley, Collingwood now holds that the starting point of philosophy is a given, underivable foundation and context of reflection that is never transcended. For Schelling, the starting point and permanent medium of philosophy is the primordial intuition of the existence of the divine nature

---

129. Collingwood, *Essay on Metaphysics*, 225–6.
130. Ibid., 10.
131. Cf. ibid., 6.
132. Ibid., 217.
133. Ibid., 6, 212, 220.
134. Ibid., 226 and note.
135. Ibid., 227.
136. Cf. ibid., ch. 2.
137. Ibid., 189–90.

that is to be accepted in faith, for, as he remarks, 'The existence of what is unconditional cannot be proven like the existence of something finite. The unconditional is the element wherein any demonstration becomes possible.'[138] By contrast, Bradley, ever the empiricist, holds the starting point and permanent accompaniment of all reflection to be the immediate, non-relational whole of feeling that he claims is the given, intuitively known, basic feature of all experience.[139] Collingwood works within this tradition, but nevertheless replaces such permanent, intuited principles with the historical variables that are absolute presuppositions or rules of faith. He transforms Schelling's intuited existence and Bradley's immediate experience into the world of cultural-practical history. The starting point of philosophy now is not ontology or phenomenology, but his presuppositional or fiducial version of historiology.

The consequence is that in *An Essay on Metaphysics* the unity of essence and existence is no longer the subject of *a priori*, deductive proof, as it was in *An Essay on Philosophical Method*. Anselm's ontological argument is not the proof of the proposition that 'God exists' but a third-person, interpretative articulation of the historically manifested absolute presupposition or rule of belief in God. It is not in the usual sense of the word a metaphysical argument but, as Collingwood puts it, an 'historical argument'.[140] The unity of essence and existence is now instaurated in philosophy, not by way of a defence of the principle of reason and its unrestricted application, nor by the Anselmian or Hegelian ontological arguments, but by way of the status of that unity as an historically manifested, fundamental absolute presupposition or rule of faith. The role Collingwood has finally found for philosophy is to uncover and acknowledge its unavoidable commitment to its own historically manifested metaphysical-theological grounds. Thus the ontological argument has become the historico-ontological argument – the argument that, whether we know it or not, the historically manifested absolute presuppositions of our practice commit us to belief in the point of philosophy.

---

138. F. W. J. Schelling, 'Stuttgart Seminars' (1810), in *Idealism and the Endgame of Theory: Three Essays by F. W. J. Schelling*, trans. and ed. Thomas Pfau (Albany, NY: SUNY Press, 1994), 199. I am grateful to Peter Harris for drawing my attention to this passage. For more of Schelling's writings on this topic, see F. W. J. Schelling, *The Grounding of Positive Philosophy: The Berlin Lectures*, trans. Bruce Matthews (Albany, NY: SUNY Press, 2007).
139. See especially F. H. Bradley, 'On Our Knowledge of Immediate Experience', in *Essays on Truth and Reality*, ch. 6. For an account of Bradley's theory of feeling, see my 'F.H. Bradley's Metaphysics of Feeling and its Place in the History of Philosophy', in Anthony Manser and Guy Stock (eds), *The Philosophy of F.H. Bradley* (Oxford: Clarendon Press, 1984), 227–42.
140. Collingwood, *Essay on Metaphysics*, 188–90.

As will emerge, it is quite another question whether or not Collingwood accepts Hegel's logic. Collingwood's historico-ontological argument still moves from idea to existence, but idea has been redefined as the historically constituted fundamental absolute presupposition of the Trinity. So his strategy could equally be described as a move from or through history to reality. For what makes the fundamental absolute presupposition of the Trinity more than a mere *ens rationis* is the characteristic post-Kantian idealist view, derived and developed out of Christian theology, that history is the actualisation of the real.

To make this last point clear, it is necessary to turn to the treatment of truth in *An Essay on Metaphysics*. Before doing so, however, it will be useful briefly to indicate something of the significance of Collingwood's view of the fundamental presuppositional status of the Trinity for his conception of history.

First, in defining the Trinity as fundamental absolute presupposition, it is important to note that Collingwood has uncoupled the notion of the self-explanatory from that of an all-containing absolute. In other words, his regressive procedure goes hand-in-hand with a notable redefinition of his earlier Hegelian conception of infinite mind, which amounts to a return to a more traditional view of the role of God as creator. For Collingwood's Trinity is not self-explanatory in the sense that it is all-containing, either as that which already possesses in its own nature (in ideal form, for example) all the determinations to which it gives rise, or as that which is the completely realised whole of all things. On the contrary, for the later Collingwood, that which is self-explanatory in its own nature is that which possesses in its nature all the reasons, but *only* in the sense of the enabling conditions, for the existence of the historical formations it makes possible. Hence, as Collingwood emphasises, his thematic concept of 'ground' in *An Essay on Metaphysics* is not that of 'cause'.[141] That is to say, the concept of cause is a specific variety of the genus 'principle' (*principium*; the Latin translation of the Greek *arche*, origin or beginning) or the genus 'ground' (*Grund*), for 'cause' implies a greater degree of dependence on the part of the effect than do the concepts of 'principle'[142] or 'ground'. Thus, defined as 'grounds', the triune conditions of actualisation are open, non-determining conditions: they are immanent grounds that make possible, but do not guarantee, the developments that arise from them. They are necessary but not sufficient conditions. So history itself is, as Collingwood always insists, 'open';[143] it is the site not of necessity but of freedom. To put it theologically, this is

---

141. Ibid., 329.
142. See Aquinas, *Summa Theologiae*, 1a, q. 33, a. 1, ad 1.
143. Collingwood, *Essay on Metaphysics*, 65.

his interpretation of the claim that creation is the creation of independent centres of free activity.

Secondly, if what has been said about the importance of Foster and Cochrane, about the logical relations among hierarchies of rules,[144] and about history as the site of freedom are correct readings of Collingwood, his historical claim concerning the fundamental presuppositional status of the doctrine of the Trinity clearly does not imply that the rise of natural science can be derived by deductive necessity from that doctrine. Equally, in line with the Augustinian and historiological tradition, neither does he allow their connection to be reduced to mere contingency or happenstance. The relation between the doctrine of the Trinity and natural science could perhaps best be described as an abductive relation. For the point is that the doctrine of the Trinity introduces a range of potentialities into Western culture, the development of some of which was enabled by myriad circumstances over long periods of time. The unfolding of these potentialities does not come about as a result of purely abstract ratiocination, but is embedded in the materiality of sociocultural history.[145] In consequence, such potentialities are not determinable prior to, but only come to be in, their realisation. As Rex Martin puts it, 'we can only go *through* the practice itself . . .'[146]

Thirdly and finally, a major consequence of Collingwood's conception of history as the site of the development of potentialities is that all historical events and determinations are in their own nature also essentially vague or open to further determination. They are open in the radical sense that their potentiality is never exhausted. On this analysis, there are no absolute nominalist individuals;[147] hence Collingwood's theories of encapsulation and re-enactment, and his Bradleyan claim against the realists that judgement makes a difference to its object.[148] Correlatively, history is Collingwood's principle of potentiality or vagueness: the law of the excluded middle does not apply to any structure, law or rule, for all are historical and thus vague. This, I suggest, is the reason why he can write:

---

144. Cf. ibid., 66–7.
145. D. M. MacKinnon is right to emphasise the Marxist tendency in Collingwood's thinking; see 'Faith and Reason in the Philosophy of Religion', in David Boucher, James Connolly and Tariq Modood (eds), *Philosophy, History and Civilization: Interdisciplinary Perspectives on R.G. Collingwood* (Cardiff: University of Wales Press, 1995), 79–91. On the present analysis, this is of course to be expected, for Marxism is itself a branch of the historiological tradition.
146. Martin, 'Editor's Introduction', in Collingwood, *Essay on Metaphysics*, xlix.
147. Collingwood, *Essay on Metaphysics*, 244–5, 263.
148. Collingwood, *Autobiography*, 44ff.; R. G. Collingwood, *The Principles of History: And Other Writings in Philosophy of History*, ed. W. Dray and W. J. Van Der Dussen (Oxford: Clarendon Press, 2001).

> The aim of logic is to expound the principles of valid thought. It is idly fancied that validity in thought is at all times one and the same . . . and that in consequence the truths, which it is the logician's business to discover, are eternal truths. But all that any logician has ever done, or tried to do, is to expound the principles of what in his own day passed for valid thought among those whom he regarded as reputable thinkers. The enterprise is strictly historical.[149]

To put the vagueness point another way: Collingwood's many-sided, metaphysically saturated term 'historical' is in one of its aspects his principle of revisability.

This brings me to the problem of the treatment of the notion of truth in *An Essay on Metaphysics*, closely related as that is to Collingwood's post-Kantian idealist view of history.

Absolute Presuppositions, Criticism and Truth

The problem of the status of the concept of truth in the theory of absolute presuppositions arises because, for Collingwood, absolute presuppositions are not propositions. In consequence, he maintains that the verificationists' disjunctive account of truth as a matter of either truth or falsity holds of propositions, including metaphysical propositions, but is inapplicable to absolute presuppositions. This raises two questions. First, is criticism of absolute presuppositions possible? Secondly, do absolute presuppositions have as such any truth status?

The first question is easier to answer. Once absolute presuppositions are recognised as defined by Collingwood on the model of creedal rules, with its correlative distinction between performatives and declaratives or what he calls metaphysical propositions, then it becomes evident that criticism of them and debate about them is not just possible but necessary. As both Foster and Cochrane argue in considerable detail, such criticism and debate is an essential element in the movement of history, and both show how the doctrine of the Trinity was developed and refined in a welter of argument and counter-argument. Such arguments are, for Collingwood, arguments about the consistency of the absolute presuppositions that compose a constellation of absolute presuppositions, considered in terms of the classes of third-person, interpretative declaratives or propositions that they generate. As Collingwood's notion of the various kinds and degrees of strains that might obtain in a given constellation indicates, the criteria of the assessment of absolute presuppositions are those of the idealist theory of truth transposed into a historiological context. Coherence is a matter of the relations

---

149. Collingwood, *Principles of History*, 242.

of logical compatibility among rules, as defined earlier. Comprehensiveness is the measure of the relative adequacy or success of a constellation of rules in properly unfolding or developing its subject matter by way of the interpretative correlation of different rules in that constellation, as was indicated above in the discussion of divine creation. Besides Collingwood's own examples of strains, Cochrane's account of the mixture of classicist and Christian elements in Tertullian's account of the Trinity would be a case in point, analysing as it does the complex strains in Tertullian that subsequent thinkers had to address.[150]

In this context, it becomes quite clear how to read Collingwood's claim throughout *An Essay on Metaphysics* that the metaphysician's job is to state or report what absolute presuppositions or rules are operative in a given historical phase. This does not mean, as is often thought, that absolute presuppositions cannot be criticised, as should be obvious from the fact that Collingwood himself readily convicts of 'metaphysical error' not only certain absolute presuppositions in classical philosophy,[151] but also, among others, the absolute presuppositions involved in Kant's doctrine of the permanence of substance[152] and his theory of causation.[153] Moreover, the writings of Foster and Cochrane provide numerous instances of the incoherence and inadequacy of various presuppositions, and of the often fierce debates surrounding them. Here, as elsewhere, Collingwood's employment of the model of creedal rules, with its distinction between first-person performative rules and the third-person, interpretative declaratives or propositions they generate, completely exonerates him from the near-incredible self-contradiction of which he has been accused because he makes criticisms of absolute presuppositions![154]

The second and more difficult question is whether or not absolute presuppositions have as such any truth status, beyond the empirical-historical truth status that they enjoy when they are the properly defined absolute presuppositions of some historical epoch. The importance of this question cannot be underestimated. For if the truth status of absolute presuppositions

---

150. Cochrane, *Christianity and Classical Culture*, 229–30, 246–8; LF, 252–3, 270–2.
151. Collingwood, *Essay on Metaphysics*, 215, 221, 226.
152. Ibid., ch. 27.
153. Ibid., 328–33.
154. Apart from the fact that Collingwood had the work of Foster and Cochrane in front of him, his idealist-derived, immanentist and 'contextualist' theory of the criteria of absolute presuppositions as coherence and comprehensiveness means that he does not need a 'super-absolute' presupposition to explain conceptual change, contrary to Stephen Toulmin, *Human Understanding. The Collective Use and Evolution of Concepts* (Oxford: Clarendon Press, 1972), 76–7; see also Beaney, 'Collingwood's Conception of Presuppositional Analysis', 93. This is not to deny that, for Collingwood, 'God exists' is historically a basic 'background' presupposition.

is no more than empirical-historical, then our basic beliefs are merely the result of accidental happenstance and have no purchase on the real. Were that the case, Collingwood's metaphysics of absolute presuppositions would be a sort of historicist or relativist idealism, akin to the kind of linguistic idealism sometimes found in Wittgensteinian and postmodern philosophies of language. If not sceptical, his position on the Trinity would at best amount to nothing more than an historical fideism or dogmatism.[155] It would represent a complete abandonment of that concern with the nature of the historical disclosure of the real which so deeply concerned thinkers such as Hegel, Schelling and Peirce.

It is certainly the case that in *An Essay on Metaphysics*, Collingwood restricts discussion of the notion of truth to the logical positivist theory of truth as verification. On this view, the nature of truth is purely an epistemic relation of correspondence between propositions or linguistic structures and states of affairs, and all propositions are subject to the disjunction 'true or false'. Collingwood holds that because absolute presuppositions are first-person performative rules, not third-person declaratives or propositions, they do not stand in a relation of correspondence to anything and are not disjunctively true or false. It would be wrong to assume, however, that there is not another theory of the nature of truth heavily inscribed in *An Essay on Metaphysics*. Indeed, once Collingwood's use of creedal rules, and his orientation to the historiological tradition, are taken into account, the presence of this alternative theory of the nature of truth in *An Essay on Metaphysics* is more or less self-evident. For both the theological and historiological traditions characteristically subscribe, not to the epistemic, but to what R. J. Campbell calls the ontological theory of truth.[156] This theory of the nature of truth – in which the term 'Truth' is often capitalised to mark the difference from epistemic accounts – is fundamental to metaphysics from Plato to Peirce and Heidegger. On the ontological theory, truth is a state or relation of the real. Whether articulated in a Platonic, scholastic, idealist or pragmatist framework, the real is understood to be an activity of disclosure or manifestation.

The central point here is that, after the rise of Christianity, the activity of disclosure or manifestation is held to occur in history and to be intrinsically a matter of the movement of history. As has been emphasised, this is the crucial and distinctive feature of the Judaeo-Christian view of truth. Both on the Greek and the Judaeo-Christian view, truth is what endures and does not pass. Further, on both views the unity of truth guarantees the unity of

---

155. See among many, Beaney, 'Collingwood's Conception of Presuppositional Analysis', 85–8, 105–6.
156. This is the influential view of T. M. Knox, 'Editor's Preface', in R. G. Collingwood, *The Idea of History* (Oxford: Clarendon Press, 1946), v–xxiv.

experience. However, truth as Greek *aletheia* does not happen. Even though it is always connected to the relation of the speaker to the addressee, as in the Socratic dialogue form, truth is not something personal and is not an event. As Socrates always insists, he is a mere midwife, an impersonal conduit for that which is thoroughly impersonal: namely, that truth that is much more than an event because it is always identical with itself and is the reality that is hidden behind appearances, a reality that can be disclosed only by rational thought. In contrast, a key transformative feature of the Judaeo-Christian view of truth is that truth is not a timeless state of affairs. It must occur, and it must be unfolded and realised again and again in new situations that shed fresh light on it. It is as such intrinsically connected to actions in time. In consequence, truth is not a reality that lies behind appearances, but is something that emerges in history and is nothing other than its disclosure and realisation in the movement of history.

Seen in this theological and historiological context, Collingwood's theory of absolute presuppositions has an obvious consequence, one that is characteristic of post-Kantian idealist historiology and about which Collingwood is explicit: namely, because the real is to be found nowhere except in the movement of history, the movement of history is its unfolding and disclosure. For Collingwood, as for Foster and Cochrane, the articulation of the real is a matter of the historically immanent and mutual critique of rules, a critique that is at once theoretical and practical. It is what is held in faith or trust, and informs our practice and action, that manifests the real and is reflected upon by metaphysics and theology. As the movement of history itself, the real is more than any of its specific historical manifestations. But the real is at least what the movement of history has shown it to be, and it is nothing less than that. History is thus not reducible to mere happenstance: the unity of the real and the empirical-historical is a relation of realisation, a matter of the actualisation of potentialities.

There are of course no guarantees that the process of the interpretative critique and transformation of presuppositions will be one of genuine development. For Collingwood, as noted, history is the arena of freedom and contingency. Moreover, given our intrinsic historicity or essential historical finitude and situatedness, we cannot make choices about our absolute presuppositions. We can only come to some recognition of their nature, and it would be foolish ever to lay claim to completeness, or, for example, to 'the best of all possible kinds of science . . . for nobody knows what all the possible kinds would be like'.[157] Nevertheless, the accounts that Foster, Cochrane and Collingwood offer of the development of the metaphysics of nature and science all provide strong arguments for the

---

157. Collingwood, *Essay on Metaphysics*, 254–5.

gradual, if erratic, correction of 'metaphysical error',[158] and thus, to that extent, of the unfolding of an ever more consistent and comprehensive apprehension of the nature of the world. Indeed, once Collingwood's account of the doctrine of the Trinity as the fundamental absolute presupposition of Western thought is taken into account, the post-Kantian view of history as the articulation of the real is clearly recognisable as an intrinsic feature of his metaphysics of absolute presuppositions. For the self-referential inclusiveness or reflexivity required of any philosophical theory of reality means that the metaphysics of absolute presuppositions has to acknowledge its own historical situatedness and its own presuppositions. Thus, for Collingwood, because the doctrine of the Trinity is the fundamental absolute presupposition of our thinking,[159] and because the self-differentiating activity of the Trinity is intrinsically self-communicating activity,[160] it follows that, as an integral part of the doctrine of the Trinity, the ontological theory of truth has the status of a fundamental absolute presupposition for the metaphysics of absolute presuppositions itself. So besides the formal or logical, creed-oriented analysis of presuppositions offered by the metaphysics of absolute presuppositions in terms of the logic of question and answer, the substantive content of that metaphysics is also creedal in nature, wherein the real presents itself as self-disclosing. It is the substantive metaphysical content of the creed – the doctrine of trinitarian self-communication – that prevents the formal analysis of presuppositions in terms of the logic of question and answer from lapsing into historicist relativism, just as the logic of question and answer prevents the metaphysics of presuppositions from lapsing into irrationalism. The Athanasian Creed thus encapsulates for Collingwood both the form and the fundamental content of the metaphysics of absolute presuppositions. This is why he insists, following Aristotle, that metaphysics and theology constitute a unity.

It may be objected that Collingwood's presuppositional claims in respect of the substantive, trinitarian content of his metaphysics is in fact irrationalist, for it amounts to a form of historical fideism. Yet his position here does no more than register the implacable irreducibility of historical fact. For Collingwood, the presuppositional status of the Trinity is a matter of the givenness of historical situation, the factuality of fact. He would hoist positivism with its own petard of verificationism. Whereas Hegel and Schelling attempt philosophically to demonstrate the reality of trinitarian self-communication by giving history itself a triune structure, Collingwood,

---

158. Ibid., 218–27.
159. Ibid., 227.
160. Ibid., 218–22.

like Foster and Cochrane, interprets trinitarian self-communication solely in terms of the empirical-historical outcomes of debate and struggle. He thus maintains a considerable looseness of fit between trinitarian self-communication and the concrete contingencies of the open movement of empirical history. In consequence, he is in no danger of overlooking the interpretative complexity and even instability that always accompanies the establishment of historical fact and any appeal to historical fact. Indeed, his whole critique of positivism serves to emphasise just that, and it does so by attempting to expose the myopic and simplistic account of the factual and observable that, for an historian of his range, is so glaring a weakness of positivism and most modern naturalisms. The creedal dimension of the metaphysics of absolute presuppositions makes it a powerful assertion of the unity of the empirical and the speculative-metaphysical.[161]

It is of course the case that Collingwood nowhere formally states or expounds his own ontological theory of the nature of truth as the revelation of the real by way of the movement of absolute presuppositions in and through the materiality of sociocultural development. As with the status of the principle of reason and the concept of the self-explanatory, Collingwood leaves it to the reader to work out the implications of the metaphysics of absolute presuppositions, and in particular the significance of the status of the Trinity as fundamental absolute presupposition. Given the sweep of his claims, it is time to step back and assess the overall position he presents in *An Essay on Metaphysics*.

Faith, Reason and Metaphysics in the *Essay*

In attempting a general overview of Collingwood's thought in *An Essay on Metaphysics*, I will consider how original it might be, what cogency the central claims about the Trinity might have, and its place in philosophical debate.

There can be little doubt that Collingwood's *Essay on Metaphysics* is the culmination of a lifelong concern with the relation between faith and reason. In this respect, his metaphysics of absolute presuppositions, defined on the creedal model of rules and the concomitant logic of question and answer, is an elaboration and development of the Augustinian tradition's dual emphasis on the primacy of faith or trust in the movement of historical experience and on the complementarity of faith and reason. So understood,

---

161. The anti-Thomist view that the Trinitarian God is essentially and eternally creative is, as will be noted below, a characteristic feature of the historiological tradition from Hegel, Schelling and Peirce onwards.

Collingwood's position is neither sceptical nor fideistic and dogmatic. As his critique of various absolute presuppositions clearly indicates, he does not in the least subscribe to the complete independence of faith from reason. Equally, his metaphysics of absolute presuppositions is a rejection of the tradition of natural theology, which, following Hegel, he explicitly criticises as an uneasy compromise between faith and reason, in which the 'work allotted' to the two spheres remains unclear, and in which it is assumed that infinite and finite, God and the world of experience, are two absolutely distinct and separate dimensions.[162] Indeed, the modern philosophical context in which Collingwood develops his Augustinian theme is that of the historiological tradition, initiated by Hegel and Schelling, which denies any fundamental opposition between faith and reason, or between natural and revealed theology. This is the historical context in which his endorsement of the Aristotelian unity of metaphysics and theology is to be understood.

The work of the representative figures of the historiological tradition is distinguished above all by their elaboration of various theories of metaphysical trinitarianism. As noted earlier, once relations and not individual substances are fundamental, trinitarian relations and finite structures are no longer ontological opposites. Thus Hegel and Schelling undertake to ground the doctrine of the Trinity philosophically, over against its treatment in the Protestantism of the day as solely a matter of biblical revelation. In Hegel, the *Deus revelatus* takes centre stage. God, as mind, is shown by transcendentally necessary dialectical deduction to be essentially creative and so essentially self-disclosing: the timeless truth unfolds itself in history in a necessary movement that is the very manifestation of the divine triunity. In consequence, the finite is not the ontological opposite of the infinite, but the articulation of the infinite, and the divine movement in history, because it is a movement of disclosure, is intrinsically exoteric, or available to rational reflection. The ahistorical approach of natural theology, and Kant's phenomenal/noumenal divide, is here replaced by historiology: the *Deus occultus*, revealed only to faith, is now the self-communicative threefold God that is revealed to all in history and can only be properly comprehended as such in terms of metaphysical historiology. The relations of metaphysics and theology, reason and faith, as defined by natural theology, are thus completely reversed. Metaphysics is not the handmaiden or propaedeutic to theology, and the work of philosophical reason is not to find support or some degree of commonality for theological claims that transcend it. Rather, the historically manifested doctrine of the Trinity finds the realisation of its true content only in and through metaphysics. Metaphysics is the fulfilment of theology in that metaphysics brings into

---

162. Collingwood, *Faith and Reason*, 112–13.

reflective consciousness, and spells out the significance, of the beliefs and practices that are the self-unfolding of the real in history. It is metaphysics that provides the basis in dialectical necessity for the absoluteness of theological faith. Theology understood is metaphysics, and metaphysics understood is speculative trinitarianism.

Schelling takes the same view of the essentially metaphysical character of theology as Hegel. However, although he too establishes metaphysical principles in terms of transcendentally necessary deductions, he repudiates Hegel's historiological necessitarianism and instead emphasises the freedom of history. He interprets the Judaeo-Christian view of truth as meaning that metaphysics is in constant crisis, for it must return to, and attempt to realise, over and over again, the presence of God in the ever-constant movement of history. Philosophy is thus for Schelling 'the philosophy of revelation'. Also, as noted earlier, he fundamentally differs from Hegel in his claim that the starting point and medium of metaphysics is the primordial intuition of God in faith. He thus replaces the dialectical necessity of Hegel's exoteric reason with an esoteric ground of experience, the necessity of which is made evident only by metaphysics.

Peirce's trinitarianism departs from the respective metaphysical necessities of Hegel and Schelling, as well as from Schelling's intuitionism, because of his unqualified insistence on the hypothetical, exploratory character of metaphysical thinking, both in relation to the unrestricted application of the principle of reason and to his own threefold ultimate. What is especially striking about his position in the present context is encapsulated in his essay, 'A Neglected Argument for the Existence of God' (1908), where he comments on his lifelong elaboration of the explanatory power of triunity across a wide range of experience. In his own words: 'Now to be deliberately and thoroughly prepared to shape one's life into conformity with a proposition is neither more nor less than a state of mind called Believing in a proposition, however long the conscious classification of it under that head be postponed.'[163] As is characteristic of the historiological tradition, Peirce here repudiates any hard and fast division between metaphysical and theological faith. He does so, however, on his own terms: both the claimed absoluteness of theological faith and the claimed absoluteness of the transcendental necessities of German idealism, as well as the mutual support they lend each other in the hands of Hegel and Schelling, are here completely abandoned. The search for absolute certainties in theology and philosophy is over. Throughout 'The Neglected Argument', the heuristic, exploratory character of metaphysical-hypothetical thinking is presented as an essential dimension of theological faith.

---

163. Peirce, *Collected Papers*, VI, para. 467.

Once Collingwood's *Essay on Metaphysics* is placed within Augustinian tradition in general, and the historiological tradition in particular, it becomes possible to characterise with some precision the extent to which his metaphysics of absolute presuppositions represents an original and significant contribution to the continuous, ongoing debate on the nature of metaphysical reason and its role in experience, a debate that has driven modern philosophy since the rise of empiricism and the advent of Kant's critical philosophy.

Clearly, the Collingwood of *An Essay on Metaphysics* rejects not only Hegel's account of theology as picture thinking, but also his necessitarian view of history. Equally, Schelling's intuitive faith method plays no role in *An Essay on Metaphysics*, while Peirce's hypothetical method has, for Collingwood, its proper place in the investigation of absolute presuppositions, in terms of the third-person declaratives or metaphysical propositions that they generate (a point to which I shall return). The function of metaphysics in *An Essay on Metaphysics* is not, as in Hegel and Schelling, to save theology by bringing it into the realm of reflective consciousness. Metaphysics is not proclaimed to be the true content of theology. Rather, the function of metaphysics is to discover and interpret the nature and content of whatever absolute presuppositions or rules govern our practice. These are fundamentally theological in nature, in line with Aristotle's view of the unity of metaphysics and theology, and are to be understood on the model of creedal rules of faith or trust.

Here, insofar as Collingwood's presuppositions analysis takes the form of an analysis of the conditions of thought and practice, it is obviously nothing new as a philosophical strategy. What is new is his presuppositional account of the nature of the conditions that are the subject of inquiry.

In comparison to the regulative ideas that are the conditions of order or systematicity in Kant's first *Critique*, Collingwood's absolute presuppositions are not 'as ifs'. In the tradition of post-Kantian idealism, Collingwood rejects not only Kant's nominalist view of the primacy of particulars, which renders rules constructs of the mind and the mere products of psychological need,[164] but also Kant's noumenal realm of determinate individual entities that obey the law of the excluded middle and are held to be unknowable. Indeed, Collingwood may be said to be doing for the first *Critique* what Kant did in the second *Critique*: Collingwood himself, with suitable qualifications, likens his presuppositional analysis to Kant's treatment in the second *Critique* of God, freedom and immortality.[165]

---

164. Cf. Collingwood, *Essay on Metaphysics*, 233.
165. Ibid., 232–4.

Equally, however, Collingwood's presuppositional analysis repudiates the Kantian, Hegelian and Schellingian concern with the demonstration of permanent, transcendental or universally applicable conditions. Collingwood's absolute presuppositions are not permanent transcendental conditions, but historically constituted and historically specific transcendental conditions that as such lie outside the realm of deductive, dialectical or intuitional proof, and belong to the sphere of historical inquiry. Above all, just as much as absolute presuppositions are not regulative ideas, neither are they the deliverances of absolute mind or intuition. Rather, Collingwood's absolute presuppositions state the commitments we make in our thought and practice: that is, they are historically unfolded objects of faith or trust, which as such are best understood in terms of the model of creedal rules. While all analyses seek the 'given' in the sense of the ultimate, the given for Collingwood is not to be understood as physiological, sensory, logical, epistemic, ethical, aesthetic or emotional; instead, the given is the historical-fideal, a matter of the faith or commitments we find ourselves furnished with in our given historical situation. As with F. H. Bradley, although in a very different way, there is a strongly empiricist and specifically Humean dimension to Collingwood's metaphysics: his theory of absolute presuppositions both appropriates and completely revises Hume's account of fact, belief and their relation, expanding it far beyond its characteristic ahistorical limitations. The factual is redefined as historically saturated, and what in the Humean tradition is camouflaged as 'feeling', or in empiricist cognitive science is disguised under the rubric of 'intuition', is for Collingwood the subject of the science of absolute presuppositions: so-called 'feelings' and 'intuitions' have a history and are historiologically constituted. If philosophy begins always *in medias res*, for Collingwood this means it begins always *in medias res gestae*. The centrality of the empirical is here at once preserved and enormously extended by its redefinition as the historical.

Inscribed in the metaphysics of absolute presuppositions, therefore, is a new theory of the nature and status of faith in the form of a fiducial theory of historical-transcendental conditions. In Collingwood's hands, conditions theory becomes an historical pistology, and historiology becomes a theory of faith. The relation of faith and reason is defined by way of the account of metaphysical propositions and of the historical-conceptual inquiry into their adequate formulation and internal strains.[166] In this context, it may not be too much to say that Collingwood adds his own kind of proof of

---

166. As Collingwood put it in 1916: 'It is incorrect to say that philosophy is theory based upon fact; theory is not something else derived, distilled from facts but simply the observation that the facts are what they are. And similarly the philosophical presuppositions of history are not something different from the history itself: they are philosophical truths which the historian finds historically exemplified.' Collingwood,

the existence of God to the traditional proofs that have been elaborated in the past. Indeed, his is a proof, not just of monotheism, but of a Trinitarian God. For, as I have tried to show, the theory of the constellation of fundamental absolute presuppositions is essentially, both in form and content, an argument for the Trinity *ex ordine historiae*.

At this point, it is necessary to consider what for many readers is the most surprising and discomfiting feature of Collingwood's metaphysics of absolute presuppositions: namely, his argument concerning the fundamental presuppositional status of the doctrine of the Trinity. Though often politely ignored by commentators, this is clearly central to his thinking in *An Essay on Metaphysics*. The argument has, I think, two aspects.

First, it is the claim concerning the past historical *derivation* of natural science from Trinitarian metaphysical theology. As such, it is a matter of historical-conceptual debate. Whatever may be the truth here, there can be no doubt that Collingwood's own *Idea of Nature*[167] and Foster's work present a strong supporting case, which I have not anywhere seen seriously challenged. At the very least, the derivation argument is an eminently defensible hypothesis.[168]

Secondly, Collingwood's claim is much more than a claim to past historical derivation. For on the basis of the claim to past historical derivation, he maintains that the doctrine of the Trinity is the real and active possibility condition of Western 'science and civilization'.[169] In other words, he claims the ultimate conceptual *dependence* of science on that constellation of fundamental absolute presuppositions that is the doctrine of the Trinity.

The polemical significance of this claim is obvious. Collingwood confines himself in *An Essay on Metaphysics* to the three basic and co-equal principles or rules of unity, plurality and order or movement to which natural science is committed.[170] But this is enough: in the struggle against positivism, his conditions analysis is all he needs to make the point that these three principles or rules carry us beyond positivism and into speculative metaphysics. For these are non-empirical and so non-empirically verifiable commitments, which as such require a philosophy other than positivism and most forms of naturalism for their analysis. To bring to light the nature of our non-empirical commitments, we must, for Collingwood, engage with the

---

Faith and Reason, 85. See A. N. Whitehead, *Process and Reality: An Essay in Cosmology* (New York: The Free Press, 1978), 51.
167. So understood, it seems to me that in *Essay on Metaphysics*, Collingwood's historiology is as much a critical response to Karl Barth's fideism as to Ayer's positivism.
168. See R. G. Collingwood, *The Idea of Nature* (Oxford: Clarendon Press, 1945), esp. 8, 77, 87–8, 115, 170. Some of the materials in this work on 'the presuppositions of natural science' (pp. 29–30) reappear in *Essay on Metaphysics*, Part IIIA.
169. Collingwood, *Essay on Metaphysics*, 232.
170. Ibid., 225.

closely intertwined history of metaphysics and theology, and in particular with the role in our thinking of the ubiquitous metaphysical-theological doctrine of the Trinity.

Yet Collingwood's claim of conceptual dependence goes much further than this. In principle, the doctrine of the triunity of nature is separable from the metaphysical-theological doctrine of the Trinitarian God, on account of the non-deductive relations that hold between the components of a constellation of absolute presuppositions. Nevertheless, the doctrine of the triunity of nature has the doctrine of the Trinitarian God as its own presupposition, in the sense that the doctrine of the Trinitarian God is the rule that is followed in the triune description of nature. Here, indeed, we come to the nub and core of Collingwood's whole argument in *An Essay on Metaphysics*: that any counterclaim to the status of the doctrine of the Trinity as fundamental absolute presupposition or rule of faith in respect of science will always be found to presuppose that doctrine in some respect. Any appeal to 'the natural', or some aspect of the natural, as fundamental absolute presupposition will in his view always be found ultimately to presuppose the account of nature as a threefold of unity, difference and movement or order. The broad and basic character of this analysis, and the fact that it closely converges with central elements in Kant, Peirce and even Dewey's accounts of the concept of nature, mean that it is a claim that cannot easily be dismissed. At the very least, Collingwood's critics should bear in mind that he is by no means alone in his analysis of the threefold character of the possibility conditions of natural science. His is a bold attempt to place front and centre in contemporary philosophical debate that great, continuous and constantly developing conversation stretching across the ages, which has been practised by the thinkers of triunity, theologians and philosophers alike, from Augustine to our own times. The fact that, in the predominantly sceptical culture of the Anglo-American academy, this powerful intellectual tradition of speculative metaphysics meets with little but patronising smiles and headshaking incredulity is at least a measure of the extent to which Collingwood's account of the historico-conceptual complexities of the implicit presuppositions of our thought and practice is desperately required. His point is that the intellectual depth and reach of modern unbelief does not go as deep or as far as its proponents think, and in fact represents a serious failure of empirical-historical self-understanding.[171]

---

171. Charles Taylor (*A Secular Age* [Cambridge, MA: The Belknap Press of Harvard University Press, 2007], 275ff.) makes a similar point about the role of the Patristic doctrine of the Trinity, extending its significance far beyond the development of natural science. See also Marcel Gauchet, *The Disenchantment of the World: A Political History of Religion*, trans. Oscar Burge (Princeton: Princeton University Press, 1997); Remi Brague, *Eccentric Culture: A Theory of Western Civilization*, trans. Simon

It is usually the case, indeed, that those who would bowdlerise and save Collingwood by turning him into a respectably secular thinker fail to make a simple but all-important distinction in the use of the term 'religion': that is, between 'religion' as a set of sociopolitical institutions and practices, often regrettable, and 'religion' in Collingwood's sense as that which is believed or trusted to be of absolute value and is properly a matter of the rigorous, rationally reflective disciplines of metaphysics and metaphysical theology.

Beyond even the claim about the conceptual dependency of science, there is of course a further claim made in *An Essay on Metaphysics*, concerning not just science but 'science and civilization':[172] namely, that Western civilisation is based on Christian principles. This theme which, given the globalisation of Western ideas, nowadays has universal implications, Collingwood does not pursue in *An Essay on Metaphysics*, but he went on to develop it at length in his last work, *The New Leviathan* (1942).[173] It could perhaps be encapsulated in the assertion that in the realm of ethics and politics any attempt to find a naturalist basis for the Christian doctrine of *agape* or unconditional love for the other – the fundamental, driving, impossibly difficult ideal of the West – will always fail, and will always tacitly presuppose the trinitarian framework of that doctrine. At the least, Collingwood puts the onus on positivism and any form of naturalism to prove otherwise. In his last works, the unity of philosophy and history inscribed in the theory of absolute presuppositions does not entail a collapse into historicist relativism, but means for him the recognition of what he holds to be the true foundation of science and civilisation.

It may be objected that there could occur what might be thought to be clashes over different fundamental absolute presuppositions; for example, between pagans and Christians, or between Western and other civilisations or cultures, or between Collingwood's own metaphysics and logical positivism (which is a variant of that between theism and atheism). If such were the case, then Collingwood's claim that the metaphysical proposition

---

Lester (South Bend, IN: St Augustine's Press, 2002); Michael Allen Gillespie, *The Theological Origins of Modernity* (Chicago: University of Chicago Press, 2008).

172. Collingwood, *Essay on Metaphysics*, 232.
173. Collingwood would completely agree with Richard Rorty, in *Philosophy and the Mirror of Nature* (Princeton: Princeton University Press, 1979), 272, that 'There is nothing the philosopher can add to what the historian has already done to show that this intelligible and plausible course [of a shift in conceptual schemes or central beliefs] is a "rational" one.' The difference resides both in the depth and reach of the empirical-historical analysis proposed by Collingwood, along with Foster and Cochrane, and in the metaphysics of absolute presuppositions to which that analysis gives rise. In this context, Collingwood can be regarded as standing Rorty on his feet by demonstrating the consequences of a truer empiricism.

'God exists', interpreted in a trinitarian sense, is the fundamental absolute presupposition of science would be false. It does not take much reflection, however, to see that for Collingwood, what might look like a clash of fundamental absolute presuppositions is in fact not so. Superficially, one could think that pagans and Christians, Western and non-Western cultures, Collingwoodians and logical positivists, are committed to different fundamental presuppositions. But this is exactly what Collingwood denies. In respect of pagans and Christians, he makes it quite clear that both share the absolute presupposition 'God exists'; their differences lie further up in the hierarchy of absolute rules, though still at the 'fundamental' level. *Mutatis mutandis*, something similar would presumably be true of any non-Western culture that has taken up the practice of natural science, or, for example, decided to further women's rights. In respect of logical positivism, or any naturalism, his claim is that they do not meet the criterion of comprehensiveness and represent a complete breakdown of philosophical analysis or self-consciousness. This is because in his view such philosophies totally fail to see the ultimate, conceptual-historical grounds of the view of nature they espouse.

For all the originality and power of Collingwood's historiology of absolute presuppositions, however, two major and vexing questions remain. First, what place is there in the metaphysics of absolute presuppositions for debate about that metaphysics itself? Secondly, just what is the overall significance of the metaphysics of absolute presuppositions?

Collingwood has, I think, already answered the first question with his account of metaphysical propositions as third-person, interpretative declaratives. As he puts it: 'The analysis which detects absolute presuppositions I call metaphysical analysis; but as regards procedure and the qualifications necessary to carry it out there is no difference whatever between metaphysical analysis and analysis pure and simple.'[174] In other words: *The critique of absolute presuppositions has the same character as all philosophical argument*: it involves the testing of hypotheses concerning the adequate interpretation and formulation of absolute presuppositions and their internal strains. Moreover, *this is equally true of any critique of the metaphysics of absolute presuppositions itself*, such as would be involved in the standoff between that metaphysics and logical positivism, or indeed between speculative metaphysics and naturalism. Debates on the adequate formulation of the conditions that underpin natural science would be, as always, arguments as to which hypothesis provides the best account of the commitments that natural scientific inquiry involves. Thus debates as to whether the role of trinitarian doctrine in natural science is a matter merely

---

174. Collingwood, *Essay on Metaphysics*, 40.

of past historical derivation, or, as Collingwood asserts, of real and active conceptual dependence, would continue as before.

In this respect, everything in philosophy remains the same after the theory of absolute presuppositions. The debates do not change. Indeed, in response to the second question, it may be suggested that at the end of the day the metaphysics of absolute presuppositions does not make much difference at all. After all, even Collingwood's strongest critics generally agree that his discussions of secondary suppositions (a usefully neutral term), such as Kant's view of causation, are good, if debatable, examples of historical-conceptual analysis.[175] The crucial issue is whether or not the claim that such suppositions are absolute presuppositions adds anything of significance to the usual kinds of critical analysis undertaken in philosophy. And it is here that we come upon the central significance of *An Essay on Metaphysics*: namely, that in contemporary philosophy it constitutes a unique, original and profound meditation on the relation of faith and reason. Whether or not Collingwood's account of the status of the Trinity or of Kantian causation, or his post-Kantian idealist version of historiology and of the ontological theory of truth, are at all cogent or acceptable, his creedal theory of rules of faith or trust provides a precise, logical account of the ineluctable, fiducial elements in our thought and action, defined, not in terms of feeling, intuitions or some kind of natural practice, but in terms of the historically constituted nature of our philosophical commitments. Collingwood's 'reform of metaphysics'[176] consists in the claim that metaphysics has as its proper subject of study the first-person, performative rules of faith or trust that underlie thought and action, and the propositions they generate. The business of metaphysics is the identification of absolute presuppositions, past and present, and the assessment of their consistency and comprehensiveness. Under what might be described as the slogan 'Follow the rules!', *An Essay on Metaphysics* is a powerful challenge, not only to all empiricisms and naturalisms, but also to any philosophy that refuses to acknowledge its fiducial content and historicity.

---

175. R. G. Collingwood, *The New Leviathan, or Man, Society, Civilization and Barbarism* (Oxford: Clarendon Press, 1942). In this connection, another context in which Collingwood's *Essay on Metaphysics* should perhaps be placed, besides those discussed earlier, is the extensive debate on the nature of Western civilisation and culture that, stimulated by the rise of communism in Russia and fascism in Italy and Germany, was conducted throughout the 1920s, 1930s and 1940s. Especially relevant here would be the writings of the historians Arnold J. Toynbee and Christopher Dawson, recently the subject of renewed interest due to current conditions. See the references to Toynbee in *Essay on Metaphysics*, 98n., 227n. However, these considerations go beyond the scope of the present essay.
176. Collingwood, *Essay on Metaphysics*, ch. 7.

In conclusion, the later Collingwood's attempted reform of metaphysics resides in his original elaboration of a reduction procedure leading to the ultimate absolute presupposition, which is the self-differentiating trinitarian principle. The notion of that principle as nothing other than the movement of mind in history is of course Collingwood's post-Kantian idealist and Peircean side. Yet he is not a Hegelian or a Peircean because of his theory of absolute presuppositions or rules, and he is not a Schellingian because his fundamental absolute presupposition is not a matter of intuition. Equally, he is not a British idealist because of his trinitarianism. For the same reason, he is certainly not a purely semantic thinker, nor does he offer a 'weak' or merely 'minimalist metaphysics'.[177] And while there is no 'radical conversion' in his working career, there is a radical innovation: his introduction of the creedal model of rules into the tradition of metaphysical historiology in terms of the fiducial theory of absolute presuppositions. Indeed, if this essay has been successful in clearing the metaphysics of absolute presuppositions of the misunderstandings to which it has been subject, it is now possible to start properly to assess the cogency and implications of the metaphysics that arises from that theory of rules. What can be said is that the great strength of Collingwood's position in *An Essay on Metaphysics* is that it refuses to allow speculative metaphysics to be shut out of debate; it restores to philosophy its empirical-historical memory; it recognises the important role of theological models in philosophical discourse; and it does so by urging the centrality of the question of the interrelation of faith, reason and history in philosophical reflection. The greatness of *An Essay on Metaphysics* resides in provocatively keeping that fundamental question at the forefront of a philosophical culture that is trying hard to forget it.

---

177. See, for example, Beaney, 'Collingwood's Conception of Presuppositional Analysis', 103.

Chapter 10

Philosophy and Trinity

What cannot be left out of any consideration of Schelling, in particular the later Schelling of the *Philosophy of Mythology* and the *Philosophy of Revelation*, is to be found in a most unlikely, even shocking place: the conception of triunity or trinity as the fundamental structure and principle of actualisation of all things. In this context, I will argue that 'continental philosophy' is an Anglo-American invention. It is 'pseudo-continentalism', no more than a highly selective rendering of Western European philosophy. Born out of opposition to the dominance of analytical philosophy in our universities, pseudo-Continentalism, in fact, converges with analysis in remarkable ways. Both are advertised as revolutions in thought and both stand over against the tradition of speculative philosophy; both repeat each other's historical shibboleths about traditional speculative philosophy in respect of the completeness of reason and of reality, the priority of identity and totality, the predetermined fixity of teleology. What this amounts to is a common rejection of a chimera, which in pseudo-continental philosophy is usually called onto-theology or the metaphysics of presence, and in the analytic tradition is sometimes called speculative philosophy. Here, indeed, the analytic tradition is more radical: as I will show, it characteristically rejects any notion of a special kind of activity of actualisation as a feature of the real, whether this is understood as being, mind, will, *élan vital*, difference or the impotential. These are the vestiges of the tradition of speculative philosophy that are retained under the rubric of continental philosophy.

To see what is happening here, I will concentrate on a key feature of pseudo-continental philosophy: its suppression of fundamental themes in the Western tradition of speculative philosophy. Nowhere is this more evident than in its obliteration of any explicit or critical recognition of the centrality of the philosophical doctrine of triunity or trinity in European philosophy.

I will explain this claim in ten brief, if bizarre, theses. I shall assume the hypothesis of reality, namely, that reality is that which has a nature of its own in the sense that it is so independently of our minds or independently of whether or not we think it to be so. I shall also, and crucially, assume the hypothesis of the reality of universals. Nevertheless, some defence of both hypotheses will be advanced in what follows, which essentially addresses the questions: Why can students of continental philosophy not afford to ignore the conception of trinity? Or, to put it another way: What is the relation of the real and the constructed? I will approach these questions by way of a contrast between what I shall call 'naturalist' and 'speculative' philosophy, terms that I will attempt to define as we proceed.

Naturalist and Speculative Philosophy: Some Contrasts

My first thesis concerns the conception of 'actualisation'. It addresses the nature of existence, an issue that lies at the heart of philosophy and of our culture as a whole. My first thesis is that there are two basic theories of existence: the weak and the strong, the deflationary and the dynamical, the naturalist and the speculative.

In general, weak theorists follow Hume in treating existence as a given that is not further derivable or inexplicable. Thus, Kant maintains that '-exists' is not a real but a non-determining predicate: affirmations of existence do not add any determinate feature or content to the concept of an object, but posit an object corresponding to a concept. Frege's elaboration of the Hume–Kant view of existence in terms of the binary structure of the function dominates analytical philosophy.[1] Thus, statements of the type 'horses exist' are interpreted as quantificational statements to the effect that 'for some x, x is a horse'. On this view, existence amounts to no more than the satisfaction or instantiation of a predicate, such as '. . . is a horse'. To exist is to answer a description. Whether one is talking about prime numbers, stones or people, existence statements are defined in the same way, as saying that something satisfies a description. The weak theory of existence as instantiation is thus not properly a theory of existence at all. Existence is simply removed from the realm of reflection and replaced by an account of the logical structure of language.[2]

---

1. For a geopolitical account of the rise to dominance of analytical philosophy in the Anglo-American world, placing it in the context of the Cold War, see Philip Mirowski,'The Scientific Dimensions of Social Knowledge and their Distant Echoes in Twentieth-century American Philosophy of Science', *Studies in History and Philosophy of Science* 35 (2004), 283–326, esp. 298–311.
2. I should stress that by no means all analytical philosophers or Fregeans are weak

By contrast, strong or speculative theories of existence hold that existence is much more than the silent, featureless pendant of logical-functional structure. Strong theories deny the primitivity of the function, at least as that is usually understood, and thus refuse to assimilate the 'is' of existence to the 'is' of mere instantiation. Strong theories take '-exists' to be a very general kind of predicate. It is not a real or determining predicate, for it does not add any determinate feature or content to the concept of an object. Rather, '-exists' is a non-determining predicate in the sense that it is taken to designate that activity which is the reason why things have any determining predicates at all. Existence is here understood as 'active' existence or 'actualisation'. This is why strong theories talk of 'being'. Being can refer to a determinate or ontic entity of any kind (*to on*, *ens*). In its significant ontological usage, however, being is a gerund or verbal noun, which, like *sein* or *l'être*, translates the Greek *einai* and the Latin *esse* (to be) or *actus essendi* (act of being). These terms refer to that activity of actualisation that is held to be a constitutive condition of all things in that it provides the fundamental explanation of what makes things to be and makes them intelligible, that is, bearers of predicates. Because active existence is the condition of predication, it is not naturalistically accessible or describable, in any usual sense of those terms. Its rationale and role in speculative, and specifically triune, philosophy will be elaborated in what follows.

My second thesis concerns what happens to the subject of cognition as a result of the generalisation of the function. Whereas Kant held that the unity of judgement requires a cognitive activity of synthesis, after Bolzano and Frege it is held that the principle of the unity of judgements is meaning.

You may object that in order to grasp relations of meaning, the cognitive subject needs to engage in an activity of synthesis. But the logical analyst readily grants that, and at the same time makes a rigorous distinction between the act and the content of judgements.[3] Subjective cognitive activity there is. Indeed, a cognitive act is required to grasp even analytic propositions such as 'All bachelors are unmarried' (which is of course Kant's real point). But the *content* of these as well as of synthetic propositions has nothing to do with cognitive activity: it is decided by the given relations of meaning. No subjective activity of synthesis is required to unify meanings; all the subject has to do is to follow their given relations. Once it is held that to understand a meaning is to be able to operate with it, and that a meaning itself constitutes a rule in the sense of a decision-making procedure, there is no need to appeal to a principle of connection or synthesis

---

theorists. There is an analytic-speculative tradition that springs from McTaggart. See note 8 below.
3. J. A. Coffa, *The Semantic Tradition from Kant to Carnap* (Cambridge: Cambridge University Press, 1991), ch. 1.

over and above the meaning itself. Kant is here hoist with his own petard: having restricted activity to the cognitive subject, in contrast to traditional metaphysics, it now emerges that the activity of the cognitive subject is strictly a psychological feature of minds and has nothing to do with the objective order of meanings. The crucial point here is that rules are understood or interpreted as decision-making procedures, as automatic recipes or algorithms. Nowhere is this more evident than in the later Wittgenstein's enormously influential extension of the model of the function – specifically, the first-order function – beyond cognition to all forms of linguistic and social practice and action. Just as following the rules of a game is what constitutes a game, so by following the rules of a language or social practice we constitute our world and ourselves. The Fregean dissolution of the cognitive, synthesising subject is here extended to the realm of discourse and action, and goes hand-in-hand with the dissolution of the logical subject as a mind-, language- or practice-independent reality. In a remarkable convergence with continental structuralism and poststructuralism, both the world and human subjects or persons are thus nothing more than the effects of those functional structures that define their behaviour. On this account, the possibility of any reflective relation to rules on the part of the cognitive subject is eliminated. Further, a radically nominalist account of rule following is upheld: rules are simply a matter of 'that's how we do it'.[4] As is well known, this has the generated the enormous debate that swirls around rule-scepticism, something that is an issue only for nominalists.

By contrast, modern speculative philosophy maintains self-synthesis to be a real and universal feature of things,[5] with the corollary that all things stand in a communicative relation to one another by way of their antecedent conditions and subsequent relations. In medieval speculative thought, the act of existence of a thing was not its principle of synthesis. Universals had that task. Since the German idealists, however, speculative philosophy has maintained the activity of actualisation that is the real to be an activity of synthetic self-construction or self-organisation. Some of the implications of this general shift in the meaning of the act of existence will emerge in my next two theses.

My third thesis concerns the massive influence of the algorithmic account of rules on our view of the nature of history. I refer to Thomas Kuhn's influential analysis of historical change in science, where 'paradigm shifts'

---

4. Ludwig Wittgenstein, *Remarks on the Foundations of Mathematics* (Cambridge, MA: MIT Press, 1978), 199.
5. For a constructivist ontology of the function, see A. N. Whitehead, *Process and Reality* (Cambridge: Cambridge University Press, 1929); on which is based my article, 'The Speculative Generalisation of the Function: A Key to Whitehead' (see Chapter 4 above).

from 'normal' to 'revolutionary' science are not rational or intelligible.[6] The reason for this is that Kuhn defines 'normal science' in terms of functions or algorithms, and there is no algorithm for historical change. The algorithmic model of rules here imposes a specific historiography. In the context of naturalism, a larger point can be made: the naturalist must treat history as nothing other than contingency, and as having only anthropological significance. History may be a feature of reality, but it is no more than an intersubjective feature.

Over against such views, speculative philosophy characteristically upholds what R. J. Campbell calls the ontological theory of truth.[7] On this theory, the standard linguistic view of truth is inadequate: truth is not primarily to be understood as an epistemic relation of correspondence between propositions or linguistic structures and states of affairs, which relation is subject to the disjunction 'true or false'. The ontological theory of the nature of truth – in which the term 'Truth' is often capitalised to mark the difference from linguistic accounts – is fundamental to metaphysics from Plato to Peirce and Heidegger. On the ontological theory, truth is a state or relation of the real. Whether articulated in a Platonic, scholastic, idealist or pragmatist framework, the real is understood to be an activity of disclosure or manifestation. The criteria of disclosure are coherence and comprehensiveness, and there is no absolute disjunction between the true and the false. The central point here is that, after the rise of Christianity, the activity of disclosure or manifestation is held to occur in history and to be intrinsically a matter of the movement of history. This is, indeed, the distinctive feature of the Judaeo-Christian view of truth. Both on the Greek and the Judaeo-Christian view, truth is what endures and does not pass. Further, on both views the unity of truth guarantees the unity of experience. However, truth as Greek *aletheia* does not happen. Even though it is always connected to the relation of the speaker to the addressee, as in the Socratic dialogue form, truth is not something personal and is not an event. As Socrates always insists, he is a mere midwife, an impersonal conduit for that which is thoroughly impersonal, namely, that truth that is much more than an event because it is always identical with itself and is the reality that is hidden behind appearances, a reality that can be disclosed only by rational thought. In contrast, a key feature of the Judaeo-Christian view of truth is that truth is not a timeless state of affairs. It must occur, and it must be unfolded and realised again and again in new situations that shed fresh light on it. It is as such intrinsically connected to actions in time,

---

6. Thomas S. Kuhn, *The Structure of Scientific Revolutions*, 2nd edn (Chicago: University of Chicago Press, 1970).
7. R. J. Campbell, *Truth and Historicity* (Oxford: Clarendon Press, 1992), 56. This is an indispensable work.

as in Heidegger's conception of truth as *aletheia*. In consequence, truth is not a reality that lies behind appearances, but is something that emerges in history and is nothing other than its coming-to-be in the movement of history. On this account, because the real is to be found nowhere except in the movement of history, in the contingent materiality of socio-economic, institutional and cultural circumstances, the movement of history is itself the unfolding and construction of the real. As the movement of history itself, with all its potentialities, the real is more than any of its specific historical manifestations or formations. But the real is at least what the constructive movement of history has shown it to be, and it is nothing less than that.

Speculative Philosophy and Its Defence

My fourth thesis deals with that which I believe to be the historical and conceptual core of speculative philosophy, namely, that speculative philosophy and its history, in particular its concern with actualisation, are unintelligible without reference to the hypothesis or postulate of the principle of reason and its implications. This is the principle that 'Nothing is without a reason', or 'Everything that is the case must have a reason why it is the case'.[8]

Positively, the principle of reason invites unrestricted commitment to the search for explanation. No appeal is made here to an *a priori* rule.[9] We have only the experimental or hypothetical application of the principle of reason to the fact that we live in a puzzling world.[10] And when unrestrictedly

---

8. For this latter formulation, see Alexander R. Pruss, *The Principle of Sufficient Reason: A Reassessment* (Cambridge: Cambridge University Press, 2006), 3. I use the term 'principle of reason' and not 'sufficient reason' in order to disassociate the concept from the usual necessitarian interpretations, both of it and of Leibniz. In my view, the principle of reason is tacitly at work in a recent and unusual analytic-speculative defence of strong theory; see William Vallicella, *A Paradigm Theory of Existence: Onto-Theology Vindicated* (Boston: Kluwer, 2002). Most analytic-speculative defences of strong theory concentrate on the logical analysis of the 'is' of existence: see Peter Geach, 'Form and Existence', in *God and the Soul* (London: Routledge, 1969), 42–64, replied to by C. J. F. Williams, *What Is Existence?* (Oxford: Clarendon Press, 1981), and Michael Dummett, 'Existence', in *The Seas of Language* (Oxford: Clarendon Press, 1993), 277–307; see also Barry Miller, *The Fullness of Being: A New Paradigm for Existence* (Notre Dame, IN: University of Notre Dame Press, 2002).
9. The principle of reason is not an analytic, necessary or innate truth, so it is an experientially defeasible rule that is open or gives no knowledge in advance as to what will satisfy it. The present essay will provide grounds for rejecting any notion that we should knowingly hoodwink ourselves by treating the principle as a pseudo-Kantian *als ob*.
10. This is the principle of reason as Wiggins's 'methodological rule', which he thinks removes its speculative-philosophical implications, a view that will be challenged in

applied, the principle of reason requires that we go beyond even the most basic laws and operations of logic, mathematics and physics, for these do not account, nor do they attempt to account, for why there are laws or operations at all. This is why, under the rubric of the principle of reason, a speculative theory of reality is necessarily a theory of the actualisation of the real, a theory of the activity of actualisation; that is, it attempts to provide an explanation of why, among other things, there is order or ordination at all. Moreover, when unrestrictedly applied, the principle of reason requires that such a theory provide an ultimate principle of explanation that is self-justifying or self-explanatory in respect of its activity of actualisation, for this alone avoids an infinite regress of explanations. Whatever is held to be the ultimate or self-explanatory principle of actualisation has to meet the stringent requirement that it must possess in its own nature, or provide out of its own nature, all the reasons needed to explain its existence or activity.[11] Of any self-explanatory principle, the question 'Why?' can of course always be asked. The self-explanatory is not the self-evident. Indeed, the question as to what constitutes an adequate self-explanatory theory of actualisation is hotly debated between the different speculative schools that seek the self-explanatory. In this speculative 'explanatorist' tradition (as I shall call it) from Plato onwards, the principle of reason is best understood as operating in the way that Peirce defines as 'abduction'. In his words: 'The surprising fact C is observed/ But if A were true, C would be a matter of course/ Hence, there is reason to suppose that A is true.'[12] This is inference to the best possible explanation, usually by way of analogical generalisation.[13] The procedure is fallibilist: repeated application of abductive inference may lead to continued revision of the analogical hypothesis in the light of new discoveries and observations, as has always been the case with explanatorist theories of actualisation. On this account, the self-explanatory is neither the self-evident, nor is it based on any appeal to intuition (as, say, in Schelling). There is only the hypothetico-deductive method, in which a hypothetical model (in this case, to take one example, the unconditioned, infinite

---

this essay. See David Wiggins, 'Sufficient Reason: A Principle in Diverse Guises both Ancient and Modern', *Acta Philosophica Fennica* 61 (1996), 117–32.

11. See Ralph Walker, 'Sufficient Reason', *Proc. Arist. Soc.* 97 (1997), 109–23, on regress and the self-explanatory. This essay is a response to his cautious strictures on the latter.
12. C. S. Peirce, *Collected Papers*, ed. Charles Hartshorne and Paul Weiss (Cambridge, MA: Harvard University Press, 1932–35), VI, para. 528.
13. See Whitehead, *Process and Reality*, ch. 1, 'Speculative Philosophy', Section II. For his critique of the school of language-analytical philosophy he helped to found, see his comments on C. D. Broad, 'Critical and Speculative Philosophy', in J. H. Muirhead (ed.), *Contemporary British Philosophy* (London: Allen and Unwin, 1924), 75–100, in *Modes of Thought* (Cambridge: Cambridge University Press, 1938), ch. 9, 'The Aim of Philosophy'.

or inexhaustible unity of essence and existence) is proposed by way of remotion or regress back up a series of conditions.[14] The model is then tested by the deduction of consequences from the hypothesis, which is usually a matter of its analogical application in the form of ostensive description.

The standard objection to such a view of the principle of reason is of course that the explanatorist use of the principle of reason conflates reasons and causes. But that is to assume that causality is nothing more than physical efficient causality. It is to ignore the fact that 'cause' is an analogical concept, and thus to overlook the distinction between 'principle' or 'ground' and cause. The concept of cause is a specific variety of the genus 'principle' (*principium*; the Latin translation of the Greek *arche*, origin or beginning) or the genus 'ground' (*Grund*), for 'cause' implies a greater degree of dependence on the part of the effect than do the concepts of 'principle' or 'ground'.[15] Further, the assumption of nominalism lies behind the reason/cause distinction here. However causality is defined, it is taken for granted that rules are secondary constructs of the mind, at least in the sense that their power is exhausted by any given instance of their embodiment in individuals. The concrete individual is unquestioningly held to be prior to the rule, so that there are no supra-individual realities with an efficacy of their own correlative to that of individual interactions. Individuals are absolute and are positivistically defined as primarily physical entities.

Secondly, there is the larger objection from contingency, the claim that there is no need for an ultimate principle of actualisation at all. For what is wrong with contingency as the ultimate principle? Why is contingency not enough? From the Greeks onwards, many speculative philosophers have made contingency an essential element in their theory of the self-explanatory nature of reality. Yet it cannot be the only element, for the question 'Why not just contingency?' answers itself. The contingent is that which may and also may not be. So it is not self-explanatory: to be contingent is to be in relation to something to else, such as the laws of logic or physics. The contingent is always relative and so cannot *by itself* be a self-explanatory principle.

Perhaps what is really meant here is 'chance'. Yet if that is the case, chance is something more than an event whose cause is unknown to us, and it is more than the concurrence of two independent causal chains. As definitions of chance, both these notions simply mean 'an order whose operations

---

14. It will be clear from what has been said about abduction that I take remotion not to be reducible to reverse deduction or to conduction, though it may contain elements of both. See C. S. Peirce, 'A Neglected Argument for the Existence of God', in *Collected Papers*, VI, paras 452–93, esp. paras 458–65.
15. See Aquinas, *Summa Theologiae*, 1a, q. 33, a. 1, ad 1; see also R. G. Collingwood, *An Essay on Metaphysics* (Oxford: Clarendon Press, 1940), 329.

cannot be predicted by us' – and so we are not talking of chance in any realist or ontologically significant sense. The notion of 'chaos' cannot help either. In the first place, there can be no such thing as 'pure chaos'. Chaos is always relative chaos because, even if there is chaos of some kind, there must be determinate entities (*ens*) that have some sort of unity (*unum*) – that at is, irreducibility – about them in order for them to be chaotically related, or related at all. And if there are distinct entities, not only must they stand to one another in relations of difference (*aliquid*), no matter how minimal, but they must also persist, or display certain characters, or behave in a specific way (*res*), no matter how fleeting. To be in chaos, that is, they must possess individual identities or internal order, no matter how simple. The notion of chaos also seems to depend upon that of sequence – a sequence of events – which again entails order of some kind. It hardly needs adding that so-called 'chaos theory' is not only thoroughly deterministic but assumes that order is a given, introduced, so to speak, in one dose in the 'initial conditions'.

What contingency and chance might mean in the context of a self-explanatory theory of actualisation will be considered later. I now turn to a third objection, which is based on the claim that the logic of the function renders redundant any theories of active existence, speculative or otherwise.

To the speculative appeal to activity the weak theorist has a ready reply: that the concept of a mathematical function is a concept of the intrinsic connectivity of relations in virtue of the very nature of a functional rule. Functional rules or modern predicates are intrinsically relational in that they connect an object to a property or class. In consequence, strong questions, such as 'What is the relation that holds between a particular and a universal?', 'What is the bond that unites a particular to its various properties?', or 'How do relations relate?', become redundant. To ask such questions is mistakenly to view the concept of a relation as the concept of an abstract object or third term over and above its relata, which is the way traditional logic treats the copula 'is'. Defined in terms of functional rules or modern predicates, however, relations are structurally incomplete, partial objects that cannot occur without relata to complete them. They are, as such, intrinsically connective. Once relations are defined as functional or incomplete objects, there is no need to invoke any other principle as a glue to hold together relations and relata, functions and values. That it is the very nature of a function to have values is expressed by its variables.[16]

This objection from relations, however, completely misses its target. Because the term 'relation', like other such words in English ('composition',

---

16. See Michael Dummett, *Frege: Philosophy of Language*, 2nd edn (London: Duckworth, 1981), 174–7.

'construction', 'configuration'), is ambiguous as between the process of relating and the product that is the relation, there is nothing about the intrinsic connectivity that characterises relationality that rules out of court the speculative concern with activity as the actualisation of relations. Moreover, the concept of the intrinsic connectivity of relations obviously does not decide between, for example, a logical-realist nor some kind of constructivist account of the nature of connectivity. Hence, little of philosophical interest is decided by the given fact that there are relations, or partial, incomplete, intrinsically connective objects. Speculative philosophy does not deny, nor need it deny, that relations relate. Nor (as will emerge) need speculative philosophy deny that there is something ultimate and irreducible about unity as connectivity. What the speculative philosopher asks in this context is another version of the strong question of existence: 'Why are there instantiations of relations or connectivity?', 'What are the conditions that make relations possible?' The speculative philosopher's interest is in the fact that there are relations, and whether or not any account can be given of them over and above the fact that they are partial, incomplete, intrinsically connective objects. In asking 'What makes relational order possible?', speculative philosophers are not overlooking the intrinsic connectivity of relations. Rather, they are inquiring into the possibility of a self-explanatory account of connectivity in terms of actualising activity. Hence, the strong question speculative philosophy puts to relations remains open and is perfectly intelligible.

One final point. Explanatorist theories of existence have sometimes been accused of committing certain mistakes that some critics have read into the most general of the strong questions of existence. These are questions like 'Why is there anything at all?', or 'Why is there something rather than nothing?' Such questions, it has been said, depend not just upon the debatable claim that absolute nothingness or vacuity is conceivable, but upon the false claim that absolute nothingness or vacuity is in some sense prior to the fact that there is something, so the fact that there is something is held to need a special kind of explanation. Yet speculative inquiry need not, and usually does not, deny the priority of the actual in respect of the possible, and as the starting point of all inquiry. Rather, speculative inquiry is an attempt to see just how far reflection can go in the analysis of the actual. When disentangled from any historical connection to a doctrine of creation that already provides the answer, the question 'Why not nothing at all?' merely articulates a way of looking at actuality so as to discover what actuality requires in order to satisfy the principle of reason. It is to the nature of such inquiries that I now turn.

My fifth thesis is essentially a point of clarification, namely, that a distinction has to be made among various speculative philosophies in relation to the principle of reason. On one side, there is what I shall call the speculative 'explanatorists', who are unrestrictedly committed to the principle of reason and the conception of a self-explanatory principle. On the other side, there are what I shall call the speculative 'descriptivists', figures such as Schopenhauer, Nietzsche, Bergson, Whitehead and Deleuze.

Understood as a position self-consciously opposed as much to explanatorism as to naturalism, speculative descriptivism is a relatively modern phenomenon that starts with Schopenhauer. Like explanatorism, descriptivism offers a variety of theories of the activity of actualisation, but it abandons the concern with the self-explanatory. This has the peculiar consequence that descriptivist accounts of the activity of actualisation are ambivalent: they can either be negative and tragic, as in the case of Schopenhauer, or positive and celebratory, as with Nietzsche's will to power, Bergson's *élan vital*, Whitehead's creativity or Deleuze's *différence*. Such celebratory doctrines involve a tacit and unexplained appeal to some conception of the goodness of being or existence, a conception that (I will show) is not ignored by the explanatorists, from Plato to Peirce and Heidegger.

My sixth thesis is this: There are of course various types of principles of actualisation, explanatorist and descriptivist – monadic (Judaism, Islam, Nietzsche), dyadic (Empedocles, Democritus, Alexander), triadic (neo-Platonism, Spinoza, Deleuze) and tetradic (Plato, Whitehead). Yet there can be no question that the tradition that dominates the history of Western speculative thought is that which holds the principle of actualisation to be a triunity of three distinct, irreducible, inseparable and co-equal elements and maintains all entities to be in some sense composed of these three elements. This tradition stretches from Plato's *syntrisi* or three-in-one, through the medieval period, to the idealism of Hegel and Schelling. It is not so often noticed, however, that it has been a significant feature of modern speculative developments over the last one hundred and fifty years. I refer primarily to Peirce's triune ontology of firstness, secondness and thirdness (these terms are more or less translations of Schelling's description of the Trinity); to the later Heidegger's *das Ereignis* ('the Event'), with its triunity of *Es gibt* ('It gives'), *die Sendung* (Latin, *missio*; 'the sending') and *die Gabe* (Latin, *donum*; 'the gift'; all these terms are translations of the 'names' of the medieval persons); and to Collingwood's treatment of the Trinity in his *Essay on Metaphysics* (1940) as the fundamental 'absolute presupposition' of natural science and Western culture in general.[17]

---

17. See Martin Heidegger, *On Time and Being*, trans Joan Stambaugh (New York: Harper Books, 1972); and Collingwood, *Essay on Metaphysics*, esp. ch. 21. On Heidegger, see the indispensable article by Peter Harris, 'Patterns of Triunity in *Time and Being*: Contexts for Interpreting the Later Heidegger', *Analecta Hermeneutica* 3 (2011),

Two comments may help to dispel any puzzlement there might be at the persistence of the notion of triunity in modern philosophy. First, because the triune theories mentioned are explanatorist, they are elaborated so as to address three basic questions. These are the questions of the nature of origin, difference and order. For, in the first place, an explanatorist theory of the activity of actualisation requires a theory of the unitary origin of difference and order. That is, it requires an account of that activity which is in some sense prior to difference and order because it is the condition of difference and order. In the second place, an explanatorist theory requires an account of the actualisation of difference or individuality, of the nature of differentiation. And in the third place, such a theory requires an account of the actualisation of order. The primacy attached to these issues is of course characteristic of the triune tradition itself. But they have a certain obviousness about them that helps to indicate the rationale of the general position.

Secondly, there is a set of considerations connected with the development of mathematics and the rise of natural science. In the medieval period, the doctrine of the triune God, with its 'subsistent relations' or 'persons' (*persona* or active functions) of Father, Son and Spirit, was expounded as a supernatural or revealed mystery of faith. This is not to deny that the triune God is employed to provide a self-explanatory account of the activity of actualisation. In Aquinas, for example, all things have their *esse*, or act of being, which is derived from the Father; their individual nature (species), which is given by the Son or Logos; and their relation to other things which is given by the Spirit, the principle or gift of love or community.[18] Nevertheless, the concept of essentially relational being cuts across the Aristotelian view that finite substances exist independently and that relations are accidents. Hence, it is difficult in this context to develop a trinitarian account of all the features of the created world. By contrast, once mathematics and natural science had established the intrinsic relationality of the natural world, the relational model could unproblematically be transposed, under the rubric of triunity, not only to the analysis of the constitution of the finite subject (as with Kant's plethora of triunities),[19] but also to the whole of reality, defined as an absolute subject with three essential modes or operations

---

available at <www.mun.ca/analecta>. On Collingwood, see my 'A Key to Collingwood's *Essay on Metaphysics*: the Logic of Creedal Rules', in C. Kobayashi, M. Marion and A. Skodo (eds), *A Handbook on Collingwood* (Leiden: Brill, 2012). Peirce will be further discussed below.

18. Aquinas, *Summa Theologica*, 1a, q. 45, a. 7, resp.
19. Hegel says of Kant: 'the conception of the Trinity has, through the influence of the Kantian philosophy, been brought into notice again in an outward [read: purely formal] way as a type, and, as it were, a ground plan of thought, and this in very definite forms of thought.' G. W. F. Hegel, *Lectures on the Philosophy of Religion*, trans. E. B. Speirs and J. B. Sanderson (New York: Humanities Press, 1974), III, 32–3.

(Hegel and Schelling).[20] In a relational world, there is no longer anything exceptional or puzzling about a relational principle, which thus becomes an intrinsically immanent principle of actualisation.[21] In order to indicate the sea-change a modern philosopher such as Peirce works in the theory of triunity, transforming the medieval theory of subsistent relations or persons and the German idealist theory of the subject into an immanentist logic of events and communication, my seventh thesis extends the analysis of the principles of actualisation so far offered.

My seventh thesis is that there are three basic theories of origin or firstness in the explanatorist wing of the triune tradition. There are the supra-rationalists, who hold that the unitary origin is not only beyond specific determination but is for that reason beyond intelligibility (Pseudo-Dionysius, Scotus Eriugena, perhaps Heidegger sometimes). There are the rationalists, who describe the threefold on the psychological analogy of mind (Augustine, Aquinas, Hegel, Lonergan). And there are the 'explicabilists', as I shall call them, who hold that all things are intelligible but do not identify the intelligible with mind or rationality. Here the intelligible is the non-conceptual, for the first principle of the threefold is held to be nothing more than activity. This activity is unconditioned because it is original. So it is free or spontaneous in that it is the sole cause of its own activity. But it is activity, so it is essentially relational and teleological; for it is necessarily ecstatic or communicative in the sense that, whatever else it may be, activity is nothing less than ablative or abductive movement, movement out from itself.

The conception of the first principle of the threefold as this kind of unity of the ecstatic and the unconditioned, of necessity and freedom, is the sort of position defended by voluntarists such as Duns Scotus and Schelling (who use the psychological analogy of will rather than mind to define origin)[22] and by pragmatists such as Peirce (who reinterprets will

---

20. As Collingwood puts it: 'The doctrine of the Trinity, taught as a revelation by early Christianity . . . becomes in Kant and his successors a demonstrable and almost alarmingly fertile logical principle.' R. G. Collingwood, 'Reason Is Faith Cultivating Itself' (1927), in *Faith and Reason*, ed. Lionel Rubinoff (Chicago: Quadrangle Books, 1968), 119–20.
21. The anti-Thomist claim that the triune principle is essentially and eternally creative is a characteristic feature of philosophical trinitarianism from Schelling, Hegel and Peirce onwards. For Peirce, see *Collected Papers*, VI, para. 506.
22. Schelling is responsible for reintroducing the voluntarist tradition into the then predominantly rationalist philosophical culture of the European mainland. This helps to clarify the subsequent rise of speculative descriptivism: Schopenhauer seizes his chance, and pries Schellingian will loose from its trinitarian framework. The result is that it becomes the inexplicable, irrational origin of the world. Nietzsche sees the weakness in the notion of sheer irrational will as a creative, ordering origin, and so redefines it as the will to power. But the ball has started rolling, and other descriptivist

as action). They insist on the priority of activity to mind or thought, in particular to the laws of logic, and they maintain that spontaneous activity is a perfectly knowable, non-conceptual feature of experience. Because it is ecstatic, spontaneity or firstness is held by Peirce to generate differentiation (secondness), and both are held to give rise to ordination (thirdness).[23]

My eighth thesis is that a theory of active or dynamical and inexhaustible infinity is an essential and often philosophically transformative component of explanatorist theories of actualisation. I will take Peirce's theory of origin or firstness as a touchstone. Peirce's infinity is not the potential infinite of Aristotle and the intuitionists, where however many parts it is divided into, it is possible for there to be more. Nor is it the real categorematic infinite of set theory, involving a non-denumerable infinite multiplicity of sets in which the parts or components are really there and their number is greater than any given. Rather, Peirce's firstness is in my view a particular kind of syncategorematic infinite. That is, it is a potential syncategorematic infinite, for its absolute indeterminacy means that 'it contains no definite parts';[24] it is a continuum of potential parts only.[25] Peirce's infinite is a syncategorematic infinite of real or dynamical potentiality that is always greater than any determination whatsoever. Peirce describes free or indeterminate firstness as a no-thing.[26] That is, firstness is nothing, not as all-containing plenitude (*per excellentiam nihil*), nor as vacuity (*omnino nihil*), nor as negation (*nihil privativum*), but only as infinite free indeterminacy (*nihil per infinitatem*).[27] Peirce's firstness is not a unicity in any other sense; rather, it is the univocal concept of a dynamical free indeterminacy that as such has

---

theories of dynamical origin are not long in coming: there is Bergson's *élan vital*, Whitehead's creativity, and various contemporary forms of what can only be called irruptionism, such as those of Deleuze and Badiou.

23. For theories of triunity indebted to Peirce, see Josiah Royce, *The Problem of Christianity* (New York: Macmillan, 1913), esp. vol. II; and the naturalist triunity (existence, relation, meaning) of John Dewey, *Experience and Nature* (Chicago: Open Court, 1929). Besides Hegel (mind, object, community) and above all Schelling (*Einheit, Zweiheit, Dreiheit*), Peirce himself was deeply influenced by the triunity (*Stofftrieb, Formtrieb, Spieltrieb*) of Friedrich Schiller, *On the Aesthetic Education of Man in a Series of Letters*, trans. Elizabeth M. Wilkinson and L.A. Willoughby (Oxford: Clarendon Press, 1967).
24. Peirce, *Collected Papers*, VI, para. 168.
25. Ibid., VI, para. 185: C. S. Peirce, *The New Elements of Mathematics*, vol. IV, *Mathematical Philosophy*, ed. Carolyn Eisele (Atlantic Highlands, NJ: Humanities Press, 1976), 343.
26. Peirce, *Collected Papers*, VI, paras 214ff.
27. These distinctions should help serve as a warning to those tempted by Carnap and Ayer's mockery of speculative conceptions of the 'nothing'. See Rudolf Carnap, 'The Elimination of Metaphysics Through the Logical Analysis of Language', *Erkenntnis* (1932), 60–81, and A. J. Ayer, *Language, Truth and Logic*, 2nd edn (London: Gollancz, 1946), 43–4.

no specific nature of its own, and, in communicating itself to all things, is necessarily never the same. Moreover, because it communicates itself to all things, it follows that all difference or individuals, and all specific structures or laws, carry free or inexhaustible indeterminacy in their nature. That is, all individuals and all laws are essentially vague: they are inexhaustibly determinable determinations. In consequence, structures are always more than any of their individual instances, and there are no complete or completable wholes: as Peirce insists, for any given whole or continuity (e.g., 'All men are mortal'), the universal quantifier is to be interpreted distributively ('For each...') not collectively ('For all...').[28] Wholes are infinite in the distributive, not the collective, mode; and they are distributive wholes because they are intrinsically vague or infinitely indeterminate. The theory of vagueness constitutes in my view one of the great revolutions in the theory both of individuals and of forms or universals: even form or structure is now subject to freedom and genuine ('never before') novelty.

My next and ninth thesis leads me to the core issue. My ninth thesis is that the theory of dynamical, inexhaustible infinity provides a basis for the unity of realism and constructivism characteristic of speculative philosophy. The shortest way to indicate this is to consider Peirce's semiotics, which is intended to replace both the *Aufhebungsdialektik* of Hegel and the *Erzeugungsdialektik* of Schelling, though owing a great deal to the latter.[29] Peirce holds all communication, natural or physical and human or discursive, to be a threefold movement of sign, object and interpretant.[30] All three elements are held in his semiotics to be interdependent, co-equal elements or conditions of communicative actualisation, which means that each guides and constrains the other. Please note also that the same entity (e.g. an action) can play the role of sign, object or interpretant, depending on context. Whatever in a given context plays the role of sign functions as the relation of interpretant and object. The sign is the medium through which the interpretant apprehends the object. The sign is a dynamical power: it is vague in that offers potentialities for the determination of the object by the interpretant. Because it has its own potentialities, the sign can be reduced neither to the object, nor to the interpretant. Signs or universals are of

---

28. Peirce, *Collected Papers*, V, para. 532.
29. For an excellent comparison of Hegel and Schelling, see Edward Allen Beach, *The Potencies of the God(s): Schelling's Philosophy of Mythology* (Albany, NY: SUNY Press, 1994), 83–91, 113–16.
30. Within Peirce's general metaphysics, semiotics is a theory of 'thirdness', the realm of the actualisation of order or structure. Because all things are threefold relations, however, within the realm of semiotics signs have the role of firstness, for they are the ground of the semiotic relation; objects have the role of secondness, for they are the differences that are to be determined; and interpretants have the role of thirds, for they are ordering principles.

course material as well as conceptual, involving such things as levels of wealth in a society, technological know-how, and institutional structures, all of which can shape or mediate the relation of the interpretant to the object.

Whatever in a given context occupies the role of the object is an identifiable, determinate or definable entity with a nature of its own that is mind-independent. It is not, however, an absolute particular or completely determinate, for the object also is dynamical: it is vague in that it has infinite potentialities, which are brought out or made manifest to the interpretant by the medium of the sign. These potentialities, so far as they have been actualised in the historical interrelations of object, sign and interpretant, are properties of the object that are mind-independent. But no matter what its determinate and historically saturated nature, the object is always vague; it is a determinate determinable. Whatever in a given context plays the role of interpretant is the ordering principle of discourse, for the interpretant attempts to work out the relation of the sign and object under the guidance and constraint provided by the insistent specificities of both. The interpretant is thus a vague potentiality also, for the interpretant determines itself (as well as its object and sign, so far as possible) by its ordering or structuring work. The results of such work constitute a new object/sign for further interpretants, and so *ad infinitum* in iterative historical succession. Object, sign and interpretant are thus all three historically saturated and historically variable entities.

The upshot is that, if the movement of semiotic construction is the universal constitution of the real, then all interpretation makes a difference to its object. How much difference depends upon the point at which, in a given series of semiotic events, the interpretant intervenes. Here, in relation to human discursive interpretation, there are, I suggest, two kinds of indeterminacy to consider: epistemological and ontological. First, although all things are ontologically indeterminate or possess infinite potentiality, scientific discoveries about physical nature are best considered to be discoveries about entities that, until discovered, are epistemologically indeterminate. That is, they are discoveries about potentialities that those discoveries themselves indicate to be actual and operative prior to our discovery of them. Such potentialities could be called prevenient potentialities: they are potentialities that are actually antecedent to human action or cognition.

It is, of course, equally the case, secondly, that human interpretation can and often does unfold and actualise new, hitherto indeterminate potentialities in objects, as, for instance, with the discovery of plastic. In this respect, ontological indeterminacy refers not only to the condition of all things as infinite potentialities, but also to those potentialities that are indeterminate prior to their actualisation as potentialities in intersubjective and constructive historical activity. Such would be the case, for example, not only with the discovery of plastic, but also with the unfolding over the last two millennia of the notion of *agape* as a potentiality of human relations. Potentialities of this kind can be termed supervenient potentialities, for they emerge out of, or are supervenient upon, the intersubjective activity of human construction. Yet they are as such real potentialities. The speculative unity of realism and constructivism is based upon the claim that reality itself is semiotically constructive nature, and that human constructive activity is part of, or an instance of, the unfolding or actualisation of that larger structure.

Even this brief summary is, I think, enough to indicate the sweep of a trinitarian semiotics. The full ontological and sociocultural significance of Peirce's evolutionary semiotics as a universal theory of being or actualisation as revelation is the subject of my tenth thesis. Consider: Being or activity is not here primarily analysed as substance or as subject but as communication, the unconditional communication of freedom by the triune principle of actualisation. Unconditional communication is thus the actualising condition of substance and of subjectivity, of all determination. At this point we cannot avoid the question: Just what is unconditional communication?

There is only one answer, and this is my tenth and final thesis: being as communication is love as unconditional giving or donation, unconditional concern (*agape*).

Only in this way can the spontaneity and individuality of things and, in particular, the contingent evolution of physical nature, be properly secured. And the reason is that unconditional concern is open to what it does not control or determine. It does not stand in opposition to contingency, nor does it treat contingency as a lower moment of some absolute completeness, for unconditional concern *surrenders* itself to contingency. We see this in parental love, in all genuine love. As Peirce says in his essay on 'Evolutionary Love', 'The movement of love is circular, at one and the same impulse projecting things into independency and drawing them into harmony.'[31] The significance of this analysis of the triune principle of actualisation should now be apparent. For the ancient Greeks as well as for a philosopher such as Iris Murdoch, love, as *eros*, is the *medium* by which we come properly to apprehend and to participate in the ultimate reality. In contrast, the claim here is that the ultimate reality *is* love as infinite or inexhaustible *agape* or self-donation. This is the infinity that characterises the three principles of actualisation in their unity of co-realisation. And it is this infinite love that is the active condition of order in the universe, the ground of the complications that wherever possible accompany ordination. All specific complications or

---

31. Peirce, *Collected Papers*, VI, para. 288.

communities – not just the human mind, but mathematical order, time and space, possibly even extensity – *are* contingent. Yet ordination itself, as complication or inclusive community, is not. For these reasons, the real is not only the true; the real is essentially good.[32]

In the context of the history of our philosophy and culture, there is nothing original or mysterious about this claim. This is an ancient claim, and I have tried to indicate that not only is it a conceptually clear and powerful claim, but it is an immensely productive claim, the arena in which the hugely important, even globally transformative, notions of relations, persons, historicity, events and agapeic love as the basis of existence and of justice have been elaborated. And here is a further rationale: it is a claim that in fact tacitly informs all our attitudes, a claim by which in fact we tacitly measure all our actions. Put it like this: do you value or have high regard for that principle? If so, note that it cannot be derived from any lesser principle; it is irreducible. And its irreducibility constitutes an ethical clue to the ultimate nature of reality.

To show this, let me ask a simple question: how should we go about analysing the proposition 'Jane loves John'? A triune-semiotic analysis of 'Jane loves John' goes like this. We mean there is intense, spontaneous feeling towards another and in that respect Jane is what Peirce calls an 'emotional interpretant'. We mean also that there are actions and effort involved, and in this respect Jane is an 'energetic interpretant'. And we mean further that there is an adopted rule, habit of behaviour or ideal, in which respect Jane is an ideal or 'logical interpretant'.[33] It is the *unity* of all three that is meant by 'loves'. The interpretative and disclosing power of triune analysis is I think well demonstrated here.

Yet could we not leave it at that? In other words, why not settle for some kind of descriptivist or even naturalist theory of the triune event, as do so many of those influenced by Peirce? Does an explanatorist theory of reality have any role here? Just what does it add to the description?

Experience demands that we go beyond descriptivism and naturalism. For one of our historically saturated intuitions is that the hallmark of all genuine love is some element of unconditional concern. This is not a feeling or a disposition, for we can and should show unconditional concern to

---

32. Only by neglecting these considerations, and the whole trinitarian philosophical tradition that lies behind them, does Wiggins find it so difficult to understand with respect to ontological goodness '*what* it is that we are straining to understand'; see Wiggins, 'Sufficient Reason', 129–31. It has been a disaster for Anglo-American culture that the 'God of the philosophers' discussed in most philosophical histories and textbooks is a distorting abstraction from the conception of God most of those philosophers actually employ, develop and defend.
33. Peirce, *Collected Papers*, V, paras 473–6.

those we may be disposed to dislike, even hate. We have here an alignment of feeling and action with an ideal, where feeling is no longer erotic, nor merely an affective sentiment of sympathy, but a matter of self-surrender.

How else can this be understood except as a spiritual act, in the sense of a total orientation of our natures that transcends natural impulse? It is something more than just 'mind', something more than ordinary 'feeling', and usually involves extraordinary action. What has to be said is that where there is such love – and we can find it manifest in artworks as well as people – we have a glimpse of the *perfect* unity of feeling, exertion and rule. *Either* this is a perfection, an ideal, that is utterly without reason, is indeed quite absurd and is even self-destructive (as Nietzsche claimed, holding 'life' to be the *summum bonum*); *or* this is a perfection that has its reason – its only reason – in the ultimate order of things.

With this, I rest my case for speculative philosophy.

Postscript: My Friend James Bradley

Helmut Maaßen

Jim Bradley and I first met at the Academie du Midi in southern France in 1993. He gave a paper on Alfred North Whitehead, 'From Logical to Imaginative Cognition, Whitehead's Metaphysical Method'. At that time he was working on his Whitehead article for the *Routledge Encyclopedia of Philosophy*, in which he refers to the Dutch mathematician L. E. J. Brouwer, who is known for his philosophy of intuitionism. The Academie was founded by a group of philosophers from Wuppertal University in 1988, who had experienced the extraordinary beauty of the Midi, its landscape, buildings, Toulouse, Albi and so on, and the light, which had inspired painters such as van Gogh and Gauguin. The founding idea was to have conferences in the Midi, away from the normal workplace and atmosphere, with the Platonic experience of living together, philosophising, eating and drinking. Jim had heard of the Academie from an Oxford college friend, who had told him that he might enjoy taking part. It turned out to be true. We discussed many topics, including philosophy, and ate and drank in the congenial company of a group of international companions from Japan to France and from Britain to Canada and the US.

On Wednesday in 1993, the off day of the conference, Carl Hausman (USA), Shinnichi Yuasa (Japan), Jim and myself experienced the *menu surprise* of the Michelin cook David Moreno in his Mulin de Durban. Only products of the Midi were served, including wine and Armagnac. Clearly, we enjoyed ourselves thoroughly! After the conference, I dropped Jim off at Liège railway station, giving us ample time to philosophise and get to know each other better.

In October 1993, my wife and I visited Jim in Cambridge, stayed in his home, met friends, ate at Darwin College. Jim arranged a meeting with Dorothy Emmet, with whom he was in close contact. We talked about the

Routledge Encyclopedia of Philosophy, in which many Cambridge scholars were involved, including Jim. Among other topics, we discussed the difference between *esse* and *ens* in Thomas Aquinas, an important distinction, which Dorothy always stressed, and an important point in the development of Whitehead's ontology. When we left Cambridge, we did not realise how long it would be until we met again.

At the Silver Jubilee conference at the Process Studies Centre in Claremont in 1998, I heard a familiar sonorous voice in the DoubleTree hotel, where all the invited speakers were lodged. The topic of discussion was creativity in Whitehead's work. Since we had the same notions about the ingredients that make a conference successful, aside from good papers, our rooms became a late night meeting point with wine and cheese. Among the stimulating encounters we met Roland Faber and Hans-Joachim Sander for the first time. The Californian sun, the luxury hotel, the good papers and the long nights in Jim's or my room were inspiring and strengthened our friendship.

In 1999–2000 Jim and his second wife, Jennifer, were on a scholarship in Belgium and the Netherlands, Jim in Leuven and Jennifer in Amsterdam, both cities quite close to our home in Germany. Jim chaired a seminar on Whitehead in Leuven, supported Luca Vanzago's English version of his doctoral dissertation and organised a philosophy conference in cooperation with André Clouts on 'Whitehead and Creativity'. Among others, Bertrand Saint-Sernin from the Sorbonne and Jean-Claude Dumoncel from Caen University were there. It was rare to be joined by French philosophers at an English-speaking conference. On the way home, I drove Jim to Amsterdam, where I met his wife Jennifer and their little daughter, Isobel, with whom I could communicate in Dutch, since she was in a Dutch kindergarten. A few weeks later, my wife and I visited them in Amsterdam, enjoying their company and, of course, visiting several museums, especially the newly renovated van Gogh Museum. When they visited us, they went to the famous Joseph Beuys Museum in Schloss Moyland. During one of our smoking sessions in the study, Jim noticed that I had the theological encyclopedia *Sacramentum Mundi*, which he valued as one of the best.

Two years later, in 2002, we met in Washington, and realised that both of us had just been to the Phillips Collection. While talking about the exquisite art museum, Jim mentioned that, if he ever published a book, he would choose Wassily Kandinsky's *Succession* (1935) as the cover image. Several attempts to take Jim and his family with us to India failed, despite Jim's keen interest and our yearly trips there, to meet our Indian family.

While we continued to keep in touch, our next personal meeting took place in California in 2007. Roland Faber had founded the Whitehead Research Project and organised a philosophy conference at Claremont to which, among others, Jim and I had been invited. I was teaching during the autumn term of 2007 at Claremont, and we had rented an apartment in Pasadena up in the San Gabriel mountains. Jim enjoyed the warm Californian weather, particularly as he had left St John's with snow and the temperature below zero. When we arrived home, we had a drink on our patio, looking down on to Pasadena and the LA skyline. We drove into downtown Pasadena, an almost European city, with traffic-free roads, street cafés, restaurants, bars and, of course, bookshops. As expected, we found secondhand bookshop. We could not resist going in, and came out with such a large amount of books that we had to drive home, as walking would have been far too strenuous! Jim once more showed his deep passion for books, another passion we shared. After spending two days in our home in Pasadena, we drove to Claremont, to stay at the same DoubleTree hotel as in 1998. We followed the same procedure as before: after lectures and talks, long evenings in Jim's or my room with wine and cheese. The proceedings of that conference included our papers. Jim's paper, 'The Triune Event: Event Ontology, Reason and Love', has been republished in this volume.

In 2008 we met again at the Second Whitehead Research Project Conference, organised by Roland Faber. In the evenings the same procedure as before: wine, cheese and philosophical discussions late into the night. Jim told me that he had become more and more interested in the philosophy of C. S. Peirce. Since Jim knew German, he had read the introduction of the *Religionsphilosophische Schriften* (*Philosophische Bibliothek* 478), the German edition of Peirce edited by Hermann Deuser, and translated by Deuser and Helmut Maassen. He found the trinitarian structure in Peirce more and more convincing and found it difficult to connect to the binary approach of Whitehead.

In 2009 we visited Jim and his family in St John's, browsing through his library, enjoying a wonderful meal with other friends. Jim was resplendent in a blue velvet jacket, which his daughter Isobel had carefully delinted before dinner. Jim told me how important it is for a scholar to have stamina, not only in research, but in drinking and celebrating as well. A valid point to consider when choosing doctoral candidates! He was proud to be mentioned by John Ashton in his book on the Fourth Gospel.[1]

On 21 December 2011 I called Jim on his birthday, as I had done ever since we met. I was astonished on hearing his voice: it was not as clear and sonorous as it had been. I told Jim that we might go back to Pasadena for another visit and that he and his family could meet us there. What a wonderful prospect! Three weeks later Jennifer informed me about Jim's

---

1. John Ashton, *Understanding the Fourth Gospel* (Oxford: Oxford University Press, 1991).

cancer diagnosis, her tremendous shock and the bleak future ahead, as the cancer had spread. After a conference at Harvard, I had the opportunity to fly to St John's to meet him one last time. He was bedridden, but absolutely clear in his mind and without pain. We talked about our past, our friendship and listened to baroque music. We said farewell, three weeks before he passed away.

Rest in peace dear friend!
Requiescat in pace!

Appendix A: James Bradley's Tables of Triads and Trinities

Triadic Theories of the Ultimate Principles of Actualization

(A Snapshot of the Mainstream Western Tradition of Speculative Philosophy)

	Pythagoreans (Plato)	Neo Platonists (Proclus)	Medieval Philosophy	Spinoza	Hegel	Schelling	Peirce	Later Heidegger	Deleuze
		transcendence				immanence			
	#	#	*	#	*	*	*	*	#
	Limit (Order)	Being (One)	Father (Mind or Will)	Substance	Idea (Thesis)	Absolute Identity (Abgrund - Freedom)	Spontaneity	Es gibt	Difference
	Unlimited (Dyad)	Life (Activity)	Son (Expression, Logos)	Attributes	Difference (Antithesis)	Will	Difference	die Sendung (*missio*)	Virtuality
	Mixture	Mind (Order)	Spirit (Love)	Modes	Unity (Synthesis)	Love	Ordination (Community)	die Gabe (*donum*)	Differences
			(=God)		[=Absolute]	[=Absolute]		[=Das Ereignis]	
	completely realized reality						incomplete reality		

#Triads: usually hierarchical; 3 types of being; third is mixture.   * Triunities: always coequal; characters of all beings; third is connectivity.
Triunity in Kant's First *Critique* (of three): Intuition (Sensation, Time, Space), Analytic (Substance, Succession, Coexistence), Dialectic (Soul, World, God).
Cognate theories: F. von Schiller – *Stofftrieb*, *Formtrieb*, *Spieltrieb*; Dewey – Immediacy, Relation, Meaning; Klee- Point, Line, Plane; Freud – Id, Ego, Superego; Lacan – Real, Symbolic, Imaginary; Habermas – Life, Labour, Language

The Peircean Schema

1. The metaphysical threefold infinite, the ultimate principle of actualization:

Firstness:	Secondness:	Thirdness:
Being as Indeterminate 'No-thing' that is Undetermined or Free. Self-Motion or Spontaneity. Freedom seeks realization via determination. 6.206 Ekstatic Activity. Self-surrender. Sole origin, *unum*.	Self-differentiation of Spontaneity. The ground of Difference	Ordination Here, freedom is realized as the individual proper. 1.337, 362. The ground of Continuity, Persistence, Synthesis, Donation, Mind

The Metaphysical Threefold Infinite is the ground of, and is manifest as:

2. The cosmological threefold infinite:

Firstness:	Secondness:	Thirdness:
Unconditioned Possibility Indeterminate Freedom Distributive Infinity	Differentiation The Boundary, Contingency.	Continuity. Evolution of Systems & Individuals. Ideas, Signs, Meanings, Rules

What is strictly the firstness of secondness cosmologically, is, when viewed in the experiential or phenomenological context, the firstness of firstness:

3. The phenomenological threefold infinite:

Firstness:	Secondness:	Thirdness:
The monadic singularity of things, Presence	Reaction, Resistance, Dyadic Difference. Actuality, Events. (6.200, 201)	Persistence > Character > Rule > Sign, Meaning > Interpretation > Synthesis > Event > Individuality or System

4. The semiotic threefold (iterative) infinite:

Firstness:	Secondness:	Thirdness:
Sign (potentiality)	Object	Interpretant (ordering)

This structure of communication both expresses & governs the exchange relations *between* all threefold entities.

5. The triplicity of each member of the threefold (1.521ff.):

1. The firstness of firstness, secondness and thirdness: this is the infinite spontaneity that is present in all things in the modes of ekstatic activity, differentiation and order.

2. The secondness of difference or existence (Latin, *ex-sistere*, to stand outside) consists of two objects and their purely individual interaction. (Recall Kant's Analytic: substance, succession, reciprocity.)

3. The thirdness of the vague idea, the event of information-exchange, and the thought or rule (l.537).

6. The threefold transcendental (universal) predicates in Peirce:

1. Of any entity (*ens*): undifferentiated spontaneity (*unum*); difference (*aliquid*); order (*res*).

2. Of relations: aesthetics (*pulchrum*); ethics (*bonum*); logic (*verum*).

Appendix B: Complete List of James Bradley's Publications

1977
'Gadamer's Truth and Method: Some Questions and English Applications', *The Heythrop Journal*, 18 (October): 420–35.

1979
'Hegel in Britain: A Brief History of British Commentary and Attitudes, Part I', *The Heythrop Journal*, 20 (January): 1–24.
'Hegel in Britain: A Brief History of British Commentary and Attitudes, Part II', *The Heythrop Journal*, 20 (April): 163–82.

1980
'Feuerbach and the End of the Traditions', in *New Studies in Theology*, ed. D. J. Holmes and S. W. Sykes (London: Duckworth), 139–61.

1983
'Hegelianism', in *The New Dictionary of Christian Theology*, ed. A. Richardson and J. Bowden (London: SCM Press).
'Idealism', in *The New Dictionary of Christian Theology*, ed. A. Richardson and J. Bowden (London: SCM Press).

1984
'F.H. Bradley's Metaphysics of Feeling and its Place in the History of Philosophy', in *The Philosophy of F.H. Bradley*, ed. A. Manser and G. Stock (Oxford: Clarendon Press), 227–42.

1985
'The Critique of Pure Feeling: Bradley, Whitehead, and the Anglo-Saxon Metaphysical Tradition', *Process Studies, Special Issue on the History of Philosophy* 14.4: 253–64.

1991

'Whitehead, Heidegger, and the Paradoxes of the New', *Process Studies* 20.3: 127–50.

'Relations, intelligibilité et noncontradiction dans la métaphysique du sentir de F.H. Bradley: une réinterprétation', Part I, *Archives de philosophie* 54.4: 529–51.

1992

'Relations, intelligibilité et noncontradiction dans la métaphysique du sentir de F.H. Bradley: une réinterprétation', Part II, *Archives de philosophie* 55.1: 77–91.

'Rorty and the Image of Modernity', *The Heythrop Journal* 32: 249–53.

1993

'La cosmologie transcendantale de Whitehead: la transformation spéculative du concept de construction logique', *Archives de philosophie* 56.1: 1–26.

'Whitehead, Heidegger, and the Paradoxes of the New', *Process Studies* 20.3: 127–50.

'Whitehead, Contemporary Metaphysics, and Maritain's Critique of Bergson', *Maritain Studies* IX: 113–34.

1994

'Whitehead's Transcendental Analysis', *Process Studies* 23: 140–72.

'Transcendentalism and Speculative Realism in Whitehead', *Process Studies* 23.3: 155–90.

1996

'The Transcendental Turn in F.H. Bradley's Theory of Feeling', in *Perspectives on the Logic and Metaphysics of F.H. Bradley*, ed. W. J. Mander (Bristol: Thoemmes Press), 39–60.

'Process and Historical Crisis in F.H. Bradley's Ethics of Feeling', in *Ethics, Metaphysics and Religion in the Thought of F.H. Bradley*, ed. Philip MacEwan (Lewiston, NY: Edwin Mellen Press), 53–90.

Ed., *Philosophy After F.H. Bradley* (Bristol: Thoemmes Press).

'From Presence to Process: Bradley and Whitehead', in *Philosophy After F.H. Bradley*, ed. James Bradley (Bristol: Thoemmes Press), 147–68.

'Act, Event, Series: Metaphysics, Mathematics, and Whitehead', *The Journal of Speculative Philosophy* 10.4: 233–48.

1997

'A.N. Whitehead', in *The Routledge Encyclopedia of Philosophy* (London: Routledge), IX, 713–20.

1998

'Metafizica speculative a seriilor la Whitehead' ['Whitehead's Speculative Metaphysics of Series'], translated into Romanian by Petru Tincoca, *Krisis* 7: 70–9.

1999

'God and Argument: Strong and Weak Theories of Existence', in *God and Argument: A Collection of Essays*, ed. William Sweet (Ottawa: University of Ottawa Press), 17–26.

2001

'F.H. Bradley's Metaphysics of Feeling and the Theory of Relations', in *Idealism, Metaphysics and Community: Festschrift for Leslie Armour*, ed. William Sweet (Aldershot: Ashgate), 77–106.

2002

'The Speculative Generalization of the Function: A Key to Whitehead', *Tijdschrift voor Filosofie* 64: 253–71.

'Whitehead's Metaphysics and the Analysis of the Propositional Function', in *Process and Analysis*, ed. George Shields (Albany, NY: SUNY Press), 139–55.

2003

'The Generalization of the Function: A Speculative Analysis', in *Process Pragmatism: Essays on a Quiet Philosophical Revolution*, ed. Guy Debrock (Amsterdam: Rodopi), 71–86.

'Transformations in Speculative Philosophy', in *The Cambridge History of Philosophy 1870–1945*, ed. Tom Baldwin (Cambridge: Cambridge University Press), 436–46.

'Dorothy Emmet's "Notes on Whitehead's Harvard Lectures, 1928–29"', transcribed, edited and web-prepared with the assistance of Helmut Maassen, Stephen Gardner and Peter Norman, *European Studies in Process Thought* 1: 1–25.

2004

'Speculative and Analytical Philosophy, Theories of Existence, the Generalization of the Mathematical Function', in *Approaches to Metaphysics*, ed. William Sweet (Boston: Kluwer Academic), 209–26.

2009

'Beyond Hermeneutics: Peirce's Semiology as a Trinitarian Metaphysics of Communication', *Analecta Hermeneutica* 1: 45–57.

2010

'The Triune Event: Event Ontology, Reason and Love', in *Event and Decision: Ontology and Politics in Badiou, Deleuze, and Whitehead*, ed. Roland Faber, Henry Krips and Daniel Pettus (Cambridge: Cambridge Scholars Publishing), 97–114.

2011

'A Key to Collingwood's *Essay on Metaphysics*: The Logic of Creedal Rules', in *A Handbook on Collingwood*, ed. C. Kobayashi, M. Marion and A. Skodo (Leiden: Brill).

2012

'Philosophy and Trinity', *Symposium: Canadian Journal of Philosophy* 16.1: 155–77.

Index

abduction, 13–14, 13n, 135, 176, 251
absolute presuppositions, 190–1, 193, 205–16
    faith and reason, 234–44
    and truth, 229–34
absolute reason, 58
academic philosophy, 3
Academie du Midi, 264
activity, 117, 130, 141; *see also* mapping activity
activity of actualisation, xviii, 100, 162–8
    analytical philosophy, 245
    being as, xi
    descriptive accounts, 255
    existence as, 195
    explanatorist theory, 144
    generalisation of the function, 112
    mapping activity, 103, 104, 105
    order, 169
    Plato, 122
    and principle of reason, 139–40
    self-explanatory theory of, 134, 175, 197, 251, 256
    teleological, 186
    triunity, 177
    see also self-actualisation

actualisation, principles of, 136–9, 142–4, 176–7, 196, 255, 269
actualising principle of existence, 163–6
agapasm, 30
agape, 30, 34, 128–9, 131, 132, 241, 261–2
agapeic community, 145–8
agency, 80, 106
Alexander, Samuel, 136, 176, 196, 255
algebraic method, 59–65, 100–1
    analogy, 67–70, 75–6
    paradox of self-reference, 70–3
    pluralism, 73–4n
    schematic substitution, 66–7
algorisms, 154
algorithmic naturalism, 155, 156n
analogical application, 68, 70, 73, 75
analogical relation, 97–8
analogy, 67–8, 73, 75, 88
analogy of proportionality, 120
analytical philosophy, 7, 10, 150–3, 245
anancasm, 30
Appearance and Reality (Bradley), 40–1, 42, 43–4, 83, 84, 89, 90, 220–1
application, 97–8

Aquinas, Thomas
  esse, xviii, 17, 138, 178, 198, 256
  goodness, 122
  subsistent relations, 27–8n
  teleological development, 26
  triunity, 11, 28, 141
Aristotle
  being, 17
  Bradley on, 39
  Collingwood on, 207, 213, 233, 237
  divine being, xviii
  substance, 8
  teleological development, 26
Arnold, Matthew, 37
Athanasian Creed, 189, 233
atomistic empiricists, 19, 21, 22
Augustine, 11, 27–8n, 141, 202–3
Ayer, A.J., 190

Badiou, Alain, 136, 139, 144, 176
being, xi, 17
  Bradley and Whitehead, 82
  Heidegger, 77
  Peirce, 126
  philosophies of, 162
  question of, 130–1
  speculative philosophy, 247
  v. existence, 164
  Whitehead, 98
  see also existence
Bergson, Henri, 52–3, 58, 60, 122, 158, 175, 195, 255
Bonaventure, xviii, 17
Bosanquet, Bernard, 4, 38, 41, 84, 85, 86
Bradley, F.H., 7, 8, 18–20, 226
  abductive logic, 13
  principle of reason, 220–1
  see also 'From Presence to Process: F. H. Bradley and A. N. Whitehead' (Bradley)
Buchdahl, Dr Gerd, xii–xiii

Caird, Edward, 37
Cambridge University, xii–xiii, xiv, 2, 4

Cassirer, Ernst, 6, 10, 10n
categorial analysis, 68
categorial scheme, 60–1, 63–4, 66–7, 70, 76, 80, 94–7
cause, 165, 227, 252
chance, 252–3
chance events, xvi, 135
chaos, 135–6, 253
Christianity, xviii, 11–12, 203–4; *see also* Jewish-Christian eschatology; theology; Trinity
civilisation, 241
Cochrane, Charles Norris, 201–3, 214, 225, 228, 229–30, 232
cognition, 65, 115, 149–50
cognitive subject, 247–8
Collingwood, R.G., 7, 8, 137, 138, 178
  metaphysics, 190–4: continuum thesis, 217–18; creedal rule thesis, 221; development, 222–9; faith and reason, 234–44; hierarchy thesis, 218–19; intuitive certainty thesis, 219–20; ontological proof thesis, 220–1, 224
  theory of absolute presuppositions, 190–1, 193, 205–16: and truth, 229–34
  Trinitarian Creed, 189–90, 207–8: modern influences, 199–205
concepts, 41; *see also* event-concepts
consistency, 84; *see also* inconsistency
constant, 112
construction, 91–2, 95, 97; *see also* ideal construction; intellectual constructions
content-reflexivity, paradox of, 55–6, 70
continental philosophy, 245
contingency, 135, 170, 252
continuum thesis, 217–18
contradictories, 41
creation, xi, xvi–xvii
creative order, xv
creative process, 102

creativity, 8, 22, 94
  and being, 97
  as ultimate principle, 102, 103, 104–5, 140
creedal rule thesis, 221
creedal rules, 192, 206, 207, 209–10, 215, 230, 231
creeds, 191–3, 217; *see also* Trinitarian Creed
cultural history, 79–80

Davidson, D., 61
deconstruction, 173
Deleuze, Gilles, 122, 124, 127, 139–40, 175, 176, 195, 196
Democritus, 136, 176, 196, 255
descriptive generalization, 64, 65, 67
determinism, 26
Dewey, John, 46, 115, 150, 155
Deweyite pragmatism, 46–7
difference, 22
divine life, xviii
divine mapping, 107–8
dualism, 38
dualistic metaphysics, 18–19
dynamical object, 183

emanative cause, 123
Emmet, Dorothy, xiv, 92, 264
Empedocles, 136, 176, 196, 255
empirical world, 61–3, 64, 65, 95–6
Essay on Metaphysics, An (Collingwood), 7, 26, 189–91, 212, 220–1, 222–9, 231, 234–44
Essays on Truth and Reality (Bradley), 43, 44, 45, 83, 89–90
eternal objects, 106–8
Eternal Reason, 38
Ethical Studies (Bradley), 89
event ontology
  Dewey, 115
  Peirce's triunity, 142–5
  principle of reason, 133–6:
    and activity of actualisation, 139–40
  taxonomy of principles of actualisation, 136–9
  theories of origin, 140–2
event-concepts, 51–2, 54, 55, 56–7
events, 51, 53, 54, 55, 77, 79, 80, 150; *see also* occasions
evolution, 30
existence, xi, 198
  as activity, xviii, 12, 162–8
  actualising principle of, 163–6
  and order, 168–72
  positive nature, 82–3, 98
  as process, xiv–xv
  self-explanatory explanations of, 16–18
  strong theories, 156–62, 195, 247
  weak theories, 149–56, 195, 246
  see also being
experience, 6
  and cognition, 65
  finite centres of, 88–9
  immediate, 44–5, 46, 85, 9
  Kant, 54, 115
  Peirce, 187
  reality as, 43, 48
experimental generalisation, 161

faith, 203, 206, 217, 219–20, 224, 234–44
fallacy of unification, 46–7
feeling, 19, 22, 36, 38–42, 43–4
  epistemic status, 44–5
  historical-critical rationale, 47–9
  non-relational, 85–91
  permanent, 87–8
  vectorial account of, 92–3
  see also immediate experience
feeling of reality, 132
finite centres of experience, 88–9
firstness, xviii, 27, 32, 126, 142–3, 179–80, 182, 196, 257–9
forms, 144, 165, 181–2
forms of process, 69
Foster, M.B., 200, 201, 214, 225, 228, 229, 230, 232

Frege, Gottlob, 6, 18, 101, 104,
    150–2, 153–5, 171, 246
'From Presence to Process: F. H.
    Bradley and A. N. Whitehead'
    (Bradley), xiv
functions, 253; *see also* generalisation
    of the function

Gadamer, H.-G., 23, 23n
    language and temporality, 74–5
    theory of interpretation, 50–1
general potentiality, 108
generalisation of the function, 6, 10,
    11, 22, 100–2, 151–2, 153–5,
    167
    activity that maps to structure,
        106–8
    finite occasions of mapping activity,
        108–11
    function as mapping activity, 102–6
    significance, 111–14
generalized mathematics, 60
God, 28, 29, 31, 164–5, 176, 200
    mapping, 106–8
    neo-Platonists, 124
    Plato, 122–3
    relations, 131
    Trinity, 138, 178, 225
goodness, 122–3, 124, 126
Green, T.H., 38
ground, 50, 55, 227, 252

Hegel, G.W.F.
    Absolute idea, xix
    absolute reason, 58
    contingency, 32
    dialectic, 37, 90
    evolution, 30
    feeling, 39, 40
    historical existence of entities, 76
    love, 145
    negation, 87
    ontological argument, 221
    primordial subjects, 125
    reality, 138, 178, 199
    triad, 126–7
    Trinity, 138n, 235, 235–6
    triunity, 141, 178
Heidegger, Martin
    actualisation, 137, 141, 177
    metaphysics, xix, 20
    self-realisation, 51–2, 53
    self-realising new (radical novelty),
        54–5, 57–9, 76–80
heuristic metaphysics, 11
hierarchy thesis, 218–19
historical consciousness, 23–4, 24n,
    34
historical-critical rationale, 47–9
history, 25–6, 203, 217–18, 228, 232,
    233
    cultural, 79–80
horizontal triads, 124–5
Houser, Nathan, 27
Hume, David, 19, 38, 149, 157, 171,
    172, 238, 246
hypothesis *see* 'no hypothesis' hypothesis
hypothesis of reality, 176
hypotheticity, 72–3

ideal constructions, 85, 87, 88
ideal experiment, 83
ideas, 41
identical subject-object, 37–8, 44, 45,
    47, 48
identity, 58
imaginative generalization, 63–4
immediate actuality, 58
immediate experience, 44–5, 46, 85,
    95; *see also* feeling
immediate object, 183
inconsistency, 84, 105
individual problematic situations, 45,
    46, 46–7
induction, 135, 175–6
infinite mapping activity, 106, 108,
    110, 111
infinity, 111, 142–3, 180, 258
intellectual constructions, 72

intellectual satisfaction, 83–4, 86, 118, 220–1
internal relations, 85, 86, 93
internal triads, 125
interpretants, 183
interpretation, theory of, 50–1
intuitive certainty thesis, 219–20
irrelative, 171

James, William, 44
Jewish-Christian eschatology, 24–6

Kant, Immanuel
  cognition, 115, 149–50
  cognitive subject, 247–8
  Critique of Pure Reason, xii, 237
  existence, xviii, 246
  experience, 54, 115
  metaphysics, 9
  nature of the real, 172
  Peirce on, 187
  Trinity, 178
Kantian transcendentalism, 97
'Key to Collingwood's Metaphysics of Absolute Presuppositions, A' (Bradley), 15
Kierkegaard, Søren, 52
knowledge, theory of, 49, 65, 72
Krausz, Michael, 211n, 212
Kuhn, Thomas, 214n, 248–9

language, 50, 74–6
Leibniz, Gottfried, Wilhelm, 12, 157, 158
Leuven, 265
Liar Paradox, 76
linguistic turn, 74, 153
Locke, John, 19, 38, 213
logic, 6, 17–18
  abductive tradition, 13–14
logical analysis, 150–3; *see also* analytical philosophy
Lonergan, Bernard, 11, 12, 257
love, 29–31, 34, 125, 132, 145–8, 261–2; *see also agape*

MacKinnon, Professor Donald, xii, 4
mapping activity, 102–6
  finite occasions of, 108–11
Marx, Karl, 52
materialism, 150
mathematics, 60, 63, 68, 178, 256
me on, 32, 32n
medieval transcendentalism, 97
Memorial University, xiii, 2, 3–4
metaphysical empiricism, 9
metaphysical propositions, 209–10
metaphysics, 6, 8–9, 20–1
  analogy, 67
  critique, 53
  and theology, 235–6
  and triunity, 194–9
'Metaphysics and Things' (Bradley), xviii
Mill, J.S., 38, 39–40, 48
modern predicate, 151, 167
monism, 36, 37, 93, 173

nationality, 213
natural science, 178, 200, 228, 256
naturalism, 12, 16–17, 150, 168
  algorithmic, 155
naturalist philosophy, 246–50
nature-spirit problem, 37–8
negation, 87
neo-Platonic triads, 123–5
Nietzsche, F., 24, 52–3, 58, 76, 148, 175, 176, 196
'no hypothesis' hypothesis, 118, 134, 175, 194
nominalism, 20n, 21
non-conceptual, 113, 132, 257
non-contradiction, 14, 43, 83, 84–5, 86, 105
non-relational continuum, 44–7
non-relational feeling, 85–91
non-relational unity, 7, 19, 39
  sensationalist ground of, 40–4
novelty, 20; *see also* radical novelty (self-realising new)
numbers, 21

objects, 41
   dynamical, 183
   eternal, 106–8
   immediate, 183
   see also identical subject-object
occasions, 51, 53, 54, 55, 78n, 80, 91, 92
   of mapping, 108–11
   see also events
ontic models, 76
ontological proof thesis, 220–1, 224
ontological theory of truth, 231, 233, 249–50
onto-theology, 2, 9, 20–1, 245
operations, 108, 111
order, 168–72
   creative, xv
   neo-Platonists, 123–5
   Peirce on, 126–9
   Plato on, 121–3
   and rationality, 115–16
   self-actualising, 5, 34, 117
   self-explanatory nature of, 117–21, 129–32
origin, 140–2, 142, 143, 180, 257
origination, principle of, 197

paradox of content-reflexivity, 55–6, 70
paradox of self-reference, 55, 70–3, 78
paradoxes of the new, 55–6, 59, 77
Peirce, Charles Sanders, xvi–xvii, 26–8, 30–2
   abductive logic, 13, 13n
   being and existence, 164
   'firstness', 258–9
   metaphysical method, 174–6, 196
   'A Neglected Argument for the Existence of God', 236
   'no hypothesis' hypothesis, 118
   principle of reason, xvi, 134–5, 174–5, 194–5
   semiology/semiotics, 21, 173, 182–5, 259–60: and teleology, 186–7

speculative philosophy, 6, 8, 10
triunity, 126–9, 133, 138–9, 142–5, 179–82
Peircean Scheme, 270–1
perfect infinite, 89–90
permanent feeling, 87–8
Phenomenology of the Spirit (Hegel), 37
philosophical achievement, 3
philosophical necessity, 56, 69
philosophy, 218, 223–4, 225–6
   continental, 245
   critique, 57
   naturalist v. speculative, 246–50
Philosophy After F.H. Bradley (Bradley, ed.), xiii–xiv
Philosophy and Religion (Collingwood), 217–18
'Philosophy and Trinity' (Bradley), xvii, xix, 24–5, 29–30
Philosophy of Mind (Hegel), 39
physical feelings, 92
physics, 52, 67n
Plato, 17, 69, 115, 121–3, 137, 176, 196, 202
Plotinus, 123–4, 176, 196
politics, 79, 80
potentiality, 108
pragmaticism, xvi
pragmatism, xvi
   Deweyite, 46–7
presuppositions, 190, 203
   absolute, 190–1, 193, 205–16: and truth, 229–34
principle of reason, 9, 16, 118, 133–6, 141, 250–2, 255
   and activity of actualisation, 139–40
   Bradley, 220–1
   Collingwood, 224, 225
   Peirce, xvi, 134–5, 174–5, 194–5
   and strong theories of existence, 156–62
Principles of History (Collingwood), 229
Principles of Logic, The (Bradley), 83, 89

process, 57, 71, 102
  and construction, 92
  creative, 102
  existence as, xiv–xv
  forms of, 69
  mapping as, 108
  Whitehead on, 93–4
Process and Reality (Whitehead), 14, 53, 60–1, 66, 77, 95, 101, 102
Proclus, 123
proportionality, analogy of, 120
propositions, 79, 151–2
pseud-Continentalism, 245

radical novelty (self-realising new), 52–3, 54–9, 75
  algebraic method, 60, 68, 70
  Heidegger on, 76–80
rationality
  and order, 115–16
  Plato on, 121–3
  self-explanatory nature of, 117–21
  see also order
real, 93, 94, 232, 233
real potentiality, 108
reality, 43, 48, 133, 187
  feeling of, 132
  hypothesis of, 176, 246
  self-explanatory theory of, 134
reason, 22–3, 58–9, 170–1, 219–20
  absolute, 58
  and faith, 234–44
  reflective, 204
  see also principle of reason
reflective reason, 204
relations, 40–1, 42, 115–16, 116n, 131, 166–8, 253–4
  semiology/semiotics, 184–5
relative presuppositions, 190, 207, 213
religion, 217–18; see also Christianity; theology
Religion and Philosophy (Collingwood), 218, 222
revelation, 203–4

rules, 206; *see also* creedal rules
Russell, Bertrand
  atomistic empiricists, 22
  generalisation of the function, 7, 17–18, 104, 153, 155
  internal relations, 93
  paradox of class of all classes, 110
  Principia Mathematica, xv, 151

satisfaction, principle of, 220–1; *see also* intellectual satisfaction
Saussure, Ferdinand de, 173
Schelling, F. W. J., xix, 115, 119, 138, 141, 178, 225–6, 257
  Abgrund, 142, 180
  God, 26, 31
  identical subject-object, 37
  primordial subjects, 125
  speculative philosophy, 6, 9, 10
  theology, 236
  traid, 126, 127
  Trinity, 14–15, 235
schematic analysis, 66–7, 69–70, 70–3, 75–6; *see also* algebraic method
schematic necessity, 69
schematic substitution, 66–7
Schopenhauer, Arthur, 122, 136, 176, 195, 196, 255
scientism, 2
Scotus, John Duns, xviii, 126, 141, 187, 197, 257
'secondness', xvii, xviii, 27, 32, 126, 143, 181, 182, 196
self-actualisation, xv, 7, 93–4, 97–98, 132
self-actualising order, 5, 34, 117
self-explanatoriness, 134, 158, 166, 175, 196
self-explanatory explanation, 13, 16
self-explanatory nature of order, 117–21, 129–32
  neo-Platonists, 123–5
  Peirce, 126–9
  Plato, 121–3

self-explanatory theories, 195
self-realisation, 50–3
self-realising new (radical novelty), 52–3, 54–9, 75
  algebraic method, 60, 68, 70
  Heidegger, 76–80
self-reference, paradox of, 55, 70–3, 78
semiology/semiotics, 21, 173, 182–5, 259–60
  and teleology, 186–7
sensory apprehension, 86–7
Silver Jubilee conference, 265
simple physical feelings, 92
Smith, J.A., 199–200
Socrates, 232, 249
speculative descriptivism, 255
speculative descriptivists, 12, 13
speculative explanatorists, 12
speculative metaphysics, xi, 5, 7, 17, 118, 149, 160–1, 175
speculative philosophy, xviii, 2, 5–7, 9–11, 119–20
  activity of actualisation, 100
  defence, 250–63
  existence, 156
  and naturalist philosophy, 246–50
speculative question of order *see* self-explanatory nature of order
Speculum Mentis (Collingwood), 218
Spinoza, Baruch, 10, 124, 137, 176, 196, 255
Stout, G. F., 44
strains, 214–16
subject, 50; *see also* identical subject-object
subsistent relations, 27, 27–8n

teleology, 186–7
temporality and language, 74–6
theology, xviii, 4, 29, 131, 217–18, 222, 235–6
theory of knowledge, 49, 65, 72
'thirdness', xvii, xviii, 27, 32, 126, 144, 181–2, 182–3, 196

thought, 85–6
time, 26
  realisation of, 51–3
'Transcendentalism and Speculative Realism in Whitehead' (Bradley), xv
transcendentals, 94, 97, 169
triads, 27n
  neo-Platonists on, 123–5
  Plato on, 121–3
Trinitarian Creed, 189–90, 207–8
  modern influences, 199–205
Trinity, 1, 7–8, 14–16, 30–5, 125, 126–9, 198
  Collingwood on, 199, 211, 225, 227, 228, 233, 239–40
triunity, xvii, xviii, xx, 27n, 133, 176–9, 256
  event theory, 137–9
  Lonergan on, 11
  and metaphysics, 194–9
  Peirce on, 126–9, 133, 138–9, 142–5, 179–82
  see also triads
trust, 203, 217
truth, 24–5, 120n, 126
  ontological theory of, 231, 233, 249–50
  theory of absolute presuppositions, 229–34
tychasm, xvi, 30

ultimate principle, 102, 104–5, 135, 140, 145, 170, 195, 223, 252
unconditional communication, 261
unification, fallacy of, 46
unity, 143, 144, 180, 182
universal mapping activity, 104–6
universal mathematics, 60
universals, 21, 144, 165, 187
University of Munich, xiii

vagueness, 187, 259
values, 24
variable, 112

voluntarism, 107, 180

Ward, James, 44
Whitehead, A. N., 6, 8, 10–11, 20–3, 26
  activity of actualisation, 140
  algebraic method, 59–65, 100–1: analogy, 67–70, 75–6; paradox of self-reference, 70–3; pluralism, 73–4n; schematic substitution, 66–7
  construction, 91–2
  creativity, 177
  feeling, 92–3
  generalisation of the function, 22, 100–2: activity that maps to structure, 106–8; finite occasions of mapping activity, 108–11; function as mapping activity, 102–6; significance, 111–14
  process, xiv–xv
  Process and Reality, 14
  self-realisation, 51–2, 53
  self-realising new (radical novelty), 54–5, 57, 68
  speculative metaphysics, 7
  speculative philosophy, 6
  theory of process, 93–4
  transcendental analysis, 94–9
Whitehead Research Project, 265–6
Wittgenstein, Ludwig, 18, 21, 50, 101, 108, 110, 155, 248

EU representative:
Easy Access System Europe
Mustamäe tee 50, 10621 Tallinn, Estonia
Gpsr.requests@easproject.com

www.ingramcontent.com/pod-product-compliance
Lightning Source LLC
Chambersburg PA
CBHW050208240426
43671CB00013B/2252